LIFE AND DEATH

ON

YOUR OWN TERMS

LIFE AND DEATH
ON
YOUR OWN TERMS

L.L. BASTA, M.D.

 Prometheus Books

59 John Glenn Drive
Amherst, New York 14228-2197

The author and publishers would like to thank the following for use of their previously published material:

TABLE 8, page 142: © 1993 The Economist Newspaper Group, Inc. Reprinted with permission. Further reproduction prohibited. www.economist.com.

CHAPTER 13: This chapter, in a revised format, is reprinted from *Clinical Cardiology* vol. 23, Supplement II, page nos. II, 6–12, 14–16, 17–18, 20, and 21–25, with permission from *Clinical Cardiology*, Mahwah, New Jersey, 07430, USA.

Every attempt has been made to trace accurate ownership of copyrighted material in this book. Errors and omissions will be corrected in subsequent editions, provided that notification is sent to the publisher.

Published 2001 by Prometheus Books

Inquiries should be addressed to
Prometheus Books
59 John Glenn Drive
Amherst, New York 14228–2197
VOICE: 716–691–0133, ext. 207
FAX: 716–564–2711
WWW.PROMETHEUSBOOKS.COM

05 04 03 02 01   5 4 3 2 1

Library of Congress Cataloging-in-Publication Data

Basta, L. (Lofty).
     Life and death on your own terms / L.L. Basta.
          p. cm.
     Includes bibliographical references and index.
     ISBN 1–57392–918–2
     1. Death. 2. Medical ethics. 3. Conduct of life. I. Title.

R725.5 .B27 2001
174'.24—dc21   2001019976

Printed in the United States of America on acid-free paper

CONTENTS

FOREWORD
Henry D. McIntosh, M.D., M.A.C.C.

❧

I t is with great humility that, at the request of Dr. Lofty L. Basta, I write the Foreword for this memorable tome. Dr. Basta has taught me more, during the four years I have known him, about the compassionate care of patients than any other mentor with whom I have been associated during the fifty-five years in which I have been engaged in medical matters. Dr. Basta has taught me two lessons: (1) the importance of recognizing and so admitting that a specific therapy in a specific patient is likely to be futile, and (2) that the most important question that everyone, eighteen years of age and older, should be encouraged to answer is "How can I insure that I will depart from this life on my own terms?" He also taught me that when care of a patient is recognized to be futile, palliative care or comfort care becomes of major importance.

I reached these decisions by following the advice of the respected jurist Oliver Wendell Holmes. Justice Holmes advised, "When I want to understand what is happening today, or try to decide what will happen tomorrow, I look back." How far back did I look? I recalled that Sir Winston Churchill said, "The further back you look—the further forward you are likely to see." I looked back fifty-plus years.

My medical career began in 1946 when I entered the University of Pennsylvania School of Medicine in Philadelphia. I had just completed a tour in the military, fighting both the Germans and the Japanese, behind their lines as a parachutist, leading an O.S.S. (Office of Strategic Service)

Dr. McIntosh is former Director of Cardiology at Duke University, former Chairman of Medicine at Baylor College of Medicine, prior President of the American College of Cardiology, and currently Co-Chairman of Project GRACE (Guidelines for Resuscitation and Care at End-of-Life).

commando team. Having devoted so much effort to fighting death from enemy rifle fire, and the like, it was relatively easy to fight death due to germs, cancer cells, vascular complications, and so on. It soon became apparent, however, that, we needed better "tools." So early in my medical career, I pursued research efforts seeking new ways to postpone death, even of patients in a vegetative state. I recall early in my career, while on the faculty at Duke University's School of Medicine in Durham, North Carolina, being involved in studies designed to understand the mechanism(s) of action of cardiopulmonary resuscitation (CPR) and to improve the success of the procedure. Back then, we would never accept a Do Not Resuscitate order. I recall that after one of our early successful resuscitations, I scheduled a conference to demonstrate to the staff and students the procedure and the success thereof. The patient was presented. He had no complaints or disabilities related to the procedure or the preceding events leading to his circulatory collapse or "death" and he expressed his gratitude to his "saviors." I then called on the dean of the Duke University Divinity School, whom I had invited to the conference, to make a few comments. He stood and looked at me for about a minute without saying a word. He then said, "Dr. McIntosh, I thought that you always spoke the truth." I replied, "I always try to." The Dean then replied, "You said that the patient was dead." I agreed that I had. He then, with a loud voice, said, "Resuscitation—Yes! Resurrection—No!" Clearly, we had to redefine *death*. This was done. But we increased our effort(s) to fight it.

By reading medical history and looking further back in time, it was clear that until recent years, society granted physicians many special privileges. The public wanted to accept that medical decision making and other patient-related actions, carried out by their physicians, were guided by the *principle of beneficence*. This means that every effort of the physician was to promote the well-being of the patient. I interpreted this, back then, as meaning that I had to keep the patient alive, regardless, even if he or she was only a vegetable.

It was generally accepted, until recent years, that the public wanted to believe that only the physician possessed the requisite knowledge and judgment to make decisions regarding the appropriate treatment of a patient. This belief, by most of the public, led to the widespread acceptance of the term *medical paternalism,* which meant that the actions of the physician should be like those of a *parent* to his or her child. Most of society accepted in years past that parents would want their children to live, even if they were severely deformed and unresponsive.

History tells us that these principles of beneficence and paternalism served society for century after century as the guideposts for the ideal practice of medicine. Furthermore, history also teaches that the overriding principle, guiding a doctor's actions, until recent years, was to keep the patient alive, *regardless*.

As I recall my experiences over many years, I realize that the attitudes of increasing members of society, and some doctors, began to change about a quarter of a century ago. At that time, as a result of the activities associated with Karen Ann Quinlan,[1] the courts invaded sickrooms and began to give orders. History tells us that on the night of April 15, 1975, Ms. Quinlan, aged twenty-two, was brought to a hospital in a coma. She was placed on a respirator and, despite extensive diagnostic studies and therapy including the respirator, she remained in a persistent vegetative state. The family was very attentive, but at no time did Karen make a purposeful response.

Karen's family were devout Catholics and sought guidance regarding her care from the Church. They were told that the respirator was *extraordinary* and that they should return Karen to her *natural* state by having the respirator removed. Even if she should die, such an action was morally correct. The family requested the physician to remove the respirator but he refused for fear Karen might die and he might be accused of killing her.

Following the physician's refusal, the Quinlans asked a lower court in New Jersey to order the physician and the hospital to remove the respirator, but after a prolonged trial, that court refused. The Quinlans then sought help from the New Jersey Supreme Court in June 1976. The New Jersey Supreme Court finally agreed that the family did have the right to order the respirator be removed and it was. That was the *first time* that a court had given orders regarding therapy that did not support the orders of the physician. This case demonstrated that the Quinlans and other families with similar problems, the courts, and lawyers could become the spokespersons for a patient.

The events experienced by a second patient demonstrated more emphatically that a physician can no longer just fight death. It also demonstrated the importance of an Advance Care Plan, as described by Dr. Basta in the pages to follow. In 1983, Nancy Cruzan,[2] a young woman in her twenties, lost control of her car and was found in a ditch without detectable respiratory or cardiac function. She was attended promptly by paramedics and cardiopulmonary function was restored, but she remained in a persistent vegetative state. She could not receive orally appropriate nutrition and hydration, so a stomach tube was implanted. Despite excellent care, she remained mentally unresponsive. The family was convinced that Nancy would not want to live that way. It took the family seven years and four court trials, including one in the U.S. Supreme Court, to persuade "the powers that be" that Nancy would not want to live that way. It was finally ordered, in the fourth trial, that the tube be removed. Nancy died twelve days later.

This is the case that prompted Senator John Danforth, from Missouri, and Senator Daniel Moynihan, from New York, to guide through the Halls of Congress "The Patient Self-Determination Act" (PSDA). The act requires health-care delivery insitutions to inform patients, at the time of admission, of their right to refuse treatment through the creation of a living will and/or proxy appointments.

The events associated with these and similar cases, and my association with Dr. Basta, taught me the tragedies associated with pursuing care that is futile and the importance of palliative care. I am confident that the readers of this book will recognize, as have I, the importance of an Advance Care Plan and identification of a Health Care Surrogate for everyone eighteen years and older. I am sorry it took me so long to realize the failings of such a total commitment to fighting death as I had. I trust that my students and fellow physicians will learn the lessons that I learned from Dr. Basta sooner than I did. I am confident they, as well as the public, will if they read this book.

PROLOGUE
Dying: A Personal Note

❧

Everyone can master a grief but he that has it.
                    Shakespeare, *Much Ado about Nothing*, 3:21:28

I am a physician specializing in the treatment of heart disease who has been afflicted with cancer. As a physician, I am bound by the Hippocratic Oath to do everything I can to prolong the lives of my patients and alleviate their suffering. Over the years, steadily and imperceptibly, medical intervention to "alleviate suffering" has received a much diminished status compared to the prolongation of life in my practice of medicine and probably in most physicians' practices. Death became the prime enemy to be conquered; prolongation of life became my mission. Toward this goal, I devoted my energies, talents, skills, and passions, all mediated by the powers of the new and exciting tools of high technology.

These powers, imperceptibly but increasingly, took precedence over the antiquated and sacramental tools of medicine: touching, listening, and encouragement. The awesome powers conferring comfort, reassurance, encouragement, and maintaining a sense of well-being have been almost lost in the process.

I have become conditioned to derive my "highs" from technological achievements. No joy has ever approached that derived from opening a blocked blood vessel in a patient who has experienced a heart attack. No triumph has come close to that of bringing a heart that ceased to beat properly back to its regular and orderly rhythm through a carefully administered jolt of electricity. And I felt the greatest ecstasy of all from bringing a person back from the abyss of death by prompting a heart that had

11

stopped beating into beating again. I have loved my patients and my profession. It provided me with exhilaration, gratification, and a sense of accomplishment, as well as a decent living.

The heady success experienced by many physicians can give them a feeling of immortality. I immodestly believed, "I might not be able to walk on water, but I am willing to try, and one day I shall succeed!" One day in February 1987, that sense of immortality vanished. That morning, I noticed some discomfort in my groin and the stream of my urine was weak. Reluctantly, I approached my friend, a urologist, Dr. Roger Haglund, and asked him to examine my prostate. After the examination, I knew the diagnosis when I looked at his face; his eyes declared the diagnosis. In a soft and kind voice he said, "You have a much enlarged prostate gland. There is a large and hard nodule in one of the lobes . . . I believe it to be cancer."

Being suddenly presented with the possibility of your death works a brutal kind of magic. All the petty details of your life are swept aside. What matters is one small point of light ahead of you. You become fixated upon it. Call it awakening, transformation, or an "on the road to Damascus" experience—it is truly life-altering. Your value system becomes rattled at the core. In one moment, the once infinite, invincible, indestructible, resolute, and confident person learns finitude, vulnerability, helplessness, insecurity, and, yes, fear. I had grown to believe that the land of sickness and disease was my own; dealing with my patients' acute illness, often life-threatening and critical, and the numberless encounters with death, albeit vicarious, must have prepared me to face my mortality. How untrue! My encounter with cancer was my rite of passage into a frightening, foreign land of being mortally ill.

More than anything else, anxiety and fear took hold. It is ironic that I did not experience the classical five phases taught in medical textbooks as "typical" responses to a life-threatening illness; namely denial, defiance, bargaining, depression, and acceptance.[1] Now that I have had time to reflect, I recall that I have seen patients and their loved ones react in any one or combination of these modes; although I have rarely witnessed the whole sequence.

For me, I had but one option: to accept and deal with my illness as best as I could. The poet Rainer Maria Rilke advised, "be patient with all that is unresolved in your heart and learn to love the questions themselves." Well, I tried.

My wife and I made the trip to M. D. Anderson Cancer Center in Houston and the diagnosis was confirmed. I was advised to undergo pelvic lymphadenectomy (surgical removal of small lymph nodes in my abdomen and pelvis) to assess the grade of cancer. This was to be followed by radiation therapy (the use of high-voltage X-rays) to burn the tumor and the area around it, including the rectum and bladder.

The pundits of medical ethics preach the concepts of shared decision making between patient and physician, with the patient having ultimate autonomy to determine his or her treatment destiny. They caution against paternalization by the physician in medical decisions. Have those ethicists ever been patients themselves? The vulnerability of patients often leads them to forfeit this responsibility. Dr. Eugene Stead, a legendary physician who chaired the Department of Medicine at Duke University for twenty years, 1947–1967, was once quoted as saying

> Two years in a hospital, night and day, are necessary to see how illness looks, to see what people behind the patient look like in all circumstances. I must confess that in this era of unprecedented technologic advance, it takes a doctor to experience disease firsthand to sensitize him to the human component of disease.[2]

Well, I am a physician and now also a patient. Ask me about a heart problem, and I will answer you with confidence and authority. But, there I was, in a hospital bed, faced with death from a disease I knew very little about. The expert made a recommendation. I trusted his professional opinion, and I trusted him as a person. My answer was, as expected, "Do what you think is best for me."

I recall the thousands of times my patients relinquished medical decision making to me with the pronouncement "You're the doctor." In the practice of medicine, there is no substitute for a physician who earns his or her patient's trust. I wish we could keep it this way! This trust is the essence of that sacred and powerful bond between patient and physician called the doctor-patient relationship.

For the first time in my life, I had to experience what it is like to be a patient, to face major surgery and its sequellae, and to know what it is like to discover mortality. My center of gravity had shifted substantially and irretrievably in one moment.

It is one thing to be the valiant warrior armed with the powerful tools of high technology and well prepared to combat an enemy that you have trained to face and conquer. It is another thing altogether when the enemy is within you. How vastly different when your own body becomes the battlefield. How different to witness the fight between a cancer expanding within you and the treatments promising to cure you, but also inevitably hurting you along the way. My experience with my illness brought into question, in my mind, traditional teaching about ethics in medical schools: Beneficence (doing good), nonmaleficence (abstaining from wrongdoing), justice, paternalism (forcing decision making), autonomy, and altruism are key players in basic philosophical ethics. But abstract ethics are remote from the drama of the human encounter with the confrontation of fear and hope, surrender and denial, acceptance and rejection, depression and defiance, hopelessness and anger.

Basic precepts of medical ethics teach that the "informed consent" process has three iron-clad legs: full disclosure, patients' competence, and the exercise of free will. As a patient, I readily discovered flaws in the application of each of these components. Full disclosure is exercised by having you sign a two-page sheet of printed paper telling you that you may die, bleed, get infected, never wake up from anesthesia, etc. Competence assumes that a patient in the grip of fear and anxiety is able to deliberately evaluate and choose among various treatment options and that whatever choice he or she makes is unencumbered by extraneous influence. How vastly disassociated from reality. In the first place, the consent form is nothing but legalese jargon that helps only to minimize physician legal liability. In other words, it is not designed to inform the patient but protect the doctor. And to assume that a frightened patient is capable of proper reasoning is clearly a stretch. In his essay on reason and passion, David Hume, the famed nineteenth-century philosopher, reminds us that, in the setting of strong passions, such as hope or fear, grief or joy, despair or security, men often act knowingly against their interest. Furthermore, peoples' reaction to bad medical news is often emotional and reflexive. If it is cancer the instinctive reaction is "Take it out," "I'm going to die," "Help me." Many patients do not even want to be told the whole truth about their illness or are unable to comprehend the complexities of the medical problems. They much prefer a sincere, honest discussion with a physician whom they trust and whose integrity they can count on to guide them through the process of choosing the treatment that bests suits their particular circumstances.

My painful experience with my disease was also enlightening. I discovered that I am not afraid of death itself, but of how I might die. I dreaded a prolonged, painful existence. I realized that death is not an offense to nature but the realization of the completion of life. I know that if I were to choose, I would like to depart peacefully in my bed, without pain or suffering. I state this emphatically while I am enjoying life like never before. My disease has been in remission for several years. I am keenly cognizant of what brings meaning to life: love of family, genuine caring, and the immense pleasure of being surrounded by wonderful students and colleagues.

It is an irony that one has to experience the threat of death in order to enable one to look within to contemplate one's own mission in life with its finitude. Death is the ultimate mystery; out of beholding the unknown comes the openness to experience the ultimate and inevitable act of dying.

This book is a testament to my confrontation with the imminence of death. Although as a patient I have relinquished much medical decision making to my physician, I do not want to relinquish control over how I will die; I do not want to be "treated to death." I am writing this book to help others confront this issue and to help prepare them to make decisions that can control the final phase of their lives.

INTRODUCTION
Misplaced Medical Heroics

❧

A few years ago, before I was diagnosed with cancer and forced to really ponder my own mortality, I was attending to a "routine" emergency at the hospital. Suddenly, a "code blue" was called. The familiar alarm declared that someone's heart had just stopped beating. Along with hordes of other health-care professionals, I hurried to the patient's room where I took command of the resuscitation. The patient's heart resumed beating and Mr. Jones,* the patient, began breathing again.

There was a full moon that night. On the way to my car, I felt as if the moon and the stars were there to celebrate my triumph over death.

The next morning, the nurses informed me that Mr. Jones was fully recovered. He was alert and completely aware of himself, others, and the surroundings. I visited Mr. Jones in the intensive care unit and congratulated him for his new lease on life. It was my first eye-to-eye contact with Mr. Jones. He stared at me and didn't utter a word. I wondered why. After a long moment of silence he said accusingly, "Why did you do this to me? You have taken away from me my one chance to leave this world in dignity." He went on to tell me that he had been made miserable by lung cancer, which had spread through his body. His pain was intolerable and no longer tractable to powerful pain-killing medicine. Bodily pain, as burdensome and demoralizing as it was, he could endure. But he could not abide the mental suffering that resulted from his total dependence, inability to care for himself, and the enormous drain on his life savings that would hurt his family. "Physical pain can be numbed with medicine, but mental suffering

---

*Unless otherwise indicated, names have been fictionalized in deference to the person's right to privacy.

17

is not touched by any medicine," he said. He had been waiting for the moment of a peaceful, graceful exit. He concluded by saying, "I will never forgive you for what you have done to me." I wished at that moment that the ground could have opened up and swallowed me. I felt as if a shower of ice water had been poured on me. Tears overpowered me as I realized that the pinnacle of technological triumphs—the resuscitation of life—and the nadir in human failures—the resuscitation of a miserable existence— can meet at one point in time, and that these two extremes can become one and the same act. My encounter with Mr. Jones taught me a valuable lesson: Bringing someone back from the darkness of death, someone yearning for a graceful exit, in order to subject him or her to myriad punishments is not a miracle reminiscent of the raising of Lazarus. It is a misguided insult to human dignity. It has nothing to do with the essence of medicine, the core of which is compassion for others' well-being.

Sooner or later, I will face mortality. I want to make it perfectly clear that I do not want any health-care professional, knowingly or unknowingly, to treat me in the way that I treated Mr. Jones. I have not seen Mr. Jones since that encounter. I am sure he has long since departed this planet. But I would like to take this opportunity to say that I am eternally grateful for the lesson he taught me.

I know how I do not want to die. I do not want to die in a hospital bed, hooked up to a multitude of tubes that are connected to machines that breathe for me, produce urine on my behalf, or beat in place of my heart. I have had a great life, and I am enjoying the best years of it. I want to preserve the remainder of my life as long as I can, but not at any cost. This view is not just my own. It is shared by the vast majority of citizens that are well informed about outcomes of medical interventions near the end of life. In a recent nursing conference, I asked this question of 200 nurses, many of whom work in intensive care units. Not one nurse wished to die the way most Americans spend their last moments. Instead, they wished to die at home in a clean, warm bed. Advances in medical technology have not diminished the truth of George Bernard Shaw's conclusion in his play, *The Doctor's Dilemma*: "Do not try to live forever. You will not succeed."[1]

Discussions about the need for health-care reform have intensified recently. A majority of Americans seem to agree that something needs to be done to curb the runaway costs of health care in America. However, there seems to be no consensus about the specifics of what needs to be accomplished, nor of how to go about it. Unless we have a proper diagnosis of what needs reform, the proposed treatment is unlikely to be effective. The prescription under consideration today will yield, at best, temporary symptomatic relief, and, at worst, may prove to be countertherapeutic and too costly.

True, the United States has the best doctors, hospitals, and medical technology that humanity has ever known, but as a whole, the U.S. health-care system fails to deliver the best medicine for the public at large.[2] The United States ranks thirty-seventh among world nations for overall health-care performance, sandwiched between Costa Rica and Slovenia, according to a recent World Health Organization report (2000). The United States spends $4,187 per capita for health care, almost twice as much as France or Japan ($2,370). Yet, the mean life span adjusted for a range of disabilities is seventy years in the United States, seventy-five years in Japan, and seventy-three years in France.

An aging society with ever-increasing demand for more and better health care abetted by breathtaking technological advances promising longer and healthier lives is at the core of the problem. Earlier in this century, it took fifty years to double all existing human knowledge. In the 1970s, ten years was sufficient for an encore, and in 1985, it took only two years to double all that is known to man. Unfortunately, the promise of immortality and a technological fountain of eternal youth are as elusive as ever.

Extensive medical intervention near the end of life, in part, stems from, and is intertwined with, fear of litigation. No doubt, "defensive medicine" constitutes a substantial portion of health-care expenditure in this country. It is true that an alert legal system contributes to the excellence of medical care standards in America. On the other hand, the ease of litigation and the size of punitive damages in some well-publicized cases have rendered the medical profession extremely cautious. Physicians worry constantly about the possibility of malpractice litigation with any unfavorable treatment outcome. Routinely, they seek high-tech interventions in order to prevent any remote possibility of being sued. This self-protective behavior from physicians, while justifiable, is self-perpetuating and very costly for the society at large. Some might argue, not groundlessly, that fear of litigation may not be the main reason for excessive treatment care, but it continues to be its main excuse.

Other important factors include the public's insatiable appetite for, and unrealistic expectations from, high technology interventions and a health-care system that has undermined the time-treasured doctor-patient trust. These factors and others have conspired to produce our prevailing, wasteful, death-defying, technology-avid culture. The "do everything possible" demand from patients and their families is usually met by willing physicians ready to undertake one more high-tech, punishing intervention paid for by a health-care system, even if the intervention has a minuscule chance to produce a measurable benefit to the patient.

How did we allow ourselves, as individuals and as a society, to get into this bottomless pit? Why do we allow people to be medically treated to death, without regard to the emotional and financial consequences for individuals, families, and society?

Physicians should have predicted that overtreatment could produce permanently disabled bodies connected to malfunctioning heads; they should have forewarned the public, but they didn't. Consequently, the public demands useless, expensive care when it shouldn't. Legislators might have enacted the necessary laws to enable establishing priorities for the distribution of expensive and sparse resources, but they couldn't. And the courts (including the U.S. Supreme Court) have had the chance to guide our way through this nightmare, but they haven't (in Nancy Cruzan's case, the young woman was sustained in a permanent vegetative state).

In an era of increasingly shared medical information, medical practice is changing into a partnership between physicians and the public. Physicians no longer command an absolute moral authority in deciding the troubling issues of whom to treat and whom to let die. Neither will user-friendly health data ever be sufficient for the lay public to answer these vexing questions. Medical ethicists would like to claim these issues as being within their domain. But ethics are not freestanding universal truths; they are merely logical deductions from ideological premises colored by our cultural, religious, and personal beliefs and biases.

One of the major dilemmas facing legislators is, no doubt, how to limit care without being accused of medical rationing. The latter is a no-no in political language. Rationing (the "R" word) is the equivalent to political cyanide. Given these facts, legislators have to discover a convoluted way by which they take us to the promised land of increased access to medical care at a lower cost, without the appearance of rationing care. They have relinquished this weighty issue to the mercy of market forces with their new schemes of managed care. I am fearful that, in order to accomplish their political objective, they will pit doctor against patient.

In the process, the one clear casualty will be that the sacred bond of doctor-patient relationship will be mortally sacrificed at the altar of cost containment. The traditional role of the physician as the patient's servant and advocate who provides the best care regardless of costs will likely be subject to political manipulation. Instead, in the new world of reform, the physician will be expected to act as the agent of the big new bureaucracy, a heartless business establishment whose relentless focus is on maximizing shareholder's profit. He is expected to limit and regulate health-care delivery on behalf of the big company (or the government). The American health-care system would sustain the worst self-inflicted damage in history. According to this scenario (which is already underway), access to health care will be delivered (and rationed) according to guidelines set forth by bureaucrats. Those guidelines will be formulated with the sole intention of limiting cost. Therefore, in a peculiar way, the legislators will have used noble slogans to cover less noble goals.

It behooves us as citizens of a society that upholds the highest ideals of equality and democracy to engage ourselves in formulating these guidelines that will set health-care priorities and conserve limited resources. Relinquishing this role to bureaucrats will prove to be a grave mistake.

During the past few years, many landmark events have led to a heightened awareness about the vexing complexities of end-of-life medical issues. Among these are the Supreme Court ruling, in 1997, that American citizens do not have a constitutional/liberty right to be assisted in dying by their physicians; the enactment, in the same year, of the "Death with Dignity Act" in Oregon, which legalized physician-assisted suicide in that state; and Dr. Jack Kevorkian's unending tales in aiding patients to end their lives, ultimately in view of a large television audience. In addition, findings of the "Study to Understand Prognoses and Preferences for Outcomes and Risks of Treatment," a national multicenter study of over 9,000 critically ill and dying patients, became available to the medical community. The study highlighted many glaring shortcomings in the medical care of the dying. It showed the near irrelevance of currently used living wills and that in many instances, the patients' own wishes have been ignored. Many patients had to endure pain and suffering needlessly before their farewell.

Furthermore, many states have enacted new laws to enable the fulfillment of patients' choices for medical care. Public interest in the subject continues to escalate, with many national and philanthropic organizations having allocated sizable grants in support of the search to improve the quality of care during the last chapter of life.

In this book, I have addressed one component of the extremely complex problem of health care—medical care near the end of life. It is an attempt to explore the causes, the dilemmas, and the ethical and legal controversies, as well as the economic consequences of the excessive use of high technology and the exercise of futile medical care at the end of someone's life. This book is not intended to be a compendium of issues related to medical ethics or legal precedents relating to the care of the terminally ill. Rather it is a search to find a common ground from which we can proceed toward establishing unified policies that guide treatment at the end of life.

I do this from the perspective of a practicing cardiologist who has been part of the medical revolution of the past four decades, and as a citizen who cares deeply about our country and its future generations. In so doing, I have drawn on my own vast clinical experience and on the wisdom of many others. All medical case histories included in this book are real. Most patients are referred to by fictitious names. When true names are mentioned, appropriate permission has been obtained from their families.

The book is written for common citizens who care deeply about preserving their dignity and sparing loved ones the agony and economic consequences inherent in life-and-death decisions. Also, it should be a valuable guide for medical students and young physicians who have learned about manifestations of disordered body functions, damaged organs, and disturbed emotions. They need to know more about the fearful, hopeful, suffering, anxious human being behind the disease. Hospital ethics committees should benefit from the case studies and ethicolegal reviews.

As a physician, I have executed the "will" of thousands of patients regarding how they wish to die. As an author, I would like to help others exercise more control of the end-stage of their lives. This book is intended to educate all Americans about life-and-death issues. The topics I will address include the following:

- The need to adopt a new definition of *death* that is based on the "death of the person" rather than the death of an organ such as the heart or the brain. This information could equip all of us to better evaluate referendums on the right to die, health-care prioritizing, and other timely and controversial issues.

- The need to set up a commission composed of both health-care professionals and laypeople to grapple with issues of life and death.
- The inadequacies of existing living wills in the United States today.
- The need to adopt a new, standardized living will. I am proposing an original Advance Care Plan with a concomitant workbook section. This document could do much to ensure a death without suffering and with dignity for all.

Project GRACE (Guidelines for Resuscitation and Care at End-of-Life), a nonprofit foundation, was launched in Florida as a partnership between physicians and the lay public, with the overriding goal of developing communitywide standards for medical care at the sunset of life.[3] Project GRACE has developed an updated Advance Care Plan document, a copy of which is included in the appendix. This document has the distinction of simplicity and specificity. It has been tested (and modified) among groups of citizens with diversity in age, education level, social status, economic class, and religious beliefs. Equally important is that the Project GRACE Advance Care Plan document has found wide acceptance among health-care professionals and has proven to enhance physician-patient communication about end-of-life medical issues.

A professional publication from Project GRACE Special Task Forces is also included. This provides guidelines for determining medical futility, cardiopulmonary resuscitation, advance care planning, and palliative care.

Also included are case studies covering ethical dilemmas commonly encountered in end-of-life medical care. They should provide the public with a flavor of the vexing issues facing health-care providers as they care for the dying. Also, these case studies should be useful in teaching medical students and other health-care professionals and can serve as a valuable resource for ethics committees in health-care institutions.

Laila, my wife of forty years, has been my mentor, advisor, and critic, and has made the journey of my life so worthwhile that I wouldn't have wanted to undertake it without her. Each of my three children, Victor, Steven, and Mona, has given me valuable suggestions and guidance. And my very special grandsons, Max, Eli, and Cole, make me cherish every moment of life like never before.

Also, I wish to acknowledge with gratitude the support of the Board of Directors of Project GRACE, Executive Director Marty A. Ratliff, R.N.; partners in my private practice at Clearwater Cardiovascular and Interventional Consultants; and the excellent secretarial assistance of Susan Riedle and Lisa Weber. Limited space and imperfect recollection prevent me from acknowledging the hundreds of other persons who touched my life and influenced my thinking.

I am particularly indebted to Dan Doty, M.D.; Michael Geldart, J.D.; Irvin Kalb, M.D.; Bill Leonard, Ph.D.; Henry McIntosh, M.D.; Lu Redmond, R.N.; Ron Schonwetter, M.D.; and Robert Walker, M.D. Through their selfless dedication and exceptional talent they developed the recommendations for end-of-life care included in chapter 13.

Royalties proceeding from the sale of this book will go toward the support of Project GRACE.

1

IN SEARCH OF A NEW DEFINITION OF DEATH IN AN ERA OF HIGH TECHNOLOGY

I asked thee, "Give me immortality."
Then didst thou grant mine asking with a smile,
But thy strong Hours indignant worked their wills,
And beat me down and marred and wasted me,
And they could not end me, left me maimed . . .

Alfred, Lord Tennyson, *Tithonus*

Medical technology has advanced at breathtaking and heart-stopping speed in the last half of the twentieth century. Health-care professionals, let alone average citizens, have often been staggered by the pace of development, scrambling to keep up with the latest techniques. Because of this accelerated pace, we have not had the luxury of gaining a perspective on this technology. Indeed, our technological advances have, in a sense, outdistanced the social and ethical context in which they should be enacted. The result has been that technology often seems to control our destinies. As we shall see, advanced medical technology forced health-care professionals to adopt a new definition of life and death, with the unintended sequela of promoting miserable, terminal existences for too many people.

This chapter is designed to give the reader a sense of the accelerated pace of medical technology today, based on my own personal experience as a physician.

When I graduated from medical school in 1955, the acceleration of medical advances had just begun. But even having been exposed to this nascent technology, no medical person in the mid-1950s would have imagined the shape of today's medicine. Even the most enlightened cardiologists of the 1950s, if transported in a time capsule to the present, would be

25

bewildered in this new world and be overtaken by its wonders. The breath-taking pace of scientific advances in the diagnosis and treatment of disease has taken us to a totally new world, totally foreign to the practitioner of yesteryear. For me, it has been an enormously exciting, although demand-ing, experience to be part of this total technological transformation.

It is difficult to reconstruct the medical world of yesteryear. Just imagine a time fifty or so years ago, when the greatest drama was caused by the poliomyelitis virus (polio) for which there was no vaccine. The infection paralyzed or killed hordes of individuals, young and old. Iron lungs were used to enable these victims to stay alive while they struggled for various degrees of recovery. This scenario no longer exists—thanks to polio vaccine.

In the year of my graduation, the world was barely recovering from a devastating Second World War. War has traditionally been the great incen-tive for technological advances. Many of these advances have, in turn, spurred medical research. The imperatives of the war accelerated several engineering and technical innovations that proved to be applicable to medical research. These included monitoring devices to track vital body functions, new techniques for imaging the human body (such as methods utilized to enhance X-ray pictures) and the use of radioisotopes and ultra-sound waves in the identification of disease and in guiding treatment.

The discovery of penicillin and its use to combat infection inaugu-rated a new antibiotic era that enabled us to overcome previously lethal microbial infections. We are now able to control epidemics. Advances in war surgery led to improvements not only in operating techniques but also in anesthesia. Complex surgical procedures, deemed impossible a few years earlier, became commonplace. Trauma and orthopedic surgery witnessed enormous progress during the war. Much knowledge was gained in the areas of blood storage and transfusion. Limb prostheses and rehabilitation techniques improved life for veterans and others.

A MANIPULATION OF LIFE

Then surgeons accomplished the ultimate—something that was previously unthinkable. They began operating on the heart to remove bullets, shrapnel, and foreign bodies, thus opening a whole new frontier in surgery.

The heart was no longer considered "beyond surgery," as it had been earlier in the century. In the mid 1950s, surgeons performed operations to close congenital defects in the heart through cooling of the body. A few years later, we learned to use machines to stop the heart by cooling it at much lower temperatures, and to restart the heartbeat with warming. These machines, designed to bypass the heart and take over the functions of the lungs, ultimately were put to greater use, enabling heroic advances in heart surgery. Now, the most complex of heart defects can be corrected or at least improved using these techniques.

Soon thereafter, organ-replacing machines were invented to take over the functions of the kidneys and lungs and, gradually, renal dialysis and assisted ventilation were perfected, finding wide application and acceptance.

All these technological advances essentially resulted in a manipulation of life.

Not only were organs such as the heart and kidney manipulated in this era, but the basic unit of life—the cell—was also manipulated. Indeed, no less than the secret of life in the form of chromosomes and genes was discovered. The noted biochemists Wilkins, Crick, and Watson from Cambridge University in England were awarded the Nobel Prize in 1953 for defining the chemical composition of DNA, the material that defines us and gives us our genetic instructions. This discovery opened up a whole new vista of genetic research, which not only allowed us to uncover the secrets of relatively rare genetic diseases, but also to engineer new treatments and antibiotics for more common diseases, such as cancer, infections, and blood clots. Greater scientific wonders are anticipated as scientists unravel the intricate structure of human genes.

Many of the technological advances that have become part of the vocabulary of the common person were unheard of in the early 1950s. These advances included the advent of CT (computerized tomography) scanners, MRI (magnetic resonance imaging) devices, ultrasound imaging techniques, sophisticated nuclear imaging of the heart and brain, as well as many other diagnostic techniques. Even X-ray machines, which were considered high technology at the time of my graduation, became so advanced and the images so refined that you could hardly recognize the similarities. The use of electron microscopes and scanning microscopes, as well as new magnification and laboratory techniques, allowed the visualization of smaller and smaller subcellular structures.

CARDIOLOGY: A HEARTENING NEW MEDICAL SPECIALITY

In the 1950s, the specialty of heart disease, or cardiology, was in its infancy. Cardiologists depended on the clinical examination, chest X-ray, and the electrocardiogram (EKG), the electronic monitoring of heartbeats, to diagnose disease. In American textbooks of medicine from that era, the chapters on tuberculosis, syphilis, and typhoid fever were longer and more detailed than all that was written about diseases of the heart. Because high blood pressure is a symptomless disease, and because its causal connection to strokes and heart attacks was not yet known, big debate was still raging over whether to treat high blood pressure or whether high blood pressure was one of the varying characteristics of the individual person, like a large nose or large ears. When blood pressure was extremely high, leeches were applied to the patient's temples to suck out some of the patient's blood! And remember, this was the twentieth century, not the seventeenth century. Patients were prohibited from eating anything other than boiled rice free of salt. Today, the treatment of high blood pressure in America is a multibillion dollar industry (according to pharmaceutical company data), involving many sophisticated monitoring devices and drugs.

Before the advent of technology and the formal codification of the medical specialty known as cardiology, cardiologists relied on bedside diagnosis. The first tools of cardiologists were their hands, eyes, ears, brain— and the stethoscope, an instrument that amplifies the sounds of the heart. These early cardiologists would glean information by looking at the dancing of the veins in the neck; they would place their hands over the chest wall to discern changes in the movement of the heart. And through use of the stethoscope, they obtained information by listening to sounds produced by the heart. Generally, the more distinguished a cardiologist, the larger his stethoscope. Even today, the stethoscope is a symbol that distinguishes physicians from other professionals and laypeople.

Catheters, thin tubes that are threaded through a patient's circulatory system, were the next tool that augmented the cardiologist's diagnostic ability. In 1929, Werner Forssmann, a German surgeon, went so far as to disobey his chief's prohibition and inserted a catheter in his own heart, via a vein in his right arm. This established catherization as an important technique in the diagnosis of heart disease. He was co-recipient of the Nobel Prize in 1956 for his work.[1] A few years later, Radner used the same technique to visualize the arteries feeding the heart.[2] In the 1950s, heart catheterization enabled physicians to diagnose and evaluate congenital abnormalities (birth defects) of the heart and rheumatic valvular heart disease—the latter caused by rheumatic fever and resulting in damage to the heart valves that control blood flow. The combination of newly found scientific information with previously discovered ways to image the heart with X-rays and monitor it with electrical recording devices (i.e., EKG), established the new specialty of cardiology. The elucidation of heart problems obtained from catheterization contributed to our better understanding of information that was obtained from the patient's history and physical examination.

Initially, surgery on certain types of valve narrowing and some simple forms of congenital heart abnormalities was done while the heart was beating. These included the opening of a narrow mitral valve (the valve between the left atrium and ventricle) as a result of rheumatic disease. The valve was opened with the surgeon's finger or a special knife. A congenitally persistent defect between the two atria was closed by direct suture or by placement of a patch. More involved surgery on the heart itself would have been impractical on a throbbing organ that moved sixty times per minute. But soon, machines that allowed oxygen to travel through the body without the help of a beating heart (i.e., machines that assisted circulation of the blood and artificial ventilation) were perfected, and heart surgery for complex types of heart and vessel disease became commonplace. Thanks to the pioneer work of Forssmann and Radner, hardening of the coronary arteries has become easy to visualize and quantify using cinematographic imaging techniques. Aorto-coronary bypass surgery became possible through the efforts of the Argentinean surgeon René G. Favaloro, working at the Cleveland Clinic in 1967. Eleven years later, another maverick physician, Andreas Grunzig from Germany, introduced balloon angioplasty. A tiny balloon is threaded into the blood vessel and is carefully placed at the site of narrowing. By inflating the balloon, the narrowed segment is broadened, relieving the blockage.

Another new technological development involved electronic means to take over the pacemaker activities of the heart. These permanent pacemakers replace the heart's own electrical system when it has become dysfunctional. Pacemakers are now old-hat technology. The newest electrical system for the heart is an implantable defibrillator (a small device that is placed under the skin and connected to the heart chambers by wires). This enables the spontaneous return of the heart's rhythm whenever its beat becomes chaotic and hence life-threatening. The small device monitors the rhythm and appropriately sends a timed, measured electric shock to bring the heart back into rhythm.

At the same time, new discoveries in antibiotics applied to the treatment of heart disease, in addition to new ways to treat high blood pressure, changed the landscape even further. In 1955, rheumatic heart disease was the number one concern of cardiologists. Patients were cared for and rehabilitated in special wards and in some cases, sanatoriums. When I visited England in the late 1950s, I had the opportunity to visit Taplow Hospital outside London and observe firsthand the management of hundreds of children with acute rheumatic fever, in addition to the consequences of rheumatic valvular heart disease.

Rheumatic fever is now almost eradicated from the Western world, thanks to the discovery of penicillin, which treats the streptococcus bacterial infection responsible for rheumatic valvular disease. The number one enemy of the heart is now coronary artery disease, commonly known as "hardening of the arteries," a condition that accounts for half the deaths in the United States. Hardening or narrowing of the arteries, the blood vessels going to the heart, can cause coronary artery disease, the underlying cause of heart attacks. Just thirty years ago, one in every two patients experiencing a heart attack died of its complications.

Four decades ago, a patient with a myocardial infarction (i.e., heart attack) was treated with complete bed rest for at least six weeks. This was followed by a few months of gradually increasing activity. By the time the patient left the hospital, he or she would have become weak and depressed. Back pains, stiff joints, constant constipation, and not infrequently, hemorrhoids were inevitable consequences of this event. A heart attack meant disability for life. Contrast this with the situation today. Intensive care units have reduced the death rate due to heart attacks to one-third what it was. New "clot-busting" drugs that dissolve blood clots to open clogged arteries and prevent adverse events and other interventions have reduced death further by yet another half. Most patients with heart attacks leave the hospital in a few days. If they require further interventions, such as bypass surgery, their stay may be extended by up to one week. Most patients return to a normal, or near normal, active life. And besides bypass surgery, there are other possible interventions to open up narrowed arteries: angioplasty, utilizing tiny balloons to open up the area of narrowing, as well as laser beams and metal coils, to name a few.

For those with weak hearts, there is an armament of new and effective medicines that not only relieve symptoms of shortness of breath, but also improve the ability to exercise. And, yes, these agents also prolong life.

The greatest miracle of all has been organ transplantation, including heart and heart-and-lung transplants. Pioneer heart surgeons became recognized as heroes, held in awe for their ability to control life. In 1967 South African surgeon Christian Bernard performed the first successful heart transplant. He became an instant celebrity on a par with movie stars and world-class athletes.

These new medical advances attracted some of the brightest young minds into the healing profession. Scientific progress was supported by substantial grants from government institutions, industries, and entrepreneurs wanting to cash in on new discoveries. No doubt, these advances had a profound effect in further accelerating a process already in progress.

THE NEW TECHNOLOGY: PROLONGING LIFE AND PROMPTING A NEW SET OF PROBLEMS

Implementation of these new technologies and drugs has resulted in a longer and better life for most people. According to the National Center of Health Statistics, Hyattsville, Maryland, the mean life span of a person has increased by several years since the middle of this century. Since 1968, death from heart attacks dropped by 50 percent, and the incidence of strokes decreased by almost 60 percent in all age-adjusted groups. High blood pressure complications dropped by two-thirds, and rheumatic fever and its ravages have been almost eradicated.

Increasing the life expectancy of people through these advances was not an unalloyed boon; it caused a whole new set of problems. Although fewer people die from acute disease, more patients today are dying of heart failure than in decades earlier, in spite of advances in the treatment medications, just because they are living longer (see Figure 1). The steady increase in the inci-

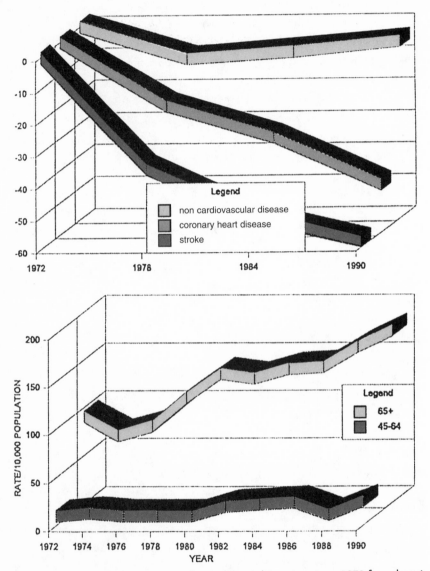

Figure 1. Percent decline in age-adjusted mortality rates since 1972 from heart disease and stroke compared to increased rates of hospitalization for heart failture (ages 45–64 and 65+, U.S. 1971–1991).

dence of heart failure has been reviewed in a 1992 article, "Prevalence and Mortality Rate of Congestive Heart Failure in the United States," by Dr. Douglas Schocken of the University of South Florida.[3] As we will see later, the increase in the elderly population and in their attendant debilitating diseases will have a profound influence on the main subject of this book. The aging of the population and the growth of the postwar baby-boom generation predicts a 40 percent further increase in the prevalence and cost of coronary heart disease in the elderly in the next three decades, according to Dr. Weinstein and associates in an article titled "Forecasting Coronary Artery Disease Incidence, Mortality and Cost," published in 1987.[4]

Not only health-care professionals but also the public at large fell in love with the new medical services. The populace demanded more and better services, and science, with its new apostles, was able to deliver. Exaggerated promises, not unexpectedly, resulted in unrealistic expectations and sometimes unreasonable demands from consumers enamored with the miracles promised by the new technologies. Hospitals found in the new technologies ways to distinguish themselves and to further their profits. The competition for the acquisition of the highest technology—CT scanners, MRI machines, heart-cath labs, and organ transplantation programs—grew at a breathtaking pace. Insurance companies paid for the services and were able to raise the premiums of willing and sometimes eager customers. Physicians learned, perfected, believed in, and almost worshipped the new technologies. They became the masters, priests, and demigods of this newfound religion. As physicians, we proclaimed ourselves the protectors of life and the enemies of death, which we sought to fight with vengeance. Death was no longer viewed as a natural end of life but as a medical failure: "The medicalization of death."[5]

THE PROFITEERS OF DEATH

In this highly individualistic, technology-driven, death-defying environment, many people profited from the new technology: the inventor and producer of the machines and devices, the drug companies, the insurance providers, hospitals, and physicians. This profit has come at a great cost to society, though. Health-care costs have escalated at a rate that is many times the rate of inflation. It grew as a percentage of the general national product, from less than 6 percent to the present 15 present in the span of three decades.[6] The genie is out of the bottle and has become a real giant. The consumer considers that he or she is entitled to the latest in technology, whether it costs a few cents or a million dollars—as long as someone else is paying for it (the insurance company for those covered with private insurance, or the government in the case of those covered by Medicare or Medicaid). Meanwhile, escalating health-care costs became a threat to the continued prosperity of our nation and its citizens, and the struggle to slow down this overheated machine has begun on many fronts.

THE SIDE EFFECTS OF TECHNOLOGY

As with every scientific advance, progress in medical science brought with it certain unique problems. Just consider the discovery of roentgen rays (X-rays). Here is a wonder tool that enabled physicians to see through skin, fat, and muscle to study bones and visualize internal organs using radiovisible dyes and the radio-opaque element, barium. Who would have predicted that this same radiation could produce leukemia, lymphoma, and other forms of cancer? Who would have thought that it would cause suppression of the bone marrow, the part of the bone that is the blood-making factory? And no one anticipated its danger to the not-yet born, its ability to cause genetic defects in the fetus.

The greatest (although, as we will see, not necessarily the most beneficial) triumph of medical technology must be in cardiopulmonary resuscitation (CPR). Forty years ago, before the publication of the classic *Fundamentals of Cardiopulmonary Resuscitation* by Drs. J. R. Jude and J. O. Elam (1965), the heart stoppage resulting in the cessation of oxygen flow meant the end of life.[7] Not anymore! Now, thanks to Dr. Bernard Lown, the noted Boston cardiologist who invented the contemporary defibrillator in 1962, when the heart stops because of a disordered electric rhythm, it can be shocked back into rhythm and the patient comes back from death to life.[8] And when the heart's electric wave ceases, the heart can be paced by an artificial generator; this is the closest medical encounter to the biblical "Pick up thy bed and walk." Similarly, when someone ceases to breathe, a machine can be used that drives breathing, and the machine settings can be adjusted to deliver the proper mixture of gases to the lungs. But maintaining blood flow through technology also has a downside.

A NEW DEFINITION OF LIFE AND DEATH

As noted earlier, as recently as thirty years ago, the cessation of heart-lung function and, consequently, vital blood flow was used to define death. According to this criterion, death occurred when the heart stopped or when the person ceased breathing on his or her own. Closed chest CPR was popularized in the early 1960s by a group of Johns Hopkins physicians. This landmark discovery replaced the often heroic adventures of opening the chest wall with the knife and squeezing the heart by hand to help it resume pumping. Also in the early 1960s, electric generators were improved through the new capacitor invented by Dr. Bernard Lown to deliver electric jolts to the heart to put it back in orderly rhythm. These two procedures found immediate application in the Western world.

The advent of this technology rendered obsolete the traditional definition of death. Faced with the challenge of finding a more fitting definition of death, philosophers and physicians looked for an alternative. Practically all body-organ functions can be substituted for by machines, except those of the brain. A heated debate ensued between those who advocated that death of a person has occurred with the loss of the higher brain functions of consciousness and awareness and those who insisted that death should be based on total loss of brain activity. The advent of the Harvard criteria for defining death provided a new perspective on death, centering on cessation of whole-brain function, including the primitive vegetative functions that take place at the subconscious level.[9] Heart-lung "death" was no longer true death, but a potentially reversible condition. In 1981, the President's Commission for the Study of Ethical Problems in Medicine and Biomedical and Behavioral Research confirmed this redefinition of death: "Irreversible cessation of all functions of the entire brain, including the brain stem."[10]

Because the use of machines to take over all functions of the body, except the brain, nullified the old definition of death, and because no alternative definition had yet been formulated, this definition of death was instantly adopted in the Western world. The new definition proved to be useful in dealing with extensive head injuries and acute brain catastrophes, such as occur in previously healthy individuals involved in catastrophic motor vehicle or motorcycle accidents, gunshot injuries to the head, and older patients with massive stroke or brain hemorrhage. It proved particularly useful in facilitating the harvesting of viable organs from potential donors for transplantation purposes. With the President's Commission report, the specialty of medical ethics was given a new life. It attracted a consortium of philosophers, humanists, legal scholars, and physicians to address the many confounding issues that resulted from this new definition. Many professionals provided much useful guidance, but some have drifted outside mainstream and practical thinking, engaging in arcane debates. These professionals often did not clarify issues for the layperson, they obfuscated them.

A DEFINITION OF LIFE THAT PROLONGS DEATH

As a result of recent technological advances and the use of the new definitions for life and death, many individuals have been kept alive when they would have died, according to the old definition of death as cessation of flow of the vital fluids resulting from heart and lung death. The 1960s and '70s produced tens of thousands of precariously living individuals who had sustained extensive brain injuries as a result of trauma or stroke, or who suffered cardiopulmonary arrest from which they were resuscitated, but during which they suffered irreversible brain damage (i.e., damage to the cerebral cortex and thus the "higher" brain functions). These individuals had probably irretrievably lost the content of consciousness and cognition, their memories, their ability to think and make decisions. But they had a persistently beating heart and circulating blood that carried enough oxygen to all their vital organs to prevent their bodies from dying. These individuals were sustained on machines that breathed for them. They were fed either by intravenous fluids or through tubes inserted into their stomachs. These passive slaves of high technology required enormous efforts and costs to sustain their miserable existences. The medical community has displayed total ethical paralysis on how to handle these horrible consequences of advanced medical technology. Health-care professionals may think they have mastered this medical technology, but by ignoring or avoiding the ethical context in which this technology should be enacted, the technology has in effect mastered them.

CONSTITUTIONAL RIGHTS
FOR THE UNCONSCIOUS

The new definition of death had far-reaching and problematic consequences, probably not fully realized at its inception.

According to the new definition of death, human beings who will probably never regain consciousness and higher brain function are nevertheless
alive and therefore entitled to all the constitutional rights granted to American citizens. A straightforward interpretation of the law of the land leads to
the inescapable conclusion that these lives, sustained by primitive brain function, must be protected and sustained at any cost and for any length of time.
Therefore, any slackness in carrying out this sacred duty would be unlawful
and would expose the treating physician to conviction for manslaughter. A
physician's professional code of honor and obligation further complicate this
matter of ending a life that is a mere vegetative life. The Hippocratic oath
obliges physicians to preserve life and not intentionally to cause death; an
intervention to end life would appear to be legally, ethically, and morally
wrong. All this conspires to make these vegetative beings and all of society,
for that matter, slaves to high-tech machines.

A REBELLION AGAINST TECHNOLOGICAL SLAVERY

Some enlightened Americans started to express their resentment against a
vegetative existence, and thus against becoming the slaves of technology.
For these people, the fear that one's final months or years might be spent
in a nightmare of confusion, dependence, and helplessness far exceeded the
fear of death. The "Right to Die" movement was born in America in the
1960s out of disdain for the proposition that a life void of dignity should
be endured as a price of medical technological advances. The Euthanasia
Society of America was established, with the overriding objective to put
control of the moment of death in the hands of those who are dying. Luis
Kutner, the society's founder, first proposed the idea of the "Living Will"
in a meeting of the society in 1967, to serve as a manifesto for the right to
die. Although their intentions are laudable, the right to die seems like a
strange claim in a society in which life, liberty, and the pursuit of happi-

ness are cornerstones of civil liberties. Death, which once was viewed as an imperative, is now claimed by some to be a "right"—a right that is to be preserved against the invasion of technology.

Counterbalancing the "right to die" movement was a new class of health-care professionals who worshipped high technology. For these people, death became an enemy to be conquered. Every human existence, except for those experiencing total brain death, was to be preserved by all means and at all costs. Many physicians viewed their primary and sacred mission to be the preservation of any vestige of life for all time. An increasing segment of the American public came to believe, justifiably, that doctors cruelly and needlessly were delaying the process of dying for various motives, some of which are highly suspect.

This new state of confusion, with polar-opposite viewpoints, continues to dominate our society today. This has been compounded by the dramatization of exceedingly rare cases of persistent vegetative state (PVS) in which there is sufficient recovery of consciousness to allow the ability to communicate, contrary to medical predictions. These cases are true medical "miracles" that defy logic. By definition, the term *permanent vegetative state* applies only when the chance of any improvement is less than 1 percent. Sensationalization of these unique cases by the media have fueled ever more unrealistic expectations from modern technology.

A HIGHER DEFINITION OF LIFE AND DEATH

The definition of death based on whole-brain death is not oriented to being a human. This definition is based on the death of an organ rather than the death of an individual, a person. Furthermore, this definition, by demanding that many people remain in a vegetative state, promotes a miserable existence for many at the end of life. The adoption of a new definition of death, based on the death of higher brain function, is one of the first critical steps toward avoiding the misery experienced by many at the end of life.

Upper-Brain Death: The Part Is More Important Than the Whole

Between the heart-lung definition of death and the newly adopted definition of whole or total brain (including brain stem) death, there is another category of brain damage that prevents the individual from ever being able to "function as a whole," as a person. This category is termed "higher brain death" and refers to that part of the brain known as the cerebral cortex. This concept, presented by the noted ethicist Dr. J. L. Bernat in the late 1970s and redefined by Dr. Stuart Youngner, Professor of Psychiatry and Biomedical Ethics at Case Western Reserve University School of Medicine and his associates in the early 1980s, deserves further discussion.[11]

Higher brain death occurs when there is permanent total loss of consciousness and cognition, when there is irreversible loss of the ability to reason, to understand, to remember, to recognize, to have passions, or to experience feelings. Many diseases affect the brain causing partial loss of high brain function. These include stroke, Alzheimer's disease, and many other diseases. These cases should not be confused with permanent vegetative state when *all* high brain functions are irretrievably lost. Another way of looking at higher brain death is that it occurs when all that constitutes a person is dead. As noted previously, the ability of high technology to take over the functions of the heart and lungs has rendered the heart-lung or vital-flow definition of death obsolete. By the same token, the ability of high technology to substitute for many lower brain functions, such as by organ-replacing machines, or by triggering spontaneous breathing, or providing support of blood pressure and regulating temperature and the level of hormones, would appear to render the "whole brain" definition of death obsolete also.

It is the higher functions of the brain that cannot be replaced or substituted for by machines. These higher functions define the person, a distinct, living being with unique intellect, will, and passions.

Figure 2 shows a picture of the brain, brain stem, and spinal cord. A brief summary of how the brain functions follows.

The brain can be divided into two basic portions: the upper brain (or cerebral cortex) and the brain stem. The upper brain consists of two large hemispheres connected horizontally by the corpus callosum. The brain stem is positioned vertically to the hemispheres and at their base.

The brain stem can be viewed as a telephone or communication center. It is actually a coordinating center that receives billions of messages from the command stations located in the hemispheres (upper brain). The hemispheres, or cerebral cortex, contain the centers of perception and senses, such as touch, taste, smell, sight, and hearing, as well as pain and

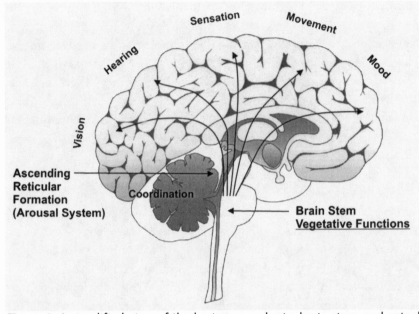

Figure 2. A simplified view of the brain: upper brain, brain stem, and spinal cord.

temperature. They contain the higher center for motor coordination—how you move your body in the world—and also the library of memory and stored experiences. They are responsible for our feelings and passions, our desires, our motivations, and our thinking.

The brain stem is responsible for basic functions, including the thermostats for temperature, breathing, blood pressure, and heartbeat. An ascending reticular arousal system (ARAS) rises from the brain stem to both hemispheres and is responsible for the state of awakening. The cerebellum, located on the back side of the brain, is primarily responsible for the coordination of movement, the commands for which arise from the hemispheres. Neither the brain stem nor the cerebellum is able to interpret or initiate measured commands on its own nor to function in an orderly fashion without the decoding and command centers in the high brain, the cerebral cortex.

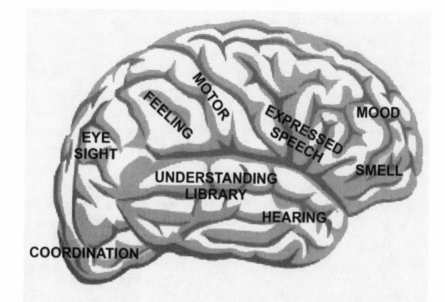

Figure 3. The upper brain: the cerebral cortex and its associated functions.

The Cerebral Cortex—Our Crown Jewel

The cerebral cortex is the crowning achievement of the brain. This "higher" portion of the brain, containing computer-like, specialized cells and neurons, is what distinguishes the human animal from all other animals. These neurons represent stations from which orders originate, messages are received, decoding of these messages occur, comparison of messages with past stored experiences occur, and a final reaction takes place. Genetic and cultural influences determine how and to what extent these small "computers" function and react. The collective characteristics of these functions in turn define the *person*. The functions of the cerebral cortex are seen in Figure 3.

The neocortex, the precursor of the upper brain, developed some 200 million years ago in protohumans, our earliest ancestors. This is not a very long time relative to the 4 billion years since the earth was born. Our human species, *Homo sapiens*, walked on the face of the earth some 50,000 years ago; moreover, serious human civilization is less than 10,000 years old. It is the neocortex, or upper brain, that prepared man to explore, inquire, memorize, reason, invent and create, assess, adjust, and perfect. Without the neocortex, there would be no "persons" as we know them.

All cells in the body require oxygen and nutrients provided by blood that is pumped by the heart. But the more specialized the cell, the more fragile it is, and the more sensitive it is to any bodily changes. The neurons in the cerebral cortex are among the most specialized of cells. Consequently, they are especially sensitive to the cessation of blood, nutrients, and oxygen, and to the effects of disease. For example, a cessation of blood flow for four to ten minutes may lead to extensive destruction, disruption, and death among these highly specialized cells. By contrast, the relatively less specialized brain stem cells, with their more primitive functions, are more resistant to the cessation of blood flow and may endure longer periods of interrupted blood and oxygen flow without showing serious damage.

Total loss of upper-brain function is sometimes referred to as vegetative state and sometimes defined as the "inability to experience self and the environment." Complete or partial preservation of primitive and unconscious reflex brain functions remain. However, there is complete unawareness of self and the environment, accompanied by what appear to be sleep-wake cycles. In addition, patients in a vegetative state show no consistent response to various stimuli, including light, sounds, touch, or pain. These patients show no language comprehension or expression. They have bowel and urinary incontinence. Unconscious reflexes, however, are preserved to variable degrees. In fact, one of the difficulties that medical professionals encounter when dealing with relatives of an individual who is in a vegetative state is how to convince the family that the patient is devoid of consciousness. For a relative, a patient who shows some eye movement, yawning, or jerking in response to a loud voice or touch could be easily misinterpreted as responding to a question or a gesture of love. But these are merely reactions to environmental stimuli rather than responses to another human being.[12]

According to a comprehensive review by a multisociety task force on permanent vegetative state of the American Society of Neurology, when the loss of upper-brain function or vegetative state is the result of head trauma, recovery is unlikely after twelve months. When a vegetative state results from causes other than head injury, recovery is exceedingly rare after three months.[13]

Individuals with higher brain death still demonstrate inner-brain reactions without the higher-brain sensibilities that accompany these reactions in normal people. They may react to light, but they cannot see; they may respond to powerful scents, but do not appreciate the smell; they may swallow, but do not enjoy food; they respond to loud sounds, but they cannot comprehend. These people do not look forward to a meal or to a drink. Males in this state may display erections, but have no desire for sex. They may yawn, hiccup, or twitch, but these movements occur without purpose. They do not comprehend, recognize, or appreciate any person or any thing in their environment. They are not capable of love, hate, rage, or happiness. They have neither memories from yesterday nor dreams of tomorrow. Yet their hearts beat, they breathe, they have warm skin, they sweat, urinate, and pass stools. They cough, yawn, display jerky movement, and appear as if they are looking at something far away.[14]

A DEFINITION OF DEATH THAT WILL HELP CONTROL OUR DESTINIES

As mentioned in the beginning of this chapter, it appears as if medical technology is at times controlling our destinies, resulting in undignified and miserable endings for many individuals. The adoption of a new definition of death that involves the higher brain function is one of the first critical steps in gaining control of our lives and ensuring death with dignity for all.

As difficult as it may be, we need, as a society, to adopt the definition that total loss of higher brain function denotes the death of the person. It is promising that one country, Denmark, and even one American jurisdiction in New Jersey, have already adopted this definition. Nevertheless, we still have a way to go. All other surrounding jurisdictions in New Jersey, for instance, as well as all other states abide by the whole-brain definition.

Table 1 summarizes the differences between total brain death (the universally accepted definition of death) and permanent vegetative state.

From this table, it must be evident that the only difference between higher brain death and total brain death is the persistence of certain unconscious reflexive activity, such as roving eyeballs, yawning, and grimacing. The question is whether these primitive, rudimentary functions constitute a life. Some well-meaning citizens, in reverence to the sanctity

TABLE 1
Comparison between Whole Brain Death and Permanent Vegetative State

	Whole Brain Death (Including Brain Stem)	Permanent Vegetative State (Higher Brain Death)
Awareness	No	No
Will	No	No
Emotion	No	No
Intellect	No	No
Ability to breathe without machine	No	Variable
Unconscious movements (yawning, roving eyeballs)	No	Yes
Jerky body movements	Yes	Yes
Sweating, growth of nails, hormone function	Yes	Yes
Heartbeat	Yes (for a while)	Yes
If sustained on life support, can grow a fetus to term	Yes	Yes

Sources: "The Permanent Vegetative State," *Journal of the Royal College of Physicians of London* 30 (1996): 119–21 and "Criteria for the Diagnosis of Brain Stem Death: Review by a Working Group Convened by the Royal College of Physicians," *Journal of the Royal College of Physicians of London* 29 (1995): 381–82.

of all life, invoke the slippery slope argument in a vehement defense to maintain such an existence.

To my way of thinking, the counterargument is more convincing: unconscious facial expressions alone without any rudiment of awareness or emotion is neither life, liberty, nor the pursuit of happiness. Allowing an unconscious existence to end in peace is hardly a slide down a slope that leads to forsaking the vulnerable and the frail.

I strongly endorse the recommendations put forward by the Royal College of Physicians of London in 1996 with particular attention to the safeguards published in a subsequent addendum report in 1997:

1. Reassessment: It is to be emphasized that there is no urgency in making the diagnosis of permanent vegetative state. If there is any uncertainty in the mind of the assessor, then the diagnosis shall not be made and a reassessment undertaken after a further time has elapsed.

2. Examination: It is important that the assessor shall take into account the descriptions and accounts given by relatives, caregivers, and nursing staff who spend most time with the patient.[15]

I would like to add to these cautionary notes the imperative of obtaining proper evaluation by an experienced neurologist to make certain of the total loss of all high brain functions.

DEMENTIA IS NOT THE SAME AS VEGETATIVE STATE

Dementia is a condition of deteriorated mentality and loss of intellectual faculties. Some degree of dementia is part of the aging process. A gradual loss of memory for names and numbers is natural and to be expected with increasing age. This can be minimized and delayed by staying socially enriched and intellectually involved through activities such as reading and group interaction.

Excessive deterioration of mental faculties can result from a multitude of brain disorders. Among these are multiple strokes, head injury, disease of the small vessels in the brain, and most typically Alzheimer's disease.

Alzheimer's disease is characterized by a slow, subtle onset and gradual but steady damage of the brain cells. In a recent article published in the *Journal of the American Medical Association*, Dr. Joseph Buxbaum, head of the Molecular Neurophysiciatry Laboratory at Mount Sinai Medical School in New York, and his colleagues shed some light on the possible cause of Alzheimer's disease.[16] These authors studied brains from seventy-nine nursing home patients. They noted that Alzheimer's patients have a build-up in their brain of beta amyloid, an insoluble form of a normal brain protein. Tangled fibers of a protein (called Tau) develop inside brain cells, damaging the internal support structure of the cell network. What causes such buildup in the first place remains elusive, however. Theories range from the influence of genetic factors, indolent virus infection, cut off blood supply, or an abnormal response of the body's immune system, whereupon the body's own defense mechanisms turn against its brain.

The beta amyloid theory is not universally accepted, however.[17] Dr. Allen Roses of Duke University and his wife, Dr. Ann Saunders, claim that Alzheimer's disease is genetically determined. They claim to have discovered a major Alzheimer's susceptibility gene (apoE4). A formidable opponent to the beta amyloid hypothesis, Dr. Roses maintains that the protein and the brain scars are the result of genetic factors and are not the cause of the disease.

More than 4 million Americans suffer from this disease and its course varies greatly, averaging eight to ten years. According to the Alzheimer's Association and the National Institute on Aging, the clinical course can be summarized in three stages:

Stage One is characterized by a gradual onset of memory impairment, language difficulty, impaired judgment, lack of spontaneity, social difficulties, depression, and outbursts of terror. This stage typically lasts two to four years.

Stage Two has the following characteristics: wandering, agitation, repetitive behavior, disorientation, twitching, seizures, and difficulty in pursuing rational thinking. Stage Two may last up to eight years with increasing disorientation, agitation, and inappropriate behavior.

Stage Three is the terminal stage and is characterized by disorientation, complete dependence, inability to recognize people, severe speech impairment, emaciation, and the total loss of body control. This stage lasts from one to three years.

It must be emphasized that while the final stage is the same for all sufferers of Alzheimer's disease, the early stages vary considerably from patient to patient. Many intelligent and socially adept individuals often develop ways to conceal their deficits for a significant period of time.

Dementia, even in its advanced forms, should *not* be considered a form of permanent vegetative state, since some high brain functions, such as hunger, thirst, feelings of happiness or pain, and a rudiment of awareness remain until the very end. The disease represents, however, one of the most heart-wrenching, chronic illnesses riddled with emotionally charged, often vexing medical decisions. Our research has shown that the vast majority of American citizens, when asked about medical treatment options in the event they develop Alzheimer's disease, would forgo all intrusive medical care, including surgery and cardiopulmonary resuscitation. This near unanimity applies to the last stages of the disease and does not necessarily apply to the earlier stages. By contrast, surrogates of patients with this condition often are reluctant to forgo treatments for their diseased loved ones contrary to the prevailing sentiments of the general public. Whether they are motivated by love, feelings of guilt, or fear of reprimand, the inescapable result is that many victims of dementia are subjected to intrusive treatments including cardiopulmonary resuscitation and placement in intensive care units and are forced to undergo medical procedures that do not enhance life's quality. We strongly advocate advance care planning and open communication between the medical professionals, patients, and their families early in the course of the disease. Better still, patients who make their wishes known before they fall victim to Alzheimer's disease are the ones most likely to have their wishes honored.

A most informative research study examining how end-stage dementia patients fare following an acute illness appeared in the *Journal of the American Medical Association*'s July 5, 2000, issue. The authors studied 118 patients with end-stage dementia, 38 of whom had hip fractures and 80 of whom had acute pneumonia. The authors compared the outcome of these patients with others, average 70 years old, having the same conditions but no dementia. Over half (55 percent) of the dementia patients were dead in six months following the acute illness, whereas only one in eight died in the group without dementia.[18]

The telling tale is that patients with advanced dementia, in this study, received as many burdensome procedures and less than one-fourth of them received medicines to relieve pain. This research sends a powerful message to the medical profession and the public: "Given the limited life expectancy of patients with end-stage dementia following these illnesses, and the burdens associated with their treatment, increased attention should be focused on efforts that enhance comfort in this patient population."[19]

And I must reiterate that proper communication and planning is paramount early in the course of the disease, and better still, before it rears its ugly head.

2

SETTING LIMITS

High Technology Interventions Near the End of Life

❦

The means by which we live have outdistanced the ends for which we live. Our scientific power has outrun our spiritual power. We have guided missiles and misguided men.

Martin Luther King Jr.

It is common to think that ethical precepts are precepts which help us live. But they also help us die. All religions, for instance, prepare us for the moment of death. It matters not whether one is Christian, Jew, Muslim, Hindu, Buddhist, or atheist. All religions, as well as humanism, recognize and protect the sanctity of life and recognize that the ultimate human justice is to place an equal value on each human life. Christians and Jews are taught about the timing of life and death in Ecclesiastes: "To everything there is a season, and a time for every purpose under heaven: a time to be born, a time to die, a time to plant, and a time to pluck up that which is planted" (Eccl. 3:1–2). The Koran advises Muslims that the dying person should disassociate himself totally from worldly affairs and anticipate the moment of meeting the Almighty:

> Mas-ala 5. At the time of one's death no such thing should be said or done which may turn his mind towards workday affairs because it is the time for him to present himself before Almighty Allah. Those present at that time should behave in such a manner that the mind and heart of the dying person may turn away from the world and be directed towards Allah.

Buddhists are taught that their prime concern is seeking the meaning of life, a peace and comfort that will enable them to face the suffering of illness and death:

A man struggling for existence will naturally look for something of value. There are two ways of looking—a right way and a wrong way. If he looks in the right way, he recognizes the true nature of sickness, old age, and death, and he searches for meaning in that which transcends all human sufferings. (Shakyamuni Buddha, p. 8)

Religions and humanist groups thus prepare us to accept death as natural and expected, and not as an unwelcome failure of our quest to seek immortality.

PHYSICIANS: PRIESTS AND PRIESTESSES OF THE BODY

If religious men and women are priests and priestesses of the soul, physicians could be viewed as their secular counterparts: priests and priestesses of the body and of the person. Just as religious men and women help prepare us for death, so should physicians. This type of caring for the total person, however, is often overshadowed by high-technology medicine.

When physicians take the Hippocratic oath, they pledge to protect the lives and alleviate the suffering of their patients. This commitment to protect lives, however, is often carried to extremes, driven by promises from physicians and unrealistic expectations from patients. Enabled by the powerful tools of modern technology, physicians keep vegetative bodies alive—in a fashion.

The attitude of medical intervention *in extremis* is prevalent particularly among young physicians who are trained less in dealing with the intricate challenges of complex illnesses and more in the acquisition of information and mastering techniques. Medical intervention that is designed to sustain a vegetative existence rather than a thinking and feeling person is an example of what I term "futile care."

The inappropriateness of futile care at the end of life was recognized and well articulated by Plato, the philosopher, and Hippocrates, the father of medicine, centuries ago. Plato chastised "the inappropriateness of persisting with treatment which leaves the surviving patient with a useless life." He went on to emphasize, "Medicine was not intended for them and they should not be treated even if they were richer than Midas."[1]

Hippocrates, in his famous oath, advises physicians to "[r]efuse to treat those who are overmastered by their diseases, realizing in such cases [that] medicine is powerless."[2] This part of the oath is rarely referred to in the day-to-day practice of contemporary medicine. Discussion about the inappropriateness of futile care have been rekindled through the realization of the limits of medicine, the inevitability of death, the horrors of intensive care or a confused life in isolation, the enormity of waste of resources at the end of life, and the mounting pressures to limit the cost of medical care by the new health-care alliances.

WITHHOLDING CARE:
SOMETIMES THE BEST TYPE OF CARING

As far back as 1927, in an address to the graduating class of Harvard Medical School, Dr. Francis Peabody, the Chief of Medicine at Boston City Hospital and humanist noted

> The most common criticism made at present by older practitioners is that young graduates have been taught a great deal about the mechanism of disease, but very little about the practice of medicine . . . or to put it more bluntly, they are too scientific and do not know how to take care of patients.

He went on to emphasize that the best form of patient care is in caring for the patient.[3] If Dr. Peabody's words were relevant in 1927, they must be much more so today. Patients, families, and young physicians must realize that withholding certain forms of treatment does not mean withholding care. In fact, many times the withholding of treatment is the best form of care. It takes a real professional to advise against more intrusive treatment; it merely takes a technician to undertake one more procedure.

A basic ethical principle (*Ex Ante Pareto*) states, "If no one is worse off with a certain choice, and at least someone is better off, then that choice should prevail." Conversely, I interpret this principle to mean that if no one is better off with a certain choice and at least someone (or society) is worse off, that choice should not be granted. According to the teachings of Hippocrates, the mission of medicine as a profession is wellness for the healthy, healing for those who are ailing, and comfort and encouragement for those with incurable disease. Ethicists and health-care professionals may disagree on the definition of futility, but a medical intervention undertaken with no hope of benefiting a patient is a misplaced intervention and could be considered unethical. Professional integrity and social responsibility should preclude a physician from recommending such a procedure. I would also add that it is unreasonable for patients or their families to ask for such treatment.

A MEDICAL FATE WORSE THAN DEATH

As all physicians and many laypeople can attest through personal experience, there are fates worse than death. Consider the case of a friend of mine, a seventy-eight-year-old psychiatrist, who suffered multiple strokes and lost all of his cognitive functions. He didn't know where he was, or what time of the day it was. He didn't recognize his family members. He didn't even know who he was. He couldn't swallow food, so a tube was placed in his stomach. He couldn't cough up secretions from his lungs, so he developed pneumonia. There was once a saying among physicians: "Pneumonia is the old man's friend." A few decades ago, pneumonia often allowed the elderly to depart peacefully. At the behest of the family and with concurrence of the treating physician, my friend, rather than be allowed to expire peacefully, was intubated and given intravenous antibiotics. A multitude of expensive laboratory tests guided the choice of drugs and treatment. He bled from his stomach and received pints of blood through transfusion. An endoscopy was performed to determine the cause of the bleeding; the threadlike tube with light at the end showed that he had developed a perforating stomach ulcer, requiring removal of the stomach. This major surgery was undertaken. Before the wound healed, he developed gangrene of the gallbladder that necessitated another major surgery—and more antibiotics—and more blood transfusions. Because he had been maintained on assisted ventilation for over two weeks, a tracheostomy was performed; that is, a hole was made in the trachea (the air pipe below the voice box) and oxygen was administered. His kidneys and his liver started to fail. Renal dialysis, a costly procedure that allows machines to filter toxins and other substances from the body, was initiated. The heart stopped after two months of struggle to maintain his marginal existence. Before this last event, I had a long discussion with the family and advised against resuscitation. The family agreed reluctantly. After death, his hospital bill exceeded $500,000 for treatment that, under the best of circumstances, would not have restored health, consciousness, or independence. This is a true but not unique story. It is an everyday occurrence in the practice of medicine in America. For those who do not believe it, ask to take a tour of any busy intensive care unit in any highly specialized referral acute-care hospital. Sustaining a life in a body that is irreversibly incapacitated and without a mind is no longer a miracle of medicine but a routine in American intensive care units. Who benefited from the prolongation of my friend's miserable existence? The patient's family and society-at-large were debited over $500,000. And some wonder why insurance premiums have been going up beyond the cost-of-living adjustment.

AVOIDING MEDICAL FATES WORSE THAN DEATH

The objective of medicine is not, and must never be, to treat people to death! Nor for that matter, to put them to death. This treatment exacts an enormous emotional and financial cost and cannot be construed as "caring" for the patient, caring for the person.

In a recent review of people who were in persistent vegetative states in 1993, the famed English neurologists, Drs. Kenneth R. Mitchell, Ian H. Kerridge, and J. Lovat from the University of Newcastle, England, asked the following rhetorical question:

> Why do we persist in the relentless pursuit of artificial nourishment and other treatments to maintain unconscious existence? Will they be treated because of our ethical commitment to their humanity, or because of an ethical paralysis in the face of biotechnical progress?[4]

Indeed, this statement should not be construed as putting a lesser human value on a person who has lost what constituted his or her personhood. Simply, it underscores that once the ingredients of reason, passions, and desires defining a person are permanently and irretrievably lost, there is no ethical imperative to sustain such an existence.

The Council on Ethical and Judicial Affairs of the American Medical Association in 1990 endorsed this view:

For humane reasons, with informed consent, a physician may do what is medically necessary to alleviate severe pain or cease or omit treatment to permit a terminally ill patient to die when death is imminent. . . . However, the physician should not intentionally cause death.[5]

Also in 1993, the American Neurological Association Committee on Ethical Affairs published a position paper that defined permanent vegetative state (PVS), classified nutrition and hydration as forms of medical treatment, stated that patients or surrogates could decide to terminate treatment, and that there were no medical or ethical distinctions between withholding and withdrawing treatment.[6]

In a recent statement, the British Medical Association recommended that consent is not needed to discontinue a treatment that is deemed to have proven futile (i.e., with no reasonable hope for recovery of higher brain functions). Also, it emphasized that a family member's views about permanent vegetative state should not be relevant to the decisions to cease treatment. (This particular statement may seem odd to the American reader. It is the rule in the United Kingdom and most European countries that useless care is not offered, and when asked for, it is not granted. This may, of course, be an offshoot of having a nationalized health-care system.) Nevertheless, I feel that in all circumstances, the physician has to inform the patient's family of the decision to forgo or cease treatment and the reasons for it. This is required as a matter of decency and in order to maintain goodwill and promote understanding among various family members and the healing physician.[7]

It must be emphasized strongly and in unequivocal terms that whenever there is a reasonable chance for some recovery, it is the physician's duty to battle death aggressively. However, when there is no reasonable chance for recovery of the higher brain, or in the case of multiple organ failure, death should be treated as a rational expectation rather than a remote contingency.

RELIGIOUS AUTHORITY CONCURS WITH MEDICAL AUTHORITY

All monotheistic religious institutions, other prevailing religions, and humanist groups generally concur with these ethical positions taken by medical authorities. Almost without exception, they recommend that the physician and the family should make the passing of a terminally ill patient as painless as possible. Of interest is that in 1980, the Vatican described contemporary high-technology applications at the end of life as "technologic attitude that threatens to become an abuse."

As early as 1957, in his address to the Congress of Anesthesiologists, Pope Pius XII noted that "while every reasonable effort should be made to maintain life and restore health, there comes a time when these efforts may become excessively burdensome for the patient and others." He also predicted that this issue would become a major one for the rest of the century. In 1990, the Bishops of Texas and the Texas Conference of Catholic Health Facilities, in their Pastoral Statement on Artificial Nutrition and Hydration, stated, "If the means used to prolong life are disproportionately burdensome compared with the benefits to the patients, then these means need not be used. They are morally optional." These pronouncements by religious authorities seem to give further credence to the proposition that death occurs when the upper brain irretrievably ceases to function or with failure of multiple vital organs. In this case, treatment is of no benefit to the patient. Indeed, such treatment will result in a medical fate worse than death. It is noteworthy that the Catholic Bishop's Committee continues to be excessively cautious about notions of letting a patient die and intending to bring about his or her death.[8]

THE RULE OF DOUBLE EFFECT

According to the ethically accepted principle generally referred to as "the rule of double effect," "effects that are considered to be morally wrong if caused intentionally are permissible if foreseen but unintended."[9] For example, administering large doses of opiates to relieve pain and suffering of a terminally ill patient may be acceptable even though such treatment may hasten the patient's death. This rule was developed by Roman Catholic moral theologians in the Middle Ages[10] and is applicable when the treating physician may not be able to avoid all potentially "harmful" consequences of treatment. The formulations of this rule of double effect underscore four prerequisites: First, the nature of the act itself must be good, such as relief of pain, and its intent must never be in morally prohibitive categories, such as ending the life of an innocent person. Second, the physician's intent must be for the good effect and not the evil effect. If there are bad consequences, such as depression of breathing caused by morphine, it should not be the intended effect, although it might be a foreseen consequence. Third, there is a distinction between means and effect. The bad effect, in this case death, must not be the means to relieve suffering which is the desired good effect. Fourth, there must be proportionality between the good effect and the bad effect, in favor of the good. The bad effects of any intervention should not outweigh any possible good achieved by such intervention.

These four conditions answer the following questions:

- Is the act morally permissible?
- Is the primary intention intended to relieve the patient's burden or to end life?
- Has the treating physician weighed his or her action in terms of burden to benefit? On balance, is the action beneficial?

The principles governing the "rule of double effect" are accepted by all official medical organizations. More importantly, while the Supreme Court unanimously ruled in 1997 in *Washington* v. *Glucksberg* that there is no constitutional right to physician-assisted suicide, a court majority effectively required all states to ensure that their laws do not obstruct the provision of adequate palliative care.[11] The Court emphasized the necessity to alleviate pain and other physical symptoms of people facing death. The Court was unanimous on the issue of the legal consequences of adequately managing symptoms through the use of opiates that are believed to carry foreseeable risk of hastened death.

> Existing state laws are constitutionally valid in recognizing a distinction between prohibiting conduct on the part of physicians that intentionally hasten death and permitting conduct that may foreseeably hasten death but is intended for other important purposes, such as relief of pain or other symptoms.[12]

By authoritatively pronouncing that terminal sedation intended for symptomatic relief is not assisted suicide, the Court has licensed an aggressive practice of palliative care.

MAY THE DEBATE ON TREATMENT FUTILITY NOT PROVE FUTILE

Unfortunately, the discussion regarding the definition of death and futility of medical care has not yet been settled. These issues are unlikely to be completely resolved until society at large comes to grips with the issues at hand. In the meantime, many respected authorities are still resisting the eminently rational definition of death based on death of the higher brain. Furthermore, enormous gaps exist among philosopher-ethicists in their definition of futility and in what they might consider as futile medical treatment and the scientific use of the term.

Futility derives from the Greek word *futilis*, which refers to a useless vessel, broader on the top than at the bottom. In ancient times, this *futilis* was used only in religious ceremonies but had no useful secular function. Futile medical care could be considered a technological ceremony, of no real use in bringing a functioning person back into the world.

A CONGRESS ON FUTILE CARE: CONTROVERSY OVERWHELMS CONSENSUS

On March 24 and 25, 1993, a distinguished group of scholars assembled at the invitation of the Congress of Clinical Societies to discuss the question of medical futility.[13] The congress was a testimonial to the differences in how futility is understood among abstract theoretical ethicists and physicians. Proceedings of the congress were published in a 1994 issue of the *Journal of American Geriatric Society*. In his paper entitled, "Necessity, Futility, and the Good Society," Dr. Daniel Callahan highlighted the differences in the understanding of futility in the United States and abroad.[14] Dr. Callahan is a highly respected leader in the ethics community. Even though he is not a physician (he holds a Ph.D.), he described it as "unfitting to perform heart bypass surgery on octogenarians." Dr. Callahan noted that individualism in America impedes Americans' embracing shared values. He asserted our need, as one society, to establish a consensus on futility and medical necessity. He has been a staunch advocate of limiting health care for the elderly who have already lived their normal life span.

Dr. Robert Veatch, another authority in the philosophical approach to medical ethics, who also is not a physician, questioned whether physicians are even capable of making futility determinations. In his paper, "Why Physicians Cannot Determine if Care Is Futile," he contends "that the physician cannot and ought not to try to determine futility." He further argues, "An appeal to justice or keeping a promise to a patient is sufficient justification to provide care deemed futile when an appeal to autonomy or beneficence is not."[15] He invoked physicians' opinions to buttress his contention. He noted that Dr. Robert Morse, speaking for physicians in the 1976 Quinlan case, argued that keeping an unconscious patient alive on a ventilator represented proper medical care. Dr. Veatch further questioned the sincerity of physicians who would now contend that such treatment is futile. Unfortunately, Dr. Veatch has ignored the historical fact that physicians' and laypeople's attitudes about certain treatments have changed over the years with increased knowledge about outcomes.

Dr. Howard Brody, a physician from the Center for Ethics and Humanities in the Life Sciences at Michigan State University, offered two basic ideas to guide physicians:

1. Treatments are inappropriate if they cause harm disproportionate to any foreseeable benefit.
2. Doctors should not fraudulently represent the knowledge or skill of medical practice to their patients and their families.[16]

Dr. John Lantos, from the Department of Pediatrics and Center for Clinical Ethics, University of Chicago, argues that the debate about futility is simply a question of economics. In his essay, "Futility Assessments and the Doctor-Patient Relationship," Dr. Lantos contends that concerns about futility stem from the emergence of a prospective payment system. The cost-containment imperatives of such a system compelled physicians to discover the once forgotten Hippocratic ethic to refrain from providing useless medical treatment.[17]

Dr. Lawrence Schneiderman, Professor of Family and Preventative Medicine at the University of California, San Diego, presented a paper entitled "The Futility Debate on Effective versus Beneficial Interventions." He offered two definitions of futility, using both quantitative and qualitative criteria. According to Dr. Schneiderman, a futile intervention based on quantitative criteria is one that has not worked in the last 100 attempts (clearly not an easy standard, unless outcome research has shown that a certain treatment has a less than 1 percent chance to succeed). A futile intervention based on qualitative criteria is one that does not achieve its desired ends, a point agreed upon by physicians.[18]

Dr. Stuart Youngner of Case Western Reserve University highlighted the difficulties between physicians on the one hand, and patients and families who desperately want to save or mend a life on the other. He noted how the motivations of even a well-intentioned practitioner who asks a patient to forsake a futile therapy may be suspect to patients and their families in the absence of a long-standing doctor-patient relationship.[19] This is particularly true in the managed care environment with its focus on cost savings.

In his essay, "Families and Futility," Dr. James Linderman Nelson of the Hastings Center presented the American society's responsibilities in this debate. He emphasized that the question of integrity pertains to families as well as to practitioners and patients. He highlighted the importance of the roles played by families, friends, and of a meaningful doctor-patient relationship in guiding the difficult decisions about futility.

Other participants in the conference highlighted the difficulties with clinical definitions, the need for social consensus, cooperation in interdisciplinary organizations, and uniform case law.

During the ensuing years, the futility debate has intensified and covered such areas as domains of definition, application, the limits of patients' autonomy versus physicians' authority, and conflict resolution. Much of the debate has been useful and enlightening. Some aspects have proved to be esoteric and Byzantine, such as philosophical arguments—impossible to apply in practice and difficult to imagine in theory. Leading experts in theoretical ethics have maintained a wide spectrum of positions. At one extreme, Dr. Veatch has continued to defend a patient's right to receive a treatment deemed useless by sound scientific medical standards, so long that the treatment has a nonmedical desired effect, such as keeping an unconscious patient on life-support singly to postpone the moment of death. At the other extreme, Dr. Callahan contends that society does not owe expensive medical care for citizens who have already exceeded "the natural life span," defined in the Bible as "three scores and ten."

In the July 27, 2000, issue of the *New England Journal of Medicine*, Drs. Helft, Siegler, and Lantos reviewed the difficult issues surrounding the medical futility concept. Whereas the title of their article, "The Rise and Fall of the Futility Movement" gives the impression that the debate about the concept is dead, these distinguished authors conclude

> The problem of making decisions about futility, as practicing physicians know, persists. Doctors all recognize clinical situations in which intervention will be futile and should tell patients and families when further treatment is futile. In many situations, the term (futile) is an extremely useful concept of how the physician feels about the patients' care. However, the fall of the futility movement reminds us that using a descriptive concept as a foundation for a policy is highly problematic and does not relieve us of our obligation to talk to patients and their families and to explain why we think further treatment will have no benefit. The judgment that further treatment would be futile is not a conclusion—a signal should cease; instead, it should initiate the difficult task of discussing the situation with the patient. Thus the most recent attempts to establish a policy in this area have emphasized processes for discussing futility rather than the means of implementing decisions about futility. Talking to patients and families should remain the focus of our efforts.[20]

But I must add that physicians and the public have to be reminded of the following unalterable truths: All life will end; since life is finite, so is medical intervention. Medicine can bring cure, sometimes; restoration of health, often; and compassion and comfort, always. Because medicine in and by itself is a perishable good, there comes a point in the care of patients where more intervention confers marginal benefit to the few, punishment to the many, and an enormous burden to the families and society. At this point, further feats of intrusive medical intervention should not be offered as treatment options. Instead, kind, caring, pain relief, alleviation of suffering, and preservation of dignity should become the order of the day. It is not only within the domain of physicians, but by necessity, their sacred duty to their patients to recognize and communicate the limits of burdensome, high technology feats. When cure ceases to be achievable, caring should intensify. Should this become the prevailing attitude from the medical profession, it would be better grounded, more rational, more defensible, and more justifiable than the relentless pursuit of feats of high-tech interventions when life has approached its inevitable terminus.

We may not be able to prevent death, but we can prepare for it and lessen the emotional and financial burden for all:

- The question of futility of a treatment is primarily the responsibility of the medical establishment. A medical intervention must have a clear goal of restoring health or improving the patient's condition. An intervention without a therapeutic goal is improper.
- Abstract ethics are subject to enormous variation in interpretation, particularly when they pertain to complex medical issues. Ethical principles guiding medical care at the end of life are not revealed to the chosen few on the road to Damascus. They must represent the shared values of our democratic society.
- A societal consensus should be the backbone for any policy regarding the perimeters of medical futility or marginal utility in order for the policy to succeed and meet wide acceptance.
- There is no substitute for a physician's professional integrity and a meaningful doctor-patient relationship in handling the vexing issues pertaining to an imminent death.
- It is about time to engage the public in the debate about such vital issues. To politicize an enormously complex issue such as this, reducing it to sound bites and slogans, does a great disservice to our citizens and our country.
- Medical students and the medical community at large must be better educated in how to discuss issues of life and death. They must be trained in communicating with patients and families under the dire circumstances of an imminent death and the concept of futility.
- Guidelines for futility should be developed by a consortium of organized medicine to be presented for review by an independent, mainstream, blue-ribbon commission that does not have a political agenda. These guidelines must take into account the patient's health status, probability of improvement with certain medical interventions, magnitude of benefit, and possible duration of the benefit, as well as possible costs in terms of length of life, complications, suffering, and total cost to society. Recommendations should then be translated into common law, accompanied by the appropriate procedures to carry out the laws.

3

THE RUNAWAY ABUSE
OF HIGH TECHNOLOGY

❦

Don't try to live forever. You will not succeed.

George Bernard Shaw

HAVE TECHNOLOGY, WILL INVADE

When it comes to the treatment of a patient with a terminal illness, the physician (with patient consent) is faced with two distinct philosophies: fighting for life at any cost (i.e., "heroically" doing everything possible), or administering optimal treatment, but treatment that is worthwhile.

The "everything possible" scenario is unfortunately too prevalent in our hospitals. Modern medical schools and medical-specialty training programs emphasize training young doctors in the use of the latest technologies. Contemporary physicians are well trained and comfortable using modern high technology. Without question, American specialists are the best technicians in the world. One could even say that the very existence of technology motivates its use. The masters of the new art of high technology are always ready; have technology, will invade. This attitude is compounded by fear or the inability of some doctors to convey "bad news" to patients and their families, physicians' focus on specific organ diseases rather than on the total patient, and viewing death as their prime enemy. Distressed family members, threatened by the loss of a loved one, are inclined to demand that everything possible be done. When one is distant from the battlefield, one can more easily be objective and rational. It is a different matter to personally be in the thick of it:

"He is too young to die, doctor . . . please, do everything you can."

"We have been together for over fifty years and I can't imagine life without her!"

"Please don't tell me that you can't do more!"

"I know God will save him. He spoke to me in my dreams last night. Just keep doing all you can, I know he is going to make it!"

"No, it is not the time for him to go! Don't say it, doctor!" These are standard, everyday pleadings from genuinely caring family members who are unable or unwilling to let go of a loved one.

Occasionally, the physician is told something like the following: "We have been married for just a few years. I am his second wife. If I let go, his children might accuse me of not standing by him. Do everything you can!" Or, "Although all of us here have agreed that there is little more that can be done, one sister in California said not to give up and to keep fighting." Or, "This is a decision that has to be made by all family members. I have a brother in Germany that we can't reach at the present time. We have to persevere until we are able to reach him."

A young physician might be tempted to perform one or two more procedures before death becomes inevitable to assure the family, as well as him- or herself, that everything has been done. With this intervention comes the comfortable feeling that the doctor has acted in a legally defensible way. Unfortunately, fear of litigation, a health-care system that undermines the doctor-patient relationship, and the seductive influence of material gain have conspired to perpetuate the "do everything attitude" regardless of whether it is in the patient's best interest.

I recall a nice sixty-seven-year-old woman whom I took care of while on call over the weekend a few years ago. Mrs. Brown had been diagnosed with cancer of both breasts twelve years previously, and both had been removed. Her ovaries were also removed to deprive the body of hormones necessary for the growth of the tumors. She had received radiation therapy and chemotherapy. A few years ago, she was also treated with a new anti-hormone medicine. Her cancer had been arrested for ten years.

Two years prior to our encounter, tumor metastases (i.e., growth of the tumor beyond the original site) had afflicted her lungs and bones; another course of chemotherapy had limited success. She was subsequently given a megadose of chemotherapy. This final blast of chemotherapy knocked out her immune system. Her physician then ordered a bone marrow transplantation. (Bone marrow is the source of the body's immune factors.) Following these procedures, it was discovered that her heart had suffered massive damage as a result of the cumulative effects of chemotherapy. She was presented to the emergency room with severe heart failure. A blood count showed that the bone marrow transplantation had not taken, and the blood count had become extremely low. At this stage, one physician might say, "We have gone as far as is reasonable. Let us now make this patient's last hours of life as comfortable as possible." This physician would have explained the situation to the family in these terms: "Everything worthwhile has been done. Any more treatment, other than that which brings comfort, is meaningless." Instead, the actual treating physician presented his recommendation to an anxious and almost distraught husband: The patient should be placed on a ventilator; her heart failure treated aggressively. This course of action was taken. A fulminant pneumonia caused by a rare organism took hold in her body. A multitude of antibiotics were administered. The patient bled profusely from her stomach. An endoscope, a tool that enables specialists to look inside the stomach, showed a bleeding "stress ulcer." Blood transfusions were given. During the episode of massive bleeding from the stomach, the patient developed a drop in blood pressure. This was partly corrected with infusions of blood-pressure-sustaining medications, but it was then discovered that the kidneys were damaged from the drop in blood pressure and had stopped producing urine. Renal dialysis was initiated to replace kidney function. The patient remained unconscious and on the ventilator. The patient's condition was described as "stable," at least on the chart.

A few days passed and the patient developed a high temperature. A new and vicious organism was found to have invaded the blood from the patient's colon (large intestine). An X-ray of the colon showed an infected sac, and her treating physician recommended that part of the colon be surgically removed. It was.

I saw the patient for the first time in this condition that weekend. I reviewed the chart and examined her. She had been on the ventilator for two weeks. This shrinking, unconscious being had twelve tubes coming out of her body. One tube was connected to the ventilator, one led to her stomach, and another tube connected a sac to her urinary bladder. Two tubes stuck out of her belly to drain the site of surgery, and one facilitated the movement of fecal matter out of her colon. Two tubes connected her to the dialysis machine, and one tube monitored the pressures within her heart. One tube enabled the continuous monitoring of blood pressure from within an artery. The rest of the tubes carried antibiotics and blood-pressure-sustaining medicines into her veins.

My examination of the patient revealed her to be unconscious, unresponsive, and unable to breathe on her own. Her blood pressure was low, her kidneys were not producing any urine. I looked at the laboratory sheet: toxins had accumulated in her blood, her bone marrow was not producing any blood cells, her liver was failing, her heart had become terminally damaged, and her lungs had become increasingly incapable of exchanging gases due to heart failure, pneumonia, and blood infection—even with the help of the respirator.

I rested my head between my hands and sighed in an audible voice, "My God. We have done everything possible, haven't we? We have undertaken what is beyond the reasonable and the ridiculous, haven't we?" I asked my medical students who accompanied me, "What legal and ethical rights does an incompetent patient have?" Some answered, "The right to life, liberty, and the pursuit of happiness." Others, well versed in ethical principles, cited autonomy, beneficence, nonmaleficence, and justice. I answered them: "The right to life? This depends upon the definition of *life*. This miserable being has suffered high-brain death for two weeks. She has been irretrievably unconscious and has lost all cognitive powers. I am told she used to be a lovely, warm, and articulate lady. I wish I had known her then. But the remains that we are dealing with here no longer fit that description."

"Well, let's agree that she has the right to liberty?" I said. "Where is liberty when you are enslaved by twelve tubes connected to a bunch of machines? Does she have the right to privacy? This nice lady has had every part of her body exposed to the multitudes. People around her, including the attending medical professionals, converse as if she is nonexistent." (When I had approached her bed, the attending surgeon was talking to the nurse about an interesting movie that he had seen the night before. Scenes of naked patients become part of the décor in our profession, as awful as it might sound.)

"Finally, does she have the right to autonomy and to shared decision making? Whose decisions? Which decisions? Which autonomy?" I paused, then continued, "Beneficence means that you do what is good for the patient and nonmaleficence is to do no harm. What good are we doing by torturing someone in the process of dying? Sometimes the act of not letting one die peacefully is the greatest harm that you can inflict on a fellow human being."

Let the pundits of medical ethics come up with whatever rights they are capable of inventing in their comfortable armchairs. It is different out here. In this medical battlefield, someone who was once a dignified, intelligent, and lovely lady has been transformed into the shell of a human being. I turned to my students and continued, "There is one right that we can't take from anyone, anytime, anywhere. This is the *right to be respected.* Yes, she still has this right and will continue to have it even after she departs from this planet."

I walked out to talk to the patient's family: a loving, intelligent, and understanding group of people. I explained the situation in detail to her husband and to the other family members. I listened to them pour their hearts out. We decided to let their loved one depart in peace—no more tests, no more procedures, no more surgery, no more interventions; just medicine that brings peace and comfort. She departed a few hours later in a closed room, covered up, surrounded by her loved ones, and as respected as one can be in an intensive care unit.

In the past, it has never been easy for me to talk about issues of death frankly and openly to a patient's loved ones. Not so since I developed cancer. I know one thing for a fact: If I ask myself whether I would want to be treated like this, the answer would be a clear and unequivocal "no." One important ingredient of the medical profession is a firm commitment to the patient not to abandon him or her until the end. It is that which makes medicine such a great profession, filled with joy and sorrow, exhilaration and sadness, but always compassionate, caring, and loving. Its moral authority derives from the fact that the patient's well-being is paramount from beginning to end.

WITHHOLDING TREATMENT
MAY BE THE BEST THERAPY

The problem with the "everything possible" doctrine of medical treatment is that it masquerades as caring. It must be remembered that withholding an unnecessary procedure is not equivalent to withholding care. On the contrary, withholding a meaningless intervention is the only rational approach to care. The best medical intervention is often no intervention at all. When the patient is approaching the end of his or her normal life span, when the afflictions are incapacitating, and when the best that medicine can offer is an extension of suffering, withholding care is the best care. In all circumstances, compassion and caring should never cease. But, the goal becomes comfort and control of suffering.

In literature on medical ethics, it is customary to find the following "benefit-risk" type descriptions of treatment:

- proportionate versus disproportionate
- ordinary versus extraordinary
- symmetrical versus asymmetrical
- gain versus risk
- benefit versus burden
- fitting versus unfitting
- necessary versus futile

These terms have been espoused by religious leaders, theologians, and ethicists. Personally, I prefer to use Dr. M. H. Weil's way of establishing whether a treatment is worthwhile. The questions that Dr. Weil, one of the world's authorities in intensive care and previously Chairman of Medicine at the University of Chicago School of Medicine, asks are as follows:

- Is the treatment rational?
- Is it redeeming?
- Is it respectful?[1]

When it is established with reasonable certainty that an individual has permanently and irreversibly lost the content of consciousness and cognition, or when further medical intervention has little promise to confer a measurable benefit to the patient, the only rational treatment is that which brings comfort and deals with the patient respectfully.

When a baby is born without a higher brain, the only rational approach, according to the best medical advice, is to let go. Unfortunately, although most parents faced with such a misfortune elect to terminate the pregnancy rather than carry the baby to term, there are some notable exceptions. Multiple studies from neonatal intensive care units have shown that a premature baby less than one pound in weight, born of a mother who abused cocaine during pregnancy, has a meager chance for survival. If through enormous efforts it survives, it will probably lead a miserable, unhealthy, and unfulfilled life at a cost to society of over $1 million. Dr. David Gary Smith, Chief of General Internal Medicine at Temple University in Philadelphia, summed up the problem in an article titled "Neonatal Intensive Care: How Much Is Too Much?" published in the *Journal of Medical Ethics.*[2]

Rational medical therapy says that when a patient approaches the end of life because of advanced disseminated cancer that is unresponsive to all reasonable treatment, the rational approach to treatment is to make the person's remaining life as devoid of suffering as possible. I believe, as Dr. Weil recommends, that when a patient is admitted to the intensive care unit with a burn that is so extensive that there is no prospect for recovery, merciful care is the appropriate care. A patient in terminal stages of AIDS infection who reaches a state of unconsciousness (due to extensive destruction of brain cells) should not be kept on a ventilator.

In my view, when someone with advanced, end-stage heart or lung disease, who is not a candidate for heart transplant, develops advanced kidney failure, he or she should not be treated with renal dialysis; this is irrational. These are not simply my personal views but are borne out of solid medical data.

I do not condone paternalism in medical practice, by which the physician makes decisions on behalf of his patients or their families without explaining to them why the decisions are made. By the same token, I do not condone the practice of doctors imposing their own views upon their patients about what constitutes an acceptable quality of life. Such judgments are outside the bounds of the medical profession. Every person is entitled to life, liberty, and the pursuit of happiness. On the other hand, for someone who has lost "higher brain" function or who is in the end stages of an irreversible disease, the use of high-tech procedures does not represent autonomy, liberty, or pursuit of happiness and *should not be presented as a treatment option.*

Yes, a family in distress not infrequently asks the question of whether there is anything else that can be done. In the example I have given about the lady with terminal cancer, was the doctor right in presenting ultimately futile treatment options to the family members when he offered the options of placing her on a ventilator, supporting her blood pressure with medicine, replacing the lost blood and treating the infection . . . and see what happens? With each additional complication, a physician who is so inclined could keep coming up with futile options. "We found a source of infection from the colon, and we can remove the colon. We can place the patient on dialysis, which will take on the function of the kidneys."

I feel the proper answer to the family should have been, "We have gone as far as is reasonable. Any intervention beyond this point would not be curative, nor will it allow her to live for any length of time. It simply will prolong the process of dying and make it unduly painful to all concerned." Oftentimes, after the treatment has failed, families have second thoughts about whether they have chartered the right course. After all, life is finite and so is medicine. Recognizing the limits of medical interventions is part of what defines good medical care.

TRUST IN A PROFESSIONAL:
THE NEXT BEST THING TO PATIENT AUTONOMY

In all my years of practice and particularly in recent years, I have rarely encountered family members who did not concur with a rational recommendation, so long as there is a long and trusting relationship and they have been reasonably well prepared for treatment outcome. I have grown to realize that the concepts of patient autonomy and shared decision making are important. However, they are not as important as the right of the patient to be respected at all times. Also, I have come to realize that the most important ingredients in doctor-patient relationships are trust and trustworthiness.

As important as they are, the concepts of "autonomy" and "shared decision making" cannot be trusted to operate as intended in the setting of the intensive care unit. This is particularly true with unexpected emergencies and when the patient's education and/or comprehension are limited. Data has shown that whereas some of the less sophisticated families develop unlimited trust in the physician and are prepared to relinquish all medical decisions to him or her, others leave all decisions in the hands of a specified family member, a religious leader such as their pastor or rabbi, or a respected friend. Many tend to be indecisive about the complex life-and-death issues, either from a lack of trust, poor communication between doctor and family, inability to understand all ramifications of treatment, lack of consensus, or sometimes outright resentment.

WILL LIMITING FUTILE CARE
LEAD TO UNLIMITED ABUSE?

Some people feel that the limitation of any medical intervention—even futile intervention—will result in a spiraling descent into abuse, the so-called slippery-slope argument. Partisans of the slippery-slope argument maintain that society must protect the lives of its citizens under all circumstances and at any cost, since this is the basic value that binds the society together. Slippery-slope advocates feel that society must protect its most vulnerable members who may therefore be neglected or even by going to extremes, be exterminated. Ironically, these people are ignoring and often violating the right of the individual to have freedom, dignity, and respect near the end of life. It would be far better to have as an advocate a rational and compassionate physician who understands the finitude of medicine and futility of futile care. Back in 1927, when Dr. Francis Peabody of Boston University addressed Harvard medical students on the "Care of the Patient," he began by stating that "the most common criticism made at present by older practitioners is that the young graduates have been taught a great deal about the mechanisms of disease, but very little about the practice of medicine, or to put it bluntly, they are too scientific and do not know how to take care of patients" . . . how true today![3]

Dr. Timothy Quill, the famed advocate of legalized euthanasia and author of *Death and Dignity: Making Choices and Taking Charge,* has some harsh words for medical ethicists who advocate life and continued treatment regardless of its futility. Although I do not agree with some of Dr. Quill's views, I quote him here to underscore a point of view with some validity: "The idealized, sanitized intentions of medical ethicists lead to bad medical practice because they neglect the reality and complexity of experience." He continues: "Current ethical and legal prohibitions reinforce self-deception, secrecy, isolation and abandonment. The humanizing of medical ethics requires greater clarity about intentions and responsibilities in the care of dying patients."[4]

PHYSICIANS BEWARE!
KNOW YOUR BOUNDS—DO NOT OVERPROMISE!

In my experience, one of the most difficult situations in clinical practice is what I like to call the 50–50 proposition. In order to clarify what I mean, I will share my precise recollection of one such recent case.

Mrs. H, a sixty-seven-year-old widow born in Scotland, lived most of her adult life in the United States. She had two bright, caring daughters and a charming granddaughter who lived close by, visiting Grandma frequently. Mrs. H was a proud, bright, independent, feisty lady. She had had heart bypass surgery twice: several years ago and four years later for the treatment of severe hardening of the coronary arteries (which provide blood to the heart muscle). In addition, she suffered two heart attacks and underwent two other procedures to open up clogged bypass veins that had been grafted into the coronary circulatory system. The second bypass surgery was extremely difficult technically, according to the surgical report. Two bypass operations had exhausted all utilizable leg veins for grafts. In addition, Mrs. H developed severe heart failure as a result of a badly damaged heart muscle and a leaky heart valve. Although still fairly young, the burden of generalized hardening of the arteries had taken its toll. The kidneys became sluggish, her blood chemistry became difficult to stabilize, and Mrs. H spent the better part of the last three months in intensive care. She was deemed not to be a candidate for heart transplantation and became desperate. "I can't go on like this!" she repeated to her relatives, nurses, and doctors. Unfortunately, I had known Mrs. H only for a few weeks prior to her last hospitalization. We spoke about Scotland (where I had part of my training), her family, and her illness. In spite of the fact that she had executed a living will less than two years prior, denoting her resentment of a permanently dependent life, and her suffering was immense, she declined an order to "not to attempt resuscitation" when I approached her tactfully about the subject.

The family asked for a second opinion of her condition. A heart surgeon, new to town, reviewed her case with us. We had a joint conference with the family.

"The only options we have are either to do something or do nothing," he said. "If we do nothing, she will die," he continued, "If we do something, we have a 50–50 chance." He went on to say that he had already presented these options to Mrs. H and that she was ready for a third open-heart surgery. The whole family welcomed this newfound hope.

I demurred: "Under the best of circumstances, Mrs. H's outlook is dismal. Even if we assume that she has a 50 percent chance of surviving surgery, the period following the operation promises to be long, stormy, and loaded with complications. Her subsequent improvement, will, at best, be extremely limited. She will never be able to lead a life of independence and, assuming the best-case scenario, she has less than a 10 percent chance of surviving one year."

The older daughter appeared startled. She asked the heart surgeon, "What is your experience in cases like this?"

"Well, I operated on a similar patient, Mr. Hunt, three months ago. They said he wouldn't survive, but he surprised us. He is alive."

"How is he doing now?" she asked me.

"He is still in the hospital in the skilled nursing facility. He is in severe heart failure. Each time we get ready to discharge him, he develops a new complication: pneumonia, urinary tract infection, clotting of leg veins, exacerbation of heart failure, and so on," I answered.

Mrs. H's daughter gazed at me and asked in a tearful voice, "What do you think?" I asked to talk to Mrs. H one more time.

"I know what you are going to tell me," said Mrs. H. "Life is a gamble, isn't it? I am ready to have surgery and whatever happens, happens," she added.

The next morning, Mrs. H underwent surgery. The operation lasted over seven hours. During surgery, a device to assist her heartbeat was inserted from the left groin; impending gangrene of the left leg developed, and another surgery to save her leg had to be performed.

After witnessing nine days of her continuing struggle in intensive care, the family decided that enough was enough, even though the surgeon wanted to persevere. A consultation with the ethics committee was obtained. Dr. Walker, Professor of Internal Medicine and noted ethicist, wrote the following in the patient's chart:★

★Reprinted with permission of the patient's family and Dr. Walker.

We are asked to comment on this difficult case of a 67-year-old white female with severe coronary artery disease, hypertension, and peripheral vascular disease. In particular, we were called regarding refusal of tube feeding for the patient by the patient's daughter. This patient has a history of multiple heart attacks prior to 1982, when she had her first bypass surgery. In recent years, her case has become more complicated by further myocardial [heart muscle] damage, repeat bypass surgeries, angina, heart-failure problems with peripheral vascular disease. On 5-26-95, the patient underwent further bypass graft surgery, mitral valve repair with intra-aortic-balloon-pump assist device. Her postoperative course has been complicated by kidney failure, low cardiac output, and mental confusion. Prior to surgery, the patient was given a 50–50 chance of surgery improving her situation. But now, nine days after surgery, the patient's cardiac [heart] status has not improved. She remains in the intensive care unit on multiple drips. Both cardiology and nephrology have assessed her prognosis as poor. In recent days, a DNR [Do Not Resuscitate] order has been written and a hospice consult placed. Currently, the patient is confused and unable to participate in discussions regarding her treatment. She did have the foresight to draft a detailed living and proxy appointment while living in the state of Washington. Her proxy is her daughter who is here at the bedside. As the patient lacks decisional capacity, all decisions regarding the patient's care should be consented to through the patient's daughter. We were consulted over the issue of the daughter refusing insertion of a feeding tube. First, it should be noted that patients have the legal and ethical right to refuse artificial nutrition and hydration. It should be also noted that the patient, in her advance directive, refused this sort of intervention in advance, conditioning it on her being decisionally incapacitated and having a terminal condition (i.e., life expectancy judged to be 12 months or less). In discussion with Dr. . . . , the patient's cardiologist and attending [hospital physician], he states that the patient is in a terminal condition. Thus, the daughter's refusal of the tube feeding goes with the patient's prior wishes. In discussion with the patient's daughter, she states that she and all her family members only want to honor their mother's wishes. She is now concerned that her mother does not wish to remain in intensive care. She states that surgery has not helped her mother's heart and that her mother is now in a situation she would have wanted to avoid. She tells me that after surgery, her mother pleaded with her to get the physicians to "stop doing things to her." The daughter is convinced that her mother would not want to continue aggressive care. She told me that she and the other family members would prefer that their mother be transferred out of the [intensive care] unit and be given comfort measures only. By contrast, there is an entry in yesterday's nurses' notes that "the patient does not want to die."

It is difficult to interpret this comment in view of the patient's disorientation and confusion. At other times, when the patient was judged to be more lucid, she indicated the opposite desire. In conclusion, we have a patient with end-stage coronary artery disease, whose heart function has not improved post cardiac surgery. She remains incapacitated in the intensive care unit. Our assessment is that the daughter is the appropriate proxy decision maker for the patient, and that she should be consulted for all decisions. In view of the patient's poor prognosis and the attending's assessment that the patient is in a terminal condition, we agree with the daughter's decision to forego the tube feeding. We do agree with the DNR status and the decision of consulting hospice. We strongly recommend that aggressive intervention be discontinued and that the patient be transferred to the floor for nonaggressive intervention and comfort care. All measures should be negotiated with the patient's daughter.

A few days passed and Mrs. H became more lucid, but more weak. I asked her, "Why did you decide to go through surgery?"

"I wanted to die—and I thought I would die in surgery," she said.

Arrangements were made to transfer her by air-ambulance to be close to her daughter. On the way out I said to her daughter, "You have done what you thought was best for her; no decision is perfect, and I would have been the happiest man if I was proven wrong."

With a choked voice, trying to overcome her tears, she asked, "What is the title of your book?"

"*On Your Own Terms,*" I said. There was a moment of silence that was worth a thousand words. A few weeks later I received a kind note from the family, in which they shared with me that Mrs. H died at home.

I turned to my students and said, "When the surgeon said 50–50 chance, he meant surviving surgery; he didn't promise health, comfort, and independence, promises that he implied but were clearly unfulfillable. Such vaguely worded misrepresentations are unethical. A patient at the abyss of death is like a drowning person groping for straws. Exaggerated promises invite unrealistic expectations that lead to unreasonable demands, often followed by great disappointments."

Sometimes doing nothing is better than doing something when that intervention is without a defined realistic and achievable objective. Patients and families should realize this. But often it is difficult for a layperson to assess medical options or realize that a specialist may be biased toward a particular procedure. It is not unethical for a physician to express his or her bias when making a recommendation. Therefore, for a surgeon to recommend bypass surgery to a patient is entirely ethical, provided the recommendation conforms with the surgeon's belief that such a course will most benefit this particular patient. Furthermore, doctors and medical professionals sometimes use, in their conversation, medical terms that may be difficult for nonprofessionals to understand. A recent research study at a leading university involved taping discussions between medical professionals and patients and their families regarding interventions. A few weeks later, most patients and family members had forgotten the content of the conversations and many did not recall that conversations about specific subject matter had taken place.

WHEN DOCTORS PLAY GOD

Some physicians need to be reminded of the supremacy of the patient's own choices. They are expected to provide their patients with sincere and honest advice, but when all is said and done, the patient holds the ultimate sovereignty over his or her own body.

Consider the case of Mr. Woodward, a seventy-six-year-old gentleman suffering from widespread cancer that originated in his right lung. The cancer ceased to respond to all available medical intervention, including radiation and chemotherapy. Mr. Woodward was transferred to hospice care with the objective of maintaining comfort and dignity. He and his family had resigned themselves to accept the inevitability of an impending death.

Mr. Woodward experienced severe headaches associated with double vision. Specialized testing showed a leaking, small blood sac (aneurysm) at the base of the brain. After an initial bleeding, the leaking stopped. A neurosurgeon was consulted and recommended an elaborate surgery to prevent any future bleeding, citing that any further bleeding may prove fatal.

The patient and his family refused the neurosurgeon's recommendation on the basis that Mr. Woodward was facing an imminent death anyway and that undergoing major brain surgery would be foolish, given Mr. Woodward's health status.

At the surgeon's insistence, one of Mr. Woodward's sons was persuaded to advocate brain surgery for his father. A date was set for the planned surgery.

The patient had already executed a living will, in which he appointed his oldest daughter as his surrogate. The patient and his surrogate became livid at the neurosurgeon's unwelcome intrusiveness and took the matter to court for adjudication. As expected, the court upheld the patient's right to refuse brain surgery with no tangible benefit to the patient, even if that surgery was not expected to cause additional unwelcome suffering.

This case illustrates an extreme example of physician's arrogance exhibited by an attitude of "doctor knows best." It also represents how some physicians are driven by self-interests and allow their greed to masquerade as altruism. They argue in favor of undertaking major procedures that do not benefit their patients. In reality, it represents a reckless disregard to the patient's best interests and the supremacy of a patient's right to control how he or she is treated.

Shamefully, the neurosurgeon failed at two levels: first, as a professional, he should have taken into account the totality of Mr. Woodward's health status, not just his brain condition. Second, at the human level, the surgeon should have been sensitive and respectful of the patient's own choices. The surgeon's attempt at forcing an unwanted and unnecessary major surgery on an unwilling patient is abominable. It is unethical, immoral, and illegal. Also, the neurosurgeon's preying on the patient's son, and exploiting the son's fear of losing his beloved father, is reprehensible. Mr. Woodward was facing a certain death in a few weeks, with or without brain surgery.

Thankfully, the likes of this case are uncommon. They should never take place.

Doctors are expected to guide their patients through medical decisions. They must do so with great sensibility to the patient's condition, with impeccable professional integrity, and with utmost regard to the patient's unique choices. True, there are not many doctors like Mr. Woodward's neurosurgeon. It is not uncommon for certain physicians to present their patients with exaggerated promises about certain medical interventions. They may cite data from the best medical centers which may apply to patients in better health conditions. Likewise, the public tends to have unrealistic expectations from medical high technology. These powerful forces often lead to unfulfillable hopes, only to be followed by profound regrets.

This unhealthy cascade must be dealt with and duly corrected through proper professional and public education. Physicians and health-care professionals should refrain from promoting high-tech interventions that do not have a clear, beneficial purpose to their patients. The public has to accept the limitations of intrusive, sometimes punishing medical interventions.

When I was a patient, I experienced two surgeries for my prostate cancer: one in 1987, another in 1991. In both instances, I followed my doctor's advice. Yes, it is my right to share in the decision making. However, this right assumes that I am able to evaluate all available options and am capable of making an informed choice among them. I felt that I was not professionally qualified to accept or refuse any particular course of therapy. In each case, my decision to abide by the choice of my doctor was based upon my trust in him. He lived up to my trust and I accepted his professional recommendation. In the case of Mrs. H and her family, I served as the trusted liaison between the medical establishment and the family. I was ultimately able to help effect a death with dignity for Mrs. H. Mr. Woodward's predicament should never have happened. His neurosurgeon did not live up to the honor of our profession.

Over the last few decades, the nation witnessed the passing of former President Richard Nixon, former First Lady Jacqueline Kennedy Onassis, and Archbishop Cardinal John O'Connor. When faced with the inevitability of an imminent death, each elected to depart peacefully in his or her own bed, surrounded by loved ones. No doubt, these and many other enlightened people provided an exemplary standard for how to face the moment of death. And, no doubt, they too had a trusted relationship with a primary physician who respected their wishes.

A NATURAL DEATH

The deaths of these famous people reminded me of a long-term friend and patient, Mr. Otha Grimes. I treated Mr. Grimes for a heart attack in 1978. Subsequently, he returned to his oil and farm business in Kansas, Oklahoma, and Texas. He bred cattle and won prizes. At age ninety-two, he had the energy of a sixty-year-old and the passion of a twenty-year-old. At this advanced age, he developed a cough and his breathing became heavy. A chest X-ray showed cancer with a large collection of fluid outside the right lung. Small lumps were palpable at the root of his neck. A biopsy confirmed incurable cancer. I shared with Mr. Grimes details of our medical findings. He asked, "How much longer do I have to live?"

I answered, "A few months."

He asked, "Can we make it any shorter?"

I said, "I do not believe in euthanasia."

He said, "Neither do I, but my wife is crippled with advanced arthritis and has heart failure. I wish not to add to her burdens. Now that I am ninety-two years old, I have outlived my peers by over ten years. It is time for me to go."

He asked to be admitted to a private hospital room and I did as he instructed. He asked that I refrain from giving him any medicine other than painkillers, and I agreed. I held his hand. He winked at me with his right eye and smiled. I was overpowered by tears. He squeezed my hand as if to encourage me, closed his eyes, and slipped into a coma.

One may ask, "What caused Mr. Grimes to slip into a coma? How would it be possible that he would be alert and conversant one moment and go into deep sleep the next?" I have no explanation except to say that the way he went proves the naturalness of death. I have seen this same phenomenon among many other older patients of Native American descent and in my native country. People who long for death withdraw from life and simply die. Mr. Grimes died two weeks later—quickly and without "lamentation or suffering." Indeed, his end was as "wonderful if a mortal's ever was." He chose an Oedipus-like death as described by Sophocles.

Richard Nixon, Jacqueline Kennedy, Cardinal O'Connor, and Otha Grimes could financially afford a couple of weeks on a ventilator somewhere in an intensive care unit. However, they could not afford the indignity and futility that goes with it. They displayed wisdom, serenity, and courage even in the face of death.

4

THE EXORCISM OF DEATH
Cardiopulmonary Resuscitation (CPR)

❧

A Man can die but once; we owe God a death.

Shakespeare, *Henry IV*, 3:2:253

A HISTORY OF RESUSCITATION

Since the dawn of history, humans have been fascinated with the idea of resuscitation.[1] Asklepios, the mythic figure, was venerated as a hero of Greek and Roman physicians from approximately 1500 B.C.E. to 500 C.E. Deifying Asklepios, first in Greece and then in the Roman Empire, made him, in essence, the god of healing who also raised the dead. The oldest written version of the myth of Asklepios was told by Hesiod in approximately 700 B.C.E. and was recounted by Appollodorus in 50 C.E.

> Asclepius . . . a son of Coronis . . . and they say that Apollo loved her and at once consorted with her, but she, in accordance with her father's judgment, chose Ischys and married him. . . . Apollo cursed the raven . . . ; but Coronis he killed. As she was burning, he snatched the babe from the pyre and brought it to Chiron, the Centaur, by whom he was brought up and taught the arts of healing and hunting. And having become a surgeon, and carried the art to a great pitch, he not only prevented some from dying but even raised up the dead. . . . I found some who are reported to have been raised by him. . . . But Zeus, fearing that men might acquire the healing art from him and so come to the rescue of each other, struck him with a thunderbolt.[2]

Since Asklepios, ancient physicians have employed myriad methods to effect the feat of resurrection.[3] A recent article by Dr. Kelly Tucker and

81

associates in the *Archives of Internal Medicine* cites various attempts at resuscitation through the ages. These authors mentioned how whipping of the dead, burning of elixirs, smearing dried excreta over the victim, incantation, and the use of fireside bellows were employed in an attempt to breathe "life" into the dead.[4] R. Boehm, a German pharmacologist from the University of Dorpat, is credited with the first reported method of closed-chest heart compressions (i.e., pushing down on the chest with both hands) on a cat to effect resuscitation. Koenig, a German surgeon, used single-handed, slow chest compressions to revive six patients after chloroform anesthesia. Another German scientist, Dr. Maass, modified this method in 1892 by applying 120 fast compressions over the breastbone, using this method to revive two patients who were presumed to have had cardiopulmonary arrest after chloroform anesthesia. In 1914, Dr. Crile, a noted American surgeon, used chest compression to revive a patient who had been anesthetized by ether to enable neck surgery. He described his method in a book dedicated to resuscitation and published in 1914.[5]

Data from experiments on dogs in subsequent years showed the feasibility of chest-wall compressions to assist the pumping action of the heart. Nevertheless, doctors resorted to opening the chest and direct hand massage on the hearts of patients who had experienced sudden death due to electrocution or similar accidents.

At Johns Hopkins University, the earliest studies in electrically shocking fibrillating hearts into regular rhythm were undertaken (fibrillation is the type of irregular heartbeat that can be fatal). A young Dutch visiting scientist, Dr. Kouwenhoven undertook these studies in 1928 at the behest of the Edison Electric Company, whose management was concerned about potential electrocution of workers.[6]

From experiments on dogs, in 1957 Kouwenhoven developed the first machine for reviving the heart rhythm by an electric shock applied through the intact chest wall.[7] Dr. Kouwenhoven, in association with Dr. Knickerbocker, was experimenting on a dog using new, heavy electric paddles to shock the fibrillating dog heart. As these scientists pressed the pedals, they noticed that the pressure caused the dog's heart to squeeze, even though it was not beating by itself. This chance observation resulted in the discovery that in humans, rhythmic compressions sixty times per minute applied to the breastbone at a force of 40 kilograms can revive an arrested heart.

On February 15, 1958, Dr. H. T. Bahnson, working with Drs. Kouwenhoven and Jude at Johns Hopkins, successfully resuscitated a two-year-old child with an arrested heart using the technique of closed-chest heart massage. Shortly thereafter, mouth-to-mouth artificial ventilation was used in conjunction with closed-chest resuscitation. In 1962, Dr. Bernard Lown of Boston discovered that direct-current electric shocks can be used safely to regulate disordered heart rhythm in place of the less safe alternating-current method.[8] He built on earlier pioneer work of research workers. By the mid 1960s, cardiopulmonary resuscitation (CPR) was ready for wide application. Initially, the success rate of CPR was 70 percent, when resuscitation was applied to victims of electrocution or when arrest was caused by anesthesia, but subsequent studies have never duplicated this figure. The success rate of CPR depends upon how soon CPR is initiated after cardiopulmonary arrest, the underlying state of health of the victim, the proficiency of the resuscitating team, the immediate availability of heart rhythm correcting devices, as well as the nature of the accident or health condition responsible for the arrest.

THE NEW RIGHT OF RESUSCITATION

As we have noted, the medical profession has been unable, so far, to develop rational and practical guidelines for life-and-death issues at the end of life. This hesitancy is also seen around the topic of resuscitation. With the wide acceptance of closed-chest CPR, Drs. Jude and Elam, the pioneering physicians, stated that the first principle for CPR was that "the patient must be salvageable" with a high degree of probability of success.[9] Their initial recommendations for CPR appeared in a textbook on the subject in 1965. Indications for CPR in the 1960s included drowning, electrocution, anesthesia, and heart attack. The criteria for who should receive CPR have undergone numerous modifications over the years, increasing its scope of application. In 1974, the American Heart Association proposed the need for documentation of any do-not-resuscitate (DNR)* orders in patients'

---

*We prefer the term "Do Not Attempt Resuscitation" (DNAR) to the commonly used DNR designation. The latter term suggests denying a patient a medical procedure and may give a false impression of abandoning the patient. DNAR underscores that CPR is either inappropriate because of medical reasons or unwanted by a competent patient.

records. CPR approached being mandatory therapy for all patients with cardiopulmonary arrest, whether they were really "salvageable" or not.

In 1976, the Clinical Care Committee of Massachusetts General Hospital developed recommendations for the treatment of hopelessly ill patients and for orders not to resuscitate.[10] DNR orders meant that, in the event that the heart stops beating or the lungs cease to function, no efforts should be undertaken to revive the heart or place the patient on assisted ventilation devices. These recommendations were published in the *New England Journal of Medicine* and had the effect of changing CPR from an intervention intended for use on victims of an acute illness or accident, leading to a premature and/or unexpected death, to a standard therapy for all cases of cardiac arrest, except for those that fulfilled the new, stringent criteria for DNR. The committee determined that DNR orders were appropriate *only* when the patient's disease *has fulfilled all three of the following criteria*:

1. The disease is "irreversible," in the sense that no known therapeutic measures can be effective in reversing the course of illness.
2. The physical status of the patient is "irreparable," in the sense that the course of illness has progressed beyond the capacity of existing knowledge and techniques to stem the process.
3. The patient's death is "imminent," in the sense that in the ordinary course of events, death will probably occur within a period not exceeding two weeks.

The committee also stipulated that the initial medical judgment regarding DNR orders be made by the physician primarily responsible for the patient, after discussion with an ad hoc committee consisting not only of the other physicians attending the patient, the nurses, and other healthcare professionals active in the care of the patient, but also at least one other staff physician not previously involved in the patient's care.

Even with the medical staff's recommendation, the committee deemed that a DNR order would become effective only upon the informed choice of a competent patient. When the patient is incompetent, *all* appropriate family members must be in agreement with the views of the involved staff. In this context, "appropriate" means at least the family members who would be consulted for permission to perform a post-mortem examination if the patient died.

Unfortunately, these guidelines represent a tremendous burden on the treating physicians, especially the guidelines developed for the incompetent-patient situation. These guidelines also imply an unfortunate message:

1. It is the right course of action to resuscitate patients any time there is a cardiopulmonary arrest.
2. Had the patient been capable of making an independent decision, it is assumed that he or she would have desired to be resuscitated (the doctrine of implied consent).

Instead of considering resuscitation to be a form of treatment that is indicated in some instances and not in others, it is assumed to be the right course for all unless otherwise clearly stated. In effect, resuscitation is regarded as the standard operating procedure. In fact, under the conditions set forth in the guidelines by Massachusetts General Hospital, even when irreversibility, irreparability, and the imminence of death have been established with reasonable certainty, a DNR order may not be the appropriate course, unless the family approves unanimously.

THE ODDS OF BEING RESUSCITATED

Our team has reviewed results of in-hospital and out-of-hospital resuscitation in an article titled "Cardiopulmonary Resuscitation in the Elderly: Defining the Limits of Appropriateness" and published in the *American Journal of Geriatric Cardiology*. Of all out-of-hospital victims of cardiorespiratory arrest, whether it occurs while the patient is in the company of others (witnessed) or alone (unwitnessed), an average of 5 percent leave the hospital alive with intact brain function.[11] Table 2, which includes results from most published large studies, shows success rates ranging from 0 percent to 12 percent. The exceptionally high success rate of CPR in Seattle (12 percent) has its explanation. Advanced Cardiopulmonary Life Support (ACLS) in Seattle is part of an intensive, coordinated, citywide training by several organizations, including schools, civic organizations, and workplaces. Also, some figures suggesting high success rates represent out-of-hospital patient triage and some do not include unwitnessed CPR. More recent reports on CPR success rates employ the "Utstein" criteria making

TABLE 2 *CPR Results: Out-of-Hospital*	
Location	% of CPR Victims' Survival
Seattle	12
Tucson	6
Maastricht area, Netherlands	6
Baltimore	11
Arrowhead, MN	5
Scotland	10
New Haven	4
Houston	7–10
Hong Kong	3
Goteborg, Sweden	9
New York City	1.4–2.1
Memphis	7.9
Boston	1
St. Etienne, France	7
Providence	0
AVERAGE	5

results more uniform, therefore allowing more reliable data comparison between studies.

Generally speaking, out-of-hospital success is likely to be highest in a midsized community and is low in a large metropolis or in a small town. It appears that midsized communities are best suited for coordinated efforts in teaching CPR and making defibrillators available at workplaces, fire stations, and other key locations.

The older the patient is, the less the chances for success with CPR. Victims over sixty-five years of age have a success rate of 3 percent to 4 percent, which is about one-third less than the pooled results. This represents a significant number of victims over sixty-five who are expected to leave the hospital alive and functional and with intact brain function. Therefore, age, per se, should not be a reason to deny CPR. On the other hand, the few studies that pertain to CPR of frail, elderly nursing home residents show that only 1 percent to 2 percent leave the hospital alive and 1 percent leave with unaltered brain function after CPR.

For in-hospital CPR, the success rate is generally reported as 10 percent to 20 percent, and for victims over sixty-five years old, the success rate is 9 percent to 12 percent. For the elderly over eighty-five years who are often in poor health, the success rate is as low as 3.5 percent and some of these patients leave the hospital with permanent brain damage.

UNREALISTIC EXPECTATIONS WITH CPR FROM PROFESSIONALS AND THE PUBLIC

Of interest is that the public has unrealistic expectations about the success rate of CPR. Under the title of "Cardiopulmonary Resuscitation on Television: Miracles and Misinformation," Drs. Diem, Lantos, and Tulsky published their findings about the success rate of CPR in television series, such as *ER*: It is a staggering 67 percent, which is more than ten times the success rate for out-of-hospital resuscitation and fifty times the success rate with the frail elderly.[12] These results are shown in Table 3. Not only the lay public but also many physicians have inflated expectations with CPR. Drs. Wagg, Kninirons, and Stewart from England asked doctors and nurses from both sides of the Atlantic about their expectations with CPR. Most respondents quoted figures that are at least twice the actual success rates.[13] These factors have the inevitable consequences of exaggerated promises by health-care professionals and unrealistic expectations by the public. They underscore the need for public and professional education.

ATTITUDES OF INFORMED CITIZENS TOWARD CPR

A study by Drs. Murphy, Burrows, and others, published in the *New England Journal of Medicine* in 1994, confirms that hospitalized, relatively healthy, elderly people have a 10 percent chance of being revived through

TABLE 3
Summary of the Percent Survival Rate with CPR

	Out of Hospital %	In Hospital %
All Patients	5	15
Over 65 Years Old	3	10
Over 85 Years Old	1	3.5
Shown in Television Series like *ER*, etc.	67	

CPR.[14] On the other hand, elderly people with long-term illnesses have a very poor chance (well below 5 percent) of being revived through CPR. This carefully conducted study showed that when *fully* informed about the outcome, including the chance of survival and possibility of impaired brain function following CPR, 20 percent of all relatively healthy patients of various ages opted for CPR in the event of cardiopulmonary arrest, but only a very small minority of patients older than eighty-six years desired CPR. The overwhelming majority (95 percent) of well-informed, elderly patients did not wish to be revived by CPR, with its attendant risk of brain damage and consequent loss of autonomy and independence. Our own research yielded almost identical results.

Our team conducted a similar study involving 298 individuals. These comprised a group of 54 elderly citizens (average age 78 years) living in an assisted living facility and 244 others who attended a mini-medical school education series. The first group of older citizens attended an informal workshop about CPR results and DNAR orders. The mini-medical school group attended a presentation on the same subject.[15]

Each of the attendees was given a questionnaire asking about his or her preference for CPR under specific medical scenarios including the following:

- Terminal illness, organs are failing, there is no reasonable hope for recovery and death is imminent and unavoidable; example, extensive malfunction of multiple organs following an accident or surgery;

- Deep coma with no reasonable hope for ever waking up;
- Permanent vegetative state when one is unaware of self and surroundings with little chance of any discernible improvement;
- Severe dementia, such as the final phases of Alzheimer's disease with permanent confusion and inability to care for self or interact with others.
- Advanced senility with decrepitude and total dependence on others for feeding, hygiene, and basic care;
- Total incapacity because of a massive stroke or multiple strokes or a disease of the nervous system that renders one wheelchair- and bed-bound with total dependence and inability to communicate;
- End-stage organ failure or systemic disease, such as the final stages of heart failure when no medicine is able to help the patient's breathing, or advanced lung disease rendering the patient immobile and in need of large doses of oxygen around the clock;
- Untreatable, disseminated cancer or infection, such as AIDS, rendering the patient bed-bound.

Analysis of the patient responses showed impressive findings: less than 5 percent of the patients did not voice an opinion, less than 4 percent of the patients over sixty years of age asked to receive attempts at resuscitation, some specifying that such attempts be carried out only for a few minutes, and almost 92 percent of patients asked that no attempt at resuscitation be carried out under any of the stated medical scenarios. The percentage of those declining attempts at resuscitation was over 94 percent among the assisted living residents and was slightly higher among women than men.

These findings fly in the face of the prevailing practice to attempt resuscitation of all cardiopulmonary arrest victims (unless clearly refused) regardless of their health condition under the doctrine of implied consent.

CONSENT DNAR VERSUS THERAPEUTIC CPR

There is no question that an individual has ultimate sovereignty over his or her body. This is an undisputed legal, moral, and ethical right of an individual. Also, a competent person has the right to refuse a medical intervention, even if the intervention is deemed beneficial by rational medical standards. This right applies to competent and incompetent individuals. When the patient is unable or incompetent to make the decision, the right is extended to the patient's appointed surrogate or a court-appointed guardian who would make choices on behalf of the patient (substituted judgment). According to the consent doctrine, when the patient's own wishes or that of his surrogate are not available or not clear, CPR should be undertaken under the premise of implied consent. This means that had the patient been able to choose, he would have chosen CPR, that is, he would opt for a chance to stay alive.

By contrast, the argument for the therapeutic CPR is simple. CPR is a medical intervention. Like all other medical interventions, CPR has to have its rational indication: an attempt to avert a premature or unexpected death.

With the therapeutic prerogative DNAR protocols, the reason for terminating treatment is to avoid "prolongation of death." These protocols, according to Robert Baker, an outspoken critic of unrestricted CPR, recognize that there is no rationale, no medical justification, no moral justification for futile interventions, even when the patient or family disagrees. I wholeheartedly agree that "[t]he mere fact that a patient, or the patient's family wishes an intervention is not sufficient grounds for the physician to maintain or initiate it."[16] When clinicians believe that an intervention will no longer serve its medical objective of prolonging life, they should so inform the patient or the patient's surrogates and then alter or discontinue the treatment. Proper communication with various family members is clearly needed to gain their approval. As with any other medical intervention, CPR should be used only for those patients who have a good chance of being restored to a conscious living state in which some degree of autonomy, even if limited, can be preserved.

Once more, court rulings, while generally supportive of DNAR orders in cases of medical futility, occasionally rendered conflicting decisions based on narrow statutory grounds. In *In re Doe* (1992), the Georgia Supreme Court upheld in the case of a thirteen-year-old girl suffering from severe brain degeneration and uncontrollable seizures with "no reasonable possibility of meaningful recovery" that physicians could not write a DNAR order.[17] The patient's parents were not married, and one of them disagreed with the DNAR order. The court supported the wishes of the parent who asked for resuscitation efforts, while at the same time concurring with the attending physicians that resuscitation efforts would have been without any therapeutic purpose in this case. Researchers have shown that mothers tend to be extremely protective of their dying children, out of a deep sense of duty, love, and hope. Maternal devotion sometimes does not yield to rational thinking or pragmatic evaluation.

In various hospitals, protocols regarding DNAR vary considerably. In some, the order is considered for all terminally ill patients. In others, more stringent limitation of its use is the norm. Drs. Waisel and Truog of the Children's Hospital, Harvard Medical School, reviewed CPR policies from four institutions in a review published in 1995. They highlighted policy differences among the following hospitals: Allegheny General Hospital, Pittsburgh, Pennsylvania; Veteran Affairs Medical Center, Seattle, Washington; Beth Israel Hospital, Boston, Massachusetts; and Johns Hopkins, Baltimore, Maryland. As the authors emphasized in their valuable study, cardiopulmonary resuscitation policies should derive from scientific thought and public negotiation.[18] At this time, they strongly support policies based exclusively on physiological evidence of futility. Allegheny General Hospital policy comes close to their criteria.

Still, most DNAR protocols in U.S. hospitals bias the decision making toward aggressive interventions (resuscitate first and ask for consent later), often with disastrous consequences to the patient, family, and society.

To further illustrate difficulties inherent in DNAR policies, I wish to share with the reader two case histories.

Mr. JW was seventy-six when he died. Six months earlier, I had had a long talk with him and his wife when he was leaving the hospital after three weeks on a ventilator for the treatment of pneumonia.

Doctor: As you know, you have severe emphysema and you will need to be on oxygen around the clock.

JW: Yes, I know that. I am hardly able to move. I can't finish a sentence without getting short of breath.

Doctor: You must stop smoking.

JW: I cannot and I will not. This is the only source of joy for me now. I know it is killing me. But I want you to know that I do not want to be placed on the ventilator again. Next time, please let me go in peace.

Doctor: After all, it is your choice. I promise to follow your directive.
           (His wife nods as if to say, "I agree.")

Four months later, Mr. JW's wife brought him to the emergency room
with chest pain. He was drenched in sweat and suffocating.

Doctor: Do you want me to place you on a ventilator to breathe for
           you?

JW: Nods, and wife screams, "He is dying, do something!"

JW was placed on full assist ventilation. He was found to have suffered
a massive heart attack, complicated by severe heart failure and cessation of
urine flow because of kidney damage. JW was started on a kidney dialysis
machine. He developed a clot inside his heart and this traveled to the
brain, resulting in a massive stroke. Despite multiple team intensive care,
JW died from multiple organ failure and systemic infection six weeks later.
His death was a harsh one.

Another patient, Mr. GH, a sixty-seven-year-old homeless person, developed out-of-hospital heart arrest. He received bystander cardiopulmonary
resuscitation (CPR). In the intensive care unit, he was sustained on the ventilator, developed kidney failure requiring dialysis, relentless pneumonia and
lung damage, gangrene of the hands and feet requiring toe and finger amputation, and systemic infection. He never recovered consciousness, and a Do
Not Attempt Resuscitation (DNAR) order was contemplated two weeks later.
An eligible relative (nephew) was found in another state after a few days of
searching (otherwise, a court-appointed guardian would have been needed).
The nephew's instructions were "continue to do everything possible." He did
not consent to a DNAR order. Mr. GH died four weeks later in intensive care.

These two cases represent everyday occurrences in the practice of
medicine and intensive care. Do these cases represent the exercise of
patients' autonomy in the choice of resuscitation? Did they serve the
patients' best interests? In the first case, was a dying patient's cry for help a
plea for resuscitation or relief? In the second case, was the relative's choice
a true representation of what the patient himself would have chosen,
assuming that he could be fully informed, able to comprehend, and had the
leisure to make an uncoerced decision?[19]

Cardiopulmonary resuscitation by necessity is undertaken under unusual circumstances. A large percentage of patients who at one time expressed a desire for DNAR change their minds when facing the imminence of death.[20] One wonders whether this change is based on rational re-evaluation of circumstances or is simply reflective of the gravity of the situation. Also, surrogate decisions are often discordant with the patient's own wishes, tainted with feelings of guilt, fear of loss of a loved one, concern about possible future accusations that they didn't show enough concern, or motivated by self gain.[21]

The common practice of "do everything possible" by which interventions are undertaken with no clear health benefit to the patient is neither rational nor humane. True, many do so out of love, sense of duty, or fear of guilt or loneliness. However, the salad-bar-eat-all-you-can approach to medical care of the dying is wasteful and cannot be sustained. Some patients' families often ask "do everything possible" out of convenience, and because there are no economic consequences to them.

For physicians, the same attitude safeguards against possible litigation, and in many instances, is rewarding financially. In addition, it satisfies a physician's passion for high-tech interventions.

Furthermore, for the minority of Americans who execute advance directives, the patient's true wishes about medical care in terminal illness are often neglected, overlooked, overruled, renegotiated, or reinterpreted. Such behavior from physicians and the public undermines the patient's autonomy and complicates an already vexing problem.

Is there a solution to this wasteful, high-technology-driven, death-defying attitude toward terminal care? Cardiopulmonary resuscitation (CPR) is a medical intervention that must have its indications and therapeutic goal. In our view, it must not be applied unless there is a reasonable hope for a conscious life with a chance that the patient will be able to pursue and achieve some degree of happiness. The prevailing policy of consent DNAR, that is, resuscitate every patient unless he is clearly terminal *in extremis* and death is imminent, and provided the patient or surrogate agreed to DNAR, needs further review. We argue that like other medical treatments, CPR should be the domain of the treating professionals, provided that they communicate their reasoning to patients and families with a good measure of sensitivity and sensibility.

Two questions have to be addressed: First, would such policy undermine the patient's autonomy? Second: Does it give undue power to physicians?

According to the American Constitution, the individual has supreme authority over his or her body. Therefore, any policy that undermines such authority is unconstitutional. It follows that life and death decisions should be left in the hands of individuals or their appointed proxies. On the other hand, the exercise of autonomy requires full information, capacity to evaluate and choose, and ability to make a free, spontaneous decision (the exercise of free will). Clearly, these conditions cannot be satisfied in the emergency room or intensive care unit. Furthermore, credible studies have shown that after patients' deaths, a large percentage of families report that their loved ones were not treated according to the patients' expressed wishes and others regret what they allowed their loved ones to endure.[22] In addition, the current restrictive policies of DNAR fly in the face of the fact that most fully informed seniors do not wish to undergo resuscitation in the event of cardiopulmonary arrest when the odds are overwhelmingly against a successful outcome and when the expected survival to discharge is less than 5 percent.

The slippery slope argument that relinquishing so much authority to physicians over matters of life and death could lead to abuse should not be a reason to suffocate a sensible discussion of this vital subject. Physicians are trained to deal with disease and death issues. Like an informed jury that adjudicates life or death in criminal cases, the treating physicians and nurses, in consultation with specialists and other health-care professionals, are suited to evaluate which patients are suitable for CPR based on the patient's functional status and prognosis.

To guard against possible misapplication and to protect against litigation, we propose that national guidelines for CPR be developed. Already, many physicians have proposed such guidelines. These guidelines will need to be reviewed and refined by a consortium of the medical establishment including the American Heart Association, American College of Cardiology, American Medical Association, and Association of Medical Specialties, among others. These decisions must be subject to supervision and review by institutional review committees. Furthermore, health-care professionals and the public at large should be better educated about the possible outcomes of CPR under various medical scenarios. The literature indicates that both the lay public and health professionals have unrealistic expectations for resuscitation.

We believe the guidelines for DNAR orders articulated by the American Medical Association are extremely restrictive.[23] On its face, the wording of the guidelines may seem to be permissive: "When efforts to resuscitate a patient are judged by the treating physician to be futile, even if previously requested by the patient, CPR may be withheld." In truth, the guidelines are quite restrictive. They provide an impediment to the use of DNAR orders rather than allow for the rational application of CPR. For example, they call for CPR in cases of permanent vegetative state when high brain functions are irretrievably lost. No counterargument is more eloquent than that of Drs. K. R. Mitchell, I. H. Kerridge, and R. J. Lovat, who in a recent review of vegetative states asked the following rhetorical question: "Why do we persist in the relentless pursuit of . . . treatments to maintain unconscious existence?" Will they be treated because of our ethical commitment to their humanity, or because of an ethical paralysis in the face of biotechnical progress?"[24] Also, the American Medical Association recommends that CPR be withheld only when there is absolute certainty about the patient's imminent death.

Rational CPR indications should not be required to pass the "absolute certainty" standard advocated by the American Heart Association. As in all human endeavors, the "beyond reasonable doubt standard" applied in legal pursuits should be the guiding standard and the patient's best interests should be the ultimate arbiter.

It seems fitting to quote Massachusetts Court proceedings from 1978. In the case of Shirley Dinnerstein, the family of an older patient suffering from advanced disease of the heart and brain arteries requested DNAR for their patient, which was not in accordance with hospital policy:

> Attempts to apply resuscitation for Mrs. Dinnerstein will do nothing to cure or relieve the illness which have brought the patient to the threshold of death—this case presents a question peculiarly within the competence of the medical profession of what measures are appropriate to ease the passing of an irreversibly terminally ill patient—this question is not one for judicial decision, but one for the attending physician, in keeping with the highest traditions of his profession.[25]

Here we are, more than twenty years later, grappling with the same question. It is time to heed this court's advice. Let us set in motion the process by which patients' best interests are duly served.

5

THE SOUR NOTE
IN THE "SWEET DEATH"

Physician-Assisted Suicide and Active Euthanasia

Commit the oldest sins the newest kind of ways.

Shakespeare, *Henry IV*, 4:5:124

From the previous chapters, it must be apparent that I strongly favor the withholding or withdrawal of medication in the case of a terminally ill person once treatment has been deemed futile. I consider it a sacred duty that physicians terminate a countertherapeutic treatment. When a physician embarks on a treatment plan, it must be with the purpose of restoring the patient to a reasonable physical health that is compatible with living. Once it is found that the treatment does not produce the desired result, the physician has no obligation to continue and commits no unlawful or unethical act by discontinuing it. Some ethicists refer to the withdrawal of life support that is deemed to be without benefit to the patient as passive euthanasia. The intention here is not to end the life of a patient, but to allow nature to take its course. In this case, death, although forseeable, is not the primary intent. In this context, the views of the patient or those of his relatives should not affect these medical decisions, as long as the physician keeps the family informed at all times. This position has been supported by many court decisions and conforms with the recommendations of the Council of Medical Ethics of the American Medical Associaton.[1] Furthermore, it is the physician's duty to alleviate the patient's pain and suffering, even if that hastens the moment of death.

Physician–assisted suicide or active euthanasia is a different matter. In physician-assisted suicide, the patient controls the time and mode of death and self-administers a lethal dose of medicine prescribed for that purpose by a consenting physician. Literally translated from the Latin, *euthanasia* means "sweet death" or peaceful death. Active euthanasia is an act by which a health-care professional willfully administers a lethal dose of a drug with the intention to end the life of a patient in order to relieve the patient's suffering. Some believe, as does Dr. Robert Gillon of Kings College, London University, that "when it is time to die, the medical profession has a series of duties and obligations to aid the patient in achieving that end as an autonomous and dignified individual. Also physicians must be willing, on occasion, to take an active role in the process of death to stop suffering, to protect autonomy, and to replace technology by real people in dying situations."[2]

In the context of the debate about persistent vegetative state in the House of Lords, Lord Browne-Wilkinson asked rhetorically,

> How can it be lawful to allow a patient to die slowly, though painlessly, over a period of weeks, from lack of food, but unlawful to produce his immediate death by a lethal injection, thereby saving his family from yet another ordeal to add to the tragedy that has already struck them?[3]

Lord Browne-Wilkinson's rhetorical question was presented to the Judicial Council of the House of Lords in England in the context of a hearing about whether it was lawful to discontinue feeding and hydration from Tony Bland, a young man with extensive brain damage as a result of suffocation in a soccer accident.

No doubt these eloquent arguments are in favor of controlled, active euthanasia. There are, however, legal, moral, ethical, and religious imperatives that must be taken into account. It is true that when it comes to animals, decent human beings make sure that their beloved pets do not suffer. Author Robert James Waller quotes Isaac Asimov on this point: "No decent human being would allow an animal to suffer without putting it out of its misery. It is only to human beings that human beings are so cruel as to allow them to live on in pain, in hopelessness, in living death, without moving a muscle to help them." And Waller reflects upon putting his favorite pet, Roadcat, to sleep in his book *Old Songs in a New Café:*

> For some days after, I swore I would never go through that again. If it came to euthanasia, I would refuse to be present. But I have changed my mind . . . you owe that much to good companions who have asked for little and who have traveled far and faithfully at your side.[4]

In my view, there has to be a difference between how we treat our patients and our pets. Dogs and cats do not understand the meaning of suffering. To them, pain is mere punishment. By putting them out of their misery, we are dealing with them humanely. People, on the other hand, deal with their suffering differently. There are spiritual, emotional, and social as well as physical components to human suffering. People in the grip of dying expect us to deal with them not humanely, but with due respect to their humanness. Many of my patients find a silver lining in the dark cloud of suffering. It is our duty to make their suffering less intense so that they may be able to resolve any pre-existing conflicts with loved ones, come to terms with their own mortality, and prepare for death in ways consistent with their faith and beliefs.

MURDER OR MERCIFUL DEATH?

It can be argued that euthanasia is not akin to murder. In murder, there is the intention to hurt; there is often hatefulness and cruelty. Euthanasia, on the other hand, is often justified by those who advocate it on the presumption that it is motivated by noble sentiments: love, caring, and mercy. Nevertheless, my beliefs, my upbringing, my faith, and above all, being a physician prevent me from administering a medicine with the intention to end a life. In the Hippocratic oath, a physician swears, "I will give no deadly medicine to anyone if asked, nor suggest any such counsel." Furthermore, the Judeo-Christian teachings place human life over virtually all other considerations. This attitude is summed up in the Talmudic passage about Adam, "to teach that if any person has caused a single soul to perish, scripture regards him as if he had caused an entire world to perish, and if any human being saves a single soul, scripture regards him as if he had saved an entire world."

For these reasons, like many other mainstream thinkers, I cannot bring myself to accept a role to deliberately, intentionally end the life of another whatever the motive may be. I must admit, however, that many times I have administered fairly large doses of painkillers to terminally ill patients in order to alleviate their suffering. I knew that this act might have hastened their death, but that would have been incidental to relieving their pain. Also, I have strong suspicions that two of my terminally ill patients, for whom I prescribed medications to alleviate their pain, might have used the medicines to end their own lives. But I could not administer such drugs with the primary purpose of causing death. Multiple recent publications from the United States, Britain, Australia, and Canada have confirmed the fact that more than half of practicing physicians are willing to administer large doses of painkillers to alleviate patient suffering, even if that hastens the moment of death. The American Medical Association, in 1992, supported this practice in an official communiqué from the Council of Ethical and Judicial Affairs, entitled "Decisions Near the End of Life."[5]

A DOCTOR OF DEATH

Dr. Jack Kevorkian, the "death doctor," has received much publicity as a physician who actively abets the suicide of strangers. Personally, I have great difficulty validating a physician like Dr. Kevorkian, who has taken the Hippocratic oath to protect life yet dedicates himself to helping others die. I find it difficult to condone the conduct of a physician who specializes exclusively in the act of mercy killing and videotapes the moments of his patients' deaths.

Kevorkian embarked upon a crusade, hoping to change the law prohibiting doctor-assisted suicide. He believes that this law is intrinsically immoral; therefore, he feels a greater duty to violate it. Indeed, in many instances his actions have been supported by the court, such as when Michigan Judge Cynthia Stephens supported the right to suicide of two terminally ill plaintiffs: "This court cannot envisage a more fundamental right than the right to self-determination."[6]

The publicity surrounding Kevorkian and his suicide machines is indicative of how ill at ease physicians and society in general are with doctor-assisted suicide. At the very mention of "euthanasia," many groups, including members of the medical profession, throw up their hands in horror. Like many other attempts to reach consensus regarding end-of-life medical treatment, these issues are greeted with cries of the "slippery-slope" hazards. Similar expressions of alarm occurred in the past regarding discussions about withholding interventions from patients whose deaths are imminent, withdrawing machines when treatment is hopeless, or when considering the cessation of feeding and hydration when life is near its close.

When Dr. Kevorkian, in 1990, attached one of his suicide machines to Janet Adkins, a fifty-four-year-old woman with Alzheimer's disease, his proclaimed reason was that he was honoring her wishes. She no longer enjoyed life and feared a gradual, unrelenting decline with progressive disability. According to Kevorkian, his role was merely to facilitate Mrs. Adkin's own use of the suicide apparatus to end her own life.[7]

The suicide apparatus first delivered an intravenous infusion of saline (salt) solution. An anesthetic (thiopental) was ready to flow when Mrs. Adkins pushed the button; the potassium chloride, which caused a lethal heart rhythm disorder, automatically followed one minute later. Because he designed the device so that the patient could trigger the sequence, Kevorkian has been accused of aiding Mrs. Adkins in taking her own life.

Dr. Kevorkian's license to practice medicine in Michigan was revoked in November 1991. Without a license, he no longer had access to thiopental or potassium chloride and hence could no longer use his machine. Since Kevorkian has a fear of flying and dislikes driving long distances, he limited his activities to the state of Michigan. In an attempt to stop him, John Engler, the governor of Michigan, signed a law banning assisted suicide in December 1992. The law makes assisted suicide a felony punishable by four years in prison and a $2,000 fine and was to take effect on March 15, 1993. However, a sudden spate of Kevorkian-assisted deaths (seven in two months) led legislation to introduce the measure and make it effective immediately on February 25, 1993. A special commission was appointed to further study the issue of physician-assisted suicide.

Michael Schwartz, Dr. Kevorkian's attorney, speaking for his client, challenged the constitutionality of the law. Kevorkian has commented that the legislators are making fools of themselves and expressed contempt that they would even think of perpetrating human misery by law. "It is the arbitrary codification of an edict for the sole benefit of a barbaric religious clique," said Kevorkian's attorney.[8] Dr. Kevorkian never ceased his activities.

A new wave of criticism of Kevorkian erupted after it was revealed that Hugh Gale, a seventy-year-old client of Kevorkian, might have changed his mind shortly before his death. Mr. Gale, a victim of advanced heart failure and emphysema, sought Kevorkian's assistance with suicide. Mr. Lynn Mills, an activist in Operation Rescue, while preparing for an anti-Kevorkian campaign, found in the garbage of a Kevorkian associate a form entitled "Final Action." In this form, Kevorkian described the last moments of the life of his client. According to the document, Mr. Gale placed a mask on his face and initiated the flow of carbon monoxide (a toxic gas) from a machine prepared for him by Kevorkian. After forty-five seconds, Mr. Gale became flushed, agitated, and short of breath. He asked that the mask be taken off. The mask was removed. Twenty minutes later, Mr. Gale indicated that he wanted to restart the process to end his life. Thirty seconds after starting the second time, "he again became flushed and agitated." His pleading to "take it off" was not honored, and he died eight minutes later. The incident, which was subsequently refuted by Mrs. Gale, Kevorkian, and his attorneys, caused a firestorm of criticism from the Washington-state based Christian Defense Coalition. Reverend Patrick Mahoney declared that "Gale did not die with dignity, he died an agonizing death asking that the mask be removed. This was clearly a murder taking place. Mr. Gale did not want to die." The allegations prompted many discussions about Kevorkian's activities, and he was banned from continuing his activities with physician-assisted suicide.[9]

Task forces in Canada, the United Kingdom, and many U.S. states were appointed to further study the appropriateness of physician-assisted suicide in selected instances. So far, there is a general agreement that letting a hopelessly ill patient die is both proper and humane. But there is a difference between letting one die and causing one to die.

The ban on doctor-assisted suicide did not stop Dr. Kevorkian from assisting more patients to take their lives. Supported by public-opinion polls showing a slim majority in his favor and court rulings from three separate county circuit judges in Michigan, Kevorkian seemed unstoppable. The Michigan Court of Appeals, in May 1994, invalidated the legislative ban on assisted suicide. The court also ruled that there is no constitutional right to suicide and that suicide assistance amounts to murder. Three weeks later, on May 30, 1994, the Michigan Supreme Court placed the appeals court ruling on hold.

In one of his many court appearances, Kevorkian was found "not guilty" in the case of the suicide of Thomas Hyde, thirty-year-old man totally paralyzed as a result of a degenerative neurologic disorder. The man died from inhaling carbon monoxide provided by Dr. Kevorkian. The jurors heard Hyde's taped, anguished plea for a merciful death, along with Kevorkian's videotaped confession of aiding him.

The Michigan Commission on Death and Dying submitted its final report in the fall of 1994. The commission comprised twenty-three members with a wide spectrum of interests. Not surprisingly, three conflicting positions emerged. One, supported by five members, called for a total ban on assisted suicide. Another position, supported by nine members, called for a "Death with Dignity" act, by which assisted suicide would be legal in the case of terminal disease or irreversible suffering. The person would need to have engaged in repeated requests for assistance in dying and undergo examination by two physicians, a psychiatrist or psychologist, a social worker, and a pain management specialist. The third position, supported by nine members, only suggested procedural safeguards in the event of decriminalization of physician-assisted suicide.[10]

Dr. Kevorkian continued his devotion to the mission of making physician-assisted suicide legal. He received numerous new requests to end the lives of people suffering enormous mental or physical pain, caused by total body paralysis, disseminated cancer, or deteriorating mental function. Kevorkian's legal wrangling was relentless and seemed unlikely to stop as long as he was able to maintain the fight. Eventually, Dr. Kevorkian did himself in. In a display of extreme defiance, he videotaped himself assisting his last victim to die and televised it on *60 Minutes* to millions of viewers. He was convicted of second degree murder and is serving his jail term. By putting Kevorkian in jail, the Michigan court refused to allow him to blur the line between the patient's wish and the physician's act.

According to an article published in *Time,* dated May 31, 1993, out of frustration or fear of helplessness, an increasing portion of the American public views physician-assisted suicide as a reasonable "treatment." They applaud Kevorkian's acts and statements and thereby express their defiance of the perceived inconsistency in medical practice: treating people to death while they are unable to voice their wishes and yet denying those who ask for a graceful exit the means to achieve their wishes. The first is committed under the doctrine of implied consent and the latter is denied as unlawful. Other health-care professionals also champion Kevorkian: "He tells us exactly where the health-care system stinks," proclaims one professional, Dr. Annas, a recognized authority in judicial and ethical issues of medicine and professor at the Boston University of Medicine and Public Health. "He is a total indictment of the way we treat dying patients. . . . We don't treat them well and they know it. . . . This mistreatment is a combination of deceit, insensitivity and neglect. . . . Worse, doctors ignore patient's suffering." Many feel that Dr. Kevorkian is a refreshing antidote to those physicians who, for whatever motive, employ one last treatment intervention—even if the chances of it working are one in a million.[11]

When people are asked how they wish to die, most would say the following: "I choose to die quickly, painlessly, at home in my bed, surrounded by family and friends. I choose a graceful exit." Then ask them how they expect to die: "In a hospital, in an intensive care unit, violated by many tubes, on machines, and in pain." Although the question about active euthanasia has come to the forefront in America, where more elderly die in the hospital and are likely to end up in an intensive care unit, the problem is universal. In Canada, Sue Rodriquez was suffering from an incurable neurological degenerative disease that attacks the brain and the spinal cord. She was completely paralyzed and could not walk, breathe, or speak. She asked in 1992 for someone to be legally allowed to help her die. The Canadian Supreme Court denied her wish by a slim majority. She died in February 1994, with the help of an anonymous doctor.[12] Of interest is the fact that less than two years earlier the same court had granted another patient with a similar condition the right to be allowed to die by disconnecting her from the ventilator. In *Nancy B. v. L'Hotel Dieu de Quebec,* the patient, a twenty-five-year-old woman, was permanently paralyzed from nerve degeneration (Guillan-Barre syndrome). Her life was dependent on the ventilator. The patient asked to be disconnected, and her family approved. In January 1992, the Supreme Court of Canada granted her request under the "Causation Rationale" (i.e., no crime would be committed by persons who complied with patient's informed consent to allow death through "nature taking its course").[13] Conversely, Ramon San Pedro of Spain sustained a crippling neck injury in 1968. Since then, he has lived in a "locked state." He is conscious but can only move his head. In vain, he has pleaded repeatedly to the medical and legal establishments to put him out of his misery. So far, two Spanish courts have refused consent for assisted suicide.

DEATH ON DEMAND

The debate about active euthanasia (mercy killing) and physician-assisted suicide (prescribing a medication with the intent of assisting a person to take his or her own life) is by no means new. In recent articles in the *Archives of Internal Medicine* and in the *Annals of Internal Medicine*, Dr. Ezekiel Emanuel, Director of Ethics at the Dana Farber Cancer Institute in Boston, reviewed the history of euthanasia in the United States and Great Britian.[14] Dr. Emanuel noted that euthanasia was an everyday encounter in the Greco-Roman empire, where "many people preferred death to endless agony." The practice of euthanasia in ancient times ran contrary to the Hippocratic oath "not to prescribe a deadly medicine even if they asked for it." It must be noted that the ascent of Christianity in the twelfth century reinforced Hippocratic teachings that "Life is a gift from God that has to be preserved." However, British and French philosophers of the seventeenth and eighteenth centuries attacked prohibitions against euthanasia out of defiance to the Christian religious authority. In an essay titled "On Suicide," David Hume, the legendary philosopher of the eighteenth century, wrote, "Suicide may be consistent with our duty to ourselves, no one can question, who allows that age, sickness or misfortune may render life a burden, and make it worse even than annihilation"[15] These and similar writings seemed to have a limited resonance among the general public.

Dr. Emanuel reminds us in his article that in more modern times, with the introduction of powerful analgesics such as morphine, and with the discovery of anesthetics in the nineteenth century, it was suggested that these drugs might be used to "mitigate the agonies of death." The use of morphine preparations, chloroform, and ether anesthetics to relieve the pain of dying found wide use in Britain and in the United States (especially during the Civil War). Soon after, advocates for a peaceful, quick "death on demand" promoted the idea that patients should have the right to end their lives. In 1870, Mr. Samuel Williams advocated the use of anesthesia to intentionally cause death:

> In all cases of hopeless and painful illness, it should be the recognized duty of the medical attendant whenever so desired by the patient, to administer chloroform, or such other anesthetic so as to destroy consciousness at once, and put the sufferer to a quick and painless death.[16]

Dr. Emmanuel noted that, in 1899, Simeon Baldwin, in his presidential address to the American Social Science Association, advocated euthanasia by criticizing the "pride of many in the medical profession to prolong such lives at any cost of discomfort or pain to the sufferer."

Dr. Emmanuel described how discussions about euthanasia came to the forefront of public debate early in this century: a wealthy woman, Anna Hill, whose mother was dying from cancer, campaigned for the legislation of euthanasia in Ohio. Her campaign prompted the introduction by State Representative Hunt, of "an act concerning administration of drugs, etc. to mortally injured and diseased persons." In 1906 a heated debate erupted in the news media. The *British Medical Journal* characterized America as

> Land of hysterical legislation, in which the legislation of euthanasia is put forward every now and then by literary dilettantes or by neurotic intellectuals whose high-strung temperament cannot bear the thought of pain. The medical profession has always sternly set its face against a measure that would inevitably pave the way to the grossest abuse and would degrade them to the position of executioners.[17]

The Ohio Hunt Bill was rejected by an overwhelming margin.

According to Dr. Emanuel's review, several instances of euthanasia on demand were publicized. Also, many leading newspapers carried commentaries on the subject. An editorial on this subject entitled "Dr. Norton on Euthanasia" appeared in the *New York Times* in January 1906. After denying that human life is always necessarily "sacred" and charging the physician with having carried too far his commendable desire to prolong the existence of his patients, Dr. Norton declared

> That no thinking man would hesitate to give a fatal dose of Laudanum [a pain killer] to the victim of an accident from the torturing effects of which recovery was impossible, that no reasonable man would hesitate to hasten death in a case where a cancer has reached the stage of incessant pain and the patient wants to die, that it is the plain duty to shorten, not to prolong the life of an old person whose mind has become a chaos of wild imaginings productive of constant distress not only to the sufferer, but to all who live with and attend him.[18]

The article concludes eloquently with this commentary:

> . . . and where would Dr. Norton get his physicians who could always tell with certainty the outcome of an accident or disease? . . . It is an

utter waste of time to worry about the few cases where a man with perfect wisdom would be justified in giving "the happy death" to another, since the man with perfect wisdom is yet to be invented or developed.[19]

The debate on euthanasia was revived in Britain the 1930s by the president of the Society of Medical Officers, at which time Dr. C. Killick Millard proposed a statute to legalize euthanasia in Britain.

THE DOWN SIDE OF EUTHANASIA

The debate about euthanasia took a new twist in Germany. In 1920, Dr. Hocke, a German professor of psychiatry, and Mr. Binding, a German lawyer, coauthored a book entitled *Permission to Destroy Life Unworthy of Life*. They argued that certain people with mental illness or physical infirmity, including deformed children, lead "unworthy lives." For these people, Hocke and Binding argued, "Death is a compassionate healing."[20] They went on to make the point that these "unworthy lives" represent a financial drain on society while polluting the gene pool. Hocke and Binding's views became part of the Nazi agenda and justified the notion of genetic cleansing, as well as that of mercy killing.

The Nazi experience, particularly the role of German physicians in genocide, biased the public debate about active euthanasia for some time.

THE REVIVAL OF "HUMANE" EUTHANASIA

The debate about humane euthanasia was rekindled in 1972, when a Netherlands physician (Dr. Postma) administered a large dose of morphine to his senile, crippled, deaf, mute, paralyzed mother upon her insistence, through repeated pleading through gestures, that he relieve her pain. Dr. Postma was given a sentence of one week in jail and one year probation. The incident rekindled the debate about euthanasia and brought it into the public forum in the Netherlands, eventually leading to the wide acceptance of euthanasia in Holland. In 1973, the Royal Dutch Medical Association issued this statement: "Euthanasia should remain criminalized but the physicians should be permitted to engage in euthanasia for dying and suffering patient as a *force majeure,* when there is conflict between duties to preserve life and duties to relieve suffering." In 1987, the Dutch Parliament established the Remmelink Commission to review and advise the parliament regarding the practice of euthanasia in Holland.[21] The commission interviewed over 400 physicians and submitted its report in September 1991, recommending that physicians who engage in euthanasia cannot be prosecuted as long as they follow certain guidelines. The commission also felt that the practice of euthanasia should be brought into the open to guarantee against its abuse. In America, in 1988, the *Journal of the American Medical Association* published a case entitled "It's Over, Debbie," in which an anonymous young physician claimed (perhaps falsely) to have given a young woman who was dying of disseminated cancer a large dose of morphine, then watched her die painlessly. The two recent cases of Dr. Timothy Quill in the United States and Dr. Nigel Cox of Britain have fueled debate about the issue again on both sides of the Atlantic.[22] (These cases will be discussed later in this chapter.)

The problem with legalization of active euthanasia stems from the difficulty of striking a balance between two opposing views, each of which has compelling reasons to be heard.

The euthanasia argument is summed up eloquently by Dr. Dan Brock, Professor of Philosophy and Biomedical Ethics at Brown University:

> If self-determination is a fundamental value, then the great variable among people on this question makes it especially important that individuals control the manner, circumstances, and timing of their dying and death.[23]

The argument follows that if physicians are allowed to withdraw life-sustaining treatment from their dying patients, why not hasten their moment of death? After all, "human life is sacred, but only to the extent that it contributes to the joy and happiness of the one possessing it, and those about him." These advocates would agree that it ought to be the privilege of every human being to cross the river Styx in the boat of his choosing, when further human agony cannot be justified by the hope of future health and happiness.

The principal argument against euthanasia is that society has a vested interest in protecting all its members and in ensuring that all members of society have equal human worth under the law. It is one thing to have the right to commit suicide or to be left to die, but to be helped to die or made to die by a physician is a different issue. One of the central Christian beliefs is that life is a gift from God that individuals guard but do not own. It is a basic good on Earth. Furthermore, many believe that human suffering, by itself, is a wellspring of redemption and therefore has value. However, the question remains as to whether protracted human suffering inflicted by manmade machines is necessary, and at what point should it be considered excessive? Where should the boundary between death and meaningful life be drawn? This is the ultimate challenge.

Public and professional opinion polls are shifting toward support of euthanasia. A slim majority of the American public is in favor of legalizing euthanasia with ample safeguards. A collaborative study between Harvard School of Public Health (Boston) and the *Boston Globe* regarding the public's attitude on euthanasia involved over 1,000 participants. The study showed two-thirds of the public favor physicians being permitted to give a terminally ill patient in pain a lethal injection to aid in dying. Of the public, 20 percent supported assisted suicide or euthanasia for advanced, painful, irreversible disease.[24] The passage in November 1994 of a law legalizing physician-assisted suicide in Oregon supported these polls. A recent survey of 2,500 readers in *Yours,* a U.K. pensioner's magazine, found that nine out of ten readers thought the doctors should be allowed to end the lives of terminally ill patients and wanted the law changed in Britain. More than 50 percent said they would help a friend, relative, or spouse to die in such circumstances. Surprisingly, religious faith, social class, and place of residence had little bearing on people's views about euthanasia in Great Britain. Because of the much stronger influence of organized religion in the United States, it is unlikely that active euthanasia will meet with as much overwhelming support here. A report published in the *British Medical Journal* in February 1993 revealed that of 1,100 adults surveyed in Britain, 70 percent called for euthanasia to be removed from criminal law. The Canadian Parliament, which turned down euthanasia legislation four times, has appointed a commission to study the subject and gather public information.[25] Of interest is the revealing statistic that in the Netherlands, where active euthanasia is not punishable by law, more people long for assisted suicide because of mental anguish rather than intolerable physical pain.

As shown earlier, several studies from the United States, Britain, and

Australia find that roughly one-third to one-half of practicing physicians and consultants were asked by patients to hasten the moment of death, yet few of them have helped their patients die. It is clear, however, that Europeans and Australians are more accepting of the idea that some form of legislation allows euthanasia in certain circumstances. In the United States, laypeople and health-care professionals remain uneasy about the subject of euthanasia. This subject must be approached deliberately and cautiously. Supreme Court Justice Brennan's closing words in the Cruzan case are eminently relevant here: "The greatest dangers to liberty lurk in insidious encroachment by men of zeal, well-meaning but without understanding."[26]

EUTHANASIA: THE HOLLAND EXPERIENCE

Not infrequently, I have heard individuals refer to the "savage system" of legalized euthanasia in Holland. But in Holland (the only European country in which euthanasia is not prohibited) the legislation and the medical community have taken ample measures to ensure that active euthanasia is not applied arbitrarily.[27] Technically, euthanasia was illegal in Holland until 2001, when the original law prohibiting the ending of a life by a physician was finally repealed. In 1994, a law was passed which protects physicians who undertake euthanasia under certain conditions from prosecution and requires them to report these cases for purposes of monitoring. There are strict criteria for determining who would be eligible for physician-assisted mercy killing.[28] Also, the system has ample safeguards against abuse. According to these "carefulness requirements," the patient's request for euthanasia must be made "entirely of the patient's own free will," without pressure from others. The patient must be "well informed" and capable of weighing the alternatives. Furthermore, the patient must demonstrate an enduring longing for death, rather than an impulse to die that is due to, say, a temporary depression. In addition, the patient, "must experience his or her suffering as perpetual, unbearable, and hopeless," and the physician must be able to conclude reasonably that the patient's suffering is unbearable. Finally, the physician is required to consult at least one experienced colleague who previously made a decision regarding euthanasia. In many instances, the patient is referred for psychiatric evaluation; a cooling-off period is required prior to carrying out mercy killing.

In spite of that, 11 percent of all physicians in the Netherlands refuse to practice euthanasia. Those who do carry it out do so once or twice a year at the most, and they describe it as a "very emotional and heart-wrenching experience." In spite of the acceptance of euthanasia in the Netherlands and the fact that every physician undertaking it must file a detailed report in each instance, reported cases of euthanasia have accounted for only 2 percent of all deaths since the new laws were enacted. According to opinion polls in the Netherlands, quoted in the *Economist* and in *Biolaw,* 80 percent of the population support the right of terminally ill patients to ask for euthanasia and only 10 percent oppose it.[29]

In 1996, I made a fact-finding visit to Holland. I spoke with several physicians, many of whom had been involved in euthanasia. Also, I spoke to several laypeople. I have the impression that younger physicians are more accepting of euthanasia than older ones. All the physicians I talked to, without exception, indicated how seriously the medical establishment has approached the problem and that only a minor proportion (25–30 percent) of patients who ask for euthanasia end up receiving it. On the other hand, many cases of euthanasia go unreported. An editorial, "The Dutch Way of Dying," in the *Economist* of September 17, 1994, cited the reasons why admirers have hailed the Dutch experience and why critics say the safeguards are ineffective. They comment that Holland is skidding down a slippery slope toward licensed killing. The editorial cites an official report that found that in addition to 2,300 reported cases of euthanasia in Holland in 1990, a further 1,040 people had their deaths hastened without making a formal request for intervention. This is a clear violation of the stated guidelines. The article quotes Mr. Johan Legemaate, Legal Council of the Royal Dutch Medical Association: "We have succeeded in creating a large amount of openness and accountability."[30] It is to be noted, however, that the current laws have been enacted by a Parliament comprised predominantly of Socialists and Christian Democrats. There is a real concern that the law may be reversed if a more conservative government assumes power in Holland. This fact seems to underlie why some physicians still do not report cases of euthanasia. They fear the repercussions of a change in government. Even though the Dutch have accepted euthanasia as an available option, there is a mounting consensus among physicians calling for more stringent self-regulation. Many influential voices prefer the patients who wish and are eligible for euthanasia be allowed to self-administer the lethal dose of barbiturate or morphine. In other words, place the final act in the hands of patients and not physicians. It thus appears they condone physician-assisted suicide but not euthanasia (mercy killing).

WILL AMERICA CONDONE
PHYSICIAN-ASSISTED SUICIDE?

An ordinance that would legalize physician-assisted suicide with somewhat ample preconditions and safeguards was approved by the Oregon voters in November 1994. A similar ordinance was defeated previously in the states of Washington and California.

The study of California's Proposition 161 on physician-assisted dying is of special interest. This initiative was presented to California voters in November 1992, and was defeated by a margin of 54 percent to 46 percent.[31] A year earlier, a similar bill was defeated in Washington state by a narrower margin of 52 percent to 48 percent. The initiative would have legalized physician-assisted suicide under certain circumstances. The Attorney General of California prepared for the voters an official title and summary of the measure:

> Terminal illness—Assistance in Dying. Initiative Statute: Permits revocable written directive authorizing a physician to terminate life in "painless, humane, and dignified manner" by mentally competent adult after terminal illness diagnosed. States procedures for witnessing and revoking directive and requesting medical assistance in dying. Precludes physicians, health professionals, and facilities from civil or criminal liability if initiative's provisions followed. Provides requesting or receiving authorized aid, not suicide. Allows physicians and health professionals to refuse to end life if religiously, morally, or ethically opposed. Prohibits existence or nonexistence of directive from affecting sale, renewal, cancellation terms, or premiums of insurance policies. Estimate by Legislative Analyst and Director of Finance of fiscal impact on state and local governments: This measure would result in some unknown savings due to decreased utilization of the state Medi-Cal program and other public programs, including county programs.[32]

Polls taken just before the election suggested that the vote on the initiative was too close to predict. One newspaper story, appearing a few days before the election, ran the following headline: "Outcome of Death Measure May Rest on 11th-Hour Ads." A $2.8 million campaign against the proposition was proposed by the Roman Catholic Church, including the state's Catholic bishops, Catholic hospitals, and individual Catholic church members, who were urged to donate directly to the campaign. The organized support in favor of the initiative raised $215,000, less than one-tenth as much money. Both sides sought to sway voters in the final days of the campaign by airing paid advertisements. One of the opposition's thirty-second television ads stated that Proposition 161 "allows physician-assisted suicide in secret, with no witnesses, no family notification, no psychological exam, and no medical specialist." The ad has whispering voices in the background asserting: "No witnesses; no one will know." Other television ads focused on the possibility that physicians would err in diagnosing terminal illness. One ad stated, "If a diagnosis is wrong, someone you know may choose physician-assisted death by mistake. Death by mistake." Other spots in favor of the proposition featured patients diagnosed as terminally ill arguing that if physician-assisted dying had been available, they might have asked for a lethal injection.

A large amount of cash was raised by those who opposed the legislation. The opposition carried numerous television and radio ads, while the proponents, with a mere $55,000, were only able to run a single radio ad in the final days before the vote. The ad featured Dr. Griffith Thomas, a Los Angeles physician-attorney who had served on the joint committees on biomedical ethics of the county bar and medical associations. It aired several times daily but only on a few stations in Los Angeles and San Diego, according to the *Los Angeles Times*. California Proposition 161 was defeated.

The Oregon "right to die" legislation differs from the proposed legislation in California in some critical respects:

- The patient request for euthanasia must be in writing.
- The request must be witnessed.
- A consulting physician must certify that the patient's condition is terminal.
- A fifteen-day waiting period must elapse between the patient's request and obtaining the suicide prescription.
- The physician must ensure that the patient's decision is voluntary by providing information about diagnosis, prognosis, other options such as hospice care, and referral to a state licensed psychologist or psy-

chiatrist if there is any suspicion that the patient may be asking for assisted suicide because of depression (a treatable illness) and not because of suffering caused by the underlying disease.[33]

This issue, even in Oregon, remains controversial. Not surprisingly, various Oregon groups similar to the California coalitions against euthanasia voted to defeat the initiative. The populace of Oregon voted in favor of "physician-assisted suicide" with the aforementioned safeguards by a very slim majority. Interestingly, it has been said that Oregon is the most "secular" of all American states, except for Nevada. More recently, a similar ordinance was enacted into law in the northern district of Australia in spring 1995.

SECONDARY PHYSICIAN-ASSISTED DEATH VERSUS PRIMARY PHYSICIAN-ADMINISTERED DEATH

Discussions about active euthanasia first came to the attention of the medical community through isolated instances such as the incident related in "It's Over, Debbie," published in the *Journal of the American Medical Association* in 1988, and more recently with the widely publicized cases involving Dr. Jack Kevorkian. Because the stories about Dr. Kevorkian and his patients are well known, I will review only the case of Dr. Timothy Quill, published in the *New England Journal of Medicine* in 1991, and that of Dr. Nigel Cox, tried in England in 1992.

Dr. Quill, a primary-care physician and director of a hospice in Rochester, New York (now professor at the University of Rochester), challenged the medical community in an article entitled "Death and Dignity: A Case for Individualized Decision Making."[34] Quill admitted aiding a leukemia victim, Diane, to take her own life. He prescribed a dose of barbiturates sufficient to cause her to stop breathing. Prior to the suicide, all treatment options had been explored, tried, and rejected. The patient and family were counseled, and it was determined that the limits of palliative care, from the patient's perspective, and to Dr. Quill's satisfaction, had been reached.

This case resulted in a heated debate in the medical and lay communities. Quill was exonerated by a grand jury that found no grounds for prosecution. The New York Health Department, after careful review of the case, refused to sanction Dr. Quill, who since then has become an out-spoken advocate for thoughtful, discriminate, physician-assisted suicide.

By contrast, Dr. Cox, a British rheumatologist, promised his patient relief of pain from her disabling, painful, acutely deforming rheumatoid arthritis.[35] Her suffering continued to be immense and unrelenting, and Dr. Cox tried every measure to alleviate the pain. According to court records, he noted in the patient's chart, "She still wants out, and I don't think we can reasonably disagree." Increasingly large doses of morphine did not relieve the pain and Dr. Cox realized that, by continuing with con-ventional medications, he would not fulfill his pledge to alleviate her pain in her final days. Out of compassion, he injected her with two ampules of potassium chloride, which brought about her death. He recorded his act in the patient's chart. A Catholic nurse, after reading the doctor's note, reported the matter to the Solicitor General and Dr. Nigel Cox was charged with and tried for murder. The prosecutor argued that giving injections with the primary intent of relieving pain and suffering is per-missible, even if this resulted in hastening the foreseen death. This is referred to as the "rule of double effect." But he argued that Dr. Cox gave the injection with the *primary* intent of killing his patient in order to relieve her suffering, a clear violation of the law. The jury was instructed to ignore Dr. Cox's motive of compassion and to focus on his intent. The jury found Dr. Cox to be guilty. Deep sighs broke the dead silence of the courtroom as the judge addressed the jury at the end of the verdict, "There are times when, speaking for myself and, I strongly suspect, speaking for all of you, a criminal trial is an almost overwhelming burden."[36] The judge imposed a sentence of twelve months but suspended it. Subsequently, Dr. Cox's conduct was reviewed by a committee of his peers and his license to practice medicine was reinstated.

Some may view Dr. Nigel Cox as a felon who crossed the line be-tween what is legally right (to let a terminally ill patient die) and what is legally wrong (to cause the death of a terminally ill patient). Some may view him as a martyr who must have agonized over his pledge to a trusting patient in extreme, uncontrollable pain. It must have been a heart-wrenching experience for him. I believe most will view him as a decent man, a great physician who might have broken the letter of the Hippo-cratic oath but who was loyal to its spirit.

PROPOSED GUIDELINES FOR ASSISTED SUICIDE

In the wake of these cases and following the defeat of California's Proposition 161, Drs. Quill, Cassell, and Meier proposed a policy for assisted suicide in the context of "care for the hopelessly ill." They suggested the following guiding principles to determine the correctness of euthanasia, in conjunction with a meaningful doctor-patient relationship:

- Patient must have a condition that is incurable and associated with severe, unrelenting suffering.
- Patient must not be asking for death because of failure to get treatment that could relieve his or her suffering.
- Patient must "clearly and repeatedly" ask for assistance in dying.
- Patient's judgment must not be distorted by a problem, such as depression, that is reversible in a way that would substantially alter the situation.[37]

These are similar to the guidelines set forth in the Dutch law of doctor-assisted suicide and conform with the newly enacted ordinance of physician-assisted suicide passed in Oregon.

A June 14, 1994, article in the *New York Times* described how AIDS patients seek solace in suicide but may risk added pain if they fail to commit it. In the article, AIDS patients relate the horrors some HIV-infected patients go through as they approach the moment of death. There are tremendous psychological stresses associated with AIDS—financial insecurity, homelessness, joblessness, and social isolation. "I will be dead, no question," one patient said. "I can't continue this way. . . . It's awful. It's worse than being dead." This AIDS patient has stated that the act of stockpiling drugs necessary to effect his own suicide "has made my every day better, much, much better. It has diminished my horror, as though I was facing an enemy on a battlefield stark naked and now I have my armor."[38]

The argument is indeed powerful and compelling. In spite of this, as a physician, I find it hard to support the proposition of active euthanasia. But I understand and empathize with those who condone it in very limited circumstances and with ample strict safeguards.

Franklin Miller and John Fletcher, of the University of Virginia, in an article titled "The Case for Legalized Euthanasia," offer a compromise position on euthanasia. I quote: "Decisions to die by euthanasia are too ethically problematic to be left to the privacy of the physician-patient relationships." Furthermore, they say,

> We oppose the position of leaving the law against euthanasia unchanged while conducting a social experiment . . . on grounds of respect for law and public accountability, we recommend legalizing voluntary euthanasia subject to prior committee review.[39]

A RULING FROM THE WASHINGTON STATE COURTS

No doubt, active euthanasia will be hotly debated over the next few years in the United States. We have really just begun to address this controversial subject. The debate will be fueled by a recent ruling from a district court in the state of Washington, which in May 1994 overturned a statute prohibiting assisted suicide. The court cited explicit use of abortion as an analogous situation. The court rationalized that since abortion is a legal right and the decision to bear a child is a matter of private choice, so is the right to choose the moment and method of dying. A summary of this landmark case follows.

In this case, the plaintiffs were a coalition of three terminally ill patients, five physicians, and the Compassion in Dying Organization. The patients included a retired pediatrician with cancer that had metastasized to the bones, a forty-four-year-old artist dying of AIDS, and a sixty-nine-year-old retired salesman with terminal emphysema. In its deliberations, the court referred to a ruling on abortion: *Liberty Interest under Planned Parenthood* v. *Casey* (114 S. Ct. 909, 1994). I quote from the subsequent ruling:

> Personal decisions relating to marriage, procreation, contraception, family relationships, child rearing, and abortion are constitutionally protected. These matters, involving the most intimate and personal choices a person may make in a lifetime, choices central to personal dignity and autonomy, are central to the liberty protected by the fourteenth amendment. At the heart of liberty is the right to define one's own concept of existence, of meaning of the universe, and of the mystery of human life. Beliefs about these matters could not define the attributes of personhood were they formed under compulsion of the state.[40]

The court went on to point out that the opinion in *Casey* involved a woman's right to choose abortion. This case did not precisely address the question of the liberty issues inherent in a terminally ill person's choice to commit suicide. However, the court found the reasoning in *Casey* highly instructive and almost prescriptive on the latter issue. Judge Barbara Rothstein noted that, as in abortion, the court's duty is not to impose a particular moral standard. "Some of us as individuals find abortion offensive to our most basic principles of morality, but that cannot control our decision. Our obligation is to define the liberty of all, not to mandate our own moral code. The underlying constitutional issue is whether the state can resolve these philosophic questions in such a definitive way that a woman lacks all choices in the matter."[41]

The judge further found the decision of the lower courts, in denying the plaintiffs the right to assisted suicide, inconsistent with *Casey*.[42] She granted the plaintiffs the right to assisted suicide, stating that a decision to end one's life is the ultimate act of self-determination. She ruled that the current law against physician-assisted suicide in the State of Washington is unconstitutional.

PHYSICIAN ASSISTED SUICIDE: THE OREGON EXPERIENCE

In 1997, the United States Supreme Court ruled that American citizens do not have a constitutional/liberty right to physician-assisted suicide.[43] The Court further stipulated that states are free to ban it or to permit it. Oregon has chosen to permit physician-assisted suicide in certain circumstances.[44] The Oregon Death with Dignity Act, passed in October 1997, allows the physician who has primary responsibility for managing a patient's terminal illness to prescribe a dose of lethal medication which the patient may administer, provided certain conditions are met: death should be expected within six months and this must be confirmed by a consultant. Also, the patient must make two oral requests and one written request for assisted suicide over a period of fifteen days. Referral to a mental health professional is required if either the attending physician or the consultant is concerned that the patient's judgment may be impaired by a mental disorder.

In 1998, twenty-four Oregonians were given prescriptions for lethal doses of medication. Of these, sixteen died after ingesting their medicine. The rest either died naturally without taking the lethal medicine or elected not to take it at all. In 1999, of thirty-three Oregonians who were given such prescriptions, twenty-seven took their own lives. Participation was not found to be associated with low educational level, lack of insurance, or poor access to hospice care.

Only 12 percent of the 1998 patients were married. This raised concern that physician-assisted suicide would be asked mostly from patients lacking social support, regardless of the severity of their disease. In 1999, the percentage of married patients was forty-four. Autonomy and the desire to control the moment of dying was the most important factor driving terminally ill patients to ask for assisted suicide.

In 1999, over half the patients who asked for physician-assisted suicide raised the issue of pain and suffering as a contributing factor. In many instances, however, the fear of suffering was more pressing than present pain.

Doctors have granted one in six requests for lethal medications, and only one in ten requests eventually resulted in suicide. This underscores how reluctant physicians are in responding to requests to assist their patients in ending their lives. "Physicians frequently made palliative care interventions which were helpful to patients and caused them to change their minds about assisted suicide," reported Dr. Linda Ganzini, a geriatric psychiatrist at the Portland Veterans Medical Center, and her colleagues in a recent article in the *New England Journal of Medicine*.[45]

One-third of patients had to go to more than one doctor for help. More important, however, is that of the 165 patients who asked to be helped with suicide, more than one-third did so because they perceived themselves as a burden to others. Only three of these received a prescription, suggesting that the physicians were reluctant to grant requests for assistance under these circumstances.

In the same issue of the *New England Journal of Medicine*, Drs. Amy Sullivan, Katrina Hedberg, and David Fleming from the Oregon Health Division of the Centers for Disease Control and Prevention reported on the second year's experience with legalized physician-assisted suicide in Oregon. The authors concluded,

> In the second, as compared with the first year of legalized physician-assisted suicide in Oregon, the number of patients who died after

ingesting lethal medications increased, but it remained small in relation to the total number of persons in Oregon who died. Patients who requested assistance with suicide appear to be motivated by several factors, including loss of autonomy and a determination to control the way in which they die.[46]

The Oregon experience has lent credence to both sides of the debate for and against physician-assisted suicide. On the one hand, the law to legalize physician-assisted suicide in Oregon did not open the floodgates to mass executions or to a slippery slope by which the undesirables go first. Less than 4 out of every 10,000 deaths occurred by lethal drug prescription. Most of these deaths were quick and uneventful. On the other hand, the experience shows clearly that with adequate attention by the physician to control the patient's pain and anguish, it would not be necessary to consider the option of ending the life of another; indeed, most of those who pursued this way of exit turned out to be "control freaks," obsessed with the notion of autonomy and their desire to be in command of all aspects of their life and death.

Dr. Dick L. Willems and colleagues of Vrige Universiteit, Amsterdam, The Netherlands, compared physicians' attitudes from the United States and from The Netherlands toward physician-assisted suicide. They noted that physicians from The Netherlands are much less strict in allowing physician-assisted suicide, particularly to patients who perceive themselves to be a burden to others.[47]

THE DUTCH WAY OF DYING IN THE NEW MILLENNIUM

On November 28, 2000, the Dutch Parliament finally approved a bill legalizing euthanasia, thereby establishing The Netherlands as the first nation to openly let doctors end their suffering patients' lives upon request.

According to an Associated Press release, the law stipulates that foreigners would not be able to meet the strict standards required by the law for allowing euthanasia, a stipulation that fends off concerns that the Netherlands could become a haven for patients flocking from foreign lands to have their lives ended by Dutch doctors.[48]

The bill passed the Dutch Lower House by a majority vote of 104–40, and won approval by the Upper House by a landslide on April 10, 2001. It became law.

With the law, The Netherlands formalized the tolerance it has held toward euthanasia. Some criteria in this law have been quite relaxed from previous requirements for euthanasia. The bill sets the following guidelines for carrying out euthanasia or assisted suicide:

- Physicians must be convinced the patient's request is voluntary and well considered.
- They must be convinced the patient is facing unremitting and unbearable suffering. The patient *does not have to be terminally ill.*
- Patients must have a correct and clear understanding of their situation and prognosis.
- The physician must reach the conclusion, together with the patient, that there is no reasonable alternative that is acceptable to the patient. The decision to die must be the patient's own.
- The physician must consult at least one other independent doctor who has examined the patient.
- The physician must carry out the termination of life in a medically appropriate manner.

These criteria differ from earlier guidelines in many respects. There are no strict requirements in either the indication or in the procedure of ending a patient's life. It is left entirely to patients and their physicians. Ending a patient's life becomes another treatment option like any other medical intervention. For example, the patient's suffering need not be due to relentless physical pain. It may represent mental anguish, a sense of loneliness or helplessness, or even a feeling that one has become a burden on others and society. There are no provisions for psychiatric evaluation or consultation and no waiting period.

This liberal stand has been hailed by the Dutch Minister of Health, Els Borst: "Doctors should not be treated as criminals. This will create security for doctors and patients alike." She added, "Something as serious as ending one's life deserves openess."[49]

The Dutch legislation provides an option for patients to leave a written request giving doctors the right to use their own discretion of whether to carry out euthanasia when patients themselves can no longer decide. The law further empowers patients as young as sixteen to seek euthanasia in consultation with their parents. Children aged twelve to fifteen must have parental consent.

The only safeguard provided by the law is the establishment of a committee consisting of three people, a physician, a lawyer, and an expert in medical ethics, to review cases in order to ensure that the criteria are met.

Not surprisingly, groups in favor of euthanasia and physician-assisted suicide welcomed the new Dutch law; the Denver-based Hemlock Society and the London-based Voluntary Euthanasia Society hailed the measure with statements like these:

> "We are very excited. . . . We have admired what the people of Holland have been doing for the past 20 years."

> "They have been carefully and openly helping people to die."

> ". . . this is a courageous step for the incurably ill."[50]

Opponents from within the Dutch Parliament derided the decision:

> "This is a black day in the history of our parliament. . . . We believe as Christians that our lives are not in our hands. . . . We must wait for God's leadership."[51]

The Vatican described the law as "a sad record for Holland. . . . It violates human dignity." Lori Hougens, representing the Washington-based National Right to Life committee, scoffed at the law by saying, "It is cheaper to kill people than to take care of them."[52]

It is noteworthy that although physician-assisted suicide is legal in Oregon and euthanasia is legal in Holland, other countries also condone these measures. Switzerland, Columbia, and Belgium tolerate euthanasia. Australia's Northern Territory approved the practice in 1996, but the federal Parliament revoked the law in 1997. In the U.S. House of Representatives, in a back-door approach, passed a bill in October 2000, "The Pain Relief Promotions Act," which has provisions that would undermine Oregon's legalized physician-assisted suicide, but has little chance of being enacted into law. This bill has the potential of limiting access to optimum pain relief for terminally ill American citizens by rendering physicians culpable if the patient's death is perceived to be hastened by pain-killers. If passed, this bill would be detrimental to proper care for the dying. Fortunately, the bill is opposed by the majority of senators.

MORE ABOUT THE DEATH DOCTOR

A correspondence to the editor of the prestigious *New England Journal of Medicine* appeared in the December 7, 2000, issue with revelations about Dr. Jack Kevorkian's cases.

Drs. Lori Roscoe and Donna Cohen from the University of South Florida, in collaboration with Dr. Dragovic, the Pontiac, Michigan, medical examiner, reported the characteristics of sixty-nine persons who died with the assistance of Dr. Kevorkian in Oakland County, Michigan, between 1990 and 1998. The study excluded the more than thirty other cases where death was investigated and studied elsewhere.

The correspondence stated

> Most patients in the United States who receive assistance from a physician in committing suicide or who undergo euthanasia are terminally ill men over the age of 65 years who have cancer, neurologic disease, or end-stage heart or lung disease. The patients who died with Kevorkian's assistance had similar diagnoses; however, only 25 percent were terminally ill, according to the autopsy findings. Seventy-two percent of the patients had had a recent decline in health status that may have precipitated the desire to die. Seventy-one percent were women, a finding that is noteworthy because suicide rates are usually lower among women than among men.
>
> Persons who were divorced or had never married were overrepresented among those who died with Kevorkian's help, suggesting the need for a better understanding of the familial and psychosocial context of decision making at the end of life. Altogether, our findings underscore the vulnerability of women and groups of men (i.e., those not married and those coping with serious illness) to physician-assisted suicide and euthanasia, particularly when clinical safeguards are lacking.[53]

These troubling findings underscore the perils of relinquishing the weighty life and death decisions to someone like Dr. Kevorkian, a zealot whom some consider to be driven by macabre weirdness.

WILL THE DEBATE ABOUT
"SWEET DEATH" EVER DIE?

The only certainty about the debate on euthanasia and physician-assisted suicide is that it will continue. In this debate, I hold the views so eloquently expressed by Dr. Kathleen M. Foley of Memorial Sloan-Kettering Cancer Institute. Dr. Foley, a national leader for a physician-patient partnership for good dying, wrote

> If legalized, physician-assisted suicide will be a substitute for rational, therapeutic, psychological, and social interventions that might otherwise enhance the quality of life for patients who are dying. The medical profession needs to take the lead in developing guidelines for good care of dying patients. Identifying the factors related to physicians, patients, and the healthcare system that pose barriers to appropriate care at the end-of-life should be the first step in a national dialogue to educate healthcare professionals and the public on the topic of death and dying. Death is an issue that society as a whole faces, and it requires a compassionate response. But, we should not confuse compassion with competence in the care of terminally ill patients.[54]

End of life decisions are not going to get easier for individuals and society. They constitute a spectrum, the colors blurring subtly and often confusingly into one another, thus making it difficult to discern where to draw the line. For some, the principle of autonomy entitles a dying patient to treatments deemed futile by medical standards.[55] For others, withholding treatment and withdrawing useless care have different connotations.[56] Some view feeding and hydration to be different from the other forms of therapy.[57] For many, including the courts, withdrawal of treatment is ethical, whereas deliberately hastening the death of a patient is murder, while to many, both carry the same intent and lead to the same foreseeable result. And for an increasing segment of society, the option to end one's life (assisted or not) underscores one's right to a dignified exit when one's terminal chapter is riddled with anguish and pain.[58]

6

THE EXORBITANT COST
OF DYING IN AMERICA

❧

The days of our years are three-score years and ten; and if by reason of
strength they be four-score years, yet is their strength labor and sorrow;
for it is soon cut off and we fly away.

Psalms 90:10

Most of the recent innovations in medicine have been employed
to extend the life of people past middle age. Dr. Daniel
Callahan, Director of the Hastings Center in New York and outspoken
critic of wasteful medical care at the end of life, quotes Dr. Jerome Avorn,
Health Economist of the Harvard Medical School, who writes, "With the
exception of the birth control pill, most of medical technology interventions developed since the 1950s have their most widespread impact on
people who are past their fifties—the further past their fifties the greater
the impact."[1]

Over the past three decades, health-care costs in America have
increased threefold as a percentage of the gross national product. Today,
America devotes one-seventh of its gross national product to health care;
most of these expenditures are spent on the oldest segment of the population. One of the most widely quoted statistics in medical and economic
circles derives from the 1986 publication from the Center for Health Statistics. The data showed that 30 percent of Medicare expenditures are
incurred during the last year of life. Furthermore, for the 6 percent of the
elderly Medicare patients who die each year, 40 percent of medical expenditures go for care during the last month of life, and 50 percent of all medical costs are spent during the last two months.[2] According to one of

America's leading economists, Victor Fuchs, "One of the biggest challenges facing policy makers for the rest of this century will be how to strike an appropriate balance between care for the dying and health services for the rest of the population."[3]

IS HEALTH IN THE UNITED STATES
THE BEST IN THE WORLD?

In the United States, we spend more health dollars per citizen than any other nation on earth, but we are not healthier and we do not live longer than people in most civilized nations. Dr. Barbara Starfield, affiliated with the Department of Health Policy and Management at Johns Hopkins School of Hygiene and Public Health, comments on the deficiencies in the United States health-care system in an article published in the *Journal of the American Medical Association*.[4] Dr. Starfield reminds us of the Institute of Medicine's report "To Err Is Human" where as much as 20 to 30 percent of American patients receive unnecessary surgery or other interventions and that 44,000 to 98,000 among them die each year as a result of medical errors.[5]

Dr. Starfield compares the American health-care system with twelve other countries. The United States ranks twelfth (second from the bottom) on overall performance surpassed by Japan, Sweden, Canada, France, Australia, Spain, Finland, The Netherlands, the United Kingdom, Denmark, and Belgium. Germany ranked thirteenth among this distinguished group of nations.[6]

The Year 2000 World Health Organization's report using disability-adjusted life expectancy shows similar data. The report ranked the United States as fifteenth among twenty-five industrialized countries.[7] The World Health Organization measured each nation's overall health system performance by its achievement of three goals: the provision of good health, responsiveness to the expectations of the population, and the fairness of individuals' financial contribution toward their health care.

Health was measured by life expectancy adjusted for the likelihood of a range of disabilities and produced the following ranking:

1. Japan: 74.5 years
2. Australia: 73.2 years
3. France: 73.1 years

4. Sweden: 73.0 years
5. Spain: 72.8 years

24. United States: 70 years

Responsiveness was judged by a nation's respect for the dignity of individuals, the confidentiality of health records, prompt attention in emergencies, and choice of provider.
1. United States
2. Switzerland
3. Luxembourg
4. Denmark
5. Germany

Financial fairness was measured by the equal distribution of the health cost faced by each household.
1. Colombia
2. Luxembourg
3. Belgium
4. Djibouti
5. Denmark

54. United States

The full report is available on the World Health Organization Web site, http://www.who.int/.

High spending does not necessarily translate into a better health system, according to the World Health Organization. Among the fifteen top-rated nations, the amount spent on health care as a percentage of the overall economy and on a per-person basis varied widely. These differences are detailed in Table 4.

Yes, America has the most technologically advanced and most responsive system in the world. It has the best doctors, the best hospitals, and the best-equipped intensive care units. Also, the relatively poor health-care performance cannot be blamed on the fact that Americans "behave badly," smoking, drinking, and perpetrating violence. This accusation is not supported by data. In fact, Americans tend to smoke less and consume less alcohol than most other Western countries.

	TABLE 4 *Top Ranking, Not Top Dollar*		
Country	Health spending as percentage of GDP	Per capita spending	Population
1. France	9.8%	$2,369	59 million
2. Italy	9.3	1,855	57 million
3. San Marino	7.5	2,257	26,000
4. Andorra	7.5	1,368	75,000
5. Malta	6.3	551	386,000
6. Singapore	3.1	876	3.5 million
7. Spain	8.0	1,071	39 million
8. Oman	3.9	370	2.4 million
9. Austria	9.0	2,277	8.2 million
10. Japan	7.1	2,373	126 million
11. Norway	6.5	2,283	4.4 million
12. Portugal	8.2	845	9.8 million
13. Monaco	8.0	1,264	33,000
14. Greece	8.0	905	10 million
15. Iceland	7.9	2,149	279,000
37. U.S.	13.7	4,187	276 million

Highest spending per capita: United States ($4,187)
Lowest spending per capita: Afghanistan ($2); Rank 173

The reasons for the poor performance of the health-care system are no doubt complex and multifaceted. However, an important component can be attributed to the fact that Americans undergo more surgeries, consume more medications, and are hospitalized more often than citizens of other better-rated nations.[8]

No wonder *The Economist* hailed the British system as the "British Bargain" for producing the same life span as the United States for its citizens at one-third the cost: $1,400 versus $4,200. (See figure 4.)

FIGURE 4
Life Expectancy in Relation to Spending as
Percentage of GDP in 7 Western Countries

Source: OECD Health Data 2000

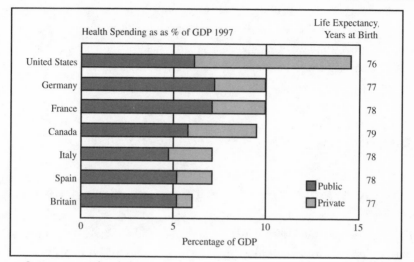

One may applaud the access to such care that we have in America, but the following American medical case illustrates the wastefulness of such access under certain circumstances.

This case involved the treatment of a middle-aged woman who lived a reckless life. This woman was infected with a tuberculosis organism that was resistant to conventional antibiotic therapy (drug-resistant tuberculosis is one of the deadliest threats in America today). In addition to high blood pressure, she was also infected with the AIDS virus and had very little immune system activity. She did not take her medications to treat either the high blood pressure or the tuberculosis, although these medications were dispensed to her free of charge. She was brought to the hospital in a high-blood-pressure crisis that resulted in acute heart failure; she was placed on a ventilator to assist her breathing. It was discovered that the high-blood-pressure crisis (a result of her refusal to take high-blood pressure medications) had caused irreparable damage to her kidneys. The patient's family requested that she be placed on permanent dialysis. The patient declared, in a defiant gesture, that she intended to have unprotected sex with others in the future and that she did not intend to take her med-

---

*Life expectancy is almost the same in all Western countries.

icines under any circumstances. In other words, she intended to distribute HIV and resistant tuberculosis infections and consequently death, to the community. At the same time, she was entitled to receive dialysis! And receive it she did. She died two weeks later.

This and similar cases beg the vexing question (outside the scope of the practice of medicine) of whether one is entitled to all the rights and privileges of citizenship without being asked to make a return to the society. Since Plato's time, it has been recognized that in order to enjoy the rights of citizenship, one must fulfill one's duties toward society and to others.

Consider also the following case of absurd access to medical intervention. No story can approach this one told to me by my friend, Dr. Philip Altus, Professor of Medicine at the University of South Florida.

SAVING A LIFE THAT WILL TAKE OTHER LIVES

The case of Mr. M, age thirty-seven years, has bequeathed us an unrelenting debate about the following ethical issue: Should doctors take into account a person's morals and character when considering eligibility for a heart transplant or a scarce medical treatment?

Mr. M was ostensibly a New York shopkeeper, born in the Dominican Republic. In July 1993, he was charged with six murders, one attempted murder, and six kidnappings. Police claimed his gang was also responsible for many other crimes, including several murders. Three of his followers were convicted to life without parole; others received less severe sentences.

In court, Mr. M pleaded that he was too sick to start the trial because of advanced heart trouble and that he was expected to die within a few months. The judge decided, on medical grounds, to forgo a trial and released him on his own recognizance, reasoning that if the man were terminally ill and was going to be in intensive care there was no reason not to release him so that he could be with his family and have whatever comfort he could.

Subsequently, Mr. M enrolled in the heart-transplant program at Temple University in Philadelphia. His lawyer stopped the police from passing on information about his past to the heart-transplant team. Philadelphia surgeons gave Mr. M a new heart, not knowing that he was the suspected ringleader of a brutal drug gang responsible for at least twelve murders and numerous kidnappings. Mr. M continued to attend the Temple University heart-transplant clinic on a regular basis for two months. He vanished at the end of July 1994, even though he was wearing a surveillance device. Without drug treatment, which cost $20,000 per year, Mr. M was expected to die in a few weeks.

Two months after the operation, police rearrested Mr. M and reinstituted charges. A New York judge released him on $250,000 bail so that he could continue to obtain treatment in Philadelphia. The judge added, "If he flees, he flees; too bad. I think we could determine (then) that it would be virtually suicide."

Physicians debated whether Mr. M's moral character should have ruled out the operation. However, Dr. Arthur Caplan, director of the Center for Bioethics at University of Pennsylvania, said in an interview to the news media, "I don't care if a person has been shot in the process of a holdup or if he is a child molester. Medicine has no business trying to judge the moral worth or the character of people." He added his own deduction: "Very soon you'd stop treating couch potatoes or a person who had a criminal record as a child."[9]

To many, this statement from a respected ethicist is surprising. It supports the position that reckless, unreliable, shady characters are entitled to scarce, expensive societal resources at the same time that they may be wasting these resources at best, or continuing to destroy society at worst. Not surprisingly, soon after this case became publicized, another convicted felon, Dewayne Murphey, sued the government for $20 million in damages; he had developed severe heart disease and did not have long to live. The authorities in Minnesota refused to allow him to be considered for a heart transplant while serving four years imprisonment for drug trafficking.

DARING TO SPEAK THE "R" WORD:
RATIONING HEALTH CARE

Our society has the right and duty to determine how to establish priorities in the allocation of resources that are and will always be scarce. According to the national transplant registry, in 1995, 6,200 people in America were on waiting lists for new hearts: 34 percent got them, whereas 12 percent died before a suitable heart could be found. It must never be forgotten that the care of heart-transplant recipients does not end with the

TABLE 5		
People over Age 65 Years in America		
Year	% population	% use of health-care cost
1980	11	29
1986	12	31
2000	15	40
2040	21	50

Source: Adapted from E. L. Schneider and J. M. Gurainik, "The Aging of America: Impact on Health Care Costs," *Journal of the American Medical Association* 263 (1990): 2335–40.

surgical procedure; the recipient must be responsible for his or her own self-care. It requires a great deal of self-discipline and the motivation to engage in regular, rigorous follow-up for several years at a substantial cost.

We are an aging society. An article in *The Economist* asserts that the cost of health benefits and other social services are six times as much for a person over sixty-five years than for one less than eighteen years old. Based on data from the Office of National Statistics, people over sixty-five years constituted 11 percent of the population in 1980, they constituted 15 percent of the population in the year 2000, and they will constitute 21 percent of the population in the year 2040. In 1985, people over age 65 years consumed 30 percent of health-care costs. In the year 2000, they were expected to consume 40 percent, and in the year 2040, they will consume 50 percent of all health-care expenditures (see Table 5).[10]

The problem of medical and monetary excesses is real and demands immediate attention; the proposed solutions, however, are problematic, because they circle around rationing, which is unacceptable to the majority of Americans. Dr. Muriel Gillick, director of the Hebrew Rehabilitation Center for the Aged, in an article entitled "The High Costs of Dying—A Way Out," quotes a review of seventy-five national opinion polls, which reveal that Americans "want more medical care in the future, including insurance for catastrophic events, high-technology medicine, and long-term care."[11] If medical care rationing is not acceptable to us as a society, can we come up with a system of rational medical care that satisfies expectations without sacrificing quality? This will no doubt be the challenge of the decade and beyond.

Richard Lamm, Colorado's former governor, went to the extreme to state publicly that the very elderly, chronically ill members of society have a moral duty to be more sensitive to the needs of younger generations and to be prepared to accept an inevitable death with serenity. He added,

> It is sad that we now have a system that allows the elderly to consume far more medical resources than we give to children. It is not only fair but desirable to have a different level of care for a 10-year-old than for someone who is 100. Should not public policy recognize that some people have far more statistical years ahead of them than others? I feel it is morally repugnant to use $100,000 or more of our kids' limited resources, as I'm on my way out the door.[12]

According to *The Economist*, the aging of the population will represent an ever-increasing burden on young individuals. Whereas in 1970, one hundred able-bodied workers supported seven elderly individuals in the United States, in 2050, one hundred workers are expected to support thirty-eight elderly individuals. If we, as a society, do not face up to this enormously complicated challenge, we will be faced with a formula for generation warfare (see Table 6).

Will the younger generation faced with obligations to raise their children and also take care of their aging parents be able to strike the necessary balance to carry out the two obligations faithfully? Or will they find that the ever-increasing demands of health care for their frail, aging parents too big a burden to carry? Will they view the ever-increasing cost of maintaining a terminally ill or permanently unconscious parent or grandparent a just expenditure or will they view that the aging members of society as usurpers of limited resources that may be better allocated to younger members of society?

The economic burden of caring for elderly people who still have higher brain function is great, but no one is protesting this economic investment. On the other hand, the use of futile care, however, for a ninety-year-old or a nine-year-old is both economically and ethically untenable. Unfortunately, the widespread use of useless interventions has convinced some people, such as those in the medical cases that follow, that it is an entitlement, a right.

Mrs. Doe, a gregarious ninety-two-year-old woman, was my patient

TABLE 6	
Number of Elderly for Every 100 Employed Persons in the United States	
Decade	Number of Elderly per 100 Employed Workers
1970	7
1990	19
2050	38
Source: Adapted from The Economist, 1993.	

for over ten years. She had been a music teacher. She had a loud laugh and an eloquent vocabulary. During one of her visits to my office, Mrs. Doe instructed me to make her death as peaceful as humanely possible when her time came. Several months later, she suffered a massive stroke, afflicting a key location in her brain stem, and quickly lapsed into a deep coma. In order to fulfill Mrs. Doe's prior expressed desire, I had a conference with the family. I knew these people very well and considered them friends. I explained the gravity of the situation, stating that death was imminent and inevitable. I advised that we should not place her on a ventilator machine and it would not be necessary to treat a newly developed pneumonia. I believed that I had faithfully represented Mrs. Doe's wishes and clear instructions. I remember that day very clearly. It was a Tuesday. The family stunned me by asking that I place Mrs. Doe on assisted ventilation until the following Monday. Her daughter added, "We want her to stay alive until next week by any means and at any cost."

"Why are you asking me to do what your mother wanted to avoid?" I asked.

The daughter calmly answered, "Our children are scheduled to play in an important school football game next Saturday, which is being held out of town. My mother's death at this point would be disruptive. My children have been looking forward to the football game for weeks."

I objected to their request and politely asked that I dismiss myself from her care if they insisted, and the daughter did insist. Mrs. Doe was placed on a ventilator with full resuscitation orders and a multitude of tubes, just to keep her alive for a few days. I do not regret the fact that I could not do what the daughter asked. I have a clear conscience. Poor Mrs. Doe, and all the rest of us who had to pay close to $100,000 to delay the moment of death for a few days. A very expensive football game!

Consider next Mr. Williams, a sixty-eight-year-old man with advanced, end-stage heart failure. Mr. Williams had spent more than two of the previous three months in the hospital. For the last week, he had not been able to sleep, even in the sitting position, because of a sense of smothering. He required a large dose of oxygen on a continuous basis. He had ceased to respond to a multitude of medicines given in large doses intravenously in an effort to strengthen his heart muscle. In the past, his heart would respond to these medicines by showing an improvement in pumping blood, but not anymore. His body had withered away, and he had become very weak. His breathing was labored; he could only speak a few words at a time; his hands and feet were cold; his pulse was fast and weak; and his blood pressure had become quite low. All of these are signs of poor pumping function of the heart. An ultrasound image confirmed that the heart had become extremely weak, pumping very little blood. Furthermore, the heart valves, which keep blood in the proper heart chambers, were now allowing blood to leak backward. All of this indicated that death was imminent. Mr. Williams was too old to be considered for heart transplantation. I talked with Mr. and Mrs. Williams at great length, explaining the precarious nature of Mr. Williams's heart condition and how it was beyond the stage with which we could expect any improvement. I recommended to Mr. and Mrs. Williams that no resuscitation efforts be undertaken when the heart stopped. Also, I advised to make Mr. Williams's last days as comfortable as possible, even if that resulted in the shortening of his life, emphasizing that peace and comfort should be paramount at this stage. They agreed.

Two days later, Mrs. Williams stopped me in the hallway. "I changed my mind," she said. "I want you to do everything possible for my husband. If the heart stops, try to revive it. If you have to place him on a ventilator, please do." I asked Mrs. Williams that we visit in a private conference room. I thought that her change of heart represented a profound love for her husband and reflected the difficulty and pain associated with a "let go" decision. But I was mistaken. She declared, "Upon checking with my husband's boss, I found out that Mr. Williams's insurance will pay all expenses associated with his hospitalization. He has already met his deductible, and there will be no additional cost to him." I answered that my recommendations regarding Mr. Williams were based solely upon his medical condition.

No consideration was given to whether he or someone else would pay for unnecessary care. I further explained that placing Mr. Williams on a ventilator in his present condition would be contrary to good medical judgment and I could not be expected to carry out any treatment if I did not believe that the treatment would benefit the patient. She finally agreed to allow me to exercise my best medical judgment, but reluctantly.

THE FINANCIAL AND MORAL BANKRUPTCY OF UNNECESSARY CARE

I am told by an economist friend that any service that is offered for free will be abused by consumers, the perception being that it does not cost anyone anything. The truth is, everyone pays for it. But perceived "freebies" are not the only factor that drives the use of futile care. There is no doubt that physician peer pressure and the fear of legal repercussions also drive its use. There is also the "heroic" motivation to try a procedure, even if there is only one chance in one thousand that it will work. In some cases, financial incentives are powerful motivating factors for physicians to utilize expensive high-tech procedures. The more procedures a physician performs, futile or not, the higher his or her income. Unfortunately, self-interest can masquerade as altruism, as if doing more procedures, useful or not, is a manifestation of caring. Finally, the mere existence of these tools may motivate their use.

It has been argued that if patients who are potential candidates for unnecessary interventions are provided with financial alternatives much of the useless care at the end of life might be forfeited by them and their families. For the sake of the argument, let us assume that futile care at the end of life costs the system 10 percent of its total health-care expenditures, which is a reasonable assumption. Also suppose that at age twenty, individuals are asked to choose between two alternate health-insurance policies: one costs $2,000 per year and covers all health-care needs except for unnecessary care at the end of life, and the other policy costs $2,200 annually, with the added benefit that the policy will cover useless terminal treatment in addition to other necessary health care. I wonder how many people would buy the second policy. How many people would pay an extra $200 per year, with a yearly escalation of 5 percent, just to render their dying more prolonged and/or more punishing? Suppose we offer individuals approaching the end of life the options of choosing to be treated to death with no hope or award $100,000 for a grandchild's education or a charity of their preference?

When we relinquish our "right" to useless care, we do, in effect, invest in our grandchildren. Can we relinquish that additional expense as a gift to generations to come? Can we, as we approach the end of life, willingly forgo unnecessary, burdensome treatment to take care of the health of the unborn or the education of the young? Or are we becoming, without our consent, the grabbers and usurpers of limited social goods as we exit from this world?

This is a pertinent question for our generation to ponder with open minds and caring hearts. Very few rational and reasonable people would want to be subjected to treatments that are clearly useless. This should be a relatively clear-cut issue. Other health-care issues are less so, such as when a dismal treatment outcome is less certain, although the odds are stacked against a favorable outcome. The following two cases exemplify more problematic situations.

In 1986, a seventy-six-year-old woman successfully received a liver transplant at the Presbyterian University Hospital in Pittsburgh and made headline news. The cost of the surgery exceeded $200,000 dollars, when the prospects for a decent quality of life and length of remaining life were quite limited. The woman died a few days later. In 1993, Siamese twins, both doomed eventually to perish, were operated upon in Pennsylvania to salvage one while the other died immediately. The one claimed to have been saved, Angela Lakesburg, had complex anomalies of the heart that could not be corrected completely. Previously, the twins had been evaluated by a specialized center in Chicago, and the possibility of surgery was rejected because of the complexity of the operation. It was felt that, given the best possible scenario, the surviving twin would have a life expectancy that did not exceed a few miserable years. In Pennsylvania, a multihour surgery was undertaken by multiple teams of surgeons. A million dollars was raised to enable the high-tech support of the surviving twin. She died on a ventilator after ten months of surgeries and a torturous postoperative course at a cost of over $1 million.

DARING TO SPEAK THE "P" WORD:
PRIORITIES IN HEALTH CARE

Dr. Norman Daniels, the noted health economist and professor at Tufts University, suggests a life-span approach to health-care allocation.[13] Drs. Tristan Engelhardt and Michael Rie, anesthesiologists at Massachusetts General Hospital, went further to suggest a formula for use by society to establish priorities of care based upon the outcome of a specified intervention and the cost involved.[14] The formula takes into account probability of cure (P), quality of life (Q) with treatment and expected length of lifespan (L; assuming the treatment proves successful). These are weighed against the cost of treatment (C). His formula is expressed thus:

$$\frac{PQL}{C}$$

The higher the number, the more worthwhile the treatment. For example, an intervention that costs $100,000 promises to increase life span by fifty years in 80 percent of cases, with a good quality of life in 90 percent of treated patients. Then

$$\frac{PQL}{C} = \frac{80 \times 90 \times 50}{100,000} = \frac{360,000}{100,000} = 3.6$$

Contrast this to another intervention that costs $100,000, promises to increase lifespan by five years in 20 percent of cases and leads to a good quality of life in 10 percent of cases. In this case

$$\frac{PQL}{C} = \frac{20 \times 10 \times 5}{100,000} = \frac{1,000}{100,000} = 0.01$$

According to this example, the first intervention would be much preferred to the second by a 360:1 margin. A similar formula guided the newly designed Oregon health-care model in establishing treatment priorities applicable to all citizens receiving state-supported medical treatment.

In the Oregon model, 709 paired medical conditions and treatments were evaluated. Priorities for care were given to the unborn, child care, and curable conditions. Out of 709 conditions, 586 were found to be eligible for state support, and the rest were rejected because of poor outcomes in relation to cost. These cases included newborn infants with no upper brain (anencephaly), advanced cancer not responding to therapy, deep coma, and advanced vegetative states.[15]

Table 7 shows a classification of medical interventions based upon cost and outcome. At the top are conditions and treatments that have the highest return for invested dollars. At the bottom are conditions with increasing costs and diminishing returns.

Some would view the Oregon plan as a form of unacceptable rationing by which the worth of human life is measured in terms of dollars. Others would argue that with limited health-care resources, society has to establish reasonable priorities for care. Otherwise, we may end up spending a good portion of the nation's resources on expensive care that gives little benefit to society at large. Through implementation of scientifically sound outcome criteria in the setting of priorities, society at large (but not necessarily a particular individual) will gain. After all, a good health-care system must carefully balance equity, cost, and quality and must give priority to disease prevention and children's welfare.

Even a prioritization of medical interventions and conditions will not render all cases clear cut. Medical care is always based upon reasonable, not absolute, certainties. The essence of the art of medicine is in weighing probabilities.

The difficult question is where to set the limits: for example, how many hundreds of people should be kept in a mindless vegetative existence at a cost of $100,000 per year per patient in the hope that one might show a late recovery, which is rarely significant? Clearly, this is not a decision for physicians to make, since it is beyond physicians' authority to allocate expensive resources. These decisions are for the patient's family to make, unless certain clear guidelines are formulated by society. To quote Paul Menzel, the noted health-care economist, "Whether to pay the real cost of saving a life in old age will always be an open question . . . but facing up to the real costs of what we are doing is not!! We must face up."[16] One of the most challenging exercises in medicine is to be able to determine early in the course of acute disease which patients are likely to survive in an intensive care unit, thereby enabling the physicians to identify early on

TABLE 7
Health-Care Costs and Outcomes

Low cost, high gain
    Preventive care
    Immunization

Moderate cost, excellent outcome
    Common surgeries
    Treatment of common disease in the young
    Treatment of common infections including pneumonias
    Treatment of high blood pressure, asthma, diabetes, and reversible medical
       illnesses

Moderate cost, good outcome
    Managment of
        Acute heart attacks
        Early heart failure
        Early emphysema
        Early cancer
        Early liver disease

High cost, limited outcome
    Heart failure
    Disseminated cancer
    Advanced kidney disease

Very high cost, very poor outcome
    Premature cocaine babies
    Extensive brain injury
    Massive strokes

Extremely high cost, futile care
    Multiple end-stage organ failure (heart, lung, liver, kidney)
    Premature infant (one pound or less)
    Advanced, uncontrollable systemic infection
    Over 90% total body burn

which patients will not benefit. An Acute Physiology-Chronic Health Evaluation method has been developed (APACHE scale) and modified further to APACHE II and III. [17]

During a recent visit to England, I observed how physicians are forced into establishing priorities for intensive care. With declining resources, recent hospital closures, and a limited number of intensive-care beds, doctors have to make hard choices. Dr. David Bihari of Guys Hospital has developed a refined computer program, the Riyadh Intensive-Care Program (RICP), to aid in establishing priorities. According to a recent evaluation of the program by Drs. Atkinson, Bihari, and associates from Guys Hospital in London, the program is likely to produce 5 percent mistakes in judgment.[18] By one standard, the program is deemed extremely valuable in guiding intensive care admissions. On the other hand, one can easily imagine the controversy that would be created by such a computerized program were it considered for use to guide care in the U.S. intensive care units.

TACKLING THE LAST TABOO: CALCULATING THE VALUE OF A LIFE

Before I became interested in the ethical and economic issues related to life and death, I did not know that societies make decisions to hire policemen based upon a cost-benefit ratio. Even local communities hire lifeguards to monitor beaches in order to prevent people from drowning based upon the potential number of lives saved: The greater the hazards of drowning, the better the justification to hire lifeguards. When car companies place air bags in their vehicles, they take into account the cost of the bags in relation to the potential for lives saved. In a recent issue of *The Economist*, I encountered an interesting table relating how much a country is willing to pay to save a life after a car accident, expressed as the cost of a road accident (see Table 8). I am sharing this information to emphasize the point that human societies have already calculated the value of life of a fellow human being under certain circumstances. In the same vein, societies have to determine how much should be spent to pursue an expensive treatment that promises less in life-saving potential, along with the maintenance of a reasonable quality of life. In general, a medical intervention that costs less than $40,000 per year of life served is considered cost-effective.

No subject in medicine evokes such controversy and is riddled with such passions and biases as does what constitutes an acceptable quality of life. A life worth living is a uniquely personal thing. Furthermore, equality of human worth is the basis of freedom and democracy. In the United

TABLE 8

The Value of Life: Cost of a Road-Accident Death by Country

Country	Cost (× $1000)
United States[a]	2,500
Sweden[a]	1,236
New Zealand[a]	1,150
Britain[a]	1,100
Germany[b]	928
Belgium[b]	400
France[b]	350
Holland[b]	130
Portugal[b]	20

[a]Willingness-to-pay basis.
[b]Human-capital-business.
Source: Adapted from "The Price of Life: Why an American's Life Is Worth Twice as Much as a Swede's," The Economist 329, issue 7840 (December 4, 1993): 74.

States, we have a Constitution that not only values the right to life and liberty for all individuals, but also recognizes these individuals as the fabric units of this country ("We, the people").

As much as our diversity and individualism confer a richness of heritage and greatness to our country, they also produce a heterogeneity that, at times, borders on chaos. If you consider the variety of our heritages, religions, ethnic backgrounds, and other factors, it is no wonder that it has become quite difficult to formulate standards by which an acceptable quality of life, a life worth living, can be defined. Psychosocial and spiritual attitudes vary enormously between citizen groups. These attitudes are grounded in people's faith, ethnic background, and level of education. However, when it comes to end-of-life medical care, there is much similarity among mainstream citizens.

In my numerous lectures on this subject to the public, I have rarely met someone who would like to stay "alive" at any cost when he or she has permanently lost the ability to recognize self and surroundings or interact meaningfully with others. In fact, I have seen hundreds of cases like that of Dr. Z, a Ph.D. who taught archeology at a southern university. He was an international lecturer and published extensively on the subject of comparative behavior in primitive societies. Fifteen years ago, at age seventy-two, he retired and moved his family to Oklahoma to be close to their only daughter, an articulate, bright, young woman who was an associate editor of the local, premier newspaper.

I saw Dr. Z in consultation over ten years ago. He was complaining of increasing angina pectoris, chest pains due to lack of oxygen to the heart. Because chest pains came with mild exertion, he was unable to take his daily swim. At that time, my examination showed him to be a pleasant man who could follow most of our conversation, but showed early signs of forgetfulness. His wife and daughter had to repeat names and events in order to keep him aware of persons and things. I performed a procedure on Dr. Z's coronary arteries in order to prevent the chest pains, and he resumed his daily swimming. A few months later, Dr. Z tripped and broke his left hip. He was hospitalized. By this time, he had become clearly forgetful and intermittently confused. He kept repeating the same questions over and over and talked continuously about old events in his life.

He was discharged from the hospital several weeks later and was advised to continue physical therapy at home. For over a year, the family had to struggle to take care of Dr. Z. One day, he left the house and was found after several hours of aimless wandering. His wife started to show signs of weariness. His daughter's marriage became strained because of her ever-diminishing attention to her husband and their child.

One day, during a scheduled office visit, it became apparent to me that Dr. Z's dementia, caused by Alzheimer's disease, had progressed significantly. He had become incoherent, totally confused, and incontinent. He did not remember my name, where he was, or the purpose of his visit. He used abusive language when he talked to his wife and daughter. I talked to them frankly: "Dr. Z has a rapidly progressive, degenerative brain disease. He has deteriorated considerably." They nodded. "His management at home is going to be very difficult," I said. Mrs. Z's strained smile disappeared. Her face became contracted and tears overcame her. "You can't imagine the nightmare I am living in at present. But what can I do?"

"We have to consider placing Dr. Z in a nursing home," I said. The wife and daughter broke down.

The mother almost choked in a flow of tears. "But I promised him that I would not place him in a nursing home," she said in a cracked voice, while still crying. "He is a very special man. I love him so much."

"I understand your pain and the predicament that you find yourselves in," I said. "I face this dilemma all the time. Had Dr. Z been in his usual sound mind, would he have wanted to put you through this burden?"

"No," Mrs. Z said, and in a lower voice, she mumbled, "but he asked me not to place him in a nursing home."

I told them that they had to face the painful truth. "What is living with you now is not Dr. Z. It is a mindless, belligerent being. Dr. Z, as you knew him, is dead. This may sound insensitive, cold, and callous, but it is the truth. He is not suffering as much as you are, because he is unaware of what is happening to you or to him."

Dr. Z's stay in the nursing home was not easy on the family. His wife and daughter visited him every evening and ate dinner with him. The pain was not over, but it was bearable. Every now and then, Mrs. Z would express her feeling of guilt and tears would run down her cheeks. She missed the real Dr. Z, the intelligent, witty, articulate, charming man. She felt pity for what he had been transformed into and wished that he had died when he had had the heart trouble a few years earlier.

THE DIMINISHING RETURNS OF MEDICAL INTERVENTION

Unfortunately, the story is not over yet. In the fall, the nursing home medical staff was planning to give vaccine shots to all residents. They planned to vaccinate Dr. Z with a shot to prevent pneumonia, in order to lessen his chances of dying from lung infection. Pneumonia is one of the most merciful ways to go. As the old physician's saying goes, "Pneumonia is the old man's friend." What if he developed a heart attack? Or suppose his heart stopped? Should his attendants start CPR, transfer him to an intensive care unit, and place him on a ventilator machine to breathe for him? Or should these heroic efforts be forfeited with the rationalization that Dr. Z as we knew him is no longer there?

How many more people will be allowed to have a much diminished, stretched-out existence, for how long and at what cost? Should Dr. and Mrs. Z have to go bankrupt to sustain the existence of someone who was once loved, revered, and capable of giving so much love and inspiration?

Frankly, I told the family that I would not want my existence to be extended in such a situation. My life would have already outlasted its usefulness and meaning. If I reach this point, I would not want to be given flu or pneumonia vaccines, would not wish my infections treated if I developed any, would object to resuscitation if my heart stopped, and would want to have as comfortable an exit as possible—the sooner the better! However, I cannot and must not make similar decisions in my care of Dr. Z. As a physician, I should never apply my notions about life's quality in my care of another human being. It is the patient, through advance care planning or his appointed surrogate, who should guide treatment under these conditions.

The problem is that, when faced with an enormously complex problem that relates to a loved one, we cannot, and for that matter, are not expected to think rationally. Our emotions and passions overtake us. Unfortunately, we confuse true love with demonstrated love. True love considers first and foremost the right of the loved ones to be respected.

What is the cost of sustaining Dr. Z's existence? It is reasonable to assume that Dr. Z could live several more years with proper nutrition, hygiene, nursing supervision, preventative vaccination against infection, and other medical care as the need arises. The cost of nursing home care is roughly $50,000 per year, which adds up to $500,000 over ten years. For all other medical interventions, including treatment at the end of life, add the reasonable estimate of $200,000 for the remainder of his life span. The total cost amounts to $700,000. And what do we show for it? A miserable existence for Dr. Z, a painful experience riddled with guilt and unjustified feeling of shame for his family, and $700,000 less in resources for society are the bitter fruits of protracted deterioration.

One can apply the same calculations and determine the enormous costs involved in the partial salvage of a patient in a persistent vegetative state (several million dollars) or the cardiopulmonary resuscitation of a frail elderly patient at the sunset of life (several hundred thousand dollars for each life saved).

L. Churchill, the author of *Rationing Health Care in America*, notes

> Neither should we extend our lives at the margins if by so doing we deprive nameless and faceless others a decent provision of care. And such a gesture should not appear to us as a sacrifice, but as the ordinary virtue entailed by a just, social conscience.[19]

Churchill concludes, "If the next generation is to flower and flourish, we must practice the wisdom of giving ground when our time comes."

A VIABLE SOLUTION: ADVANCE CARE PLANNING

I cannot conclude this discussion without underscoring the fact that, in patients who have not lost their ability to think for themselves, quality-of-life issues are theirs to decide. Some patients have the strength and will to rise above life's travails, to embody what the poet Ben Jonson describes:

> To struggle when hope is banished
> To live when life's salt is gone
> To dwell in a dream that's vanished
> To endure, and go calmly on.

These individuals are real heroes and they display the triumphs of the human spirit, serving as inspiration for us all. For others, the cross is too heavy to bear. These patients include those with intractable pains, "locked-in states" (when the patient is conscious but is totally paralyzed), and those with advanced AIDS. They need counseling, encouragement, and relief of pain. In spite of all sincere efforts, many yearn for a death like that in Samuel T. Coleridge's poem *The Rime of the Ancient Mariner*:

> How well he fell asleep
> Like some proud river, widening towards the sea,
> Calmly and grandly, silently and deep,
> Life joined eternity.

When a rational individual, faced with the fear of hopelessness, pain, financial insecurity, enormous psychological stress, and social isolation, makes a decision that life need not be prolonged, this person's wishes have to be granted. A fully informed, competent patient has an unquestionable right to refuse treatment as long as he or she fully understands the consequences of such a decision. No wonder that many rational and well-informed individuals find that a debilitating end-of-life infirmity is a fate worse than death.

Advance care planning and proper communication with our physicians and family members can help ensure for each of us a death with dignity. Advance care planning also can benefit society by precluding the option of futile care and the enormous costs it entails.

7

SHOULD AGE, PER SE, BE REASON TO LIMIT MEDICAL INTERVENTIONS?

Last scene of all that ends this strange eventful history:
Is seemed childishness and mere oblivious, sans teeth, sans eyes, sans taste, sans everything"

Shakespeare, *As You Like It*, 2:7:139

In the year 1000 C.E., the estimated average life expectancy of a human being was thirty years. At the start of this century, life expectancy increased to fifty years, and it has now exceeded seventy-five years. This substantial increase in longevity is evident worldwide, but is more manifest in economically advanced countries of Western Europe, the United States, and Japan. The biblical ideal life of "three score and ten," rarely achieved in the remote past, has fallen below the average life expectancy in recent years. Furthermore, it is estimated that the human life-span would become 100–120 years if disease, accidents, and self-destructive behavior were eradicated, although this is clearly an elusive goal.

Not only are people living longer, but also most are leading healthier lives. Many are able to pursue new challenges of learning, exploring, traveling, or just having a good time. You see oldsters who are healthy at golf courses, tennis courts, health clubs, spas, and dance halls. Retirement is no longer viewed as a time of decline and isolation; on the contrary, many view retirement as an opportunity to reap the benefits of many years of hard work and struggle. Unfortunately, senility and decrepitude can be postponed, but not indefinitely. With the sequellae of natural aging come failure to remember or reason, loss of physical stamina, loss of appetite, and eventually physical decay leading to death.

147

Life-spans vary enormously among human beings. Human differences in physical stamina, intelligence, and other attributes account for the differences in the length of useful life. Dr. Karen Ritchie, a leading dementia expert who runs the Eugeria project in southern France, recently undertook a fascinating study that she published in the *British Journal of Psychiatry*.[1] In November 1993, she examined the mental status of the world's oldest woman, J.C., then aged 118 years. J.C. was born in Arles, France, in 1875. The *Lancet* medical journal noted in an editorial that, at the time of J.C.'s birth, a republican constitution was being reestablished in France and the Paris Opera House had just been completed. The first bacteria were discovered a year before her birth, and the telephone and phonograph were invented a year after her birth. She was thirteen years old when Vincent Van Gogh moved to Arles. She outlived her husband, her daughter, and her granddaughter. She was independent until age 115 and lived alone until age 110. Apart from some compromise in hearing and eyesight, she was always healthy. She celebrated her 120th birthday in February 1995. Although the recent increase in life span is usually attributed to improved nutrition and sanitation, these factors could not totally explain J.C.'s long life. Dr. Ritchie's assessment indicates that J.C. had attended school until the age of sixteen and was of middle socioeconomic class. She had always consumed a Mediterranean diet rich in vegetables, fruit, fiber, and olive oil, shown in other studies to be associated with a lower incidence of certain diseases. Clinical examination by Dr. Ritchie showed J.C. had a satisfactory degree of attention, expression, memory, language, and reasoning, and a normal to superior IQ. She was alert and curious, and she seemed to have an extensive knowledge of early events in her life and of her relatives. Brain scans, however, showed generalized decay of J.C.'s brain that was not commensurate with her high level of intellectual functioning. Dr. Ritchie interpreted the findings to support the notion that people of average or above-average intelligence who remain socially active retain considerable intellect in spite of senile atrophy of the brain. It should be noted that J.C.'s life, with its absence of major degenerative diseases such as cancer, vascular disease, and dementia, does not represent normal aging. But her end stage can really be considered to be successful aging with its "terminal frailty."

But older people whose ages fall way short of 120 years derive considerable benefit from elaborate and costly medical treatment. For example, with modern treatment of heart attacks, 80 lives per 1,000 patients over seventy years old can be saved. The success rate with valve replacement in the elderly (who are susceptible to developing narrowing of certain valves that control blood flow in the heart) is 90 percent. In a carefully selected group of patients older than 70 years, deaths from surgery can be as low as 1 percent. Also, 95 percent of these patients benefit from coronary artery bypass surgery administered appropriately for treatment of hardening of the arteries. Relief of artery narrowing using balloon angioplasty carries a risk of well below 1 percent. These interventions can provide otherwise healthy, older patients with many additional years of enjoyable life.

In light of this success in the United States, the Royal College of Physicians in London published a report in 1991 entitled "Cardiological Interventions in Older Patients." In this report, the college recommends expanding medical services similar to services available to older Americans to older British patients with heart problems.

Professor Ulrich Gleichmann of Ruhr University, Bohum, Germany, and his associates reported Germany's experience with the treatment of heart disease in the elderly. He showed that, in Germany, more than one-fifth of all bypass operations and nearly one-fourth of valve surgeries are performed on patients over seventy years old. He further emphasized the excellent results encountered when patients are selected carefully.[2]

However, the total picture is not all roses; there is a dim and problematic side to it manifested in the larger number of patients who undergo useless or marginally useful interventions that contribute nothing to the quality of life. The elderly population is by no means a homogeneous group. Not all people show signs of aging at the same pace. There are those individuals who suffer biological aging while in their forties and fifties as a result of debilitating chronic illnesses such as severe hypertension, diabetes, or kidney disease. Others endowed by nature with a healthy genetic makeup and who follow a healthful lifestyle advance gracefully into their eighties. For most, the process of aging in older years depends on whether one is fortunate enough to escape the ravages of cancer or hardening of the arteries that strike in the fifties and sixties. Heart surgery has taught us that otherwise healthy older patients have outcomes similar to those of young patients. On the other hand, frail patients and those with diseases involving multiple organs face disastrous outcomes from major surgical interventions. The same applies to cardiopulmonary resuscitation for hospitalized patients who suffer cardiac arrest. Among the healthy and old, 10 to 15 percent survive resuscitation and are discharged alive from the hospital. The percentage drops to half with each organ failure. Only 1 to 2 percent of the resuscitated frail elderly leave the hospital alive without significant brain damage. The problem is where to draw the line. Is there a magical threshold or a reliable test that can help achieve the desired effects?

THE MEDICALIZATION OF DEATH

Just a few decades ago, death at all ages was not uncommon. Thanks to improved nutrition and sanitation, together with the advent of vaccination and antibiotics, the death of young children today has become an anomaly. Fifty years ago, a family with an average number of children had a 50–50 chance of experiencing the death of a child. Today, in Western societies, the loss of a child has ceased to be a normal, anticipated part of family life. We have grown accustomed to position dying at the close of a long, long life. When death occurs before life is experienced to its fullest, it is looked on as untimely. So, while to our ancestors deaths were part of the experience of living, to us death has become a remote contingency.

In a recent article published in the *Journal of the American Medical Association* Dr. Jack McCue makes this exact point: "The naturalness of dying at any age has become a foreign concept."[3] Furthermore, he addresses a more problematic issue: Dying, which was once viewed as natural and expected, is now perceived as an unwelcome part of medical care. Dr. McCue argues that the event of death has been distorted from a natural event of great societal and cultural significance into the end point of untreatable or inadequately treated disease or injury.

P. Aries, in *The Hour of Our Death,* concludes that our current attitudes and beliefs, which he names "the medicalization of death," derive from social and scientific changes that cannot be considered wholly beneficial.[4] The percentage of patients dying in hospitals has increased steadily over the past few decades. Some patients are taken to the hospital while in the process of dying, simply out of fear of facing death at home. Machines have the power to control the time and method of death in many cases; the supremacy of nature, with its unpredictable timetable is thus tamed and controlled. A concerted effort to change this attitude about death is underway in America.

Some Americans have risked popularity by courageously addressing this controversial issue. Richard Lamm, the former governor of Colorado and present director of the Center of Public Policy and Contemporary Issues at the University of Denver, argues in one of his publications, *America in Decline*,

> No nation spends as disproportionately on the elderly. America spends eight times more on health care for those over 65 as on those under 65. No other industrial nation spends more than four times more.
>
> No nation spends as much on death and dying. We spend 11 percent of our Medicare dollars on the last 40 days of our lives—often merely to delay the inevitable.
>
> No society has as unrealistic expectations, i.e., that we can cure anything, even death, and that money should not be a consideration.[5]

Lamm's comments are timely and appropriate: "We are using our limited capital to give hip replacements to people with Alzheimer's disease, to remove cataracts from people dying in hospices."

Daniel Callahan, Ph.D., director of the Hastings Center and author of several books on care for the elderly, notes

> The indefinite extension of life combined with an insatiable ambition to improve the health of the elderly is a recipe for monomania and bottomless spending. It fails to put health in its proper place as only one among many human goods. It fails to accept aging and death as part of the human condition.[6]

In one of his several publications on the subject, Dr. Callahan reports on his experience with a group of Swiss physicians. Dr. Callahan observed that no heart surgery is undertaken in Switzerland on patients over the age of seventy years.[7] This might have been true several years ago, but not anymore. Heart surgery is now available in Switzerland to the "healthy old," and heart transplantation is considered appropriate for some selected patients over sixty years old. It appears as if Europe is now following our lead rather than the other way around.

Dr. Callahan suggests three principles to remedy what he considers to be the problem of misallocation of health-care resources:

1. Government has a duty, based on our collaborative social obligations, to help people live out a natural life-span, but not to help
   medically extend life beyond that point.
2. Government is obligated to develop under its research subsidies,
   and to pay for, under its entitlement programs, only the kind and
   degree of life-extending technology necessary for medicine to
   achieve and serve the aim of a natural life-span.
3. Beyond the point of a natural life-span, government should provide
   only the means necessary for the relief of suffering, not those of
   life-extending technologies.[8]

In another proposition, Dr. Callahan asked whether our society should
leave crucial life-and-death decisions in the hands of individuals or let
them be decided, at least in great part, by commonly shared cultural
notions of what is and is not fitting. These cultural ideas should then be
implemented in ordinary medical practice.

AGE: NOT AN ABSOLUTE CRITERION
FOR HEALTH-CARE ALLOCATION

No doubt, Dr. Callahan's probing questions are cogent, probing, and
timely. His notion that some expensive interventions are not fitting beyond
a certain age is not groundless. However, getting an arbitrary limit for what
constitutes a "normal life-span," beyond which medical interventions
should be directed solely to help the patient in the process of dying, is, in
my view problematic.

In the first place, a normal life-span is contingent on many factors,
especially genetic constitution and lifestyle. Therefore, a normal life-span
could be one hundred years for one person, forty years for another, and
only a few days for an unfortunate infant. Second, to establish arbitrary
age-limit guidelines for the allocation of medical benefits degrades human
worth and violates self-evident, unalienable human rights. It can be argued
that our current system provides a health-care allocation bias favoring the
old. All those over age sixty-five are entitled to comprehensive care, and a
large proportion of children are disenfranchised and do not have access to
basic care. But to impose an injustice on a previously favored segment

cannot be a fair remedy for an existing unfair one. Yes, a system that denies preventive care to the young is an outrage, and the loss of a young life from a potentially curable illness is a travesty. However, to deny a longer, productive, happy life for a seventy-year-old person because he or she is close to the "normal life-span" is unrealistic and unjustifiable.

Limiting intrusive care for someone who has irretrievably lost his or her intellect, will, and passions is a different matter. This applies to all ages. Futile care is bad medicine, regardless of age.

The length of "years of benefit" from a medical intervention, however, justifies the allocation of expensive rare resources in favor of younger individuals. Priority for organ transplantation should be given to younger individuals. Any policy of rationing, however, should meet stringent conditions, including that the policy and its rationale be approved by the public. Also, it should never be taken literally and without consideration of all mitigating circumstances.

WHEN MEDICAL INTERVENTION IS WASTED ON THE YOUNG—NOT OLD

To illustrate my point regarding the invalidity of using age as an absolute criterion, I would like to share with the reader the following two cases: one an elderly patient, one relatively young. These patients were cared for by the same physician. I saw both of them in my capacity as a consultant to the primary physician a few years ago.

Mrs. Campbell was a very bright eighty-one-year-old widow, well known in the philanthropic community for sharing her time, talent, and resources for children's causes and the arts. Mrs. Campbell was admitted to the hospital because of shortness of breath and chest tightness that came on with exertion. She had become quite limited in her activities. Clinical examination showed her to be generally healthy except for a narrowing of a heart valve that controlled blood flow. An ultrasound study showed the valve to have been transformed into a piece of stone through calcium deposits. A tiny hole allowed the blood to be minimally pumped by a laboring heart. Laboratory tests showed all other body organs to be in an excellent condition.

I recommended heart surgery to replace the narrowed heart valve with an artificial one. She was reluctant, stating, "My husband died six months ago from heart failure. He had undergone two open-heart surgeries, one twelve years ago and the second four years ago. I would rather die a slow, natural death."

Her primary physician agreed with her decision, based primarily on her age. "She is eighty-one," he said, "already beyond the normal life-span."

I did not accept the decision without a further conversation with the patient in the presence of her primary physician. "You are quite healthy, except for this condition," I said. "Without heart surgery, your deterioration is expected to continue steadily, and death will occur within a few months. The chances of a surgical success are 95 percent, and you may be able to enjoy several years of good health." She pondered the decision and decided to receive the artificial valve. She is now enjoying life and continues to participate in several volunteer activities for the good of society.

The second patient was an unfortunate thirty-two-year-old woman. I was asked to see her during her third hospitalization in fifteen months. She was a drug addict who used heroin intravenously and sniffed cocaine. She used unclean needles for the heroin injections. More than a year ago, she was hospitalized for treatment of an infection of a heart valve, the one between the right side of the heart and the blood vessel leading to the lungs. She received six weeks of intravenous antibiotics. She was advised against self-injections with dirty needles. Nine months later, she was readmitted to the hospital for a similar condition, caused in the same way. A different kind of microorganism, which usually resides in the intestine, destroyed another valve on the right side of her heart. Another six-week course of intravenous antibiotics was initiated. She was again admonished not to use dirty needles. She came to the hospital for a third time four months later with a similar condition, caused by yet another kind of microbe. This time the infection had destroyed another heart valve: the aortic valve on the left side of the heart. Patients can tolerate destruction of heart valves on the right side of the heart, but not the aortic valve. Quickly, and expectedly, she developed heart failure. Her physician asked me to evaluate her for immediate heart surgery. I hesitated to recommend surgery. If past behavior is the best indicator for future behavior, I reasoned, predictably this patient would return to the habit of using intravenous drugs. In the first place, artificial heart valves have a higher propensity to be infected than normal valves, and in the second place, she would have to take a blood thinner reliably for the rest of her life. I shared with her physician my doubts about her future behavior and compliance with the treatment.

"She is only thirty-two," he argued vehemently. "I will convince her to be a good girl from now on." His tone was confident. Further, he cited a basic principle of medical ethics, that is, "distributive justice" requires the physician to treat all individuals with the same respect, regardless of the patient's social status, education, race, or background. Based on that principle, she was entitled to the same treatment as any other patient. Of course, I agreed.

She received an artificial heart valve in the aortic area, completed a full antibiotic course, was given instructions about the use of the blood thinner, and was told never again to self-inject with dirty needles. Three weeks and $50,000 later, she was brought dead to the emergency room because of heart arrest. An autopsy showed the $10,000 valve to be infected and clotted.

These two patients, one eighty-one years old and the other thirty-two years old, each received a gift from society: major surgery and an expensive artificial valve. The first patient used it to benefit herself and society. The second patient squandered it—what a tragedy!

In the same vein, I wish to reiterate that age per se should not be the deciding factor for the appropriateness of CPR. CPR should be the proper intervention when death is premature and unexpected. It is proper to avert the death of an otherwise healthy eighty-year-old patient suffering from a heart attack. CPR is inappropriate in a younger patient with irreversible massive brain damage or end-stage disease afflicting multiple organs.

Ultimately, procedures for setting limits for unnecessary, marginally effective, or inappropriate care requires treatment standards based on sound scientific evidence and the exercise of the physician's professional responsibility toward the best interests of his patients. Also, these decisions have to be subject to the patient's expressed preferences and convictions, and should never be based solely or predominantly upon the patient's age. After all, it is not how old you are that matters, it is how you are old.

HOW OUR DYING
CAN HELP THE LIVING

❧

Life, if well used, is long enough.

Seneca De Trivitate, *Vitae* II:49

DISCOVERING NEW LIFE
BY CONFRONTING DEATH

As strange as it may sound, my experience with cancer has been enlightening and enlivening. Others may have found cancer to be an awful thing, a curse to be dispelled, a nightmare to be fought. The occurrence of my cancer, on the other hand, has taught me who I am and who I am capable of becoming. It brought discipline into my life. It enabled me to look back, and it showed me the price I had to pay to rise to the top. Throughout my professional career, there were times when I did not care whom I was stepping on, if, in the process, I could reach the stars. It did not matter if there were victims as long as I was declared victor.

Cancer has changed all this. I rediscovered my wonderful family. I wish we had more laughs and fewer confrontations in years past, but now I cherish every minute I spend with them and with my three grandsons, Max, Eli, and Cole. With every passing day, I derive more joy out of life than I ever dreamed I would. I am thankful for every day, for the beautiful sunrises and sunsets, for the birds, the skies, the evening breezes, and for every little pleasure that life brings with it. I am grateful for the time I spend with my wife, Laila, for her grace, selflessness, optimism, and love. I am grateful for every meal, every smile, every laugh, and every expression of friendship. Most of all, I am grateful for the little nameless, numberless acts of kindness and love from good-hearted "ordinary" people.

I do not have to fight cancer; I am grateful for it. Yes, two major surgeries and radiation in between brought with them considerable physical pain, but that is the price for being human, thank God. The deeper the wound, the tougher the scar.

THE COLLISION OF TECHNOLOGY AND HUMAN VALUES

In the news media, it is customary to refer to patients dying of cancer as if they have lost an arduous battle or as if they have displayed enormous courage in their fight with their disease. I am neither a fighter nor a hero for having cancer, I am merely human. The one thing that cancer has taught me is how fragile we all are. It is part of the human condition. It made me think about the finish line, and I discovered that as a society, we are doing a poor job meeting our fate. We are wasting billions of dollars just to buy a miserable end, so that more of us can have a harsh exit, a fate worse than death. It need not be this way—clearly, there must be a better way, and it is within our grasp. We have to rediscover that death is naturally inevitable. We need to prepare for it, accept it, and even welcome it.

NATURAL DEATH VERSUS TREATMENT TO DEATH

The fact that, technically, all Americans can have access to the latest in technology regardless of class, color, or race has been hailed as the living example of substantive social justice in America. On the other hand, when death is imminent, the way patients are treated varies enormously from patient to patient, and depends on the patient's education, level of understanding, socioeconomic background, and beliefs. Interestingly, some studies suggest that the better-educated patients are more likely to demand less intervention at the close of life. The wishes of the family and the physician's bias also influence treatment. Even if we had all the resources to treat everybody to death, the wholesale application of high technology at the end of life would not be just. Performing invasive procedures on someone who does not have the capacity to consent or refuse can be justified only if that intervention has a reasonable chance of benefiting the patient or restoring his or her health and independence. Love for high technology and fear of lawsuits cannot stand as justification for the torture of hordes of decent people and the waste of society's valuable and limited resources. Neither we in the United States nor anybody else in the world has unlimited resources to sustain, for any length of time, the squandering of resources at the end of life. Leland Kaiser, a noted contemporary philosopher, warned, "The final crisis on this planet is the collision of technology and human values. . . . Technology has no ethics, but the people who employ the technology have to develop ethical standards for its use." What we need is a public policy, developed by ordinary laypeople with advice from lawyers, theologians, ethicists, and physicians, and enacted into law by Congress. This consortium needs to establish guidelines for the wise and rational allocation of resources at the end of life. This has been best expressed in a statement made by Lord Mustill of the Judicial Council of the House of Lords in England in the context of the case of Tony Bland, a young man in a persistent vegetative state whose treating physicians wanted to discontinue treatment.

> The whole matter cries out for exploration in depth by Parliament and then for the establishment by legislation not only of a new set of ethically and intellectually consistent needs, distinct from general criminal law, but also of a sound procedural framework within which the rules can be applied to individual cases.[1]

Is our Congress capable of debating and enacting such laws? We Americans have been accused of being too individualistic to see beyond our own self-interests. To put it bluntly, we are seen as so self-centered that we cannot function as one society working together for the common good. It is in our best individual interests to rid ourselves of the fear of being treated to death, a course that will bankrupt our families and future generations in the process. Unfortunately, end-of-life treatment issues are so complex, so emotionally charged, and so controversial that they do not lend themselves to sound bites, slogans, or headlines. Also, they can be readily politicized to scare people off and achieve voter support. This is too significant a subject to be reduced to some politician's sound bite.

THE IMPERSONAL USE OF TECHNOLOGY VERSUS THE PERSONAL TREATMENT OF THE PATIENT

The medical community has, by and large, refrained from discussing these issues with the public. We physicians owe it to our patients to share, in detail, what is meant by *coma*, *vegetative state*, and *terminal illness*; what treatment entails and its possible cost and outcomes. We owe it to them, not as a matter of courtesy, but as a duty, if we are to be deserving of their trust. The birth of the Euthanasia Society of America and the emergence of the "death doctor" are living testimonials to our failure as a profession to carry our duty of educating the public about life-and-death issues and to fulfill their desires to exit life with dignity and respect. The breathtaking pace of science and technology has caused us to forget the "personal" treatment of the patient. "The application of the principles of science to the diagnosis and treatment of disease is only one limited aspect of medical practice. The treatment of disease may be entirely impersonal; the care of a patient must be completely personal," Dr. Francis Peabody reminded us in 1927 in a series of lectures titled *The Care of the Patient*.[2] There is no medical, legal, ethical, or moral justification for the use of unnecessary interventions in hopelessly ill patients. This type of intervention constitutes an impersonal use of technology—not the personal care of the patient. This serious failure of the medical community is underscored by the fact that a book describing how to end one's own life, *Final Exit*, was a best-seller in the United States. Do reasonably informed people have to scream in our faces to interrupt our relentless pursuit of high technology to preserve an existence that, left undisturbed by high technology, would end in peace? That is not, and should not be, the mission of medicine. I can hear the poet Rainer Maria Rilke warning us

> Just another moment left!
> But what they are doing to me, they're always taking the rope
> And cutting it!
> The other day it was so good!
> And there was already a little bit of eternity in my intestines.
> They hold this spoon in to me,
> This spoon of life.
> Well I want it, and I don't
> I'd better throw up.

I know that life is just fantastic fun,
And the world is a foamy mug;
But I don't really get strength from it,
It just makes me dizzy.
It heals others, it makes me sick.
Grasp that some can't stand it.
For at least a thousand years now
I'll have to fast.[3]

GUIDELINES TO ENSURE QUALITY OF DEATH

First and foremost, a generally acceptable definition of medical futility must be agreed upon between the medical community and the public at large. Clear and unambiguous guidelines regarding treatment of terminal illness should be developed for universal use by the medical community. The definition of medical futility cannot and must not be left to ethicist-philosophers alone. Our leading ethicists espouse views so varying that it is difficult to reconcile them. On one hand, Dr. Veatch, the dean of Kennedy School of Ethics, maintains that keeping a brainless child on a ventilator is not medical futility and that doctors should not be allowed, and for that matter are incapable, to decide whether a medical treatment is futile. On the other extreme, Dr. Daniel Callahan, the chairman of the Hastings Center, maintains that discussions of medical futility cannot be dissociated from medical necessity and that it is not fitting to consider bypass surgery for older people who have completed a normal life span.

Guidelines in the United States are necessary to reconcile these opposing views. Such guidelines were developed in Denmark in 1985 and in many other Western communities. Doing so in the United States would alleviate physicians' fear of litigation. I believe that the concept of *upper-brain death* should be adopted as one definition of death, as it is in many European countries. The definition stipulates that permanent loss of consciousness and cognition constitutes death, and any further treatment will, therefore, be considered futile. This concept is strongly supported by the recent philosophical views by J. P. Lizza[4] and the critical review by A. Halevy and B. Brody.[5] Furthermore, I propose for the purposes of future deliberation that treatment of the following conditions be considered futile treatment:

1. End-stage disease afflicting two organ systems (heart-lung-liver-kidney) such as
   - End-stage heart disease + end-stage kidney disease
   - End-stage heart disease + end-stage lung disease
   - End-stage endocrine disorder + end-stage heart or kidney disease
2. Patients with advanced dementia (with loss of capacity to recognize self, others, and the environment) who, in addition, have an end-stage disease of one major system (e.g., end-stage heart disease)
3. Disseminated cancer not responsive to chemotherapy or radiation therapy
4. Advanced systemic (i.e., throughout the body), uncontrollable infection complicated with end-stage organ failure, including AIDS
5. Advanced senility, decrepitude, total dependence associated with end-stage disease of one major system

Under these circumstances, high-technology assistance devices, major surgical procedures, and major interventional procedures should not be applied unless they are strictly used to alleviate pain and suffering, such as in the case of amputation of a gangrenous limb or antibiotics to cure a painful bladder infection. Laboratory tests, antibiotics, and blood transfusions would no longer be considered viable treatment options. No resuscitative measures would be undertaken in the event of cardiopulmonary arrest. Terminal pneumonia may not be treated, if the patient's prior instructions indicate so. I realize that this list needs further examination and refinement. Opinions must be solicited from professional organizations, other conglomerations such as the Congress of Clinical Societies, and their proposals then need to be debated in public forums.

THE "IMPOLITIC" ISSUE OF DEATH

Unfortunately, our political system has been incapable of tackling the difficult issues related to life and death. In an editorial in a leading medical journal, Arthur Caplan, Ph.D., an ethicolegal expert from University of Pennsylvania, describes America as a wasteful, extremely individualistic, technology-driven, death-denying society.[6] Death was not always denied in Western civilization. According to the Greek philosopher Epicurus, "For the common man or woman, death, the most awful of evils, is really nothing, for so long as we are, death has not come, and when it has come . . . we are not." But for our contemporary legislators, the mention of technology and death can ruin a career in politics. When Richard Lamm, the former governor of Colorado quoted earlier, ran for Congress, he brought up the issue of waste of medical resources at the end of life. He suggested that society had to take measures to prevent this waste. His statement was used by his political rivals to instill fears that Mr. Lamm was against the old, the frail, and the disabled. Mr. Lamm fell from grace and was defeated. That was a cautionary tale: Never again would any politician who holds or aspires to hold office bring up the question of curtailing the costs of treatment of terminal illness. The issue is very much subject to manipulation and misinterpretation and, therefore, misuse by political rivals. Futile medical care at the end of life has become an unmentionable topic—taboo. And whenever the issue is raised, it is almost guaranteed that there will be a political lobby to cry "foul" and claim discrimination against the old, the frail, the disabled, and the weak in our society.

This subject, as controversial as it may be, is a ticking time bomb. It cries out for demanding public policy, grassroots coalition. This book is an invitation for one such effort, but do not depend on politicians to get the ball rolling. As long as there are no term limits for legislators' services, our politicians will tiptoe around the subject, hoping that it will go away. The dismally useless "Patient Self-Determination Act" enacted by Congress in 1990, was an effort to defuse the issue.[7] The act stipulates that patients should be informed about their rights to refuse treatment whenever they are admitted to a hospital. The right of a competent person to refuse treatment was recognized early in this century in this country, but so far, the self-determination act has had very limited effect on the practice of medicine. How can an elderly patient, or any patient, comprehend all possible scenarios that may follow a procedure or a hospital admission? What benefit can be derived from engaging in a cold, routine conversation about life-and-death issues at a time when we want the patient to harness all energies and good spirits on behalf of a planned procedure or surgery? Bringing up details about life-and-death issues at this time may even be cruel. These difficulties are well articulated by Drs. Jeffrey S. Tobias and his colleagues of the Meyerstein Institute of Clinical Oncology, Middlesex Hospital in London, in an article, "Fully Informed Consent Can Be Needlessly Cruel."[8] In all cases, it reflects poor taste. In a recent issue of the *Journal of Medical Ethics,* I encountered an interesting article entitled "Preventive Ethics."[9] The authors of this article recommend that treating physicians discuss the possibility of brain death with every pregnant woman in the event that she should be involved in a fatal accident, and the dilemma of whether to sustain the patient's heart and lung function to sustain the fetus. I find this to be an extreme example of poor taste that borders on absurdity.

It is unrealistic to think that physicians can cover every possible contingency with every patient everywhere and at all times. And if it were possible, I wonder whether it is at all decent. Where is the good old patient-doctor relationship? Physicians need to ask themselves, "Who are we? Slaves of medical etiquette or disciples of medicine?"

THE PRESENT LIVING WILL: NOT A VIABLE GUIDELINE TO ENSURE QUALITY OF DEATH

In its present form, the living will that applies to a patient when death is imminent and unavoidable is a new testimonial to the failure of the medical community to live up to its sacred mission. Why on earth should anyone need to execute a document asking physicians not to continue to invade his body when the intervention is not indicated and imposes an unnecessary burden on the patient, his or her family, and society?

In the present forms, with their scope focused totally on terminal illness *in extremis,* living wills are meaningless. Responsible physicians do not need living wills to prevent ineffective treatment from being given. Treatment should cease once it is determined to be useless. Physicians should not need notarized documents with two witnesses in order to withhold or withdraw treatment when the patient's status proclaims what Christina Rossetti described in "song" in 1862:

> I shall not see the shadows,
> I shall not feel the rain,
> I shall not hear the nightingale sing on,
> As if in pain; and dreaming through the twilight
> That doth not rise or set,
> Happy I may remember and Happy may forget.

The scope and application of living wills should change. Advance care planning may be utilized as an expression of one's personal preferences and might address the treatment of potentially reversible diseases such as pneumonia. Additionally, living wills could direct the use of life-saving measures in the context of

> advanced weakness with total dependence, senile decay, accident, heart problems, or similar situations that have led to severe invalidity that he (or she) would become permanently incapable of taking care of himself (or herself) physically and mentally . . .

The foregoing is taken verbatim from Denmark's living will.[10] These conditions do not, by themselves, represent futility and ordinarily should never be considered reason enough to unilaterally limit treatment by the physician. But for those of us who value personal dignity and independence more than outstretched existence, a much diminished quality of life may not be acceptable.

THE EXTRAVAGANT HEALTH-CARE SYSTEM IN THE UNITED STATES

No other country on earth devotes so much energy and money to take care of the critically ill than does the United States. True, we have more victims of violence and AIDS in our hospitals compared to other countries, yet this cannot justify five times as many intensive-care beds (relative to population size) compared to the Western Hemisphere country with the next highest of intensive care unit (ICU) bed count. Many more ICU beds do no help us to live longer or healthier than people in England. Whether we spend $50 billion or $100 billion on futile care is immaterial. These billions are spent to purchase misery, and these precious billions of dollars are taken away from our children and from future generations. As our society ages, the demand on high technology will increase unless we change our methods of applying high-tech care. We need to learn to discipline ourselves and to allocate our resources wisely. Unless this is done, our nation will face a generational fight in the allocation of scarce, expensive medical resources. In the near future, fewer working people will be supporting more and more of the retired, the senile, and the decrepit.

I wonder whether I would have been able to publish this book were it not for the fact that I am over sixty years old and have cancer. Sooner or later, I shall join those of humanity who have passed away before me. We cannot but ask ourselves: Can we achieve wisdom and peace in our unrelenting combat with the aging process? Much of the progress in medical science has not produced vitality and happiness, and the fountain of youth remains as elusive as ever. Will we ever temper our unrelenting pursuit of immortality? Will we elderly show generosity and consideration for future generations or each be fixed on his or her fate? How many societal resources are we going to exhaust as we exit from this life? Will each of us cost the system hundreds of thousands of wasted dollars as we leave?

A society in which each individual competes for limited resources without regard to others is a society that will bring itself to its knees and is headed for collapse. Members of the society, young and old, cannot behave as if they are entitled to their rights without making a return to the society at large. And, we, the older generation that has enjoyed the blessings that our nation has bestowed upon us, must lead the way.

HEALTH-CARE REFORM: LET OUR ELDERS LEAD THE WAY

Aristotle defined a civilized society as a group of individuals who enjoy being together, are useful to each other, and have as their prime aim the common good. How can we, the elderly, be part of this formula? We could begin by initiating the discussion of establishing priorities for medical care. First and foremost, we have to eliminate the wasteful high-tech brinkmanship that only distorts and prolongs the process of dying. End-of-life treatment policies will affect all members of society, but inevitably will affect primarily the elderly segment. The acceptance of death must be part of dealing with our humanity. A peaceful death must become the natural conclusion of a meaningful life. It is an imperative for the good of society. If we, the older members of society, can help build the momentum necessary to tackle this difficult subject, we would be making a return to society at large, for the common good.

It must be clear that rationing of health care should never be at the sole discretion of the physician. As health-care resources become more limited, pressure will mount on physicians to unilaterally ration health care. It must be emphasized that it is society's responsibility to set health-care priorities, although physicians' organizations should be part of the dialogue. For instance, establishing priorities for admission to intensive care, when circumstances dictate, is required from, and expected of, experienced physicians. In fact, Florida courts found a hospital liable for negligence in the case of *Von Stetina* v. *Florida Hospital* when the patient was denied admission to intensive care in the place of other, less acutely ill patients.[11]

We already have a policy of rationing in one area of medicine. Establishing nationwide priorities has worked fairly well in the case of organ transplants. The number of potential recipients far exceeds the number of potential donors; triage in this case is both legal and ethical. Despite the clear necessity for rationed care, and despite the role physicians must play in enacting this, physicians must be, and should remain, their patients' advocate at all times. This sacred relationship must be preserved in any system that society elects to adopt. In Denmark, practice guidelines regarding futility and end-of-life issues are formulated by a committee comprising seventeen individuals, predominantly laypeople, with almost equal representation from both genders. The committee is guided by public opinion polls and also consults with physicians, nurses, social workers, and chaplains, as well as ethicists and law professionals. It advises the Parliament about guidelines on the definition of death, allocation of scarce resources (including life-sustaining treatment), as well as other health issues. The committee also has the duty to disseminate information and educational material. Can we agree on a commission comprised in a similar way to study our collective values and make recommendations for appropriate legislative action? In this way, the judgment of a committee composed of a number of chosen laypeople is used to satisfy the substitute judgment standard for the society as a whole.

A common criticism of doctors is that they often provide patients with fraudulent representations that lead to unfulfillable and unrealistic expectations about the efficacy of a futile treatment. Unjustified hope leads to unreasonable demands. This criticism is not groundless and, in many cases, is justified. Medical schools have to take seriously training of the young physicians in how to communicate with their patients clearly, truthfully, and thoughtfully. The moral weight of the doctor-patient relationship must be taken very seriously. Professional integrity should never be overshadowed by vague notions of professional authority.

I remind my students of the most poignant demonstration of a doctor-patient relationship: Lying on a table is a naked patient, overtaken by anxiety and anticipation, overburdened by the enigma of his illness, in the presence of a fully dressed, calm, informed, secure physician asking questions and giving instructions. In this scene, the patient should be viewed as king and the physician as his devoted servant. This captures the essence of a doctor-patient relationship. Neither passion for technology nor the fear of the legal shutters should influence this sacred bond in which the patient's interests must remain paramount.

Conversations with patients and families in distress are never easy: A mix of patient ignorance or confusion about what can be achieved, as well as the inability of the physician to express himself clearly, impedes discourse between patient and physician. Another impediment to this relationship occurs when physicians obtain their medical information about ethics from ethicists who have not been faced with the plethora of decisions doctors make on a day-to-day basis. Decisions from patients and families are usually based upon their understanding of incomplete, simplified, brief, biased information from a physician. A patient about to be placed on a ventilator for the treatment of pneumonia does not have the thousands of medical articles at his disposal to read and evaluate before making his or her decision. The principle *primum non nocere* (first do no harm) could have been applicable to ancient medicine but not to high-tech interventions. Every procedure a physician performs, every survey he or she undertakes, every medicine he or she prescribes has hazards, side effects, and sometimes serious complications. I have great respect and even reverence for theoretical ethicists. I learn from their writing, although I must confess sometimes I have difficulty understanding them. However, in the world of intensive care, or when life is at stake, theoretical ethics has its limitations. It troubles me when a highly respected ethicist (e.g., Dr. Veatch) recommends that a permanently comatose eighty-seven-year-old or a brainless newborn be maintained on a ventilator in the name of justice. What about social responsibility? How could a doctor justify an expensive treatment with no hope of any benefit, such as in these cases?

A definition of *futility* is the prime responsibility of organized medicine. Not groundlessly, physicians are asked why the question of futility is important now. Why did doctors resist attempts to take unconscious patients off the ventilator twenty years ago and some are now championing the drive? It may seem bizarre and self-serving for physicians to carry the banner of establishing priorities for medical care when they avoided similar efforts before. Frankly, because of escalating costs, physicians can no longer evade this issue. No one could have predicted the enormous escalation of health-care costs over the past three to four decades. With the wide use of CPR and artificial ventilation, medical miracles have become possible. But who would have predicted that thousands of mindless victims would be left in persistent vegetative state or comas?

The breathtaking progress of medical science is quickly eliminating acute disease as the main killer. Most cases of pneumonia are cured. Acute heart attacks, which were 50 percent lethal to victims before intensive care, now kill fewer than 10 percent of their victims. Patients today live longer and die slower, many in isolation, confusion, anguish, and pain.

Physicians, self-proclaimed advocates of life (without having a chance to review the Hippocratic oath to discover that terminal comfort is also part of their duty), have been fighting death, preserving life, and defending any vestige of it. But physicians alone cannot establish guidelines for life-and-death issues.

LET US ASSESS FUTILE CARE AT A PUBLIC FORUM

Yes, the economic imperatives are great, and our country has realized that the wild application of technology in cases of futility or marginal utility must be tamed. Yes, the rapid growth of managed care is applying new, sometimes wrongful, pressures to limit expensive care. But generational responsibility, rationality, and social conscience more than any other motive necessitate that we put an end to the madness of futile care. There are limits to what can be expected of medicine. Not all care can or will be beneficial. The vexing questions about when to withhold, when to withdraw, and whom to resuscitate are part of the clinical landscape. They have spawned a troubling debate among abstract thinkers, but ultimately the limits have to be set through public consensus, with the help of primary-care physicians and specialists. Unfortunately, these weighty issues are conspicuously absent from national deliberations about health-care reform. This troubling phenomenon must be remedied as soon as possible or the consequences will be disastrous.

It is time to reform health care without sacrificing the core values of medicine. Our nation is in the process of rediscovering the values that made this country great. Let us resurrect the values that made our medicine great: (1) a strong, trusting doctor-patient relationship in which the moral authority of the physician is neither overlooked nor undervalued, and in which the doctor's devotion to his patient's best interests is never suspect; (2) scientifically superior, technologically advanced medicine that is applied judiciously, as well as skillfully.

In the context of futile medical care, we need to establish unified, proactive CPR procedures based upon our extensive current knowledge of outcomes. We should be prepared to modify the guidelines as new technologies develop or as research clarifies some of the treatment outcomes of interventions for us.

In order for these changes to be effective, full participation from the lay community, legal authorities, theologians, ethicists, and legislators is needed. Yes, it is the physicians who have the responsibility to help guide the development of these procedural guidelines, whereas it is society's responsibility through its elected institutions to finalize and empower these guidelines. It is customary for medical ethicists to promote the idea of autonomy as the basis for asking the patient to choose the way he or she wishes to be treated at the end of life. The basic premise of autonomy (according to Immanuel Kant) is, however, that people participate in designing the laws that govern them. Therefore, society's role in developing these guidelines should reinforce, and not undermine, our individual autonomy in a democratic society.

ABANDONING ABSOLUTES IN MEDICAL CARE

The whole subject cries out for establishing standards, procedures, and protocols that take into account "reasonable probabilities" rather than absolutes in the practice of medicine. For example, the likelihood of a one-pound cocaine baby surviving, even with prolonged intensive care, is less than 10 percent and at a cost of $1 million dollars. If this baby survived, the chances are high that it will be mentally retarded and subject to multiple medical problems. The weight of these facts directs us to use our efforts and resources to save babies of two pounds or more; these babies have an 80 percent chance of surviving at a cost of $50,000 each and a very good chance of becoming healthy. The same principles can be applied at the end of life and for the application of resuscitation efforts.

THE NEED TO PUT A PRICE ON HUMAN LIFE

It might be argued that such an exercise stifles medical progress and would bury our hopes and dreams of future medical progress in the green hash of cash. The argument goes on to say that human life, whatever its definition, is priceless, and that it is immaterial whether it costs a few cents or several million dollars to save a life. The argument further claims that while the cost-effective syndrome masquerades as prudence, it will have the effect of demeaning the value of human life by placing a price tag on it. Although there are obvious truths to this argument, it must be emphasized that no country and no civilization, whatever their wealth, can afford to waste resources by trying to expand the limits of life beyond reason at both ends: babies who weigh less than one pound and citizens over 100 years of age. It is imperative that a society set its priorities straight.

A COMMISSION DEDICATED TO DEAL WITH END-OF-LIFE TREATMENT

The time has come for a national commission, properly selected from community leaders, to be empowered to develop goals and procedures for treatment near the end of life. Let it be named the Quinlan commission in honor of Karen Ann Quinlan, whose mother was the first to challenge the high-tech maintenance of unconscious existence. The commission should be relatively independent and broadly representative, but should not be seen as representative of any particular special interest group. It should be appointed in a way similar to that of Justices of the Supreme Court. It must be insulated from political pressure or interference by lobbyists. It may work with small work groups that interface with medical authorities, legal scholars, ethics specialists, economists, and theologians representing dominant religions and scientists. It will have access to opinion polls, health statistics, and other pertinent information. The commission should develop substitute judgment standards for care of the incompetent and the

terminally ill. The commission should be charged with the duty to recommend, review, and modify health-care legislation and establish priorities
for medical care, including home care and hospice care. This commission
would represent society's will, in addition to disseminating a uniformly
designed Advance Care Plan (living will) that has practical applicability and
legal power to limit treatment when death is near rather than imminent,
in order to limit unnecessary and unwanted care at the end of life. In addition, the commission should establish strategies and instructional materials
to disseminate information and educate the public at large. A similar commission was established in Denmark in 1988 and one in Sweden recently.
The Swedish commission was able to establish the following "difficult priorities in health care":

1. That all human beings have equal worth.
2. That society has a duty to protect the weakest and most vulnerable
   among its citizens.
3. That cost-efficiency and maximum return to society for the
   amount of money spent on health care should prevail.

The German wife of a friend of mine has told me that a similar commission with a consensus viewpoint on health care at the end of life can never
be implemented in America. She stated that Americans are too individualistic to come to a consensus on such issues. She noted that although our
Constitution begins, "We the people," we Americans are so heterogeneous
and so self-centered that we have lost our sense of community and of the
"common good" that binds other societies together. I resent her reasoning,
not only because I love America and am proud to be an American, but also
because, if she is right, it will mean that we are a nation on the decline.
No force is as powerful in bringing a civilization to its knees and hastening
its collapse as a bunch of self-centered grabbers, cheaters, and usurpers of
the public good. I do not believe we Americans are this way. I feel that the
use of futile, high technology at the end of life was inevitable for a time.
As it always is with Americans, fads come and go; fascination with high
technology has been a fad carried to its extremes. A correction is overdue
and must be forthcoming.

Although there is no religion, heritage, tradition, race, or belief that
unites us in America, the fact that we are Americans is a force powerful

enough to bring us together. If you do not believe me, just remember that when you travel anywhere in the world, Americans become instant friends with other Americans. Something compelling unites us—a force beyond description. Our love of country, our pride in being Americans is the glue that keeps us together and gives us the energy to dream about a better tomorrow for future generations.

More than 150 years ago, Alexis de Tocqueville, in his immortal classic, *Democracy in America*, wrote

> . . . when an American asks for the cooperation of his fellow citizens, it is seldom refused; and I have often seen if offered spontaneously, and with great goodwill. . . . All this is not in contradiction to what I have said before on the subject of individualism. The two things are so far from combating with each other that I can see how they agree. Equality of condition, while it makes men feel their independence, shows them their own weakness; they are free, but exposed to a thousand accidents; and experience soon teaches them that although they do not habitually require the assistance of others, a time almost always comes when they cannot do without it.[12]

The time has come for the older people in our society to band together and lead the way toward a secure future. In order to achieve this, we must, among other things, stop the wasteful allocation of resources at the extremes of life. We are an aging nation, and health-care needs for the elderly will grow steadily into the next century. We have a responsibility to guide our country in its quest to reallocate its expensive medical technology wisely. If we continue to add the cost of futile care at the end of life to our increasing health-care needs, the time will come when the younger generation will not be able to cope with our demands. They may in these circumstances feel compelled to abandon us.

Our elder generation is comprised of heroes who valiantly defended America during World War II and beyond. We are the owners of America's great scientific revolution, and among us are the architects of America's quest to become the unquestionable beacon of decency in a war-torn world. It is our sacred duty to lead our beloved country through this political minefield, developing the necessary laws and procedures to stop the needless waste at the end of life. In the process, we will have, as individuals, preserved our dignity as we exit this planet.

SUMMARY OF PROPOSED SOLUTIONS

The following list summarizes the contributions needed from various contingents in our society to arrive at guidelines near the end of life:

1. *Duties of the medical societies*

   - Establish guidelines for medical futility or marginal utility
   - Develop guidelines for out-of-hospital CPR and in-hospital CPR
   - Develop guidelines for the withholding and withdrawal of care
   - Review the definition of brain death

2. *Duties of lay blue-ribbon commission*

   - Review medical guidelines developed by the medical establishment, debate them, modify if necessary, and recommend their adoption
   - Disseminate public education about health-care issues
   - Propose laws for adoption of guidelines
   - Monitor the implementation of policies and procedures

3. *Duties of Congress*

   - Enact laws for the universal adoption of guidelines
   - Enact laws to establish the procedures for adoption of guidelines
   - Adopt a uniform health-care decision bill and a uniform Advance Care Plan document
   - Establish a central registry for those who execute such documents
   - Require health-care professionals to consult the registry on a regular basis
   - Ensure that patients' expressed wishes are legally binding within reasonable limits

Albert Einstein once wrote, "Strange is our situation here upon Earth. Each of us comes for a short visit, not knowing why, yet sometimes to divine purpose. . . . One thing we do know, is that man is here for the sake of other men."[13]

All of us will someday face death. The way we die and the guidelines or lack of guidelines for death with dignity will either bankrupt future generations or allow us to invest in those generations to come. It is my sincere hope that this book will help all Americans make the right choice for themselves and their loved ones to forgo the relentless, futile, and often cruel pursuit of high-tech prolongation of the process of dying.

9

CONTROLLING OUR
MORTAL DESTINY
The Birth of the Living Will

❧

Just as I select my ship as I am about to go on a voyage,
so I shall choose my death when I am about to depart from life.
Lucius Annaeus Seneca

THE LIVING WILL: AN INDICTMENT OF
PHYSICIANS' ETHICAL PARALYSIS

The accelerated development of new methods to reverse death and sustain life has, as we have seen, left the medical community totally paralyzed to handle the unwanted consequences of high technology in medicine. Doctors in the recent past declare their proper position as patients' advocates without fully understanding what that position entails. They were not prepared to consider the termination of ineffective, countertherapeutic measures, even if the patient or family requested it. This prevailing attitude was exemplified by the testimony of Dr. Morse in the case of Ms. Karen Ann Quinlan, who in 1975 at age twenty-one suffered a cardiopulmonary arrest as a result of accidentally ingesting a combination of prescription medications and alcohol. After the cardiopulmonary arrest and coma, Quinlan was in a persistent vegetative state, with loss of all meaningful cognitive brain functions. Her parents sought permission from the court to let her die naturally by discontinuation of mechanical ventilation, which they thought was sustaining her hopeless condition. Dr. Morse, Ms. Quinlan's treating physician, justified that maintaining the permanently unconscious Ms. Quinlan on a ventilator was the right treatment and that

177

he had a duty to provide it. Ms. Quinlan's parents prevailed. Nine years after removing the ventilator, Karen Ann Quinlan died without regaining consciousness. The public has attributed to physicians various motives to account for this perverse attitude: financial greed; a passion for technology that leads doctors to use invasive procedures to excess; insensitivity to the suffering they may inflict on patients; and/or fear of malpractice litigation. These have resulted in physicians' eagerness to suggest all treatments that have the slightest possibility of improving the patient's condition.

While the medical community was responding tentatively to these issues, a momentum was gaining among the general populace. This grassroots movement metamorphosed into political action. Living wills originated in the "right to die" movement in the United States. In 1967, at a meeting of the Euthanasia Society of America, Luis Kutner, founder and president of the society, first proposed the idea of the living will.[1] Soon, it became clear that the living will was really an expression of the right to self-determination rather than a manifesto for the right to die. Subsequently, the Euthanasia Society of America abandoned its traditional advocacy for active euthanasia and directed its efforts more to protect the right of the terminally ill and to promote the living will. The following prototype document was the result:

> Death is as much a reality as birth, growth, maturity, and old age—it is the only certainty of life. If the time comes when I, _____, can no longer take part in decisions for my own future, let this statement stand as an expression of my wishes, while I am still of sound mind.
>
> If the situation should arise in which there is no reasonable expectation of my recovery from physical or mental disability, I request that I be allowed to die and not be kept alive by artificial means or "heroic measures." I do not fear death itself as much as the indignities of deterioration, dependence, and hopeless pain. I, therefore, ask that medication be mercifully administered to me to alleviate suffering, even though this may hasten the moment of death.

This pioneering will has the virtues of brevity and simplicity. Clearly, the person executing the will knew what he or she wanted. "I wish to be spared the pain, indignity, and cost of unnecessary care at the end of life." In other words, "I long for an Oedipus-like exit, a graceful exit." Most citizens have experienced the horrors of a prolonged, high-tech death of a loved one, a relative, a friend, a neighbor, or a work associate. In their minds, heroic measures equate with high-technology interventions. "Physical and mental disability" means loss of independence and the ability to reason.

Not unexpectedly, the intent, spirit, and promise of this will was virtually lost in the feud among doctors, lawyers, theologians, ethicists, families, and society. Doctors viewed it as too ambiguous and nonspecific; lawyers noted its shortcomings regarding the issue of being legally binding; ethicists analyzed it, criticized it, and ostracized it; and families ignored it. Nevertheless, it represented a precious starting point for a society getting tired of the entrenched idea that people should be medically treated to death.

LEGISLATION ADDRESSING THIS VITAL ISSUE

In 1976, the California Natural Death Act reaffirmed the patient's right to refuse futile treatment while exempting physicians from liability. That every human being of adult years and sound mind has a right to determine what shall be done with his own body was affirmed early in this century.[2] The preamble of the California Natural Death Act states:

> The ability of modern technology to prolong life beyond its natural limits can, in some cases, produce no more than precarious or burdensome existence while providing nothing necessary or beneficial to the patient . . . thereby enabling physicians to legally withhold or withdraw treatment from an unwilling terminally ill patient . . .

Subsequent to the California Natural Death Act, many other states adopted similar acts, such as "The Natural Death Act" and "Advance Directives." The basic ingredients in these acts are as follows:

1. A competent patient has the right to refuse treatment. The patient is deemed competent when he or she is able to comprehend, evaluate, and choose between treatments. This underscores the patient's autonomy and the right to "shared decision making."
2. An incompetent patient has the same rights as a competent patient. The right to refuse treatment and the "right to die" are interpreted by the courts to be within the right of liberty and privacy and are included or implied in the Bill of Rights.

The California Natural Death Act contains a prescribed form of Living Will. It further stipulates for the instructions to be binding, the declarant should sign the directive at least fourteen days after having been diagnosed as suffering from a terminal condition: "which means an incurable condition caused by injury, disease, or illness, which regardless of the application of life-sustaining procedures would, within reasonable medical judgment, produce death, and where the application of life-sustaining procedures serves only to postpone the moment of death of the patient."

The concept of the living will, or advance directive, proposed by the American Euthanasia Society, was popularized after the enactment of the California Natural Death Act. This legal document "directs" health-care professionals in "advance" as to the wishes of a person regarding medical intervention in the event that he or she becomes incompetent. The intention of a "living will" is to prevent unnecessary, intrusive, death-postponing intervention at the end of life. Most states require that the document be executed by the patient while he or she is still competent and that it be witnessed. In many states, the "living will" is honored only for a few years, after which it has to be renewed or updated by the patient to remain in effect.

A second-generation form of the living will allows for a durable power of attorney to be granted to someone chosen by the patient. This designated person is given the authority to make medical decisions on behalf of the patient when the latter becomes incompetent or unable to make them.

A CASE OF SUBSTITUTE JUDGMENT

Short of living wills, the courts held to certain standards in order to grant or deny withdrawal of life-supporting measures for incompetent patients. These are

- the subjective standard
- the substitute judgment standard
- the patient's best-interest standard

The subjective standard requires clear and convincing evidence that the patient would not have wanted to lead a medically sustained existence of unconsciousness or severe infirmity. An example is the 1986 case *Brophy*

v. *Massachusetts*.[3] Mr. Brophy was a fireman who was involved in saving a victim from perishing in a burning truck and transported him to a Boston hospital. The victim lived for approximately three months in a burn unit. The town of Easton, Massachusetts, gave Brophy a medal for his heroic act. Mr. Brophy expressed his regret that the man he had rescued was leading a subhuman, miserable existence and that he would not have wanted a similar fate for himself. Brophy subsequently threw the commendation in the wastebasket and explained to his wife, "I should have been five minutes later. It would have been all over for him." Brophy told his brother, "If I am ever like that, just shoot me, pull the plug." Years later, Brophy became permanently unconscious from a stroke. Before he slipped into a coma, one of Brophy's five children visited her father at Goddard Hospital. When Brophy pulled himself up to a half-sitting position in order to kiss his daughter, she scolded him for not lying still. Brophy told his daughter, "If I can't sit up to kiss one of my beautiful daughters, I may as well be six feet under." The court took Mr. Brophy's prior public statements as clear and convincing evidence that he would not have liked to have his vegetative existence sustained. He did not need to execute a living will; Mr. Brophy was allowed to die through the withholding of life-support measures.

THE NEED TO EXECUTE A WILL
WHEN YOU ARE WILLING—AND ABLE

By contrast, the U.S. Supreme Court denied the removal of medical support from Nancy Cruzan, the young Missouri lady mentioned earlier, who sustained extensive, irreversible brain injuries in an accident.[4] The Missouri law required "a clear and convincing evidence" that the patient, while competent prior to the accident, would have desired the discontinuation of medical intervention that would only maintain a permanently unconscious existence. In 1988, the Missouri Supreme Court ruled that no such evidence existed. In a five-to-four decision, the U.S. Supreme Court upheld the Missouri court decision. The decision, written by Chief Justice Rehnquist and quoted by Alan Meisel, said,

> Missouri requires that evidence of the incompetent's wishes as to the withdrawal of treatment be proved by clear and convincing evidence. The

question then is whether the U.S. Constitution forbids the establishment of this procedural requirement . . . the state has "a general interest" in protecting life.

Meisel continues,

> Justice Rehnquist went on to emphasize the due process clause requires the state not to repose judgment on these matters with anyone but the patient herself. Close family members may have a strong feeling—a feeling not at all ignoble or unworthy, but not entirely disinterested either—that they do not wish to witness the continuation of the life of a loved one which they regard as hopeless, meaningless and even degrading. But there is no automatic assurance that the view of close family members will necessarily be as the patient's would have been . . .[5]

The lesson here is that if you are an adult who lives in a state that requires the rigorous standard of clear and convincing evidence, you had better execute a legally valid document indicating your wishes about end of life issues—or you are wasting your ink![6]

IMPLICIT CONSENT TO BE TREATED TO DEATH

Until a few years ago, not every state had a living will statute. New York, Michigan, and Massachusetts were among the last to enact advance directive statutes, although some of the most progressive legal proceedings came from their courts. Of interest is that New York courts have accepted the validity of generic living wills in certain circumstances even before the state had legislation of its own. Alaska and Alabama did not have a health-care proxy law until recently. In states that have living will laws, it is presumed that unless you have executed a legally valid advance directive or given unquestionable specific, oral instructions to the contrary, every attempt will be made to prolong your life, regardless of what you or your family would have wanted. The doctrine of implied consent supposes that lack of instructions to limit treatment equates to consent to being treated to death. Furthermore, New York and Missouri have both specifically denied family members the authority to refuse life-sustaining treatment for patients with extensive brain damage. Without advance directives, hospitals and nursing homes feel committed to use all available technology for fear of allegations of negligence. A living will is therefore promoted by the legal profession as a way to prevent your family from having to fight with hospital staff at a time of enormous distress. Living wills might also serve as a means to "save the family" from crushing medical costs.

THY WILL BE DONE—THROUGH A PROXY

Occasionally, the courts based their decisions about treatment near the end of life on the less stringent substitute judgment standard.[7] This standard stipulates that the judgment of a surrogate or an appointed proxy be taken as equivalent to the patient's own, when the patient is incapable of voicing his or her own desires. Generally, the views of someone appointed by the patient to have a power of attorney in health-care decisions are binding, as long as the surrogate's views are deemed rational and reasonable by a competent medical authority. In the Karen Ann Quinlan case, discussed earlier, the views of the mother were upheld by the court according to the substitute judgment standard. In this case, the more rigorous "clear and convincing evidence" standard did not apply, since it is not required by the state of New Jersey. Even in the Cruzan case, Justice Brennan presented a strongly worded dissent to the Supreme Court decision: "They have discarded evidence of (Nancy's) will, ignored her values, and deprived her of the right to a decision as closely approximating her own choice as humanly possible."

Justice Antonin Scalia issued a separate concurrent statement: "I would have preferred that we announce, clearly and promptly, that the federal courts have no business in this field. . . . The point at which life becomes "worthless" and the point at which the means necessary to preserve it become extraordinary or inappropriate are neither set forth in the Constitution nor known to the nine justices of his court any better than they are known to nine people picked at random from the Kansas City telephone directory."[8]

LET THE PEOPLE RULE

If that is the case, one cannot but ask the rhetorical, yet extremely pertinent question: Why not submit to the judgment of the vast majority of the

American people? Poll after poll has shown that all segments of the public, including members of all major religious groups, overwhelmingly support the right of the hopelessly ill to be allowed to die. Yet the courts often hand down decisions that contrast with the tenor of the times.

"PATIENT'S BEST INTEREST": A NEW STANDARD

More recently, various courts have increasingly adopted the "patient's best interest standard" to guide the management of a permanently unconscious individual. Much useful guidance can be gleaned from the case of *Airedale NHS Trust* v. *Bland* judgment in February 1993.[9] Mr. Tony Bland, a young man, was trapped against the stadium fence during a Liverpool soccer game. Multiple rib injuries resulted in the cessation of effective breathing. His brain was deprived of oxygen for a long enough time to cause permanent brain damage. The patient's recovery was limited, and it became obvious that Mr. Bland would continue to linger in a persistent vegetative state. Recognizing that the treatment was futile, the physicians wanted to remove existing support measures. The case was brought in front of the Judicial Council of the House of Lords in England. A thoughtful and probing discussion followed. The best way to summarize the proceedings is to provide the reader with excerpts of statements by members of the House of Lords. The upshot of the case was that physicians were granted the right to allow Mr. Bland to die in peace, without further life-support measures. The following are excerpts and quotations from hearings of the Bland case in the House of Lords:

> To presume that the incompetent person must always be subjected to what many rational and intelligent persons may decline is to downgrade the status of the incompetent person by placing a lesser value on his intrinsic human worth. (Lord Goff of Cheiveley quoting the Supreme Judicial Court of Massachusetts[10])
>
> The doctor cannot owe to the patient any duty to maintain his life when that life can only be sustained by intrusive medical care to which the patient will not consent. (Lord Browne-Wilkinson)
>
> If it is not the interests of an insentient patient to continue the life-supporting care, the doctor will be acting unlawfully if he continued the

treatment . . . and would perform no guilty act by discontinuing. (Lord Lowry)[11]

Several relevant cases that came before the American courts were treated similarly. Even Nancy Cruzan of Missouri was allowed to die peacefully upon withdrawal of life support. Soon after the Supreme Court hearings, the state of Missouri withdrew from the Cruzan case, stating, "It has no interest in the outcome of this litigation." The Missouri law was changed by the state legislature and no longer requires the "clear and convincing evidence" standard. This was a welcome legislation that received wide support from the citizens and the media, and provided a welcome relief to the Cruzan family.

PHYSICIANS: IMMUNE FROM THE LIABILITY OF WITHHOLDING CARE

In spite of the seemingly conflicting court rulings on this issue of futile care, it must be stated that no physician has ever been indicted, let alone convicted, for withholding care deemed unnecessary by reasonable medical standards. This may seem odd when one considers the prevailing view among practicing physicians that they should overtreat patients for fear of legal repercussions.

In the case of *Barber* v. *Superior Court of the State of California*, heard by a Los Angeles court in 1983, nurses complained to the state prosecutor that physicians withdrew treatment, including feeding and hydration, from a terminally ill patient and "watched him die." The court dismissed this case on the basis that there was

> no evidence in the record to show that the defendants were acting either in a malignant, selfish, or foolhardy manner to take the life of another. In this case, we do not have willful starvation as the proximate cause of the patient's death. To say that the attending physician sat back and watched a person starve to death is to ignore the state of bad health of Mr. Herbert.[12]

In no case was the support for the physician withholding treatment as strong as in the case of *Spring* v. *Massachusetts Supreme Judicial Court* in 1980.[13] In this case, the court not only upheld that an incompetent person has the same right to respect, dignity, and freedom of choice as competent people, but also it took it upon itself to send a message to treating physicians: "little need be said about criminal liability; there is precious little precedent, and what there is suggests that the doctor will be protected if he acts in a good faith judgment that is not grievously unreasonable by medical standards."

Legal scholar Dr. Alan Meisel, professor of law and medicine, University of Pittsburgh and the author of the *Right to Die* legal compendium in 1989, summed up a developing legal consensus in an article in 1992.[14] He indicated that the bulk of court opinions have been generally supportive of a general principle that determination of the futility of care is a decision to be made by the medical profession. These opinions would suggest that physicians are under no obligation to seek consent from patients or families before withholding or withdrawing care that is deemed ineffective. Nevertheless, we strongly recommend that physicians communicate adequately with patients and families at all times. Also, physicians are not exposing themselves to legal liability if their decision is reasonable by conventional medical standards and in good faith.

WITHHOLDING TREATMENT: WHO DECIDES

Occasionally, court decisions have not supported the autonomy of health-care professionals to make decisions regarding appropriate medical intervention. Take the case of Helga Wanglie, an eighty-seven-year-old Minnesota woman, maintained in an unconscious state by the use of a ventilator.[15] In 1989, Mrs. Wanglie was hospitalized for a hip fracture. During that hospitalization, she sustained a series of pneumonia attacks for which she had to be placed on a ventilator. She was weaned off the ventilator and transferred to nursing-home care. She suffered cardiac arrest and was resuscitated. This intervention left her in a persistent deep coma, with machine-assisted ventilation and a stomach tube for feeding. The hospital physicians deemed her case hopeless and advised the discontinuation of assisted ventilation. Her husband refused to have her disconnected from the ventilator. The court upheld his decision as a reasonable and loving act. Clearly, Mr. Wanglie could not bear to allow his wife, his lifelong companion, to die. The problem in this case appears to have been that the hospital asked to remove Mr. Wanglie as surrogate and guardian for Mrs. Wanglie on the basis of incompetence. The court found Mr. Wanglie to be competent and, therefore, his decision was upheld. Interestingly, Drs. Veatch and Mason-Spicer, from the Kennedy Institute of Ethics at Georgetown University, argued in 1993 that the treatment in this case should not be viewed as medically futile, as long as it postponed the moment of death. They engaged in lengthy philosophical argument of what constitutes "medical versus normative" futility. At any rate, the court was convinced and ordered the hospital to continue ventilator treatment for Mrs. Wanglie. Her heart stopped beating a few days later.

Also, in the 1987 case of *Evans* v. *Bellevue Hospital,* a New York court refused to order the termination of intravenous treatment for the comatose patient's AIDS-related infection, in spite of the directives in his living will. The court's reason was that "[a]lthough the underlying disease is incurable, the specific infection is treatable with drugs." This ruling caused a firestorm among the AIDS community, the press, and the medical profession.[16] The prevailing sentiment was that the court ruling undermined the patient's right to refuse treatment under any circumstances, let alone when such treatment serves only to prolong the process of an inevitable and imminent dying.

CONFLICTING CASES

Subsequently, many cases were brought to court in which family members demanded the continuation of life-support measures in spite of a determination that the treatment was deemed futile on medical grounds. The rulings, in many cases, were to continue assisted ventilation. As expected, most of these cases involved individuals who died days or weeks after the rulings, and after several hundred thousand wasted dollars. Some patients, however, lingered on for months or years, with no medical benefit in sight. The ultimate in contradiction is seen in the rulings regarding M. Saikewicz in 1977[17] and the case of Baby K in 1993.[18] In the Baby K case, the court ruled for unreasonable treatment. In the Saikewicz case, the court ruled against an eminently reasonable treatment.

Mr. Saikewicz was a mentally retarded, institutionalized young man from Massachusetts. He developed leukemia, a form of cancer of the blood cells that, that with proper treatment, has a good chance for cure. Physicians who diagnosed Mr. Saikewicz's condition recommended that the treatment be initiated as soon as possible. Mr. Saikewicz's appointed guardian refused on the basis that the treatment was fairly intrusive, requiring injections and intravenous infusions that would have required Mr. Saikewicz to be confined to bed for several hours every day while receiving the medication. Furthermore, it was argued that the treatment might have very disagreeable side effects of nausea, fever, and vomiting. The physicians argued in court that Mr. Saikewicz's guardian was being unreasonable in denying the patient potentially curative treatment. The court upheld the guardian's request citing that, the "best interests of the patient would be served by not treating his leukemia. The negative factors of treatment outweighed the benefits, and it would be in Joseph Saikewicz's best interests not to undergo treatment."

By contrast, in the case of Baby K of Fairfax, Virginia, the mother refused to terminate her pregnancy, despite the prenatal diagnosis of anencephaly, or lack of a brain.[19] Babies with anencephaly uniformly die within days or weeks of birth. Baby K was born by caesarian section on October 13, 1992. Baby K would never grow up to see, hear, feel, or be aware of anything. The mother was not married to the father, who was opposed to efforts to keep the baby alive. Baby K needed to be maintained on a ventilator. The hospital decided to wait a reasonable time in the hope that the family would realize that aggressive treatment should be terminated. The medical staff informed the mother that no treatment existed for the anencephalic condition and that no therapeutic or palliative purpose was served by the use of a ventilator. The mother continued to insist on ventilator treatment against the advice of many. The hospital attempted to resolve the matter through the legal system.

The hospital's request to cease therapeutic intervention was supported by the American Academy of Pediatrics, the expert board on children's medicine. In spite of this, the court ruled in favor of the mother, citing

> The use of a mechanical ventilator to assist breathing is not "futile" or "inhumane" in relieving the acute symptoms of respiratory difficulty. . . . To hold otherwise would allow hospitals to deny emergency treatment to numerous classes of patients, such as accident victims or those who have cancer or AIDS, on the grounds that they eventually will die anyway from those diseases and that emergency care for them would, therefore, be "futile."

Then the judge referred to Baby K's anencephaly as a handicap or disability. He further affirmed that the mother's decision would have been scrutinized only if the family had sought to terminate or withhold medical treatment for a minor or incompetent adult. In this case, the mother's strong Christian conviction was that all life has value and should be protected. She also believed that God, rather than human beings, should determine the moment of death. Baby K lived for two and a half years, much of which was maintained on the ventilator.

As usual, medical ethicists weighed in on both sides of the issue. Included in the court records is Dr. Grodin's view on this intervention, with which I agree: "Sustaining the life of an anencephalic baby is the ultimate inappropriate use of health care resources." On the other hand, Dr. Robert Veatch, the dean of the Kennedy Institute of Ethics in Washington, D.C., who testified on behalf of Baby K, while conceding that an anencephalic baby should be regarded as brain dead, raised the following philosophical question: "Whether there is value in preserving a vegetative life is not a technical question to be left to *experts*. It is a matter of personal philosophy, religion, and judgment." The court ruling was based upon the testimony of Dr. Veatch.

These unusual and bewildering decisions could have been averted had we, as a society, accepted the concept that death occurs in the event of higher brain death with irretrievable loss of consciousness and cognition, or in the case of irreversibly unconscious or "never to become conscious" individuals.

"A CONSCIENCE OF SCIENCE" THAT TRANSCENDS CASE-BY-CASE RULINGS

This lack of general agreement in court decisions reflects the legal practice of dealing with issues on a case-by-case basis. Court cases differentiate what is legally right from what is legally wrong based upon specific circumstances and not upon criteria and definitions accepted by the society at large. Society cannot, however, hold the legal establishment responsible for the lack of guidelines. To some extent, the medical establishment should be held responsible for these conflicting, incomplete, and often puzzling legal decisions. The medical community has failed to educate society and pioneer the adoption of general principles and standards. Yes, these are very complex issues that cannot possibly be reduced to headlines, sound bites, or slogans. Yes, we live in a society with an ever-present fear of being misunderstood, misinterpreted, or misquoted. Yes, incomplete information, distorted information, or misinformation is rampant. Although these fears are not groundless, they cannot justify the dangerous dissociation of the medical establishment from the society-at-large. To quote John Galbraith, the noted Harvard economist, author, and professor emeritus, "Although there is no religion of science, there should be a conscience of science, a scientific code regarding the uses to which inventions are put, in order to warn politicians and the public of their terrible consequences." We, as a medical community, must not continue to adopt and implement new and more powerful tools of technology without conscious regard to the consequences of our actions. We can no longer afford to have our medical technology outrun the ethical context in which it should be practiced.

We should heed the experience of many European countries, including The Netherlands and Denmark.[20] There are ethics councils in these two countries composed mainly of people from the mainstream public whose overriding charge is to guide public policy and community debates in health-care issues. In these two countries, upper-brain death (or absence of an upper brain) is accepted as death, as it is in many other European countries. In these societies, withholding or withdrawing treatment is to be expected and goes unchallenged once higher brain functions have been irretrievably lost. This change of attitude has occurred even in Germany, where citizens have been ridden by guilt for the atrocities committed by their countrymen during World War II, and presumably have been reluctant to precipitously define guidelines for allowing death. Consequently, they had strict laws against discontinuation of life-support measures. On September 13, 1994, Germany's constitutional court ruled that doctors could withdraw treatment from terminally ill patients and thereby hasten their death, as long as this was the patient's wish.

Can rational, systematic, well-thought-out policies be enacted in the United States? Or have we become as the cynics like to describe America: a wasteful, extremely individualistic, heterogeneous, medication-loving, procedure-avid, technology-driven, death-denying country? Is it possible that we, in America, can achieve public consensus on issues of life and death without sloganizing or politicizing the matter? Can we agree on a set of standards that guide our care during the sunset of our lives without fear of the heavy hand of the law or interference by men of zeal, well-meaning but with poor understanding? My hope is that this book will offer guidelines for achieving a consensus on life-and-death matters.

10

DOES THE "LIVING WILL" DESERVE TO LIVE?

❦

> It's not that I'm afraid to die, I just don't want to be there when it happens.
>
> Woody Allen, *He Is Still Alive: Death*, 1975

I n over forty years of medical practice, I have taken care of tens of thousands of people. I have talked with many about life-and-death issues. I have lectured about advance medical directives and have held many public forums about this subject matter.

In many instances, during my medical practice, I entered a note in the patient's chart indicating his or her preferences when life is coming to a close and when death is near or imminent. In other instances, patients have brought me signed and notarized documents, instructing me as to what I should and should not do. In most cases, I included the documents in the patient's chart but also had a private talk with the patient about the subject matter. I often discovered that what the patient really meant was not clearly expressed in the signed, notarized document. Without exception, a patient who hands you a living will wants to tell you "When the end is near and inevitable, make me comfortable, make this final event as short, painless, and peaceful as possible. Most importantly, I want to be assured that I will not become a burden on the ones I love, and I want to be remembered as a person worthy of respect."

In this country, we all cherish our autonomy. I am no exception. I want to take part in treatment decisions at all times, including when I am near the end of my life. True, my wife knows exactly how I feel about life-and-death issues, as do my children and my treating physicians. Nevertheless, I wanted to leave my wishes expressed clearly in writing. To me, this is a most serious business. I have cancer. Even though it is now in remission, I am afraid I might end up dying a horrible death.

I spent hours drafting what I thought was a document that reflected my feelings and covered in detail the possible medical contingencies. After all, I am a physician, and I have unlimited access to medical literature.

In preparation for writing this document, I learned all there was to be learned about my affliction: cancer of the prostate. But I also realized then that I, as a sixty-two-year-old male, could have a heart attack; consequently, this contingency was covered also. It is possible that I might be involved in an accident, have a stroke, or develop another cancer. I covered it all, developing what I thought was a model, water-tight, multipage advance directive. I took it to my lawyer to have it witnessed and notarized.

My lawyer's secretary greeted me with a beautiful smile and asked that I leave the document for review. She advised me that Mr. Smith (not his real name) would deliver the notarized document to my office on his way home. Sure enough, the next day, my friend, Mr. Smith, delivered a document, but not the one I authorized. What an insult, I thought!

I read the form delivered to me and recognized that it was the standard Oklahoma Advance Directive. I became livid. How dare Mr. Smith do that to me! He had totally ignored my original request for him to notarize my own, original living will, the one that I had painstakingly composed and substituted it with this document, written in legal jargon with thirteen signature entries. I visited Mr. Smith and conveyed my dissatisfaction, disappointment, and dismay while I struggled hard to repress my anger. He said, "Your will is not valid in Oklahoma. It is not binding. It will not stand up in court." He added that the one he sent me is the one he has been using for other clients. It is the standard, new and revised Oklahoma Advance Directive. It conforms with the Oklahoma Rights of the Terminally or Persistently Unconscious Act and is designed to protect the most vulnerable in society against possible abuse. I indicated to Mr. Smith that I am not afraid of being neglected or undertreated. On the contrary, I have composed my directive document in order to avoid an unnecessarily harsh death—to protect myself against unwelcome interventions that would serve only to transform my dying into a medical nightmare. I want to live a full life, I added, but end it with a good dying to the extent possible. I suggested to him, politely, that we execute another, somewhat more generic form of a living will. I chose a standard will that I have used for some patients. I have adapted this document from an earlier one suggested by Sissela Bok, the noted medical ethicist, in 1976 and published in the *New England Journal of Medicine*.[1] It reads

> I, *L. Basta*, want to participate in my own medical care as long as I am able. But I recognize that an accident or illness may some day make me unable to do so. Should this come to be the case, this document is intended to direct those who make choices on my behalf. I have prepared it while still legally competent and of sound mind. If these instructions create a conflict with the desires of my relatives, or with hospital policies or with the principles of those providing my care, I ask that my instructions prevail. I wish to live a full and long life, but not at all costs. If my death is near and cannot be avoided, or if I have lost the ability to interact with others and have no reasonable chance of regaining this ability, such as in severe dementia or extensive stroke, or if my suffering is intense and irreversible, such as with disseminated carcinoma or advanced decrepitude or if I have become permanently dependent upon others for my feeding and personal hygiene, I do not want to have my life prolonged. I would then ask not to be subjected to surgery or resuscitation. Nor would I then wish to have life support from mechanical ventilators, intensive-care services, or other life-prolonging procedures, including the administration of antibiotics, blood products, and/or artificial feeding and hydration. I ask that this applies to any and all medical complications whether related or unrelated to my original condition and regardless of whether these complications may seem reversible such as pneumonia, bleeding, or a heart attack. I would wish, rather, to have care that brings peace and comfort, even if it hastens the moment of death, and which facilitates my interaction with others to the extent that is possible, and which brings peace. In order to carry out these instructions and to interpret them, I authorize *Laila Basta* to accept, plan, and refuse treatment on my behalf in cooperation with attending physicians and health personnel. This person knows how I value the experience of living, and how I would weigh incompetence, dependence, pain, suffering, and dying. Should it be impossible to reach this person, I authorize *Victor or Steve Basta* to make such choices for me. I have discussed my desires concerning terminal care with them, and I trust their judgment on my behalf.

Date: _____ Signed: _____

Witnessed by: _____

And by: _____

Mr. Smith was less displeased with this form but was demonstrably concerned. After a short pause, he warned, "Do you know that this document gives too much power to your wife?" In an apologetic tone he added, "I know that you have a good marriage, but I would not recommend this form to my clients."

I responded by acknowledging the document's shortcomings. It requires a rare level of understanding and open communication between spouses. Few spouses have the capacity not only to understand, but also to undertake the hard life-and-death decisions in absolute conformity with that of their loved one. I assured Mr. Smith that my wife and children understood my value system and that I trust them to make the right decisions on my behalf.

I added that for many people, a more detailed medical-scenario–specific document may be preferable.

I gave my lawyer, for reference, another form suggested in 1989 by Drs. Ezekiel and Linda Emanuel, directors of the program in ethics and professors at the Kennedy School of Government, Harvard University, realizing that this form appears quite complex. It covers four different scenarios of terminal illness, coma, persistent vegetative state, and advanced dementia (such as Alzheimer's disease). There are twelve different entries that go with each choice. Although this document has been well formulated, my patients—including the better educated among them—found it quite confusing and/or were intimidated by it.[2]

At present, we recommend a different and more simple, medical-scenario–specific document that was developed by Project GRACE for universal use. A copy of this document is included in the appendix and more will be discussed about it later.

THE LIMITATIONS OF EXISTING LIVING WILLS

There are multiple and major problems with currently used forms of advance directives. These problems are elaborated on in many studies. First, there is the problem of ambiguous language. When wills talk about disability, what do they mean—loss of a limb, a small stroke, dimmed eyesight, failing hearing? What is meant by mental disability? Is this simple depression, forgetfulness, or total dependence? What specifically is meant by artificial means and does the document proscribe all artificial intervention? An artificial pacemaker for an otherwise healthy heart might give an individual ten or more additional happy years; an artificial joint may significantly improve a miserable existence and enable mobility and travel. What is meant by heroic measures? An otherwise healthy person afflicted with severe pneumonia may have to be assisted by a ventilator for a few days to affect a cure; this is an eminently reasonable form of heroic action. Assisted ventilation may also be a lifesaver in a curable episode of asthma, laryngitis, or reversible muscle paralysis. What does it mean when people talk about hopeless pain? With medicines available at our disposal today, there should rarely be such a thing. The vague description of disability (physical or mental) has rendered the living will legally unbinding, ethically problematic, and medically too ambiguous to be effective.

Another problem is the limited use a "living will" has in directing medical intervention. Standard forms of "living wills" have been transformed from "personal testaments" into "legal documents" drafted by lawyers written in legal jargon to be binding in courts. A common person would not be able to decipher the language and is often intimidated by the wordiness of the document. They are supposedly designed to direct physicians to withhold or withdraw care when the patient is *in extremis*. Because of this transformed design, they have little place, if any, in directing the treatment of patients, either because they do not anticipate all medical contingencies or they apply only when the treatment has proven futile and death is imminent, with our without intervention.

WHEN DISREGARDING A LIVING WILL IS ETHICAL

To further illustrate some of the difficulties with living wills, let me cite the following cases.

I recall a sixty-three-year-old woman with no children of her own who was admitted to the hospital for treatment for a type of irregular heartbeat that is ordinarily neither fatal nor crippling. The patient arrived with her nephew, a handsome and articulate young man. She emphasized, "First of all, I want you to know that I do not want to be kept alive by artificial or heroic means. I am ready to go when my time comes. Also, I brought my nephew, who is a lawyer, to make sure that you honor my wishes." She handed me a notarized piece of paper—a generic "living will."

I assured her that she was quite healthy except for this new irregular heart rhythm. I did not see any reason for her to talk about death at present. Her condition at the time was not serious, but I did fully understand her wishes, which would be honored at the appropriate time. We started the patient on a medicine that regulates heart rhythm. The medicine is a derivative of quinine and is called quinidine.

Just to prepare the reader for what is coming, I will point out that a very small percentage (less than 5 percent or 1 in 20) of patients placed on this medicine develop a much more serious heart rhythm disturbance, called *torsades de pointes*, which can be lethal and must be treated as an emergency. Sometimes electric shocks, or *cardioversion*, must be delivered to the heart to jolt it back to normalcy. No doubt, many people would consider electric cardioversion to be a heroic measure; all would consider it a form of resuscitation. Sure enough, at 3:00 A.M., the nurse called me to declare that Mrs. Jones had developed three episodes of *torsades de pointes*. She lost consciousness during two of them and required electroconversion (electric shock resuscitation). We continued our efforts to control this life-threatening heart irregularity, knowing full well that we had disobeyed, to the letter, the patient's living will that we had pledged to honor. Would it have been more appropriate to allow this lady to die of complications caused by our treatment when such a complication could be overcome and reversed?

Mrs. Jones recovered. She is still active, and as far as I can tell, is able to enjoy life as much as before. On her most recent six-month visit to my office, she reiterated how happy she was to be alive and well.

Consider next the case of Mr. Hall, who gave me a copy of his "advance directive." This document clearly indicated that, when the moment came, he did not want to be kept alive by artificial means. Subsequently, Mr. Hall passed out while mowing the lawn. His son started CPR and the ambulance brought him to the emergency room. When I saw him, he was pale and lethargic but not comatose. He could respond to questions in a feeble voice with slow, shaky, short phrases. He was clammy and sweat beads covered his face. His heart was beating very slowly, less than thirty beats per minute (the normal is about seventy beats per minute), which barely sustained him. A thorough evaluation revealed that he had no other major health problem. The EKG showed that the electric pathways of his heart were decayed, but the heart muscle was still intact. The heart is like a car motor and needs the equivalent of a battery, spark plugs, and electric wiring to initiate the heartbeats. Also, the heart needs its gas pipes, the coronary arteries, to bring gas to the motor, the heart muscle. One can have an intact motor but bad wiring, or in other situations, bad gas pipes, which are referred to as hardening of the arteries. I explained the problem to Mrs. Hall, Mr. Hall Jr., and to the rest of the family; all agreed on Mr. Hall's behalf to place a permanent pacemaker in his heart. Twelve years have passed and Mr. Hall is still alive and active, thanks to "artificial means"—an artificial pacemaker placed in his heart.

Finally, consider Mr. Wood, who is a lay leader in our church. Mr. Wood is alive today because of two separate bypass operations—the first performed in 1985 and the second in 1991. Mr. Wood's brother was not as fortunate. He suffered a heart attack that resulted in massive upper-brain damage. He slipped into a deep coma and was maintained on a ventilator in the intensive care unit until he died a few weeks later.

After this sad experience, my friend, Mr. Wood, asked me to let him go in peace if his heart stopped. That was three years ago. A year later, Mr. Wood started to experience smothering chest pains with the least amount of exertion. The pains became more frequent, lasted longer, and started to awake him from sleep. I suggested that we repeat the coronary angiograms (pictures of his blood vessels) in order to study his heart arteries and the bypass grafts. In a bypass operation, one blood vessel, such as a leg vein that is not blocked, is used to "bypass" a coronary (heart) artery that is blocked. The angiogram showed that one of the bypass grafts had developed severe narrowing. I recommended that we open it up with a procedure called *balloon angioplasty* and *stenting*, in which a balloon inflates the blocked artery and a scaffold in the form of a metal coil is inserted to keep the vessel open. He agreed to it. A tiny balloon was advanced into the narrowed bypass vessel and positioned carefully in the middle of the narrowing. We inflated the balloon to open up the narrowed spot. Angioplasty causes a temporary interruption of blood flow and oxygen to the heart. The heart did not like the temporary cessation of blood flow, and it began beating irregularly, a condition known as *ventricular fibrillation*. The fact that the heart fibrillated (began beating in a disorganized fashion) is a common occurrence during a procedure such as the one we were performing. As a cardiologist, I may panic when I see somebody bleed from his nose, but not when I see a heart fibrillate. This is my territory.

In this situation, proper medical intervention involves deflating the balloon and shocking the heart. The use of electric-shock resuscitation will bring the patient back to life. Had we followed Mr. Wood's instructions, as set forth in his advance directive, electric shock would not have been used, and Mr. Wood would have been dead. Of course, I shocked the heart.

All these real-life instances serve as cautionary tales: Living wills should *never* be implemented blindly; neither should they be disregarded completely. Theoretically, a poorly worded living will could result in withholding useful therapy about which the patient has not been fully informed. I do not know of any such cases and have never heard of any. This hazard may become real, I fear, with the mounting pressures to limit medical treatment costs in a managed-care environment. Should that ever happen, it will be a real tragedy!

ABIDING BY THE SPIRIT, RATHER THAN THE LETTER, OF THE LIVING WILL

A competent patient has the right to refuse treatment, but such refusal has to be predicated upon that patient having full information about all possible scenarios relevant to his or her condition. The patient should also be able to comprehend and evaluate these scenarios and the therapeutic options. Given these strict provisions, there will still arise scenarios that are deemed remote at the time. Not infrequently, physicians are faced with complications that would have been only remotely possible and even inconceivable in the course of treatment.

Advance directives, as well intentioned as they might be, do not allow for all possible contingencies, as stated previously. Therefore, living wills should not be taken literally and should never be implemented blindly unless the patient is terminally ill or permanently unconscious. In most of these latter cases, treatment should be deemed futile whether or not a living will exists. This position is supported by many scholars, among whom is Dr. Wicclair, the noted author of *Ethics and the Elderly*.[3]

THE LIMITATION OF LIMITED ACCESS

Another problem with living wills is the limited access that emergency health-care professionals have to them. I cannot recount how many times an emergency call results in an ambulance dispatch. Emergency medical technicians encounter a person who has recently died (i.e., has experienced cessation of heartbeat and breathing). CPR is initiated at the scene, and the patient is transported to the emergency room. Although the patient is found to be unconscious, further resuscitative measures revive the heart. Later, family members show up to tell me that Mr. X had a living will. It's too late. You cannot reverse the course of events until you are satisfied that the resuscitation treatment (which was started without the patient's consent in the first place) has proven futile. Presently, I advise my patients who do not wish to receive CPR to advise their loved ones not to call 911 in the event of cardiac arrest.

POWERS OF ATTORNEY: BE SURE TO EMPOWER THE RIGHT PERSON

We noted earlier that a durable power of attorney allows a designated person to make medical and legal decisions on behalf of an incompetent person. Again, this legal measure is far from perfect. The requests of the designated person must be evaluated carefully by the treating physician. Even if the patient gives a durable power of attorney to a close relative, directions from this surrogate should be followed only if they are deemed legally sound, morally just, and ethically right.

I experienced the imperfections of the durable power of attorney while treating a seventy-six-year-old woman, Mrs. Fields, who was admitted to the hospital because of transient ischemic brain attack, a mini-stroke. For a brief while, she lost eyesight in her left eye and developed some weakness of her right hand. She recovered. Upon examination, the stethoscope revealed noises heard over the big blood vessels on both sides of the neck, suggesting severe narrowing of these vessels carrying blood to the brain. This was further confirmed by an ultrasound imaging device. The amount of blood reaching the upper brain was barely keeping up with the needs of the brain. This is a condition that can be corrected with surgery that cleans up the artery; this procedure carries a low risk for the patient. Mrs. Fields refused medical intervention in spite of repeated pleas to consider surgery in order to prevent an imminent stroke. She asked to be discharged from the hospital and continued to smoke two to three packs of cigarettes daily. A week later, she developed paralysis on the right side of her body and lost her ability to speak. Because of difficulty in swallowing, a small tube was placed in her stomach to feed her. Throughout her illness, she never lost consciousness. She recognized her family and knew who I was. She watched sunsets in the evenings and woke up in the morning at regular hours. She expected her meals to be served on time and became angry at her attendant when they were late.

Mrs. Fields was a wealthy woman, a recognized socialite in the community. She looked and acted like a lady. She had the reputation of being very stubborn. A few weeks after she had the stroke, her daughter asked to see me in my office. "Why are you allowing my mother to be kept alive by artificial means? Don't you know that my mother would never have wanted to live like this? Unable to communicate . . . dependent . . . helpless . . . pathetic?" I tried to calm the daughter down, but she kept pounding on my desk and the decibels of her voice became higher and higher as she continued to express dissatisfaction with my care. I waited until she finished and asked her to sit down. Then I spoke, "As far as I'm concerned, your mother is alive. She is able to appreciate people and things. Her consciousness is substantially intact and her ability to reason appears to be preserved to some extent. She has passions that she shares and desires that she expects to be fulfilled, and she appears to derive pleasure from being alive. You may not consider this to be an acceptable quality of life, but that is your view, and it might have been your mother's view prior to this stroke. But who am I and who are you to judge whether a life is worth living? It would have been different if your mother had lost her personhood completely and her existence depended upon the function of her brain stem. But as long as she has some attributes that constitute personhood—consciousness, awareness, and feelings to share—she has all the rights that you and I cherish. We owe that to our shared humanity. If you do not agree with me, ask me to cease to be your mother's physician." She stood up and left. I have not heard from her since.

WHEN THE LIVING WILL
DOES NOT GO FAR ENOUGH

Consider another case that illustrates yet another limitation of existing living wills. Mrs. Morgan, an eighty-six-year-old woman, was brought from the nursing home for my consultation. The attendant noted that Mrs. Morgan, a widow with no children, was passing blood with her stools. While competent, she executed a standard, state-approved advance directive. The directive pertained to terminal illness, imminent death, comas, and persistent vegetative state. She had been placed in the nursing home by her niece, who could not cope with her aunt's severely deteriorated mental status. Recently, she was confused all the time. She could not tell the time, day, or year. She did not remember her late husband's name, and her vocabulary became limited to a few words that she uttered incoherently. Still, she could feel pain, cold, heat, and hunger. Her condition did not conform to the provisions of the signed living will that proscribed medical intervention. In order to find the cause of bleeding, the physician attending Mrs. Morgan performed a procedure and subsequently discovered a tumor that, upon further examination, proved to be cancer. It took the attending physician two days to locate Mrs. Morgan's niece, who lived in another state; she was too busy to leave work for a few days but wanted everything that was medically necessary to be done.

Since Mrs. Morgan was anemic, she required blood transfusions. Major surgery was used to remove her cancerous colon. During the surgery, a metastatic nodule, another form of spreading cancer, was noted to have lodged in her liver. Surgery was followed by a cascade of complications. Mrs. Morgan became delirious, belligerent, and combative, requiring constant sedation. Restraints were placed on both wrists to prevent movement. She developed acute pneumonia, because she was unable to clear her lungs with a productive cough. She was placed on a ventilator. She required several antibiotics that caused her sluggish kidneys to deteriorate further. Because she was bedridden for several days, a clot formed in a major vein in her right leg. The clot became loose and traveled to the blood vessel supplying her lungs. A special filter was placed in the big vein in her belly to prevent further clots from migrating toward the heart. The kidneys continued to deteriorate. Her heart showed signs of failure, and she died after over three weeks of enormous suffering.

One cannot help but ask why a person who is only able to experience pain should be subjected to all of this torture? For what purpose? Would it not have been more humane to let her die peacefully in her sleep? Was her niece acting in the patient's best interest?

EMPOWERING THE POWERLESS

Human frailty in the person empowered to carry out someone's living will can also foil the intent of this document as it stands today. Consider the case of Mr. Harrison: "They wouldn't let him die!" his daughter tearfully told me, in a broken voice, the first time I met her. I reached out to a box of tissue, picked up a handful, and handed them to her. She wiped away her tears and pointed to a picture on the wall. "My poor dad, the doctors wouldn't let him die!" she said. I looked at the picture. There was a handsome, tall man with an overpowering figure. She went on to tell me about her eighty-six-year-old father.

Mr. Harrison was a dignified, proud man. He enjoyed golf, fishing, and hunting, which he had engaged in regularly until two years ago. His beloved wife died after a long, debilitating battle with cancer; they had been married for sixty-two years. He became reclusive and was overtaken by grief. His prolonged bereavement culminated in a stroke that left his right side paralyzed. He was unable to express himself verbally or through writing, a huge blow to his dignity. Mr. Harrison was moved to his daughter's house. The loving daughter attended to his needs with devotion. But all the fun in life was over for Mr. Harrison. He cried with the least provocation and, at times, without any apparent reason.

At one time, his daughter recalled that he pointed to a toy gun and put his left index finger to his head, as if to say, "I wish you would help me put an end to this prolonged unhappiness." He could not reciprocate gestures of love and caring and his life, according to his daughter, became devoid of fun, love, or dignity.

Mr. Harrison had executed a notarized living will and granted his daughter power of attorney for health-care decisions. Twice that year, Mr. Harrison was admitted to the hospital for treatment of pneumonia. Pneumonia is a treatable condition and, in Mr. Harrison's case, his condition was neither hopeless nor terminal. During the previous hospital admission, Mr.

Harrison had to be placed on a ventilator for three days, but this time his pneumonia was treated early enough. Mr. Harrison had spent ten days in the hospital and it was time to bring him back home. I asked the daughter whether she was certain that her father would not have preferred to die of pneumonia. Promptly, she answered "yes." She sighed and continued: "But he never asked me before he had the stroke to allow him to die of pneumonia if he became totally dependent. This much I know: If that were me in his place, I wouldn't have chosen to go on like this. I love him." I held her shoulder as a gesture of encouragement. To this day, I cannot forget her words: "A life devoid of fun, true love, and dignity is a fate worse than death." Nevertheless, when a tough but humane medical decision needed to be made, the daughter was incapable of doing so; she lacked the ability to make the tough decision.

These cases are illustrative of ordinary events and not the extraordinary; they represent everyday encounters in the life of a busy practitioner.

Patients execute living wills with the intention to spare themselves and their loved ones indignity, pain, and expense at the end of life. But "living wills," in their present form, fall short of producing the desired benefits and do not avert the horrible consequences that they were designed to prevent in the first place. The medical profession's prevailing attitude is to interpret the living will with great caution. The ever-present fear of litigation from erroneously second-guessing a patient's intentions causes an overcautious and often guarded interpretation of the living will. Also, whenever family members wish to override the document in favor of medical interventions, physicians have tended to go along with more, albeit marginally beneficial, medical care.

Consider the last two cases discussed. Did the niece of Mrs. Morgan and the daughter of Mr. Harrison not act properly? In the case of Mrs. Morgan, it can be argued that the niece did not have much interaction with her aunt, was too disengaged to properly evaluate her aunt's situation, and took the safest course available: My aunt has cancer; let's have the cancer removed. In the case of Mr. Harrison, the daughter knew that her father would not have wished to linger in his state of dependence. She loved him but could not find the courage within herself to ask the attending physician to forgo treatment of pneumonia with the temporary use of assisted ventilation.

LIVING WILLS—NO SUBSTITUTE FOR
NATIONAL GUIDELINES ON LIFE AND DEATH

Durable powers of attorney and living wills, as they stand now, remind us of our failure as a medical profession in the face of technological advances, and they provide an indictment of our society and its legal system for not instituting clean and consistent guidelines for treatment that is deemed inappropriate at the end of life. It is morally outrageous for citizens to have to go to the trouble of executing a document that has the semblance of legal power in order to tell the treating physicians "I have seen others who had horrible deaths as a result of unrelenting pursuit of high-tech interventions. Please spare me the agony." It need not be this way. It is sad that decent people are denied a decent way to exit life in peace. And the saddest indictment of all is the indisputable fact that the medical establishment, guided by esoteric, diametrically opposed ethical pronouncements or fearful of legal consequences, has consistently failed to respond to the incessant pleas of rational citizens. I was horrified to hear the secretary of my friend, the chief of cardiac surgery, describe her worst nightmare to me: "My daughter has leukemia. All attempts to cure her, including a bone-marrow transplant, have failed." Then with tears in her eyes and a choked voice, she continued, "I know that her death is near and in a few months, she will be no more. She is at home engaging in her favorite hobbies. But my greatest fear is that someday, if she is found dead or unconscious, the ambulance will be called and she will be revived. My nightmare is that she will be placed on a ventilator and enslaved by machines for weeks on end before she is pronounced dead." She went on to say, "I have put signs all over the house that indicate that I do not want such a horrible end for my daughter," and as tears flowed down her cheeks, she continued, "I love her so much!"

How amazing is our present state of medicine? Are we incapable of taming our high-tech instruments so that they serve our human needs? Have we rendered ourselves passive slaves to a monster that we have created? In a recent conference on the care of patients with heart disease, I asked 200 nurses attending the conference as to their personal preferences regarding terminal care. Of these, 98 percent did not want to be resuscitated if the chance of subsequent recovery and independence is less than

5 percent, and none wished to be subjected to CPR when the chance for a favorable outcome is less than 1 percent. Nevertheless, the present standard for CPR is to resuscitate everyone with a cardiac arrest anywhere, in or out of the hospital, often without regard for their wishes.

The weakness of contemporary living wills should be obvious by now. In the first place, they are designed to assert one's autonomy in making decisions for health care. In the second place, they are intended to preserve one's dignity at the end of life, spare one unnecessary intrusive interventions, and in many instances, relieve loved ones of the burden of excessive cost for futile care. They fail on both counts.

The concept of patient autonomy overrides all other considerations from an ethicist's point of view. But is this really practical? It is true that a competent patient has the right to refuse treatment. But what percentage of competent people refuse rational treatment aimed at redeeming their health and well-being? What percentage of patients faced with complex health problems are able to evaluate various medical scenarios and choose their treatment from that menu? In many cases, there is one best option, and almost always patients elect that option, particularly when they have a trusting relationship with their doctor. The best means to preserve a meaningful autonomy for the patient is to foster that sacred doctor-patient relationship. This relationship, however, is threatened by extinction in our business-like environment, with its HMOs and other managed-care alliances.

In the situation in which the patient is unconscious or becomes incompetent, the best way to treat him or her should be to apply the "best interest standard." The perspective that allows proxy decision making is deeply flawed, according to John Hardwig, of the program in medical ethics, College of Medicine, East Tennessee State University.[4] Surrogates are often guided by their own feelings rather than by the desire of the patient they represent. Their decisions are often tainted by feelings of guilt, fear of reproach, or desire for self-gain. Even genuine love can adversely affect a decision if the proxy is unable to let go.

Perhaps no one team has studied wills more than Drs. Ezekiel J. Emanuel and Linda L. Emanuel of the Kennedy School of Government, Harvard University. They have promoted the idea of the advance directive since its inception, proposed forms with various medical scenarios, and studied the effects of living wills on the practice of medicine. In two recent publications, "Advance Directives: What Have We Learned So Far," and "Advance Directives: Do They Work?" they reviewed the influence of living wills on patient care.[5] In the first place, only 25 percent of Americans have living wills and less than one-third of these have a provision for a durable power of attorney. Most revealing of all is that living wills achieve their intended results only when patients, their families, and their physicians have an open discussion about life-and-death issues that cover specific scenarios and detailed courses of action. And, I venture to say, the lucky ones among us who have such a relationship with their physicians and loved ones do not ever need to execute a living will. Many celebrities, such as former President Richard Nixon, former First Lady Jacqueline Kennedy Onassis and John Cardinal O'Connor had dignified deaths, in their comfortable beds, surrounded by loved ones. Numerous articles were written about how peaceful their deaths were, and many writers ascribed it to the fact that these individuals had executed a living will. No distortion can be further from the truth; their graceful exits had little to do with living wills and everything to do with the fact that they each knew exactly how they wanted to be treated at the end of life. They shared their views clearly and unequivocally with their families and physicians. They died on their own terms.

No testimonial for my thesis can lend stronger support than findings from the controlled trial to improve care for seriously ill, hospitalized patients: the SUPPORT study (Study to Understand Prognoses and Preferences for Outcomes and Risk of Treatments), published in 1995 in the *Annals of Internal Medicine*, and in 1994 in the *Journal of Clinical Ethics*.[6] This study evaluated whether advance directives (or the Patient Self-Determination Act) affect resuscitation decisions and the use of resources for seriously ill patients. The study involved over 3,000 patients treated in ten leading medical centers, including Harvard, Johns Hopkins, Duke, UCLA, and Case Western Reserve Universities. Researchers found no significant association between the existence of advance directives and decisions about resuscitation and concluded that advance directives (in their present form) were irrelevant to medical decision making near the end of life.

In a subsequent analysis from the SUPPORT study, Dr. J. M. Teno and his associates emphasized three main barriers to the use of advance directives.[7] One of these barriers is that advance directives are still not well integrated into our health-care system. It is true that the Patient Self-Determination Act passed by Congress has required that living wills, durable powers of attorney for health care, and Do Not Attempt Resuscitation orders be included in the patient's medical records. The SUPPORT study has shown, however, that even when these documents are included in the medical records, they had little impact on medical care. Researchers noted that patient preferences toward cardiopulmonary resuscitation (CPR) were not translated into practice and that among those who elected to forgo CPR, only half had Do Not Attempt Resuscitation orders written.

A second and important barrier to the use of advance directives is their lack of specificity. Dr. Teno and his associates analyzed the contents of 688 directives of patients in five hospitals. The vast majority (87 percent) of the documents had general statements indicating that the patients did not want to prolong dying through the application of heroic measures or artificial means. Only 13 percent went beyond the general statements; 5.6 percent had specific instructions about the use of life-sustaining treatment, and 3.2 percent referred to the patients' current medical situation. If one takes into account that only one-third of all hospital patients had advance directives, it follows that the document was useful in guiding medical treatment in one patient out of each hundred hospitalized with an end-of-life condition.

I cannot emphasize strongly enough that physicians are extremely squeamish about interpreting vague and nonspecific statements.

The third barrier to the effectiveness of advance directives is the difficulty of predicting when a given patient is near the end of life. Most advance directives embody the concept of not using life-sustaining measures when they would be futile. Difficulties arise when the documents require physicians to certify that the patient's condition is terminal. Others include statements of "certainty" or "no hope," or some such phrase. These conditions create impediments to the utility of advance directives and may perversely produce the exact opposite of an advance directive's desired purpose. Very few human judgments can stand the absolute certainty standard. Here, as in many other similar human endeavors, the "beyond reasonable doubt" standard should apply.

WHAT DO DYING PATIENTS WANT AND EXPECT?

A recent article titled "Quality End-of-Life Care, Patients' Perspectives" appeared in the *Journal of American Medical Association*. The authors acknowledged that "Quality end-of-life care is increasingly recognized as an ethical obligation of health care providers. However, this concept has not been examined from the perspective of patients."[8] The authors interviewed 126 patients belonging to three groups: those maintained on dialysis, sufferers of AIDS, and residents of long-term care facilities. Patients identified five domains of quality end-of-life care in the following order of importance:

- receiving adequate pain and symptom treatment
- avoiding inappropriate prolongation of dying
- achieving a sense of control
- relieving burden
- strengthening relationships with loved ones

The authors concluded, "these domains, which characterize patients' perspectives on end-of-life care, can serve as focal points for improving the quality of end-of-life care."[9]

WHERE IS THE APPROPRIATE PLACE FOR ADVANCE CARE PLANNING?

Based upon our current knowledge, we believe that an Advance Care Plan can be useful and even essential in guiding medical care during the last chapter of life.

It should be part of the routine health care of all concerned patients and be an integral component of the medical record. It should be a medical-scenario–specific document, yet, at the same time, written in simple English that is easily understood by patients.

A big gulf still exists between patients' way of expressing of their wishes and physicians' understanding. Patients should discuss their Advance Care Plan with their physician(s) and also with their appointed surrogates.

An Advance Care Plan should not be focused on medical futility at end-of-life. In fact, a treatment deemed futile should not be offered by physicians nor expected by the patient. Instead, an Advance Care Plan should focus on patients' own choices when a treatment is of marginal utility, for example, whereas intrusive medical intervention may be deemed futile in a patient with end-stage Alzheimer's disease, a patient in earlier stages of Alzheimer's disease *may elect* to forgo CPR, intrusive medical care for another incidental ailment, or even the treatment of a pneumonia.

An Advance Care Plan should be uniform within the community, portable from hospital to hospital and preferably, also from state to state. A central Internet-based registry for Advance Care Plans to which medical professionals can have immediate access will go a long way toward facilitating the use of Advance Care Plans.

Palliative care and alleviation of pain and suffering should be an integral part of care for dying patients, regardless of whether they have an Advance Care Plan. A partnership between physicians and the public and an intensive, coordinated program of public and professional education is essential to enhance the utility and effectiveness of Advance Care Plans.

11

THE DOCTOR-PATIENT RELATIONSHIP IS IN NEED OF REPAIR

❧

Some patients, though conscious that their condition is perilous, recover their health simply through their contentment with goodness of the physician.

Hippocrates, Precepts, ch. 6

A meaningful doctor-patient relationship is an imperative in order for patients, physicians, and society in general to deal with the enormous problems of end-of-life issues. Before I delve into this discussion any further, I would like to cite a doctor's perspective about the practice of medicine in past years as compared to the practice in contemporary times.

In his book, *Inside Medical Washington,* Dr. James Sammons, an influential physician who presided over the American Medical Association, describes his practice of thirty years ago in Baytown, Texas:

> It was a wonderful time to be a doctor in the United States. It was what I like to think of as the golden age of American medicine, a time when we were conquering disease and no advancement seemed out of the question or beyond our reach. . . . Unfettered by regulation that told us what we could or could not do, physicians simply went out and did it. In return, our patients had a strong degree of faith in their family physician, and that made it sheer pleasure to be a physician. There was very little government (or insurance company) interference in the practice of medicine.[1]

Contrast this with an editorial, "Case Management: A Disastrous Mistake," which appeared in a leading medical journal. The editor describes the ever-present peril of implementing a yet untested and hardly tried health-care system in the United Kingdom:

> Imagine a school which has been through some rocky times but whose
> staff was beginning to pull together at last. Suddenly, in an arbitrary
> attempt to raise standards and without prior testing, they are split up into
> teachers, who continue to provide education, and teaching assessors, who
> decide what should be taught and whether it is being provided effec-
> tively. The assessors are specialists in one subject only and yet they are put
> in a position of judging all their colleagues; their verdicts have no right
> of appeal. Any school that adopted a system like this would disseminate
> in rowdy rancor within weeks.[2]

The article further describes the managed-care system as an unworkable
system that will only alienate the medical profession from patients. Managed
care's sole objective is cost savings. Care for the elderly is a prime target for
reduced health-care resources. In the name of futility, or better still, marginal
utility, many medical services are expected to be cut. No doubt, there is
ample waste in our current health-care system. But one should fear the
fraudulent representations of much useful care as futile by health-care professionals, whose only criterion for care is cost-effectiveness. Consequently,
the greater fear is that the traditional trust between patient and doctor will
become irretrievably eroded. That would create a tense and hostile environment in which a once noble and esteemed profession falls into disgrace.

Unfortunately, the weighty issue of how these new health-care deliv-
eries will affect care for the elderly has been conspicuously left out of
national deliberation about health-care reform until very recently. A
health-care system that rewards physicians for providing less medical care
for their patients is a corrupt system. The motivation of even a well-intentioned practitioner who asks a patient to forsake a futile therapy may
become suspect under such a system. Decisions to limit care must be based
totally on the doctors' professional judgment and their unwavering devotion to the best interests of the patients. The moral weight of the doctor-
patient relationship should be taken seriously at all times.

HOW IS THE WORLD OF MANAGED CARE
CHANGING THE PRACTICE OF MEDICINE?

An article entitled "California's Anguished Doctors Revolt," appeared in
the British journal *Lancet* in 1995:

California's doctors are so aggrieved with their lot . . . with health care organizations and other intermediaries. These bodies have the power to pick and choose doctors and to determine which services will be provided. Contracts have been terminated suddenly, "gag" clauses in the contract prevent doctors from criticizing their employers' organization, and there are fears that a high proportion of doctors will find themselves out of a job in the next few years.[3]

As one of the doctors put it to a reporter, "We are just guppies in a tank of sharks that already control the market." Indeed, in today's medicine the doctor is different, the patient is different, and society is different. The more important question, however, is whether medicine's core values ought to change with the change of society. And how would that affect the treasured doctor-patient relationships and medical care at the end of life? The essence of medical practice is captured in the oath formulated by Hippocrates (c.460–400 B.C.E.), an oath that physicians take upon graduation from medical school:

I will use treatment to help the sick according to my ability and judgment, but never with a view to injure and wrongdoing. I will keep pure and holy both my life and my art. . . . In whatsoever houses I enter, I will enter to help the sick and I will abstain from all intentional wrongdoing and harm especially from abusing man or woman, bond or free. And whatsoever I shall see or hear in the course of my profession in my intercourse with men, if it be what should not be published abroad, I will never divulge, holding such things to be holy secrets.

Furthermore, the Hippocratic oath's instructions include the following:

Sometimes give your service for nothing, calling to mind a precious benefaction or present satisfaction. . . . For where there is love of man, there is also love of art. . . . For some patients, though conscious that their condition is perilous, recover their health simply through contentment with the goodness of the physician . . . and it is well to superintend the sick to *make them well,* to care for the healthy to *keep them well,* also to care for one's own self, so as to *observe what is seemly.*

The essence of the art of medicine derives from the pursuit of preserving health for those who are well, care for the sick and suffering, and comfort for the dying. Its values are guided by moderation, self-restraint, compassion, patience, understanding, discretion, and prudence. It demands truthfulness, sharing information with patients, compassion, encouragement, and fostering an appropriate measure of hope.

Leon Kass, Professor at the University of Chicago, in an article entitled, "Neither for Love nor Money: Why Doctors Must Not Kill," eloquently describes a professional:

> Professing oneself a professional is an ethical act for many reasons. It is an articulate public act, not merely a private and silent choice . . . a confession before others who are one's witnesses. It freely promises continuing devotion, not merely announces present preferences, to a way of life, not just a way of livelihood, a life of action not only of thought. It serves some high good, which calls forth devotion because it is both good and high, but which requires such devotion because its service is most demanding and difficult, and thereby engages one's character, not merely one's mind and hands.[4]

The doctor-patient relationship must be one of trust, predicated upon the patient's faith that his or her doctor's devotion to the patient's best interests is unconditional and unwavering. The patient expects his or her doctor to uphold the principles of devotion, respect, confidentiality, and beneficence. These principles are rooted in antiquity, centuries before Plato and Hippocrates. Ptah-Helep, the ancient Egyptian philosopher-physician, in his maxims dated 2000 B.C.E. instructed doctors "do not scoff the blind, do not forsake the lame, do not sneer at a man in the hand of God. Go unto him—do not abandon him."[5] The same qualities were ascribed to Asklepios, the Greco-Roman healer and hero of medical caring. According to the famed German-American scholars E. J. and L. Edelstein, Asklepios was an archetypical physician hero of the common people, not the aristocrats.[6] His honorific was "a great joy to men, a soother of cruel pangs and a lover of all people, regardless of station." An inscription at the Athenian temple to Asklepios on the Acropolis reads, "These are the duties of a physician . . . he would be like God savior equally of slaves, of paupers, of rich men, of princes, and to all a brother, such help he would give."[7] These same tenets are found in Plato's *Republic*: "No physician in-so-far as he is a physician, considers his own good in what he prescribes, but the good of his patient; for the true physician is also a ruler having the human body as a subject, and is not a mere money-maker."[8]

Will this sacred bond between patient and doctor endure in a society in which the rights of man became the rights of consumers? Will it survive in the new schemes of managed care with their relentless focus on limiting expenditure rather than on diverting resources to the severely ill?

Despite medical advances on an unprecedented scale, despite changes in societal and institutional methods of health-care delivery, the essence of medicine remains unaltered since the days of Hippocrates: Healthy people desire to maintain their health, the ill desire to be whole, and the terminally ill seek comfort and encouragement. The contract between patient and doctor is one that seeks to promote wellness for the healthy and wholeness for the one who is ailing. Wholeness, it must be emphasized, means that the body is working sufficiently well, its powers to sense, think, feel, desire, move, and maintain self are intact. Since man walked on the face of the earth and was able to appreciate the mysteries of life, death, and the universe, he searched for ways to deal with illness recognizing the limits of medicine and the inevitability of dying. Again, since the time of Hippocrates, the healer was advised to refrain from advising treatment that is not aimed at a degree of wholeness as expressed in the Hippocratic Corpus: "Whenever the illness is too strong for the available remedies, the physician surely must not expect that it can be overcome by medicine. To attempt futile treatment is to display an ignorance that is allied to madness."[9]

Also, Plato reminds us in *The Republic*, "For those whose lives are always in a state of inner sickness, Asklepios, the divine physician of ancient Greece did not attempt to prescribe a regime that would only make their life a prolonged misery."

No wonder the noted Georgetown physician/ethicist Dr. Edmond Pellegrino, in *A Philosophical Basis of Medical Practice*, published in 1981 in collaboration with Dr. Thomasma, describes medicine as "the most scientific of the humanities and the most humane of the sciences."[10] By realizing the inevitable finitude of life itself, physicians must realize that intrusive medical intervention is a perishable good. Therefore, admitting the finitude of medicine is no disgrace. It simply acknowledges the concrete certainty of death.

But the relationship between patient and physician has evolved in many ways since the days of Plato. Today's patients are much more informed and today's physicians command awesome powers afforded to them through technologic advances. In centuries past, it was customary for the physician to have full control over medical decision making. This paternalistic attitude is best exemplified in Leo Tolstoy's essay "The Death of Ivan Ilyich, 1886":

> The whole procedure followed the lines he expected it would: every-thing was as it always is. There was the usual period in the waiting room and the important manner assumed by the doctor . . . and the weighty look which implied, "You can just leave it to us and we'll arrange mat-ters—we know all about it and can see to it in exactly the same way as we would for any other man."

Paternalistic attitude in medical care is both archaic and unethical. On the other hand, treating the doctor-patient relationship as one between provider and customer ignores the inevitable vulnerability of the patient in most situations of illness. It is rare for a person facing a major illness or a complex surgical intervention to be able to negotiate in a way a consumer is able to do in a retail store or a supermarket. Therefore, the cornerstone of a proper doctor-patient relationship is a partnership that ensures full respect for the patients' individuality, sensitivity to the patients' cultures and beliefs, recognition of the patients' sovereignty over their own body and due regard to the patients' capacity to make judgments for themselves.

A RELATIONSHIP WITH A PHYSICIAN SPECIALIZING IN PATIENTS, NOT JUST DISEASE

Why should we hold on to this quaint, labor-intensive, component of health care? What is the danger of replacing it with a cold, impersonal, novel system? And in what way would the change of health-care systems affect treatment near the end of life? To illustrate how a strong doctor-patient bond ensures that one's wishes are honored, I would like to share with the reader two case histories that I presented to my medical ethics class.

The first case involves Mr. JW,★ a seventy-six-year-old gentleman who smoked three packs of cigarettes a day for forty years. Mr. JW developed severe emphysema and chronic inflammation of the air pipes. He con-tinued to smoke in spite of his doctor's advice. The lung condition con-tinued to deteriorate until he could hardly engage in any physical effort

---

★This patient is also referred to in the chapter on Cardiopulmonary Resuscitation (CPR)

without becoming short of breath. He became vulnerable to a recurrent lung infection (i.e., pneumonia). In the year before his death, he was hospitalized four times to receive intensive-care therapy with antibiotics, treatments to facilitate breathing, and various other drugs for other conditions. The last of these hospitalizations required Mr. JW to be placed on assisted ventilation (a mechanical breathing machine) for almost two weeks, and it took great efforts to wean him from the ventilator.

Mr. JW received oxygen from a tank day and night. He became chairbound and could not sleep flat on his back in bed anymore. Prior to discharge from the hospital, the treating physician had a long conversation with Mr. JW in the presence of his wife. The gist of the conversation went as follows: "Mr. JW, you know we have been lucky this time. It was a close call."

"I know it. It is nice to come back from the ashes . . . the raising of Lazarus, sort of . . ."

"Not quite . . . modern medicine can produce miracles but rarely the kind of 'Pick up thy bed and walk.' On a serious note, you will feel quite weak for a long time, several weeks, maybe several months. Rehabilitation will be very slow. I arranged for a home nurse to visit you once a week to monitor your progress."

"O.K."

"And you will be on oxygen therapy at two liters per minute all the time, around the clock."

"How much will he be able to do?" asked Mrs. JW.

"Not much. He will be almost chair-bound. We'll arrange for him to have a chair that he can use as a bed during the night. This time we prevailed. But now you will have to stop smoking. It is killing you. If you continue to smoke, we may not have another chance."

Mr. JW leaned over with his head between his hands as if pondering a thought. He looked up and said: "Look, doc, I have known all along that cigarettes will kill me one of these days. I also know that I do not have much longer to live. I shall be weak and limited but nevertheless, smoking is one of very few pleasures that I look forward to. If I have a choice between a slightly longer but more miserable life without a cigarette, I choose the shorter life. I will continue to smoke." He paused while struggling for a few more breaths and continued, "I want you to know, I do not want to go through this again, never again would I want to be on a ventilator. If this happens to me again, make me comfortable but let me die."

"I understand and I promise you that we will see to it that your wishes are honored."

Mr. JW continued to smoke and was cared for at home. As expected, he had a recurrence of lung infection a few weeks later and was brought to the emergency room in severe distress. Mr. and Mrs. JW were met by the treating physician. Mrs. JW pleaded, "Please do something to help my husband breathe. Don't let him suffocate to death. He needs to be placed on the breathing machine."

The doctor turned to Mr. JW, who was in obvious distress, fighting for his breath, half-conscious and drenched in sweat. The doctor asked, "Do you want me to put you on the machine to breathe for you?" The breathless patient nodded as if to say, "Please save me, I am drowning."

I had related this case to my medical students. I asked them: "Who of you would place Mr. JW on the ventilator?" To my surprise, the response was unanimous. Not one student had any hesitation. The attending physician had made the same decision and Mr. JW was placed on the ventilator.

The next day, it was discovered that Mr. JW had suffered a heart attack. Forty years of heavy smoking not only destroyed his lungs but took a heavy toll on the blood vessels that provide the heart muscle with necessary oxygen. Excessive smoking causes these blood vessels to narrow, and a major coronary artery became totally clogged up. Part of the heart muscle died, and the already severely damaged lungs became flooded with water.

Tedious adjustments in the ventilator machine became necessary. A small plastic tube was placed in Mr. JW's heart to monitor its pumping function and pressures. Multiple medicines had to be given through multiple tubes, placed in multiple veins, located in multiple places. A tube placed in the bladder monitored urine flow, and another, placed in the stomach, enabled feeding.

Disorders of his heart rhythm required multiple electric shocks and frequent changes in medicines. A clot formed inside Mr. JW's heart, traveled to his brain vessels and caused a stroke. Bacteria invaded his lungs and from there found their way into his bloodstream. His vital organs failed one after the other: lungs, heart, kidneys, liver, and finally his brain ceased to function.

Three weeks of unrelenting fighting culminated in the realization that the effort had been futile. Mrs. JW asked that the doctors allow her husband to die without further "heroic" efforts.

I engaged in a "postmortem" discussion with my medical students about this patient. Was Mrs. JW wrong in asking that her husband be placed on a ventilator? Of course not. She could not bear to see him suffer. An objective, well-reasoned evaluation of the situation, however, would lead to the conclusion that such intervention was doomed to be futile. It is one thing to evaluate the situation from a distance, dissociated from the immense feeling of helplessness, and another matter when you are driven by the gravity of the moment and the passion to hold on to a loved one. Were the doctors at fault? My students justified the doctor's intervention on two grounds: First, they felt that the patient revoked his previous health-care directive by asking the doctor to place him on the ventilator. Second, they felt that the physician would be setting himself up for legal liability had he not intervened as asked. I challenged them on both counts. "Asking a smothering, half-conscious patient whether he wants to be afforded relief is an inappropriate question," I said. "It is a given. This unquestioned duty of the medical profession could be extended with the aid of medicines rather through a tube connected to a breathing machine. When you give the suffocating patient one option for relief and the patient elects to opt for it, this is not consent. Also, pretending that a half-conscious patient fighting hard for breath is able to think, evaluate, and rationally choose and consent is ridiculous," I added. Unfortunately, what happened with this patient exemplifies an everyday occurrence in intensive care units and emergency room settings, and in my view, degrades the solemnity of a life near its close.

Had this patient had a really meaningful relationship with his physician, he would have been spared the indignity, travail, and cost of the last three weeks. The treating physician should have made every effort to make Mr. JW comfortable with oxygen and morphine. Breathing could have been helped by a hand-held bag (ambu bag). If asked, he should have reminded Mrs. JW of the patient's explicit desire of not wanting to endure such an ordeal. The doctor should never have asked Mr. JW such a direct and leading question as "Do you want to be placed on a machine to relieve you?" while the patient was half-conscious and in dire distress. Patients in this state of mind are not able to reason; they need relief. Instead, the doctor should have said, "I will do everything to make you comfortable." That is what Mr. JW explicitly asked for and was promised just a few weeks earlier. After all, in the words of the philosopher, G. W. F. Hegel, life has value only when it has something valuable as its object. I told my students, "Life can be revered not only in its preservation, but also in the manner in which we allow a given life to reach its terminus."

I proceeded to share with my students the story of another of my patients to illustrate the point.

Mrs. Williams, a very kind, sixty-two-year-old lady, lived a life of pain and physical incapacity because of her intractable medical problems. She had a form of psoriasis, a scaly skin condition, that was so extensive and so severe that almost all of Mrs. Williams' body was covered with dry scales. The skin bruised and bled upon the least contact. Sloughed portions of the skin formed scabs, under which bacteria found a fertile field that enabled them to produce numerous little abscesses. Furthermore, psoriasis is associated with joint disease; Mrs. Williams' psoriasis afflicted all her joints with a vengeance, destroying her knees, hips, and the small joints in her hands and feet. She could not open a jar or squeeze a lemon without pain and she could hardly write her name. In spite of her enormous incapacity, she displayed courage, optimism, kindness, and love for her family. She had been married to her husband for forty-five years and had two loving daughters, aged forty and thirty-eight. Mrs. Williams received a multitude of treatments all her life. A year earlier, she had updated her living will and instructed her family to abstain from heroic measures at the close of her life. Recently, she was hospitalized for a stroke that involved the area of the brain responsible for the coordination of body movement. All of a sudden, she was seeing double images, could not speak intelligently or hold herself up in bed, and was no longer able to feed herself.

I was asked to see her in consultation to evaluate whether the stroke was caused by a blood clot that originated in the heart. I examined Mrs. Williams and obtained an ultrasound image of her heart. It became clear that Mrs. Williams had developed an infection of the mitral valve on the left side of the heart. The infection rendered the valve leaky. Also, the mitral valve developed a large "vegetation," a nest of material infected with bacteria. It was clear that the valve infection arose from one of the many skin abscesses that had plagued her over the years; the same organism was found in bacterial cultures obtained from her skin and blood.

Under ordinary circumstances, a physician should treat the heart valve infection with antibiotics administered intravenously. After the infection is brought under control, surgical removal of the infected valve and its replacement with a mechanical valve would have been the proper course. A prosthetic heart valve would bring two distinct, new problems, however. First, it is more likely than a normal valve to pick up infection from the blood. Second, it would require treatment with anticoagulants (medicines that prevent blood clotting). In Mrs. Williams's case, these would represent big problems since she already had a high propensity to bleed and would risk the real danger of experiencing another infection in the new valve from bacteria invading her blood from abscesses in her skin. When I considered these problems, in addition to a recent crippling stroke on top of extensive joint deformity, not to mention the punishment of major heart surgery, I decided to recommend against surgical valve replacement. I discussed with Mr. and Mrs. Williams the treatment options and my reasons for my recommendation, in spite of the dangers of not removing the infected valve. These included the risk of heart failure and further clots traveling from the heart valve to vital organs, including the brain. Mrs. Williams accepted my recommendation and declined surgery. That same evening, I received a call through the answering service. One of Mrs. Williams's daughters was on the line, and she was livid. I asked the daughter to see me at the hospital the next morning. "Why do you want my mother to die?" she asked. "Dr. X, the heart surgeon, was here yesterday and said that the only way to save mother is by replacing the infected valve with a mechanical one." The daughter went on to tell me, "I have convinced mother to have the operation as soon as possible."

I told her the surgery would have been the rational choice had her mother been otherwise healthy. "Your mother's other health problems will impose enormous challenges during surgery." The daughter made it clear to me that they were ready to face the consequences.

As expected, surgery proved to be a big mess. The breastbone was so fragile that it fell to pieces while the surgeon was attempting to split it with a saw. Bleeding could not be controlled and the tissues broke down like toilet paper. After six long hours in the operating room, Mrs. Williams was transferred to an intensive care unit bed and was connected to a multitude of tubes and machines. The next few days were a series of punishments with bleeding, disordered heart rhythm, lung infection, and sluggish kidneys. On the tenth day after surgery, with Mrs. Williams still in intensive care, the daughter choked with tears, told me, "My mother doesn't want to live anymore."

I asked, "What makes you think so?"

"Whenever I try to talk to Mother, she turns her head away from me. She wants to tell me that I caused her all of this suffering," she said. I squeezed her shoulder for encouragement. Mrs. Williams continued to deteriorate and died in the intensive care unit.

Two weeks later, upon entering my office, my secretary informed me that a lady was waiting for me in my office. Mrs. Williams's daughter told me, "I came to apologize to you. I wish I had listened to your advice. My mother's image in the intensive care unit with all of those bottles, tubes, and machines and with her body exposed keeps haunting me in my sleep. I know I made a mistake by putting her through this ordeal."

I shared with her that many other well-meaning and loving people go through what she had been through. I showed her a copy of the March 18, 1995, *Lancet*. The journal quotes a recent survey published in *Social Science and Medicine*, showing that of 3,700 relatives and friends of people who had just died, 28 percent of the respondents had expressed the view that an earlier death would have been preferable.[11] We agreed that patients' families, when considering choices, often do not entertain the most plausible and realistic scenarios, but the most favorable one, even if that one is quite remote and unrealistic. They do so because they are motivated by noble feelings of love and caring, as well as by fear of loss and separation. I admitted that physicians inevitably make mistakes. That the practice of medicine is not an exact science is unarguable. The art of medicine is based on weighing probabilities and derives from the theories of Thomas Baye, an eighteenth-century English clergyman. Though patient care is a long way from horseracing, he used the analogy in an instructive manner. His first theorem proposes, in horseracing terms, that the likelihood of picking a winner from the field is proportional to the prevalence of favorable characteristics in the horse (past performance, preferences for hard or soft going, handicaps, and the jockey). Just as there is not "one horse in a race," dealing with odds in the management of a patient poses a similar dilemma. It depends on the characteristics of the patient and the physician. It is uncommon for a treatment option to be the only possible one. There is usually an outsider in the competition, and sometimes the outsider wins. These issues have been eloquently reviewed by Dr. Chiswick in an article entitled "The Science of Making Mistakes."[12]

With a sense of relief, Mrs. Williams's daughter paused and then asked,

"But why did the surgeon not present the options to us objectively. Why did he recommend surgery?'

"Bias and passion for surgery are not unethical so long as the motive is the well-being of the patient. Physicians presenting the facts, and individuals analyzing them, base their decisions not only upon the facts, but also upon the way they are presented and the complex human emotions and experiences that shape them," I said.

I gave her the following example. Suppose the surgical intervention in your mother's case had a 5 percent chance of success. Any one of the two following presentations would be accurate, honest, and ethical.

Scenario 1: "As you know, your mother has enormously complex health problems. With medical treatment, we have a fair chance of eradicating the infection from the heart valve. The risk of having another stroke will not be obviated and likely, your mother will develop heart failure. The latter will be made better with medication, and hopefully, we will achieve enough improvement to allow her to engage in a rehabilitation program to deal with her stroke. I cannot recommend valve replacement surgery since her chances to survive surgery are less than 5 percent. Also, surgical intervention in her case will be attended with enormous logistical difficulties with bleeding, infection, pneumonia, and worsening of her stroke."

Scenario 2: "Your mother's heart valve has been chewed up by organisms. It is leaking and soon will throw her into heart failure. The hazard of recurring stroke with this valve is real. Any additional stroke will likely kill her. We have a one in twenty chance to save her with surgery. It is not a big chance, but it is the only one."

Both scenarios are sincere but they are likely to result in two different decisions.

She pondered the thought and said, "But how can we, the laypeople, make the right decision about ourselves and our loved ones?" I gave her a long-winded answer, as if I were lecturing to my students: "Ethicists will tell you about the right of the patient to shared decision making. Notwithstanding, proper medical decisions are often complex, multifaceted, and emotionally charged. Your mother's predicament, if any, came about because the physician primarily responsible for her hospital care did not know her as a person long enough and was not attuned to her personal values. He was more knowledgeable about her disease than about the patient herself. She had a living will, but the document had little relevance to her final illness. The essence of medicine is not just to combat disease and carry out procedures. That would reduce medical practitioners into a bunch of slavish technicians without intelligible goals. A *doctor*, according to the dictionary, is 'a teacher, one who is skilled in healing.' Attending to the patient's individual perception of what constitutes the meaning of life and how it is affected by crippling illness is an important component of the healing profession."

She straightened up in the chair and said, "But Mother did not have a primary physician. She was seeing a skin specialist and an arthritis specialist before all this happened."

I told her that any of these specialists could have been her primary physician. He would have been aware of her limitations, helped her with her disability, and assisted her in dealing with her pain. I am a cardiologist, and in my practice, over 5,000 patients identified me as their primary physician. Your primary physician is the one you have come to trust, the one with whom you share your values and preferences when it comes to decisions of when to wage a fight and when to die. There is no substitute for having a meaningful doctor-patient relationship.

THE TYPE OF MEDICAL PRACTICE MAY INFLUENCE PATIENT-PHYSICIAN COMMUNICATION

A study entitled "Discussion of Preferences for Life-Sustaining Care by Persons with AIDS" was published in the *Archives of Internal Medicine* in May 1993. Dr. Jennifer S. Haas and collaborators collected data from patients in the Boston area at Massachusetts General Hospital, Harvard University, and Boston University Hospital. These authors assessed the determinants of communication about resuscitation between persons with Acquired Immune Deficiency Syndrome (AIDS) and their physicians. The study involved three groups of patients, one at a staff-model health maintenance organization (HMO), one at an internal medicine group practice at a private teaching hospital, and one at an AIDS clinic at a public hospital. The study found that 72 percent of all patients desired to discuss preferences for life-sustaining care with their physician. Such desire was not dependent upon race, severity of illness, place of care, or medical treatment. Patients were less likely to have had an open discussion about their illness if they were cared for by a HMO rather than a clinic. However, the authors emphasized that better patient-physician communication is needed across the board.[13]

Managed care is now becoming a fixture in the delivery of health care. It is exigent that this type of care delivery not stifle patient-physician communication, for this unique, intimate dialogue is still the best assurance for quality of health care, quality of life, and quality of death.

In a superb article, Dr. Dale Larson from the Department of Counseling Psychiatry, Santa Clara University, California, and Dr. Daniel Tobin from the Veterans Affairs Health Care Network, Upstate New York–Albany, summed up the evolving practice and theory of end-of-life conversations between doctors and their patients.

The authors identified serious barriers to end-of-life discussions. These barriers relate to patients and families, health-care professionals, and the health-care system. The authors noted that patients may conceal the full extent of their pain, feelings of self-blame, anger, fears about the prognosis, and other difficult experiences that may pertain to end-of-life discussions. The authors note that patients often avoid end-of-life discussions because of the perceived stigma and embarrassment, shyness, confusion, fear of death, or cultural prohibitions. Family members can also block or complicate end-of-life conversations when they are unable or unwilling to accept the advanced nature of the patients' diseases or the patients' own preferences concerning end-of-life care. They can overestimate the chance of cure or fear potential regret and unreasonably demand that the physician "do everything." Also, medical information available to patients and families through the popular media and the Internet, sometimes not entirely accurate or relevant, can complicate these discussions.[14]

Health-care professionals and physicians might avoid end-of-life conversations because of their fear of causing pain to their patients and families, or reluctance to be the bearer of bad news. Health-care professionals may lack knowledge of advance directive laws and training in delivering bad news. They may view death as an enemy to be defeated, anticipate disagreements with the patient or family, have medical-legal concerns, or feel threatened by end-of-life discussions. Drs. Larson and Tobin concluded that, generally, physicians lack competence and comfort in addressing various end-of-life treatment issues.

Furthermore, the structure of the medical care system discourages productive end-of-life conversations. End-of-life discussions are not a routine part of care and physicians rarely have time to incorporate these issues into their busy schedules. Furthermore, care is frequently conducted by multiple physicians in multiple sites such as the office, hospital, or home. The nature of our health-care system is that it is often unclear who is responsible for initiating and documenting end-of-life care discussions. Also, the United States health-care system does not significantly compensate physicians for psychosocial conversations, including end-of-life discussions. The problem is compounded by a decreasing contact time and fewer long-term relationships between physicians and their patients.

Drs. Larson and Tobin provide a prescription to enhance end-of-life conversations between health-care professionals and patients and their families. Physicians should be responsible for breaking any bad news and to initiate the necessary conversations with patients and their families, realizing that physicians may need to involve other health-care professionals, social workers, clergy, and if needed, psychologists. Physicians and other health-care professionals should receive adequate training in order to acquire the necessary skills to conduct these difficult conversations.

The authors espouse a patient-centered approach to the delivery of medical care emphasizing the need to understand the meaning of the illness to the patient by "seeing through the patient's eyes." They further emphasize the need to focus on quality-of-life issues rather than on prolonging life at any cost, when life approaches its close, physicians' prime concern should be patients' comfort, preservation of dignity, and fulfillment of the patients' own wishes.

If the focus of medical care should be duly on the total patient and quality-of-life for the dying patient, the next case exemplifies common instances in which this rule is violated, when no one can identify who is the responsible physician or what the treatment plan is.

JP, a ninety-one-year-old nursing home resident, was brought to the hospital with severe shortness of breath, fever, and total confusion. He was seen in the emergency room and was diagnosed with acute pneumonia. The blood oxygen level was noted to be quite low. The patient was intubated and placed on a ventilator.

Review of the medical record showed that JP had a history of a large stroke that rendered him totally dependent. In addition, he had severe narrowing of the aortic valve, the valve through which the blood flows from the left side of the heart to the aorta; he had had a previous heart attack, had been in heart failure, and had a seizure disorder and severe kidney damage. Lately, he had been unaware of who he was or where he lived. His senile wife had poor understanding about her husband's condition and asked that "everything be done" because "he is all I have in the world—if he dies, I will kill myself."

Soon, there were five teams of specialists supervising JP's care: a pulmonologist, an infectious disease specialist, a cardiologist, a neurologist, and a kidney specialist. All agreed that the patient was terminal. A distraught wife, unwilling to accept the reality of her husband's condition, and reluctant-to-speak physicians, fearful of the consequences of not doing enough, resulted in a myriad of interventions—every doctor baby-sitting the designated organ of his specialty and none attempting to reason with the patient's wife about the ultimate goal of treatment.

After three weeks, the intensive care unit head nurse contacted the wife's minister, in spite of the objection of one of the treating physicians, and convinced the treating team to obtain an ethics consult.

A team comprising a member of the ethics committee, a social worker, and the hospital chaplain was joined by the wife's own minister and formulated a staged plan of action while meeting with the wife on a daily basis.

A few days later, JP was sedated and extubated. He died peacefully. His wife did not kill herself. A church team was assembled to provide support during the bereavement process. What the family needed from the outset was a trusting doctor-patient relationship, one which would recognize that the best form of patient care is "caring for the patient—and his family."

Since the dawn of history, physicians have been held in high esteem, enjoyed a high social and economic status, and earned the trust of their countrymen. According to Greek myth, Athena gave Asklepios the Healer a bottle of blood from each of the Gorgon Medusa's arm veins. Athena advised Asklepios to use blood from the right arm to comfort and to heal and admonished against the use of left arm blood, lest it should bring about pain and suffering. Asklepios was further gifted by Hygea with powers to prevent disease and maintain health, and was taught by Panacea the art of perfecting the use of soothing simples.[15] These skills were and continue to be the cornerstones of the practice of medicine. Being a doctor was never meant to be the garden of earthly delights. Dealing with

acute illness, unexpected emergencies, human suffering, and the daily vicarious encounters with the dying are not exactly anodynes of pleasure.

It is unrealistic for medicine to always produce the exact, hoped for
results.[16] Dealing with the complex and intricate vicissitudes of illness and
the inevitability of death is what makes medicine such a great profession
referred to by ancient Egyptians as "the necessary art"; an art whose aim is
"sometimes cure, often relief, and always caring."

COVENANT FOR OUR TIMES

I would like to conclude this chapter by a modern physician-patient
covenant espoused by a team of leading physician ethicists and published in
the May 17, 1995, issue of the *Journal of the American Medical Association*.

> Medicine is, at its center, a moral enterprise grounded in a covenant of
> trust. This covenant obliges physicians to be competent and to use their
> competence in the patient's best interests. Physicians, therefore, are both
> intellectually and morally obliged to act as advocates for the sick wher-
> ever their welfare is threatened and for their health at all times.
>
> Today, this covenant of trust is significantly threatened. From within,
> there is growing legitimation of the physician's materialistic self-interest;
> from without, for-profit forces press the physician into the role of com-
> mercial agent to enhance the profitability of health care organizations.
> Such distortions of the physician's responsibility degrade the physician-
> patient relationship that is the central element and the structure of clin-
> ical care. To capitulate to these alterations of the trust relationship is to
> significantly alter the physician's role as healer, carer, helper, and advocate
> for the sick and for the health of all.
>
> By its traditions and very nature, medicine is a special kind of human
> activity—one that cannot be pursued effectively without the virtues of
> humility, honesty, intellectual integrity, compassion, and effacement of
> excessive self-interest. These traits mark physicians as members of a moral
> community dedicated to something other than its own self-interest.
>
> Our first obligation must be to serve the good of those persons who
> seek our help and trust us to provide it. Physicians, as physicians, are not,
> and must never be, commercial entrepreneurs, gateclosers, or agents of
> fiscal policy that runs counter to our trust. Any defection from primacy
> of the patient's well-being places the patient at risk by treatment that may
> compromise quality of or access to medical care.

We believe the medical profession must reaffirm the primacy of its obligation to the patient through national, state, and local professional societies; our academic, research, and hospital organizations; and especially through personal behavior. As advocates for the promotion of health and support of the sick, we are called upon to discuss, defend, and promulgate medical care by every ethical means available. Only by caring and advocating for the patient can the integrity of our profession be affirmed. Thus we honor our covenant of trust with patients.[17]

12

THE HARD CHOICES ABOUT
END-OF-LIFE MEDICAL CARE

To die well is the height of wisdom of life.

Sören Kierkegaard

Comfort or "palliative care," which addresses the multiple physical, psychological, and spiritual dimensions of suffering, should be the standard of care for the dying. This concept is not only humane, but also supported by position papers from the Council on Ethical and Judicial Affairs of the American Medical Association, the Council on Scientific Affairs of the same organization, and the American Board of Internal Medicine.[1]

The general acceptance and rapid growth of hospice care in the United States and Europe is a welcome testimonial to the ever-increasing need to provide comfort care that preserves peace and dignity at the end of life. When addressed by a skilled multidisciplinary team, dying patients and their families receive adequate relief, support, and solace. The overriding goal should be to keep the patient as free of pain as can be achieved while enabling the patient to communicate and maintain a certain degree of independence for as long as possible.

In some instances, the process of dying can be quite harsh and the suffering so intense and intolerable that ordinary comfort measures are not sufficient to produce an acceptable level of palliation. Under these circumstances, physicians should be prepared to seek consultation from experts in end-of-life care and possibly even consider terminal, unconscious sedation, and cessation of feeding and hydration.[2] It must be emphasized that such radical measures should be the exception and not the rule. They

231

are reserved for severe, unrelievable end-of-life suffering and must be approached in concert with, or at the behest of, the patient, if competent, family, or appointed surrogates.

Advance care planning for end-of-life care should be encouraged, and better yet, become part of the preventive or routine care of all adult, competent citizens. Advance Care Plans (ACP) should be medically specific to the scenario and as much as possible, encompass most end-of-life situations. Many of these situations have very special importance to a large segment of citizens. Failure to respect these former decisions by imposing unwanted medical treatment, continued life support, or forced feeding and hydration constitutes unwanted bodily invasion of a competent person and is a gross violation of personal freedom and rights.

One caveat is in order here. Physicians must make sure that their patients' refusal of treatment and other interventions are valid and that they represent the voluntary, uncoerced, informed choices of patients who have decision-making capacity (hence the importance of advance care planning).

Physicians have a right, and possibly a duty, to support continued treatment when it is considered to be medically appropriate. However, once they are assured that the patient has made a valid refusal, doctors are morally required to withhold (not give) or withdraw (discontinue) treatment, regardless of whether they believe that the patient's choice is good or bad. If a physician has moral or religious objections to honoring the patient's valid refusal, the physician can transfer the patient to the care of another physician.

Both physicians and families must, therefore, take advance care planning very seriously. We encourage every citizen to discuss his or her Advance Care Plan (ACP) document not only with his or her physician, but also with other relevant family members.

The right of a patient or surrogate to refuse life-sustaining treatment, including mechanical ventilation, is firmly established in American law and bioethics. Many physicians are reluctant to undertake the act of disconnecting patients from life-sustaining machines. Sedatives and painkillers should be administered in doses that fully relieve pain and suffering of the terminally ill patient. In addition, agents causing temporary paralysis of muscles may be needed in some cases, particularly those dependent on artificial ventilation, to ensure that the process of withdrawal of unneeded or useless life support is peaceful in its totality. Many physicians (myself included) find it difficult to discontinue ventilator assistance and watch patients suffocate. Even brain dead individuals often show jerky movements. Such scenes are particularly heart wrenching when they involve children and young people. Every available means should be employed to render the process as serene as possible.

In 1997, in *Washington v. Glucksberg*, the United States Supreme Court had determined that citizens do not have a constitutional right to physician-assisted suicide. Furthermore, it affirmed that individual states are free to ban or affirm it. Oregon has chosen to permit physician-assisted suicide in certain circumstances.

The United States Supreme Court reversed a prior opinion from the Second Circuit Court, which contended that New York State's law prohibiting assisted suicide violated the equal protection clause of the Constitution's Fourteenth Amendment. The Circuit Court's opinion stated

> Withdrawal of life support requires physicians or those acting at their direction, physically to remove equipment and, often to administer palliative drugs which may themselves contribute to death. The ending of life by these means is nothing more nor less than assisted suicide.[3]

The Supreme Court, however, firmly endorsed the distinction between refusal of treatment and assisted suicide, thereby rejecting the logic of the Second Circuit Court that the state lacks any rational grounds for prohibiting assisted suicide for competent terminally ill patients. The Supreme Court further emphasized that artificial feeding and hydration is no different from other elements of standard medical care. A competent adult patient has the right to accept or refuse any and all medical treatments, including artificial feeding by vein or through a tube placed in the stomach. Therefore, failure to honor patients' refusal of medical interventions amounts to forced treatment or forced feeding. In other words, a patient's right to forgo any treatment (even if it is deemed beneficial) is based on the principle of personal sovereignty over one's body and is included in the right to be free of unwanted bodily invasion.

In 1997 and 1998, bills on assisted suicide were introduced in twenty-six states. All were defeated. Thirty-seven states currently prohibit by statute assisted suicide, including physician-assisted suicide. In addition, eight states prohibit it under the common law or a homicide statute.

Euthanasia or mercy killing is different from physician-assisted suicide in that the patient controls the moment of death by self-administering a lethal dose of medicine in the latter. By contrast, in the act of euthanasia the physician is supposed to administer the poison.

Euthanasia may be voluntary, that is, requested by the patient, or involuntary, by which the patient is put out of his or her misery without asking to die. In The Netherlands, 2.3 percent of all deaths are physician-assisted or administered; the majority of these deaths are by euthanasia and almost half are involuntary (not asked for). Horror tales abound of patients refusing to be admitted to a hospital for fear of being euthanized by their physicians. The truthfulness of these stories has been questioned. That said, the unalterable truth about the essence of the medical profession remains, however, an unwavering dedication to the beneficence and nonmalefiscence (first do no harm) for the patients we have the privilege to serve. No violation of this code can be greater than an act of deliberately ending the life of a patient. Euthanasia is illegal in the United States and should always remain so.

Dr. JoAnn Lynn, a noted expert on quality end-of-life care, advocates ten domains for quality of care at the end of life. These include (1) relief of physical and emotional symptoms, (2) support of function and autonomy, (3) advance care planning, (4) patient and family satisfaction, (5) restraining aggressive care near death (site of death, cardiopulmonary resuscitation, or hospitalization), (6) improved global quality of life, (7) diminished family burden, (8) survival time, (9) provider continuity and communication skills, and (10) support during bereavement.[4] These guidelines have been developed under the auspices of the American Geriatrics Society and endorsed by forty-two organizations, including the American Association of Retired Persons, American Cancer Society, American College of Physicians, American Medical Association, Institute of Medicine, and National Hospice Organization.

Of these domains, three are not only improvable, but also readily measurable. They include

- control of pain and other symptoms
- advance care planning; thereby avoiding inappropriate prolongation of dying and achieving a sense of control
- patient and family satisfaction.[5]

I would like to conclude this brief review with two quotations, one by noted ethicist Dr. Daniel Callahan, who in a recent article titled "Death and the Research Imperative," said

> Modern medicine . . . seems to have made death Public Enemy Number One. It is not—at least not any longer in developed countries with the average life expectancy approaching 80 years. The enemies now are serious chronic illness and an inability to function well. Death will always be with us, pushed around a bit to be sure, with one fatal disease superseded by another. For every birth, someone long ago happened to notice, there is one death. We cannot and will not change that fact. But, we can change how people are cared for at the end of life, and we can substantially reduce the burden of illness. It is not, after all, death that people seem to fear the most, and certainly not in old age, but a life poorly lived. Something can be done about that.[6]

Equally eloquent was the French philosopher Michel Foucault, who died of AIDS on June 25, 1984, at the age of fifty-seven. In his book, *The Birth of the Clinic: An Archeology of Medical Perception*, Foucault reminds us in a poetic piece of prose about life, death, and medicine:

> Medicine offers modern man the obstinate, yet reassuring face of his finitude. In it, death is endlessly repeated, but it is also exorcised; and although it ceaselessly reminds man of the limit that he bears within him, it also speaks to him of that technical world that is armed, positive, full form of his finitude.[7]

SUMMARY OF END-OF-LIFE MEDICAL CARE

Palliative care should be employed to alleviate suffering, preserve dignity, and attend to the patient's and family's psychological and spiritual needs. This should be the right of every citizen during the last chapter of life.

Unconscious sedation and cessation of food and fluids should be reserved to the very few that endure a harsh end with unrelievable suffering. It must be subject to certain safeguards.

Withdrawal of life support should be used for those in an unconscious state or having multiple organ failure with little chance of a meaningful recovery.

Withholding (not offering) medical intervention that is not likely to benefit the patient is appropriate treatment at the end of life. When to withdraw or withhold treatment deemed futile requires continued public and professional education and open, sincere communication between health-care professionals and competent patients or their appointed surrogates. Guidelines have been developed to assist physicians in deciding when to withdraw or withhold intrusive medical interventions (Project GRACE, which will be detailed in the next chapter).

Physician-assisted suicide by prescribing a lethal dose of a sedative is legal only in the state of Oregon and is subject to certain safeguards and mandatory reporting.

Active euthanasia, mercy killing carried out by the physician, whether voluntary (with patient consent) or involuntary (without patient consent) is illegal and should remain so.

Proper advance care planning should enable end-of-life care in accordance with the patient's own beliefs and preferences.

13

PROJECT GRACE
A Physician-Public Partnership for Good Dying[1]

❧

Like our shadows, our wishes lengthen as our sun declines.

Edward Young

PROJECT GRACE

In 1998, after years of discussion, the Florida Chapter of the American College of Cardiology (FCACC) launched Project GRACE for the purpose of developing Guidelines for Resuscitation And Care at the End of Life for our society. These guidelines were developed through a partnership among physicians, theologians, ethicists, legal scholars, economists, and the lay public. It is hoped that these guidelines will be implemented throughout the state of Florida and possibly eventually throughout the nation.[2] Project GRACE does not advocate euthanasia or physician-assisted suicide.

The guidelines evolved as a result of the dedicated efforts of volunteers organized into task forces who reviewed the appropriate literature, consulted with academic and community leaders, and after much discussion, consolidated their opinions and recommendations in four task forces on major subject-matter areas. These are Medical Futility, Advance Care Planning, Palliative Care, and Education/Implementation.

The members of Task Force I emphasized that despite difficulties of predicting the time of death or its certainty beyond doubt, medical knowledge now exists that permits prediction of a fatal outcome or medical futility (where life is functionally meaningless) with a high degree of probability. The possibility exists that young people may be involved in accidents or catastrophic illnesses that impair their ability to make rational decisions about their health. Also, since people are living longer, they are likely to confront health decline and situations in which additional health care may be superfluous or undesirable, or where they are physically or mentally incompetent to make a health-care decision. Hence, all individuals should be advised to make legal preparation for end-of-life situations through an Advance Care Plan (ACP)/Living Will (LW). Further, since the individual may, at some future date, lack the physical or mental ability to make a rational decision, he or she should select in advance a surrogate empowered to act in the individual's best interest in such a situation. Such preparation can protect the individual from undesired and futile therapy and can relieve his or her family from the difficulties of making decisions about limiting or withdrawing care.

Elderly patients often choose to forgo aggressive interventions, reasoning that they have lived a long life, have accomplished their goals, have come to terms with death, which, although not imminent, may be around the corner, and prefer to make a graceful exit. Such individuals should have the right to request any or all limits to CPR and life support measures, and establish a DNAR order. Furthermore, they may prefer nonaggressive management for such illnesses as heart attacks, cancer, and even pneumonia. There is an urgent need to develop legal and social mechanisms for respecting and fulfilling end-of-life choices of these individuals.

Each person is aware of cases where patients have been kept alive for days or weeks when death was certain. When the patient's prognosis is extremely poor and the expected outcome from any medical treatment is likely to be useless or even harmful to the individual, medical futility applies. The physician will use the patient's diagnoses, together with knowledge of the severity of the illness and other individual patient characteristics to assess the situation and answer three questions:

1. Is death imminent?
2. What is the best possible outcome or recovery that can be hoped for if treatment is maximally beneficial?
3. What is the probability of achieving the best possible result, or at least a good result?

If the answers to these questions point to a medically futile situation, the patient should be managed accordingly.

Task Force II focused on the form and content of the ideal ACP. Although a number of forms are available, it was agreed that none is ideal and that an effort should be made to develop an ideal form that covers specific end-of-life medical scenarios and treatment options presented in simple, plain English (or Spanish for the Hispanic community). Task Force II recommended that Project GRACE develop such a document for use by physicians and individuals communitywide, and establish a central registry with immediate access for health-care professionals. Additionally, the task force recommended that the ACP should include consideration by the patient to make an anatomic gift of one or more organs after death.

Task Force III defined palliative care as compassionate care that provides psychosocial support to a person with an incurable disease or significant functional limitations. Illness, as well as long-term care and death, are family affairs. Each family cares for its identified patient in a way indicative of their values and beliefs, and the manner in which each person is cared for will influence the cooperation of the family and ultimately how the family grieves and is able to continue living. Health-care providers must recognize diversity in families with regard to ethics, religion, cultural norms, social support systems, financial means, and health-care expectations, along with other variables.

Florida's varied population offers a challenge to appropriate and even-handed health-care discussions. Florida is a state of transients, of tourists, of snow-bunnies here for half a year, singles such as students, divorcees, single parents, the widowed, and retirees beginning a new lifestyle. The climate and relatively low taxes attract migrants from northern states and Europe, while geography and a good economy invite immigrants from the Caribbean and Latin America. The result is a multicultural population of diverse ages, economic and marital status, educational levels, religion, race, and social attitudes.

It is a truism to state that the traditional family in America no longer exists. Families move many times and members of many nuclear families live many miles apart. Care must frequently be delivered to homosexual partners, common-law arrangements, single-parent households, young singles, the widowed, the aged who have never married, and the homeless. A frequent occurrence in Florida is the couple who moved from a distance to Florida to retire, and then within a year one partner dies, leaving a new widow or widower with little connection to the community. A recent survey of the United States reported that over 55 percent of the population lives alone.

It is often difficult for the caregiver to identify the person who serves as part of the family support system. Often the patient who is chronically ill considers the closest neighbor, friend, or nursing caregiver as more of a family than his or her own blood relatives.

Communications with the physician may also be strained where family members lack medical knowledge, do not understand the situation(s), and do not know what questions to ask. They may call the physician at inopportune times and find the response unsatisfactory.

Unfortunately, some physicians lack the knowledge of how to communicate openly with the patient and family. In other cases, they may follow the tradition of guarding the privacy of medical information. Physicians and other health-care personnel need to communicate what palliative care means and explain the efforts being made to provide comfort and pain relief for the patient. Acceptance of the person identified as caregiver by the patient and family is crucial. The role carries responsibilities, for the caregiver is an influential decision maker. Although actions taken by the caregiver may not always be approved by the family, good communications are essential.

Task Force III concluded that it was essential to

- establish a standard educational program of palliative care for physicians, nurses, health-care administrators, social workers, pharmacists, and all other health-care providers. This basic course should be required in every medical, nursing, seminary, pharmacy, and social work school in the state. The course should address the problems and goals identified in this report.
- offer additional courses in each category of health care, such as pain management for physicians, pharmacists, and nurses; social variants for social workers; spiritual or emotional care for clergy or secular equivalent, and so forth. These courses should be offered as continuing education at seminars, conferences, and educational institutions. Courses on palliative care should be included in programs of continuing education taken each year by thousands of elderly citizens throughout Florida.

- use professional magazines in each health-care discipline to provide information on palliative care and incorporate educational programs for credit for continuing education unit(s).
- develop a single medical record and a case management model that can follow patients through an entire illness.
- develop disease-specific protocols to advise clinicians of timely and appropriate transition options to palliative care and support research analyzing quality of life and cost benefits of palliative care.[3]

It was realized from the outset that the backbone of this effort must be to develop an Advance Care Plan that overcomes the three major hurdles which stand in the way of utilization of the living will. These are accessibility, specificity, and applicability.

Acknowledging these challenges and realizing that a wide gulf still exists between what patients want and expect,[4] and what physicians accept and honor,[5] Project GRACE embarked upon a systematic effort to develop a new Advance Care Plan. Task Force II provided the general characteristics of an ideal plan and recommended wide testing prior to implementation.

A committee comprising legal scholars, physicians, economists, theologians, and civic leaders was established to develop a new Advance Care Plan document that has the virtues of clarity, specificity, and portability.[6] Drafts of the document were tested with various focus groups: medical students; physicians in training; practicing physicians, nurses, and other allied health-care professionals; residents of retirement communities and other middle-class neighborhoods; office and food service workers; and seventh-grade students in their early teens. The document was modified several times to enhance language clarity without sacrificing specificity.

Plans are underway to educate the public and health-care professionals about the advantages of this document. It is hoped that in a few years, all Florida physicians will use the ACP in the routine care of their patients. Continuing education programs will focus on one community at a time. Uniformity of Advance Care Plans in all hospitals in the same region will enable easy access, portability, and enhance document utilization and the realization of patients' prior expressed wishes. Negotiations are underway to establish an Internet-based central registry for patients. Health-care professionals will be authorized by willing patients to have access to the registry at the time of need.

Project GRACE has worked closely with Florida legislators in order to enact laws that facilitate implementation.[7] Furthermore, Project GRACE looks forward to partnering with other official medical, legal, and civic organizations to carry out its important mission to change the culture of dying from a technology-driven, death-denying culture to one that attends to patients' dignity and comfort as well as to their unique expectations.

What makes this proposal even more timely is the Uniform Health Care Decisions Act that has been approved by the Uniform Law Commissioners in August 1993.[8] This legislation was proposed to enable all American states to replace their existing legislation on the subject with a single statute, therefore enhancing the utility of the "living will." The proposed act further removes the unnecessary impediments to the use of a living will and widens the scope of the advance directive to encompass not only terminal illness but also end-stage disease when death is expected in a few years. The act was approved by the American Bar Association in February 1994. It is hoped that this much-needed legislation becomes adopted by most or all states in the next few years. The prefatory note sites major weaknesses in current Advance Health-Care Directive legislation, including the fragmented, incomplete, and sometimes inconsistent sets of rules and conflicts between statutes in different states, including the lack of portability of a living will from state to state.

The act encompasses the following concepts:

1. The right of a competent person to choose or refuse any or all medical treatment in all circumstances. The patient may extend all or some defined part of this power to one or more specified individuals under specified circumstances articulated by the individual.
2. The act is comprehensive and is designed to replace any and every preceding legislation regarding refusal of medical care by patient or surrogate.
3. The act is designed to simplify and facilitate the making of a living will, which may be either written or oral. A power of attorney for health care must be written but need not be witnessed or notarized.
4. The surrogate must act in accordance with the individual's expressed instructions. Otherwise, he or she should apply the patient's best interests standard in the decision.

5. The act requires compliance from health-care providers and institutions so long that the directive meets applicable health-care standards. Furthermore, an optional form is suggested for general use.
The form has entries for

a. Choice not to prolong life in case of incurable and irreversible
conditions that will result in (i) death in a short time, (ii)
unconsciousness which is irreversible with a reasonable degree
of certainty, or (iii) when the likely risks and burdens of treatments would outweigh the expected benefits.

b. Choice to prolong life: with the limits of generally accepted
health-care standards.

There are shortcomings in the above legislation. I believe that the
medical scenarios in (a) lack the specificity to make them binding to
health-care providers. Also, (b) should be automatically provided for those
who do not execute a living will. For these reasons, and in order to
strengthen the proposed legislation and provide uniformity of the document, I propose the universal use of the Project GRACE Advance Care
Plan for reasons already discussed.

In my view, the utilization of one simplified form of an ACP (that
encompasses not only terminal illness but also end-stage disease) will go a
long way to encourage the use of advance care planning. Furthermore, the
establishment of one central computerized registry of all those who execute ACPs to which health-care professionals can have immediate access
will make the ACP more meaningful and effective in the United States.

SUMMARY

Many problems undermine the utility and effectiveness of currently used
living will forms. We propose a new Advance Care Plan document that has
the following distinct advantages:

• It is written in plain, simple, easily understood English;
• A workbook is provided by which the patient becomes familiar with
end-of-life medical scenarios and therefore can make informed
choices;

- It is focused, yet encompasses a wide range of medical scenarios not only limited to terminal illness, but also covers other medical conditions when death is near but not imminent or when the patient has become totally dependent;
- It should be binding to physicians, health-care professionals, and relatives; it dispels fear of litigation that derives from ambiguities;
- It can be easily stored in the data bank of a central registry;
- It has provisions for a patient's special wishes and can be personalized;
- It allows for decisions regarding cardiopulmonary resuscitation;
- It obviates the possibility of an appointed surrogate acting contrary to the patient's desires;
- It allows patients to express their preferences regarding organ donation;
- It can be employed by physicians as part of the routine and preventative care of their patients.

I hope that this simple but all-encompassing, medical-scenario–specific document will become universally adopted in place of currently available living wills. This will conform with the spirit of the recently proposed legislation, "The Uniform Living Act." Furthermore, it will go a long way toward the establishment of a centralized national registry to which health-care professionals will have immediate access. And finally, it can do much to eliminate the needless suffering involved in futile medical care.

After all, medicine's mission is to enhance life in years and quality and not to prolong the process of dying. Is it possible for the leading medical associations and society at large to rediscover medicine's core values and the proper application of new technologies so that we may live our lives to the fullest and have a graceful exit on our own terms? Herein lies the challenge.

Recommendations from Task Forces I, II, and III follow.

TASK FORCE I: MEDICAL FUTILITY

Background and Rationale

For centuries physicians, patients, and families have dealt with end-of-life issues in an appropriate, compassionate, socially responsible manner. When a patient's illness became overwhelming, life-prolonging efforts were abandoned and the individual was allowed to experience death, a natural part of life, with dignity and comfort. During the course of struggling with the patient's illness, physicians would come to the sad realiziation that further efforts to extend quality life were *futile*. The recognition of *medical futility* by the physician, patient, and family would not in any way diminish the need for care and medical attention. Instead, it would mark a shift in the primary goal of care from the prolongation of life to the provision of physical and emotional comfort. This traditional physician-patient-family decision-making process has now become threatened by the erosion of trust that society holds for physicians and by expanding technology, which has made the recognition and acceptance of medical futility increasingly difficult.

The explosion of medical technology has not in any way altered the cardinal goals of medical care: (1) to relieve physical and emotional pain and suffering; (2) to enhance the quality and functionality of life; and (3) to extend the length of life. Technology has brought an amazing array of beneficial treatment choices, but has also led to immense pressure to offer some form of potentially *curative* therapy. Since there is almost always *something* that can justifiably be done to treat one or more of the patient's medical problems, the norm has become aggressive treatment until death. In many cases, patients are treated well past the point where treatment may be properly regarded as futile. Even though only a small percentage of people are treated aggressively beyond futility, the absolute number of people remains large because millions become severely ill prior to death each year. The impact of expensive technology at the end of life is enormous because of technology's ability to significantly prolong dying. The fact that individuals with medically futile conditions can almost always be found in every hospital's critical care unit is obvious evidence of the increasing prevalence of continued life-prolonging treatment beyond the point of futility.

In an effort to reduce the inappropriate application of medical interventions to patients who have no potential for benefit, the term *medical futility* has been increasingly used by physicians and medical ethicists. The rationale has been that informing doctors and the public that physicians have no ethical obligation to offer or provide futile interventions should result in a reduction in the inappropriate use of technology at the end of life. While the existence of medical futility is as unquestionable as the eventuality of death, the impact of the futility concept on decision making has been hampered by the lack of a clear definition of medical futility. The definition has become increasingly elusive, as technology has pushed back the limits of what can be done to prolong both life and the process of dying.

Twentieth-Century Progress in End-of-Life Care

Significant strides have been made in dealing with end-of-life care during this century. Substantial progress has been made in defining the patient's autonomy, the physician's role in dealing with medical futility, and the medical institution's responsibility to patients and physicians.

Patient Autonomy

Americans have made progress in end-of-life care by asserting their autonomy through the realization of a number of patient rights. The right to refuse medical treatment has been supported in common law and by the U.S. Constitution. In a 1914 informed consent case, Justice Benjamin Cardozo ruled that "every human being of adult years and sound mind has the right to determine what shall be done with his own body."[9] This ruling has been cited in numerous common law cases establishing a patient's *right to refuse unwanted medical intervention, even when that intervention is regarded as necessary to sustain life.* Other cases have based the right of self-determination on the U.S. Constitution's implied *right to privacy* and on the liberty interests identified in the Fourteenth Amendment. The right to refuse unwanted, life-sustaining medical treatment gained explicit constitutional recognition in the Cruzan case with the U.S. Supreme Court's assertion that a competent patient has a *constitutionally protected liberty interest in refusing unwanted treatment.*[10]

Patients have secured the right to refuse life-sustaining treatment even in the setting of nonterminal illness. In the case of Elizabeth Bouvia, a young woman with severe cerebral palsy, but without life-threatening ill-ness, the California Court of Appeals ruled that she had the right to refuse treatment with artificial nutrition.[11] Patients have established the option of controlling health-care decisions in advance of mental incapacity by com-pleting advance directives or by delegating decision-making rights to another individual who can serve as a health-care proxy with *durable power of attorney*.[12]

In cases where patients lack decisional capacity and formal advance directives, their right to be free of unwanted treatment can still be exer-cised. Surrogates may act on their behalf through two decision-making standards: (1) the substituted judgment standard, which requires a surrogate decision maker, usually a close family member, to make the decision he or she believes that the patient would have made, based on past statements made by the patient; and (2) the best interests standard, which is used when there are no applicable past statements and the surrogate is asked to make decisions based on what is judged to be in the patient's best interest.[13]

Physicians and Medical Futility

Physicians have recognized both the quantitative and the qualitative aspects of medical futility since antiquity. Hippocrates encouraged doctors to assess the quantitative aspect of futile treatment "to refuse to treat those who are overmastered by their diseases, realizing in such cases medicine is powerless."[14] Plato, however, emphasized the qualitative nature of futility, believing that the good physician would assess each case, then judge whether treatment should be given. "For patients whose bodies were always in a state of inner sickness, he did not attempt to prescribe a reg-imen, for that would make their life a prolonged misery . . . medicine was not invented for them and they should not be treated even if they were richer than Midas."[15]

Much of the modern futility debate has centered on futile cardiopul-monary resuscitation (CPR). As CPR has become the standard of care, "do not resuscitate" (DNR) orders have evolved to designate individuals in whom resuscitation is not indicated. More recently, the phrase "do not attempt resuscitation" (DNAR) has been proposed as more appropriate because it "makes clear that many attempts at resuscitation fail" and that "in some cases in which resuscitation is accomplished, the patient is left with severe mental impairment."[16] The common practice of requiring consent for DNAR orders has been questioned. Based upon the principle that doctors have no duty to provide useless therapy, some have argued that when attempting CPR would be futile, DNAR orders can be written without the consent of the patient or family.[17] However, it is desirable to involve patients and their families in such discussions at all times. Consistent with the concept of qualitative futility, K. Plunkitt and others have written that "CPR is not indicated unless there is a reasonable hope for a conscious life with a chance that the patient will be able to pursue and achieve some degree of happiness."[18]

While the CPR debate has done much to move the issue of medical futility forward, concern about medical liability has led many physicians to order and attempt futile CPR, assuming they will not be faulted for doing something for the patient in an effort to save or prolong life. However, there is no precedent for the successful suit of a physician for refusing to render aggressive care in a medically futile situation. "Analysis of the relevant case law lends credence to the argument that a physician's liability for not providing futile CPR is remote and that, in fact, a physician exposes himself to greater liability by providing such treatment. Nevertheless, where unilateral DNAR orders are to be written, it would be prudent to do so under the auspices of hospital or medical staff guidelines for their issuance.[19] In 1993, J. F. Drane and J. L. Coulehan more broadly defined as medically futile treatment that "(1) does not alter a person's persistent vegetative state; (2) does not alter diseases or defects that made a baby's survival beyond infancy impossible; (3) leaves permanently unrestored a patient's neurocardiorespiratory capacity, capacity for relationship, or moral agency; or (4) will not help free a patient from permanent dependency on total intensive care support."[20] Unfortunately, this comprehensive, succinct definition has not been widely accepted by society or the profession of medicine.

Health-Care Institutions and Medical Futility

In 1990, Congress enacted the Patient Self-Determination Act which mandated that health-care institutions accepting Medicare and Medicaid provide all patients with written information regarding their legal rights to participate in the medical decision-making process and to formulate advance directives.[21] The American Hospital Association's Policy and Statement on Patient's Choice of Treatment Options (1995) provided that health-care decision making should be based on a collaborative relationship between the patient and the physician and that the patient may exercise this authority on the basis of relevant information necessary to make a sufficient voluntary and informed decision.[22] Additionally, the Joint Commission on Accreditation of Health Care Organizations has set standards to assist health-care facilities in implementing policies with respect to obtaining a patient's informed consent.[23]

Other innovations in end-of-life care include a clearer definition of the patient's ability to provide informed consent and detailed protocols and guidelines addressing effective palliative care; provisions in several states require skilled nursing facility patients to execute advance directives in the presence of patient advocates and the development of ethics committees to assist in resolving conflicts in patient care.[24] In addition, much work has been done to craft policies on medical futility at the health facility, community, and national levels.[25]

Twenty-First Century Obstacles to Futility-Based Decisions

The controversy over medical futility may be surprising to anyone considering the issues for the first time, given that (1) physicians, patients, and families have historically dealt with medical futility well; (2) significant progress has been made in end-of-life care, as enumerated; and (3) the vast majority of individuals, if asked, express a desire to forgo treatment beyond futility. There remains, however, an increasing number of social, cultural, legal, ethical, economic, and medical obstacles to appropriately dealing with medical futility in a way that is consistently in the patient's best interest.[26]

Social and Cultural Obstacles

American society does not deal well with death and dying. Americans are often poorly prepared psychologically and spiritually for their own deaths or the deaths of loved ones. Cited reasons include fear, denial, Western individualism, lack of understanding of the meaning of life, and the lack of acceptance of death as a natural part of life.[27] Discussions about death and dying are uncommon in American families and most American children fear death as an unknown, unspoken mystery. The American attitude toward death represents an obstacle to acknowledging medical futility, which requires that individuals accept the inevitability of death. This obstacle is greater when coupled with the expectation that technological advances will overcome illness, no matter how grave.

Inadequate communication prior to catastrophic illness represents yet another major obstacle to avoiding over-treatment. A minority of adults communicates their wishes through advance directives. Advance directives often use vague language and are of little utility because they fail to address key issues such as life support, CPR, nutrition, and hydration.[28] Questions have been raised as to the ability of patients to make informed decisions regarding more explicit advance directives because some individuals change their minds over time. Also, choices may be affected by age, race, acute or recent illness, depression, vagueness of the document or its presentation, and reluctance to commit to directives in writing.[29] Particular obstacles exist in implementing advance directives in long-term residential health-care facilities. Owners often do not want any resident to die in their facility and residents become especially vulnerable to unwanted resuscitation and emergency hospital transport. Even when an advance directive is signed, it is often unavailable.

Although surrogates typically act with the utmost compassion, many are incapable of carrying out the patient's wishes. Even surrogates with long, intimate relationships with the patient may not be able to predict accurately the individual's choices or may be influenced by personal biases or ulterior motives. Surrogates may have little confidence in the physicians involved in the patient's care or a poor understanding of the medical advice offered. Finally, physicians may be to blame for not communicating effectively and consistently enough to allow surrogates to make appropriate decisions.

Legal Obstacles

One of the clearest instances of medical futility is that of brain death. The diagnosis of death is uncontroversial when made at the bedside by establishing the irreversible cessation of heart, lung, and brain functions. However, when CPR and life support systems are used, brain death often occurs despite the reversal of cardiac and respiratory arrest. In this situation, all brain function has irreversibly ceased, but air is pumped into the chest via a ventilator and the heart has, in most cases, been restarted via CPR. Because such a person is medically and legally dead, any continued or proposed intervention is, by definition, futile.[30] Objections to stopping futile intervention in these patients typically come from families who do not accept that their loved one is dead and from physicians who do not accurately diagnose brain death, but instead continue to regard the patient as alive, albeit severely injured.[31]

Brain death with total loss of brain electrical activity, however, is rare in association with successful CPR. Successful CPR, when prolonged, much more often results in a persistent vegetative state. Such individuals have severe, permanent, high brain damage to the extent that there is no responsiveness or awareness, and yet low-level brain function allows them to breathe on their own, unlike patients with total brain death. An estimated 5,000 patients with persistent vegetative state in the United States at any given time can be kept "alive" *for several years* with artificial feeding and meticulous nursing care.[32] Some physicians have proposed that the brain death concept should be expanded to include permanently vegetative patients by defining death as the permanent failure of the brain areas responsible for consciousness and cognition, arguing that the current brain death standard is a legal obstacle to the discontinuation of futile treatment.[33] Expansion of the definition of death, however, has not met with wide acceptance. The protracted, inconsistent treatment of patients with persistent vegetative state often perpetuates emotional suffering for families and poses an extremely high cost to relatives and society.

In the absence of advance directives, decisions by surrogates for those without capacity can be legally more difficult. Some states require that surrogates base decisions on convincing evidence of the patient's wishes. When the courts become involved, they understandably look carefully at the patient's medical condition or prognosis before sanctioning surrogate decisions, particularly when dealing with patients who have not expressed a clear position of abating treatment.[34] Courts have an easier task when there is clear legal precedent, such as with terminally ill patients or those in a persistent vegetative state. The more difficult case is the charged issue of abating treatment for nonvegetative, nonterminally ill patients who lack capacity.[35]

Courts have virtually always supported physicians and medical institutions after the fact when medical interventions have been withdrawn or withheld in situations of medical futility. However, they have been reluctant to intervene by requiring the withdrawal of futile care when requested by physicians or medical institutions over the objections of families or surrogates. Despite sound legal precedent for futility-based decisions, physicians continue to be more likely to acquiesce to a vocal surrogate that requests that everything be done, possibly due to concern over liability or simply to avoid confrontation.

Significant deficiencies in most living wills are likely due to the combination of legal obstacles, insufficient understanding of medical futility, and lack of appreciation for the need and purpose of advance directives by both the lay public and physicians.[36] Recent pacesetting legislation in Florida has made significant progress toward empowering physicians to deal with medical futility rationally and facilitating the implementation of patients' expressed choices.

Ethical Obstacles

Physicians have no obligation to offer futile interventions based upon the ethical principle of beneficence, which requires physicians to act in ways that benefit the patient. Since futile interventions lack benefit, there is no obligation to provide them. Furthermore, the ethical principle of non-maleficence requires that physicians avoid harming patients with futile medical interventions. The ethical principle of justice requires physicians to make wise use of health-care resources and costly futile interventions cannot be justified. An opposing ethical argument, however, is the principle of autonomy or self-determination, which holds that adults have the right to make decisions about their own bodies. A common obstacle arises when the patient or surrogate believes his or her right to decide on treatment extends equally to decisions to *receive* treatment and decisions to *forgo* treatment, sometimes resulting in inappropriate demands for futile treatment. The treating physician's ethical obligations, however, logically limit the patient's autonomous choices to those options the physician can ethically *offer*. There remains some lack of consensus as to who should have ultimate decision-making authority.

Unfortunately, medicine's innovations are often widely applied well in advance of guidelines for their use. In some instances, guidelines are never clearly formulated. Meanwhile, decisions to forgo futile treatment have been defaulted to patients and surrogates. This state of affairs has become so common that it now seems out of place for a physician to make a unilateral futility judgment.

Unilateral futility decisions can ethically be most easily justified in situations of absolute physiologic implausibility, such as attempting CPR in the setting of progressive hypoxemia from end-stage, chronic lung disease that makes adequate oxygenation impossible despite maximal ventilator settings. Once hypoxemia leads to cardiac arrest, no amount of CPR can improve air exchange. Thus, from a physiologic standpoint, CPR is absolutely futile. Most situations, however, are not physiologically futile. The judgment of futility is, instead, based on a low *probability* of treatment success and/or an extremely poor quality of life. In these situations, unilateral futility decisions are ethically less defensible, since the pursuit of treatment is based primarily on a value judgment.[37] When futility is based upon a value judgment, the well-informed patient should decide to accept or forgo treatment. The rare exception to this is when the likelihood of benefit is extremely low and the likelihood of harm to the patient is significant, such that the physician cannot ethically offer the medical intervention. Finally, whether the patient's autonomous value judgment should be overridden by excessive cost (based on justice) in situations of borderline or definite medical futility remains an unresolved ethical dilemma for society.

Ethical conflicts sometimes occur when patients lack understanding of the meaning of low statistical probability and its full implications. More commonly, conflict arises precisely because patients and physicians may draw the futility line at a different probabilistic point, such as under 5 percent versus under 1 or 2 percent likelihood of success. Some patients might require 0 percent or unprecedented success before agreeing that a treatment is futile. Unfortunately, medical science often does not allow discrimination to such a precise degree of accuracy, since little research has been done in individual prognosis prediction and human physiology is highly variable.

Conflicts can occur when physicians and patients differ on the goals of treatment. An example is the case of Helga Wanglie, a ventilator-dependent patient in a persistent vegetative state. Her physician felt that ventilation was futile because it "could not heal her lungs, palliate her suffering, or enable this unconscious and permanently respirator-dependent woman to experience the benefit of the life afforded by respirator support."[38] Her husband disagreed because Mrs. Wanglie had consistently said she wanted respirator support for such a condition. The physician's goal was to benefit the patient through healing and relief of suffering; the patient's goal, according to her husband, was simply to have her life extended. Because cases of goal disagreement involved value judgments, the patient's values should generally prevail. Based upon the above ethical arguments, an individual who is permanently ventilator-dependent, but values such an existence, possesses the autonomous right to choose to continue treatment, regardless of whether others would agree that such a life is of value. If the patient is also in a persistent vegetative state, however, one may argue that it is no longer possible for the individual to derive any value from such treatment because such patients completely lack cognitive perception. A counterargument may be posed as to the ability to predict with absolute certainty that the individual will remain vegetative forever. A circular argument ensues, ultimately involving the question of who should decide on treatment in the face of probabilistic futility. Such unresolved conflicts may rarely require a legal judgment. Based on past judgments, courts would likely support the unilateral declaration of medical futility by a physician if life support or other therapy has already been withdrawn; but would likely rule in favor of the surrogate should the case come to court before withdrawal of treatment. Both the individual and society would arguably be better served by resolving such conflicts through a local bioethics committee made up of lay and professional volunteers empowered with a *clearer, more widely accepted definition of medical futility.*

Ethical obstacles to futility decisions are even greater in cases where surrogates do not have clear past statements by the patient and are asked to make life and death decisions based on insufficient information from the patient. Surrogates commonly err on the side of aggressive care rather than assuming the responsibility for withholding treatment. The most difficult surrogate decisions are controversial treatment choices, such as withholding artificial nutrition and hydration. Though the law and medicine clearly view artificial nutrition and hydration as medical treatments, surrogates may view them as nurturing or palliative, and may have difficulty withholding hydration and nutrition on emotional, religious, or ethical grounds. When conflict arises, the challenge is to achieve consensus of all involved. Unfortunately, many physicians are ill prepared to artfully achieve the consensus required and effective, enlightened bioethics committees are often lacking.

Economic Obstacles

A majority of Americans are not directly accountable for their medical expenses by virtue of insurance, Medicare, Medicaid, or indigent status and have no economic incentive to use medical resources judiciously. There is also little economic incentive for physicians and hospitals to avoid expensive care or to avoid hospitalization of patients. The result is that there is little incentive to change the fact that most people die in the hospital, where the costs of care at the end of life are greatest. Also, most patients believe (sometimes accurately) that their only alternative for obtaining relief of physical pain and emotional suffering is hospitalization. Most patients are eligible to receive hospice care, regardless of socioeconomic resources, yet patients and physicians too often seem unaware of or unwilling to use volunteers for end of life care.[39]

Over 10 percent of all health-care expenditures are spent during the last year of life and a significant portion is spent on hospital care that is futile or of marginal utility.[40] Much of this care is delivered in intensive care units, where costs have been estimated to make up 28 percent of total hospital costs. End-of-life costs are likely to rise exponentially in the future, due to expanding technology and the increasing elder population. The number of individuals over eighty-five years of age is expected to triple between 1980 and 2030.[41] Not only must we find ways to allow cherished senior citizens a graceful exit, but we must avoid the destructive impact of expensive overtreatment on Medicare and other health-care financing systems for our aging populations as we enter the twenty-first century.

Medical Obstacles

The absence of a clear operational definition of medical futility and poor communication among physicians, patients, and families remain the most important obstacles to making futility-based decisions. Relatively little research has been done on predicting medical futility in individual patients. Historically, physicians have been trained to prolong life to the last possible moment and training programs typically emphasize treating specific diseases rather than the whole patient.[42] They often provide little or no instruction in recognizing medical futility, communicating futile situations with patients and families, engaging in shared decision making, and achieving consensus.[43] The result is that prolonging life beyond medical futility is common and young physicians come away from their training with the idea that it is ethically acceptable, thus perpetuating the paradigm of overtreatment.

Conversely, physicians must always provide safeguards to prevent withholding aggressive care when treatment is not futile. Families sometimes misinterpret an advance directive (AD) as meaning that their loved one wanted to categorically avoid all life support. Therapy is not in violation of an AD in which a patient expresses the desire not to be resuscitated in a situation of terminal illness or medical futility. What most current ADs do not, but should, address are conditions of nonterminal medical futility.

To protect against inappropriate futility judgments, a restrictive definition has been recommended that limits judgments to those of physiological futility, or treatment that is "clearly futile in achieving its physiologic objective."[44] Use of this physiologic definition is much narrower than the concept of whole-person futility, which includes treatment that may have "important physiologic effects which medical judgment concludes (nonetheless) are nonbeneficial to the patient as a person."[45] Medical futility has been more broadly defined as *care that serves no useful purpose and provides no immediate or long-term benefit.*[46] A number of court cases, however, have failed to recognize the more inclusive, *whole-person* definition of futility and have ruled in favor of a physiologic definition. Most notably, in 1993, a U.S. District Court ruled that a hospital could not refuse to mechanically ventilate Baby K, an anencephalic infant who suffered repeated episodes of respiratory failure.[47]

The ultimate obstacle to futility decisions is that physicians can *never* predict prognosis with absolute certainty. As a result, physicians typically hesitate to make life and death decisions based on uncertain data. Because some conditions, by nature, involve more uncertainty than others, physicians may have particular difficulty in judging that treatment is futile. Examples include advanced age, dementia, severe brain injury, stroke, extreme low birth weight, and congenital defects involving severe mental and physical handicaps. Especially problematic are severe brain injury and the persistent vegetative state, which are clinical diagnoses for which there are no definitive, confirmatory diagnostic tests. Many physicians feel, however, that these diagnoses can be made clinically with confidence if the patient is unimproved after three months, after a hypoxic brain injury or a cerebrovascular accident, and after twelve months following a head injury.[48]

Statistical models of medical outcomes may be used for prognostic assessment and futility judgments. However, the accuracy of most currently available statistical models is not sufficiently predictive when applied to individual patients, such that physicians often cannot be assured that an individual patient actually has the 95–99 percent probability of dying generally desired to declare death imminent. Furthermore, existing predictive models appear to be of no greater accuracy than physicians' clinical estimates of survival.[49]

A related obstacle to accurate futility judgments is the overestimation of treatment success. The effectiveness of CPR, for example is commonly overestimated by both physicians and the public.[50] This is to some extent due to the high success rate of CPR (67 percent) depicted in medical drama on television.[51] The true effectiveness of CPR is quite limited. With in-hospital cardiac arrest, general survival rates are reported at 10 to 20 percent, but are only 3.5 percent in patients over eighty-five years of age. Following out-of-hospital arrest, only 5 percent of all patients are discharged with intact brain function. Elderly nursing home patients with out-of-hospital arrest have only 1 to 2 percent survival.[52] These statistics are not widely appreciated, much less applied consistently in making CPR decisions. One study found that when CPR outcome data was shared with people, it decreased their stated desire for CPR in a variety of medical scenarios.[53]

Patients and families are often reluctant to accept DNAR status due to legitimate concern that the level of medical care will be reduced. This obstacle to DNAR decisions is likely to worsen as managed care and nursing shortages increase. A further obstacle to palliative care is that physicians are reluctant to give adequate palliative analgesia and sedation due to personal bias, concern about addiction, or fear of being accused of euthanasia if medication intended to alleviate suffering also hastens death. Another concern is that categorically withholding heroic or investigational therapy from patients who are hopelessly ill may prevent the discovery of new, effective treatments for such individuals in the future. Although it is very reasonable to argue that heroic treatment should be undertaken for the advancement of medical science, the vast majority of futile care goes unanalyzed and undocumented and contributes little to medical knowledge.

Another obstacle to futility-based DNAR decisions is the failure of hospital policy to heed professional guidelines for the appropriate use of CPR. As early as 1974, guidelines published by the National Conference on CPR stated that the purpose of CPR is the prevention of sudden, unexpected death and that it is not indicated in certain situations, such as in cases of terminal, irreversible illness where death is not unexpected.[54] The American Medical Association's guidelines stipulate that efforts should be made to resuscitate patients who suffer cardiac or respiratory arrest except when administration of CPR would be futile or not in accord with the desires or best interests of the patient.[55] Despite these official recommendations, hospital policies typically mandate full resuscitation unless there is explicit consent for a DNAR order. The result is that physicians are routinely called to the bedside of a frail, terminally ill patient on whom full resuscitation efforts have already been initiated. There is typically no effective, routine system in place for protecting individuals from such trauma, apart from case-by-case application of DNAR orders.

Unfortunately, physicians commonly fail to engage in timely end-of-life treatment discussion with patients. Early, accurate, consistent, and continuous dialogue is of paramount importance, particularly in situations of medical futility. Failure to effectively counsel patients and families can be due to many factors, including time constraints; personal dislike of discussing death; misperception that individuals do not wish to discuss such issues; the tendency to project the physician's own values onto the patient; insecurity in disclosing a lack of knowledge about the patient's prognosis; and the concern that the patient or family may insist that the physician "do everything."[56]

Lack of communication among other health professionals involved in the patient's care, such as nurses and consulting physicians, can cause inter-staff conflict.[57] Physicians often don't recognize and communicate futility early and, thus, miss important opportunities to address the issue with patients and families. Poor interstaff communication can lead to disconnected, inconsistent medical therapies, while the mixed messages given to patients and families can cause confusion and mistrust.

Defining Medical Futility

Clearly, an operational definition of futility is needed if end-of-life care is to be improved. A logical, step-wise analysis is proposed in Figure 5.

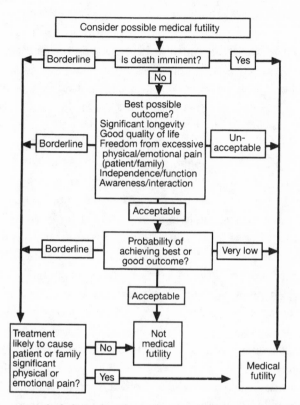

Figure 5. Recommended clinical pathway for determination of medical futility.

Physicians should consider three specific questions: (1) Is death imminent? (2) What is the best possible outcome or recovery that can be hoped for if treatment is maximally successful? (3) What is the probability of achieving the best possible result, or at least a good result? If the answer to any one of the three questions clearly points to a medically futile situation, the patient should be managed with every effort to provide comfort, support, and dignity, but not with continued efforts to prolong life. If the answer to any of the three futility-defining questions is borderline, the interventions in question should be weighed heavily against the expected negative impact of treatment, including the emotional, physical, or financial burdens inflicted on the patient, family, and society. Significant negative factors should mitigate against heroic treatment in situations of borderline futility.

Once a medically futile condition has been established, the patient and/or family should be counseled on specific treatment issues, which should always include resuscitation status, that is, full resuscitation, limited resuscitation, or DNAR. Other issues that should be discussed include highly technological measures, such as mechanical ventilation and dialysis, to simple measures, such as intravenous or nasogastric feeding and hydration. In each case, every effort should be made to genuinely reassure the patient and family that the existence of a poor prognosis will not cause a reduction in the level of palliative and supportive care. Protocols, including specific routine palliative orders, should be implemented immediately to effectively deliver the best possible care for these individuals in their last chapter of life.

Decisions regarding futility must be constantly re-evaluated. It is rare for futile situations to become nonfutile, but common for patients to evolve into apparent futility after trials of medical or surgical intervention have failed. Individuals with brain damage are typically in a coma immediately after experiencing brain insult or injury. Most recovery from such situations begins within a few hours or days, while late, miraculous recovery is extremely rare. Such individuals must be constantly re-evaluated based on best possible outcome and probability with sensitivity to the pre-event wishes of the patient and the ongoing needs of the family. If futility becomes apparent, all efforts should then be made to involve the patient's family in making choices that respect the rights and wishes of the patient while considering the realistic limitations of medical technology and health-care resources.

In an individual with end-stage heart failure with severe shortness of breath without effort, in spite of maximum treatment, however, premature death is certain but not as easily predicted as imminent. Such an individual requires a constant re-evaluation of the best possible quality of life that short-term recovery can provide and the probability of obtaining such recovery. Intermittent, intravenous inotrope infusions coupled with intensive nursing care have allowed the extension of reasonably high quality life for months with minimum time in the hospital. Continuing aggressive therapy eventually becomes medically futile when severe symptoms or emotional and financial burdens outweigh the value of survival. A DNAR order may be appropriate early in the course of therapy to allow a sudden, graceful exit and hospice, commonly underutilized for such individuals, can be extremely helpful in supporting a peaceful death in the home environment.

More emotionally charged issues in futility involve newborn children who are found at birth or in-utero to have severe congenital defects that preclude normal development and longevity. The choice to withhold life support in an anancephalic child appears appropriate to most individuals, for example, but can be extremely emotionally traumatic for the family. Management issues in children born with severe, nonsurgically correctable congenital heart disease or brain defects that predictably lead to severe mental retardation and/or short life spans without imminent neonatal death are even more difficult for physicians and families to resolve. Emphasis on a unified, supportive decision that dispels any feelings of guilt is critical.

Elderly patients commonly wish to forgo invasive medical interventions, even when futility is not yet apparent, reasoning that they have lived a long life, have accomplished their goals, have come to terms with death, and wish to fulfill personal preferences regarding their own graceful exits. They may choose nonaggressive management for any number of serious illnesses, such as stroke, heart attack, cancer, and even pneumonia. Since surrogate decisions for elderly people are difficult, physicians should take a much more proactive role in obtaining advance directives while individuals are still capable of making decisions for themselves.[58]

In dealing with a patient with severe Alzheimer's disease, Drs. J. H. Karlawish, T. Quill, and D. E. Meier recommend an approach for working with the patient's family. A "consensus-building process, grounded in dialogue among proxy, other close family members, physician and immediate caregivers" is recommended.[59] The authors emphasize an evolving dialogue, which should center around explicitly stating the goals of therapy in relation to futility judgments, and should clarify which goal(s) cannot be met, or are unlikely to be met, by the proposed intervention. Sometimes it is necessary to postpone the decision making and recommend that the participants take time to think about and discuss key issues.[60] Consensus building takes emotional release, evolution through stages of grief, acceptance, and education, all of which require time and a guided dialogue.

Despite attempts at consensus building, conflicts still emerge. Such conflicts typically arise from (1) differences in expectations of outcome; (2) difficulty in dealing with uncertainty in outcome, commonly reflected by requests to "do everything"; (3) differences in the way benefits and harms are valued; (4) denial or lack of understanding of the severity of the illness by physician, patient, or family; and (5) the tendency for physicians and families to transfer their values and perceptions to the patient.

To minimize conflict, physicians and patients should engage in shared decision making. Physicians have the ability to evaluate expected benefits and risks of treatment more accurately and objectively than patients or surrogates. However, physicians should not impose their values, religious beliefs, fears, tolerance of pain, or definition of quality life on the patient. The patient and family should make a highly informed decision as to what course of therapy is desired, within the range of reasonable treatments outlined by the physician, with the option to re-evaluate and change.

If the physician perceives that the patient or family is making a poor choice, every effort should be made to better advise the patient or surrogate, short of passing judgment on the individual's values. Once it is clear that the patient or surrogate is well informed, every effort should be made to support the decision that is made. Patients and families tend to feel guilty about such choices, no matter what is chosen, since a choice of one course of therapy necessarily deprives the patient of another and outcomes are never certain. It is the physician's cardinal responsibility to reassure the patient and family that the choice, once made, is the best and most ethical choice for that individual, since it is based upon unique, personal values.

When inevitable conflicts still occur, physicians should learn to assess *why* when a patient wants a treatment that is considered to be futile by the physician. Is it misunderstanding, disbelief, denial, mistrust of the doctor, or is it a difference in the patient's assessment of the value of a possible small duration or chance of survival? The physician should attempt to preserve or restore trust and establish a compromise when possible. All resources available should be used to resolve the conflict, including input from other physicians as well as ethical and religious consultants. Hospitals should have committees of dedicated professional individuals who are trained to assist physicians and patients when conflicts arise.

Unresolved conflicts should be dealt with by deferring to the patient or family, by recommending that the case be turned over to another physician, or rarely by arranging transfer to another institution. The best way to deal with conflicts is to avoid them through early, continuous communication. Families should be informed of the patient's condition and expected prognosis at the earliest possible time, particularly if the prognosis is poor. When medical futility is not absolutely certain, families and patients should participate in formulating a treatment strategy that might entail aggressive therapy for a finite length of time to give the patient an opportunity to improve against the odds. It then becomes much easier to accept the fact that the chosen interventions have failed and that everything of potential benefit has been done for the patient prior to agreeing that a medically futile situation exists. Physicians must also learn to deliver the message that a particular treatment is futile without giving the impression that they are abandoning their patients. They must emphasize that comfort care and attention to quality of life will never cease.[61]

Medical futility has the unique feature of being underdiagnosed and overtreated. In proposing an operational definition of medical futility and an outline of the process of shared decision making, we hope to assist physicians with the difficult task of recognizing and coping with medical futility with patients and families. When physicians, patients, and families agree that medical futility exists, aggressive therapy can be mercifully forgone and the focus of care can then shift, without feelings of guilt, to maintaining the patient's comfort and dignity. While the questions raised by end-of-life care are complex and involve important issues of ethics, autonomy, economics, and social responsibility, progress will then be made when physicians commit themselves to the accurate recognition of medical futility and to the process of shared decision making with patients and families. Physicians must take a leadership role if they are to restore trust in their ability to address end-of-life issues in an appropriate, compassionate, socially responsible manner. The physician's intimate role as the patient's advocate and loving friend, even through the experience of death and dying, remains the doctor's unique responsibility and privilege, no more and no less than it did before the dawn of modern medical technology.

TASK FORCE II: ADVANCE CARE PLANNING

Those associated with Project GRACE agree that all adults should be encouraged by their physician(s) and society as a whole to make clear statements, in legally acceptable documents, as to how they wish to be cared for when their health status, as reflected in their quality of life, deteriorates significantly, or they experience a sudden cardiac arrest.

Thus, addressing end-of-life issues first and foremost requires advance planning. A scenario-specific living will (LW), which is clearly understood by the individual, his or her relatives and caretakers, from family to physicians, is an absolute necessity. The following is an outline to help establish such an advance care planning document.

Recommendations for Advance Care Planning

All information and forms related to advance care planning (ACP) should be written in clear, concise language. If the individual for whom the action(s) implies does not readily comprehend English, the document should be written in the language understood by the individual and then translated into English. The document should be easily read by lay persons and, more importantly, understood by elderly or ill persons. Readily available trained counselors are needed to explain the forms and guide the individual in his or her decision making and finalization of the document.

The American Medical Association and other health-related organizations should lobby for a Medicare/Medicaid code and an insurance reimbursement code for counseling in ACP.

Patients (i.e., principals) should be required to discuss the document with any close, caring family and/or their appointed surrogate before signing the document. After such discussion, the surrogate should sign and date the document. The Florida Legislature defined a surrogate as any competent adult expressly designated by a principal to make health-care decisions on behalf of the principal upon the principal's incapacity.

The documents and the planning process should be discussed with the patient's primary physician so that the patient's wishes are clear and acceptable to the physician. After such discussion(s), if agreeable, the primary physician should acknowledge the content and date of the document.

If the physician does not agree with the plan(s), the patient should be informed and the reason(s) should be carefully discussed with the patient, close relatives, and any appointed surrogate. If agreement is not reached, the patient should be referred to another physician.

It should be made clear that any person executing such a document can delete options or change his or her wishes at any time. If a person does change his or her wishes, the individual must inform close relative(s), surrogate(s), primary physician(s), and other caregivers.

The document should be more precise than the traditional, vague language of the current statutory LW. The 1999 Florida Legislature reaffirmed that "[the term] advance directive means a witnessed, written document or oral statement in which instructions are given by a principal, or in which the principal's desires are expressed concerning any aspect of the principal's health care, and includes, but is not limited to, the designation of a health care surrogate, a living will or an anatomical gift."[62]

It should be noted that any advance directive made prior to October 1, 1999 (when major changes in the Florida Statues became effective), shall be given effect as executed provided such directive was legally effective when written.

The form should provide specific choices that a patient may make, with the opportunity to write in specific desires, including a desire to provide organ donations, as the patient sees fit. The LW form should be universal and should be acceptable in all fifty states. There should be a federal law guaranteeing this level of acceptance or a model act which is adopted in all states. The LW, stating the terms, should be easily accessible via a driver's license, voter registration card, and/or a national computer registry.

There should be a specific requirement that LWs be posted on the medical chart in a specific location so that they are easy for medical providers and physicians to locate. The Florida legislative statute states that "the patient's advance directive shall travel with the patient as part of the patient's medical record."

The LW should provide, and the legislature should support, a waiver of any liability for any physician or any other health-care provider who renders care or withholds care from a patient, if they reasonably believe that such action is consistent with the patient's wishes as expressed in the LW.

There should be a penalty for refusing to follow a valid LW.

Recent substantive changes in the Florida laws should enable the wide use of ACP in guiding medical care.

Recommendation for a Universal Living Will

CATEGORY I: Defines Loss of Functionality

The following are examples of scenarios that apply to conditions of terminal illness. In these situations, the individuals have lost the ability to communicate, dress or feed themselves, clean themselves, hold their urine, go to the bathroom without assistance, are not self-ambulatory, and are unable to make appropriate decisions about daily living matters.

Terminal Illness. Death is expected to occur with or without medical intervention(s). The condition is irreversible or there is no reasonable chance of recovery.

Coma. Refers to *permanent* unconscious deep sleep. There is brain damage, severe enough to render the individual unresponsive and unable to feel or communicate in any way. There is *no reasonable* chance for recovery by all generally accepted medical standards.

Permanent Vegetative State. There is *permanent* brain damage, severe enough to render the individual *unaware* of self or the environment. The patient has irretrievably lost the ability to meaningfully appreciate, understand, and communicate appropriately. There is no reasonable chance for significant improvement.

CATEGORY II: Significant Diseases that Diminish Quality of Life

Advanced Senility, Dementia, Massive Stroke, Loss of Speech, Loss of Independence. The following scenarios apply to conditions that, while terminal, do not render the person comatose or in a permanent vegetative state. In these conditions the end of life is *near* but *not imminent.* Active intervention is *unlikely* to improve the length or quality of life materially. Examples of scenarios when these losses may occur are as follows: severe dementia, advanced senility and/or advanced stroke with loss of ability to communicate, and loss of an independent life.

In this person, brain damage has been present for a while, such as with severe Alzheimer's disease or multiple strokes. The brain damage is *severe enough* to make the individual lose his or her ability to recognize others, interact with them, or make intelligent decisions. The individual is mostly confused and is totally dependent. The individual has irretrievably lost the qualities which characterized the individual as a person.

These losses include any condition with total loss of ability to communicate and that render the patient totally and *permanently* dependent upon others for feeding, personal hygiene, and all daily activities.

End-Stage Disease. Death is expected in the near future with or without treatment. Examples include the following:

• Disseminated cancer *not responsive to treatment*
• End-stage heart or lung disease, provided heart–lung transplantation

is *not* indicated or feasible. (End-stage heart disease occurs when there is loss of response to maximum medical therapy and requiring repeated hospitalization over the previous three months; end-stage lung disease renders the patient chair-bound and in need of oxygen around the clock.)

- End-stage infection such as with terminal stages of AIDS
- Disseminated infection with an organism resistant to all available antimicrobials (antibiotics)
- End-stage liver disease when liver transplant is not indicated or not feasible
- End-stage kidney disease in conjunction with advanced heart, lung, or liver disease. Dialysis is either not indicated or unlikely to improve the quality or length of life or has been instituted and has not been effective
- End-stage nervous disorder with near complete total body paralysis, near total dependence with no hope for improvement

Advanced Conditions and Disease(s) that Diminish the Quality of Life. Advanced senility, extreme frailty, total dependence, and unbearable and unrelieveable pain. These individuals are particularly susceptible to bone fractures, pneumonia, heart attacks, and strokes.

Conditions and findings included in this category make ordinary activities of daily living impossible. Examples include the inability to

- tolerate unbearable and unrelieveable pain
- clean oneself
- feed and hydrate oneself
- dress oneself
- control one's bladder and/or bowel
- communicate and express oneself
- ambulate independently
- make decisions about daily living matters

With each of the medical scenarios, the patient is given the choice whether to forgo specific medical interventions, including

- CPR (cardiopulmonary resuscitation)

- Life support measures such as assisted ventilation and dialysis, surgery, and other interventions unlikely to change the underlying medical condition
- Blood transfusion intended to treat incidental anemia
- Antibiotics aimed to treat a terminal pneumonia or a concurrent infection except for treatment designed to relieve distressing symptoms (e.g., a urinary tract infection causing dysuria)
- Tube feeding and hydration

TASK FORCE III: PALLIATIVE CARE

During the early stages of a serious illness, cure is the major goal for all concerned and treatment is generally aggressive. However, if the illness persists and cure appears unlikely, and adverse symptoms and poor quality of life become more dominant, the burden(s) of traditional medicine may appear to outweigh the benefits. This is particularly likely to be so when the therapeutic efforts that were intended to cure produce adverse symptoms that impair the quality of life and require therapy.

Such a transition period, that is, when the major therapeutic efforts are directed from traditional curative care to symptom control, may be one of the most difficult periods of caring for a patient with life-limiting illnesses, for it is not always easy to determine an individual patient's survival probability and, therefore, to date when the transition period should begin. The Study to Understand Prognoses and Preferences for Outcomes and Risks of Treatments (SUPPORT) reported that both patients and professionals overestimate the likelihood of long survival.[63] It has been demonstrated that such prognostic optimism tends to prolong the use of potentially curative therapy despite the production of symptoms contributing to an adverse quality of life.[64] So it is not surprising that, as the presence of the illness and therapeutic-induced symptoms continue, the treatment goals of the patient, the goals of the patient's family, and the patient's physician(s) may diverge.

The treatment that is directed by caregivers predominantly toward the relief of suffering, psychosocial support, and the enhancement of the patient's quality of life has been classified as palliative care. Such care is indicated not just when an illness is considered terminal but for all patients with advanced chronic illness(es), whether or not they are considered to be imminently dying.

The term *hospice care* is frequently used interchangeably for palliative care. The purist knows that the older dictionaries defined hospice as specifically and solely a place of rest or shelter, usually maintained by a religious order for pilgrims, travelers, etc. However, in more recent editions of the dictionary, *hospice* is defined as a homelike facility to provide supportive care for terminally ill patients. The word is still classified as only a noun. Reference to hospice care, where hospice is used as an adjective, is even more recent.

While a number of definitions for palliative care exist, the one developed by the Last Acts Campaign's Task Force on Palliative Care, sponsored by the Robert Wood Johnson Foundation, is considered most timely and inclusive:

> Palliative care refers to the comprehensive management of physical, social, spiritual, and existential needs of patients, in particular those with incurable, progressive illnesses. Palliative care affirms life and regards dying as a natural process that is a profoundly personal experience for the individual and family. The goal of palliative care is to achieve the best possible quality of life through relief of suffering, control of symptoms, and restoration of functional capacity while remaining sensitive to personal, cultural and religious values, beliefs, and practices.[65]

The intensity and range of palliative interventions may increase as illness progresses and the complexity of care and needs of the patients and their families increase. The priority of care frequently shifts as an illness progresses from curative goals to focus on end-of-life decision making and care that supports comfort and is consistent with the values and expressed desires of the patient.

As with any choice in health care, there exist multiple potential decisions. For the decision to transit to palliative care, the primary decision makers may be the patient, or family members, or attending and/or referring physicians, or occasionally even impersonal reimbursement entities such as Medicare, Medicaid, and contracting health plans. The decision to enter into palliative care can occur in a variety of settings such as emergency departments, intensive care units, research centers, HMOs, physician offices, nursing homes (NH), assisted living facilities (ALF), and/or patient homes.

A formalized hospice program is an attractive option for many persons desiring traditional curative care. However, patients who are averse to the word *hospice*, or who are reluctant to sign forms that redefine their insurance benefits, or who have difficulty acknowledging that they are facing the terminal stages of a disease, should ideally be able to receive palliative services under the guidance and with the support of their physician.[66] However, physician referral to or initiation of palliative care will depend on the physician's knowledge level, values, beliefs, and the availability of community resources.

For the best preparation of patients and families, physically, emotionally, and spiritually, and to assure the highest possible quality of life, it is imperative that discussions regarding palliative care begin earlier in the disease trajectory than typically occurs. The unpredictability of the outcomes of patients with chronic diseases substantiates the need to begin discussions of treatment options soon after diagnosis.

As a result of an earlier introduction of palliative interventions, in place of the compulsive continuation of traditional care, quality of life may be enhanced and costs may be reduced. A 1995 study by U.S. Healthcare demonstrated that a Congestive Heart Failure Disease Management Program, which provided palliative care to 209 members, positively impacted multiple outcomes for patients and the provider.[67] The program included a case manager, home visits and educational instruction by a nurse, parenteral medication at home (if necessary), one-year follow-up, and tracking of outcomes.

Much of the discussion on increasing care options for dying persons has focused on physician-assisted suicide. Indeed, the U.S. Supreme Court's consideration of the legality of physician-assisted suicide in 1997, the passage of Oregon's Death with Dignity Act which permits physician-assisted suicide, and the recent second-degree murder conviction of Dr. Jack Kevorkian has made physician-assisted suicide a more familiar concept than palliative care.

From the limited data available, the factors most commonly involved in requests for assistance in dying are concerns about future loss of control and being a burden to family members as well as a fear of severe pain.[68] Studies asking terminally ill cancer patients and patients with acquired immune deficiency syndrome (AIDS) about their desire for death revealed that such desires are closely associated with depression, pain, and lack of social support.[69] Comprehensive palliative care not only manages the physical symptoms of the dying patient, but also helps patients and families deal with the social, psychological, and spiritual aspects of death and dying. Advocates for the legalization of physician-assisted suicide believe that if expert palliative care were available to everyone who needed it, there would be few requests for physician-assisted suicide.[70]

The terms *physician-assisted suicide* and *euthanasia* are widely used, sometimes interchangeably, but crucial conceptual and behavioral differences distinguish the two actions. Both assisted suicide and voluntary active euthanasia are instances of assistance in bringing about the death of another person. In cases of assisted suicide, the person who dies causes his or her own death with the assistance of another person (e.g., another person provides lethal medication for the patient to take him- or herself); whereas in cases of voluntary active euthanasia, the person dies because of the direct actions of another person (e.g., death is caused by lethal injection or excessive oral medication).

At present, with the exception of the state of Oregon and despite ongoing efforts at legislative reform in several states, physician-assisted suicide and voluntary active euthanasia are illegal in the United States. Unlike the right to assistance in committing suicide, the right to refuse or to withdraw from medical treatment, even at the risk of causing one's death, is protected by the Fourteenth Amendment's Due Process clause. Furthermore, the right to refuse life-sustaining medical treatment is supported by case precedent (e.g., *In re Quinlan, Bouvia v. Superior Court, Cruzan v. Director*) and the common laws of most states. Patients (or their duly appointed surrogate[s]) who refuse or discontinue life-sustaining treatment are not seen as committing suicide/murder, but rather as dying/accepting death due to the underlying disease. Physicians who honor their patients' wishes to forgo life-sustaining treatment are similarly not seen as assisting in their deaths.

Physicians who care for dying patients may use available pharmacologic tools with the knowledge that they may hasten the time of death. While the physician's primary intent is to relieve the patient's suffering, some medications used for pain management may suppress respiratory function, and as a secondary consequence, or double effect, may hasten the time of death. However, this is a very rare event in the hands of an experienced palliative care physician administering pain medication in accordance with established protocols.[71]

Both the courts and the majority of medical professionals endorse increasing access to palliative care, not assisted suicide, as a compassionate and appropriate response to dying persons. The U.S. Supreme Court acknowledged that its refusal to legalize physician-assisted suicide was based in part on the availability of palliative care and encouraged the development of more effective and available palliative care alternatives for dying patients. In fact, the U.S. Supreme Court's ruling may be interpreted as outlining a right to palliative care and a directive to remove institutional barriers to appropriate care at the end of life.[72]

A recent Gallup Poll, however, reported that when asked if terminally ill with six months or less to live, nine of ten adults would prefer to be cared for at home.[73] Nationally, however, nearly one of five older persons die in nursing homes with many more dying in hospitals after becoming institutionalized.[74] Of all nursing home patients, 26 percent die in hospitals, unless hospice is involved in the nursing home; in such situations hospital deaths are reduced to 1 percent.

Recognizing that not all people can live and die in one place, health-care providers must also be responsible for providing a seamless transition from one level of care to another. Most people do not remain in one location during their last years of life. Regardless of their goal, illness may force them to seek interventions at different institutions of care, such as a hospital, rehabilitation center, skilled nursing facility, or an ALF. While this may be inevitable, the ability for health-care providers to provide a seamless transition may greatly reduce the ramifications of health problems.[75]

Health-care providers historically are poor communicators. This is complicated by the fact that most patients assume that all their health-care providers have conferred with each other. However, this is generally not the case and no one, including the patient, assumes responsibility for sharing all pertinent medical history with all the providers. This lack of relevant patient-related data often leads to duplication of services. Another issue encountered is the need to rewrite advance directives and other documents at every level of care. A case manager who follows the individual through the multiple levels of care may limit some of these problems.

All palliative care services need to provide continuity of health care, even between different levels of care. The site of care may not always be a choice that the patient and even the caregiver can control; however, health-care providers can minimize the negative impact of changing the care site by providing a seamless transition model.

Despite increased societal concern about end-of-life issues, there is no clear indication that care for most patients with chronic illnesses has improved. Increased attention has been given to hospice and palliative medical education; however, in practice, the majority of health profes-sionals have received only sporadic training in the principles and practice of caring for patients with advanced life-limiting illnesses.[76]

In the United States, medical conferences devote minimal time to pal-liative medicine, and only 5 of 126 medical schools surveyed in 1994 offered a separate course on end-of-life care.[77] The lack of more current data probably speaks to the lack of attention directed to such programs by the academic community. Many physicians, nurses, and students acknowl-edge a lack of skill and confidence in the area of palliative medicine and indicate a desire for more education and training on symptom control and the management of psychosocial and spiritual concerns. Very few contin-uing education courses in end-of-life or palliative care are conducted for physicians and nurses in practice.

The three medical colleges (University of Florida, University of Miami, University of South Florida) and one osteopathic college (Nova University) in Florida were surveyed about their end-of-life or palliative care education curriculum. In addition, four Florida colleges of nursing (Barry University, Florida State University, University of Florida, Univer-sity of South Florida) were surveyed to determine similar information about their curriculum.

Results of the survey revealed no standardization of education in end-of-life care or palliative care. Medical schools and nursing schools are pri-marily teaching end-of-life issues in ethics courses, but they offer little clinical instruction in the treatment of patients from a palliative care approach. There was, however, strong interest by individuals in all three medical schools to include additional palliative care education in the cur-riculum, either at the undergraduate or postgraduate level. Current end-of-life care or palliative care education in the medical schools is primarily possible because of grants (funded by the Robert Wood Johnson Founda-tion, the Veterans Administration, and the National Cancer Institute) that are time limited and based on available funding opportunities. While there appears to be no standard education, changes in curriculum are being seen; however, it is unclear whether there will be permanent changes once temporary funding ends.

If the public in general is expected to increase their acknowledgment and acceptance of end-of-life and palliative care, there needs to be acceptance by the health-care community that end-of-life and palliative care are integral parts of the health-care continuum. This will require uniform education for changes in attitudes, knowledge, and skills of health-care professionals in end-of-life and palliative care.

Although one would think that palliative care, as it is typically practiced, is less expensive than conventional medical care, there is little evidence to support this presumption.[78] If one equates care with hospice care and examines the Medicare data, the cost benefits that are seen in the last few months of life diminish the further from death patients may be.[79]

No reports have documented that high-quality palliative care is more expensive than conventional care, however.[80] According to the U.S. Supreme Court, high-quality palliative care is a right.[81] The cost-effectiveness of this form of care should be presented, at least, as not being a financial deterrent to incorporating it into mainstream medicine.

Currently, there is no defined reimbursement plan for palliative care. Palliative care is practiced by a number of physicians and other health-care providers in a variety of settings under existing reimbursement models.[82] This is not an ideal situation but it does permit some reimbursement for those involved in palliative care.

Appropriate palliative care should be administered by a skilled multidisciplinary team. Availability of such services are often limited, however, due to a lack of a reimbursement mechanism. The current Evaluation and Management (E&M) codes that physicians use for billing focus on procedures and activities and do not generally recognize time spent, thus the code limits the ability to bill for palliative care services through established mechanisms.[83] Clearly, our government and legislature need to take the necessary steps to correct this serious deficiency in our health-care system, which encourages intrusive care through built-in perverse incentives, thereby denying patients a dignified, peaceful death in their own homes.

In-patient palliative care is often provided through the Medicare Hospice Benefits (MHB) in-patient benefit. This has the limitations mentioned previously and other limitations imposed by the in-patient benefit itself, but it is a solution for acute palliative interventions for the small number of terminal patients where in-patient units or contracts exist.

Patients receiving palliative care outside of hospice programs experience many of the same previously cited problems. Obviously, demonstration of cost effectiveness will drive the development of palliative care within Medicare HMOs in a positive direction. In addition, demonstration of good quality outcomes with neutral dollar impact will move this system forward. The use of palliative care should demonstrate both of these, but data are needed. Until this occurs, Medicare HMO patients will have a more difficult time receiving any form of home health care and are unlikely to see any funding of other disciplines important to high-quality interdisciplinary palliative care.

As palliative care health services are instituted, attention must be directed toward determining the impact of the illness on the lives of the members of the involved family and the influence of the family's response to the illness on the outcome of the patient experiencing the illness. Illness, long-term care, and death are family affairs. The manner in which each person is cared for will influence the cooperation of the members of the family, and ultimately how each member grieves and is able to continue living. Health-care providers must recognize diversity in families in terms of ethics, religion, cultural norms, social support systems, financial strata, and health-care expectations.

In considering family membership, it is important to recognize, among others, the status of homosexual partners; common-law arrangements; homeless patients; single-parent households; young, single patients; the widowed; and the aged who have never married.

Another societal factor affecting the provision of palliative care is the consideration of whether one lives in close proximity to others or in isolation. The physical provision of care changes with the resident's location. A recent survey in the United States revealed that over 55 percent of our population lives alone.[84] The isolated resident is more likely to receive health care at a distance from his or her home, and providers need to recognize themselves as strangers to this type of family system.

Caregivers must recognize the word *family* as all encompassing, Those members identified and recognized by the patient will be helpful in identifying the patient's support system; however, that may not include the total membership. Infirm members who are chronically ill often consider their closest neighbor, friend, or nursing caretaker more as family than their own blood relatives. The ill patient may have made the decision to receive palliative care as the better choice over curative care, but the distant family members may not accept or agree with the decision.

To prevent worry, or to spare adult children the expense of frequent trips from work and home duties, the patient may not contact the family at the time of diagnosis, nor during the treatment process. Adult children may question the wisdom of the aged parent and his or her health-care providers, even when recognizing their inability to care for the dying in their locale. Even those family members who are totally supportive of the decisions of the patient and health-care providers may experience a sense of denial, guilt, shame, and remorse with the thoughts that they should have been more involved earlier.

The number of barriers in the family will increase or decrease depending on the openness of the communications between members, the relationships of the dying member to his or her family, and the trust and honesty with which they have lived. In a closed, secretive communication system, lack of knowledge is a barrier and becomes evident concerning not only palliative care but all end-of-life decision making, such as the selected person for health-care surrogate, living wills, expenses, desires for particular funeral rites, place of burial, and estate settlements. There are some patients who are unable to speak to their loved ones about dying. There are families who maintain denial, unable to acknowledge the closeness of death of a loved family member.

It takes tremendous energy, effort, and time to care for an ill patient in a home setting. The demands on the caregiver are enormous. Age and/or physical limitations of the caregiver can become a barrier to providing palliative care. However, the caregiver may resist respite care because of feeling guilty that he or she cannot meet the expectations of the patient, health professionals, and family. Those responsible for the palliative care must be concerned not only for the care of the patient but also the ability of the individual caregiver(s) to meet the expected needs for care without causing an adverse personal effect.

There is much that can and must be done by health-care providers and society at large to foster palliative care for those with chronic, frequently debilitating conditions. The focus of treatment should shift from attempts to postpone death to concerns about patient comfort, dignity, and quality of life.

14

ETHICAL DILEMMAS IN MEDICAL MANAGEMENT AT END-OF-LIFE

Case Studies

❦

INTRODUCTION

With little hesitation, I decided to include true stories of real patients in this book. Consistent with our philosophy and respectful of the patients' right to privacy, the identity of these patients has been concealed but the integrity of the case history has been faithfully preserved.

But why present real cases when we have an abundance of literature on the philosophical-ethical aspects of the practice of medicine? Having command of the basic rules of sailing does not make one a good sailor, nor does a keen knowledge of traffic safety rules guarantee that one is a good driver. By the same token, there is a vast gulf between the still waters of armchair theoretical ethics and the humbled waters of taking care of real people with truly complex and uniquely heart-wrenching problems. In this chapter I present the stories of people whose names and faces are familiar to me. I describe life problems that I have experienced, grappled with, toiled over, suffered for, and taken to heart. In many cases, our answers might be questioned, but these were the best decisions we could recommend. At all times we tried to be faithful to the basic precepts of medical ethics. Also, we have tried, as we always do, to strike a healthy balance between physicians' authority and patients' autonomy, ever mindful of the perils of the literal application of the cold, rigid, dissociated, esoteric, theoretical ethics to true human tragedies.

These stories of real people should provide a nonphysician reader with vivid, multicolored images of medical drama in order to further appreciate the priceless nature of a meaningful doctor-patient relationship and the importance of communicating one's own wishes with loved ones. Members of ethics committees of health-care and assisted living institutions should find this chapter to be a valuable resource when they face similar dilemmas. Medical students and health-care professionals can incorporate some of these case studies into their teaching curriculum and seminars. There can be no greater tribute to my patients' memories than to use their dying stories to educate and guide. These unnamed heroes have enriched my life and taught me unforgettable lessons. It is with humility and gratitude that I share these stories with my readers.

Additionally, I wish to extend my gratitude for the efforts of those who contributed to the case studies included in this chapter: Mark R. Chambers, M.D.; Pamela C. Crowell, M.D.; George Gamouras, M.D.; Michael F. Morrow, M.D.; Michael L. O'Neal, D.O.; Kenneth Plunkitt, M.D.; and Ron Shashy, B.S.

CASE STUDY #1

The Ethical Issue: A patient asks his cardiologist to deactivate an implantable cardioverter defibrillator (ICD) device in order to allow him to die.

A seventy-six-year-old man, JC, has advanced atherosclerotic heart disease (hardening of the arteries). He has suffered three heart attacks, has undergone aorto-coronary bypass surgery twice, and has had numerous coronary artery and bypass graft interventions over the past ten years. He has been treated for hypertension (high blood pressure) for over fifteen years, diabetes mellitus for almost twenty years, and smoked two packs a day for forty years before he stopped smoking eight years ago. Eighteen months ago he was evaluated because of recurrent syncope (loss of consciousness), which was determined to be due to episodic monomorphic ventricular tachycardia (disordered fast heart rhythm) for which JC was placed on a daily medication to keep his heart in rhythm. He also received an implantable cardioverter-defibrillator (ICD) device to successfully terminate otherwise lethal attacks. Since placement, the device has gone off three times: twice during the first six months and once during the last year.

JC made an appointment for an office visit asking to have the ICD device deactivated in order to allow him to die. He pleaded, "my life's quality is so diminished that I choose death as a much preferred alternative."

Currently he is in Class III–IV congestive heart failure. He has been admitted to the hospital three times over the last two months because of episodes of acute pulmonary edema (acute heart failure with lung congestion). He is on home inotropic infusion therapy (a medication given by vein in an attempt to make the heart squeeze better). An ultrasound examination shows a markedly enlarged heart and moderate mitral valve regurgitation (leaky heart valve). Clinical examination further shows widespread atherosclerotic disease for which JC has undergone multiple operations including an amputation below the left knee. He has moderately severe renal (kidney) failure.

The Ethical Dilemma

Should you, as the physician,

1. Comply with the patient's wishes and deactivate the ICD?
2. Absolutely refuse to comply and try to convince the patient against deactivating the device?
3. Refer the patient to a psychiatrist for evaluation and treatment for depression?

The most appropriate response is 1.

You should make sure that the patient is not suffering from depression and that his assessment of "a much diminished quality of life" is a rational one. Once these are satisfied you must comply with the patient's wishes. The ethico-legal basis for this recommendation stems from the rationale that no crime would be committed by physicians who comply with the wishes of fully informed patients to allow death through "nature taking its course."

Discussion

Patients have the right to refuse medical treatment even if that treatment is deemed beneficial to them.[1] This right is derived from the doctrine of informed consent by which the physician has a duty to disclose to the patient all treatment options, including relative benefits and risks. The patient has the right to choose (or refuse) any or all treatments. Further, many state statutes explicitly permit the patient to discontinue life support.[2] The courts, however, have made a distinction between the right to refuse treatment on the one hand and physician-assisted suicide or active euthanasia on the other.[3] In the first instance, the physician allows death to take place. In the second, the physician controls the time and means of death.

Two cases reviewed by the Canadian Supreme Court illustrate the difference. Sue Rodriguez was suffering from advanced Lou Gehrig's disease (a progressive disease causing muscle weakness and deterioration) and became wheelchair bound. In 1992, she asked that a physician be legally allowed to help her die. The Canadian Supreme Court denied her wish by a slim majority (5–4). She died in February 1994 with the help of a physician who remained anonymous.[4]

By contrast, in *Nancy B. v. L'Hotel Dieu de Quebec*, the patient, a twenty-five-year-old woman, was permanently paralyzed from Guillan-Barre Syndrome (another form of nerve and muscle degeneration). She was ventilator dependent. In a unanimous decision in January 1992, the Supreme Court of Canada granted her request to be disconnected from the ventilator under the "Causation Rationale." This states that no crime would be committed by persons who complied with a patient's informed consent to allow death through "nature taking its course."[5] The same ethical-legal principle applies to U.S. citizens.

Additionally, in the recent U.S. Supreme Court cases of *Washington v. Glucksberg* and *Vacco v. Quill*, Justice William Rehnquist, writing for the majority, asserted the individual right to refuse medical intervention that postpones death and that there is no right to determine the time and manner of one's death with the assistance of another.[6]

CASE STUDY #2

The Ethical Issue: A family member with power of attorney for an eighty-seven-year-old patient is requesting removal of the patient's pacemaker (an electronic gadget that keeps the heart beating).

RW was eighty-three years old when she received a permanent artificial pacemaker to prevent syncopal episodes (passing out spells) caused by sick sinus node syndrome (a condition in which the heart stops beating for a few seconds every now and then). She was otherwise, and continues to be, relatively healthy except for progressive dementia. Now, at age eighty-seven, she requires high-intensity institutional care to deal with her confusion, incontinence, and feeding. Her appointed surrogate, her niece, visits you in your office demanding that you remove RW's pacemaker. Her claim is that her aunt is leading a subhuman existence void of dignity, fun, or love. You agree with the niece's assessment of RW's mental status. You also know that RW is pacemaker-dependent and that removal of the artificial device will result in her instant death. The niece argues that she has power of attorney over her aunt and insists that you remove the pacemaker since it is "not serving any useful purpose."

The Ethical Dilemma

Given this scenario, you should

1. Schedule RW for pacemaker generator removal in the hospital.
2. Reprogram the pacemaker in a way that makes the pacemaker provide only partial benefit, allowing the patient's health to deteriorate.
3. Argue that the pacemaker is serving the purpose for which it was placed and that removing it or manipulating its parameters so that it would cease to function is unlawful. In fact, it is a form of active euthanasia.

The most appropriate response is 3.

Discussion

This case exemplifies the vexing nature of end-of-life decisions particularly with regard to withdrawal of effective treatment. Also, it shows that to let die, which is lawful, and to make die, which is unlawful, can blur confusingly into one another.

In this patient, the pacemaker has fulfilled its desired function by keeping the patient alive. The niece's rationale for removal or reprogramming of the pacemaker is that the patient's quality of life is much diminished so that death has become a better option for her. The niece's claim is not groundless and she has a legal right as an appointed surrogate to refuse treatment on behalf of the patient. Furthermore, neither the courts nor ethical precepts differentiate between the act of withholding or withdrawal of *useless* treatment.[7]

On the other hand, a permanent pacemaker has become part of the body and its surgical removal constitutes bodily invasion with intent to end the life of the patient. It is my view that such an action would subject the physician to charges of battery and manslaughter if not of second degree murder.[8] It may be argued that manipulating the pacemaker externally to a less favorable setting may hasten the patient's death without causing her instant demise. Such an intervention on the behest of the niece would be wrong since it is inappropriate for a physician to *willfully harm* his patients, an act that is clearly against his oath (*primum non nocere*).[9] I strongly advise against tinkering with pacemaker parameters to satisfy the niece's demands. Surrogate demands often do not conform with the patient's own wishes and are sometimes tainted with considerations other than the patients' best interests.[10] It can be argued that RW's life is not without fun. She enjoys her meals, goes out for a daily walk, and is not in distress. She is neither terminally ill nor is she in a vegetative, unconscious state. Also, a permanently placed device to carry out the function of a failed sinus node (natural pacemaker) is different from a *temporary life assist device* (such as a ventilator) placed in hope that the patient will recover that function and eventually be weaned off the ventilator. The physician should relinquish the care of the patient if the niece insists that he undertake a course not consistent with his beliefs.

CASE STUDY #3

The Ethical Issue: A terminal/dying patient endures repeated shocks from an artificial implanted cardioverter-defibrillator (AICD) unit.

EF, a seventy-eight-year-old retired executive, has a long history of heart disease. In 1972 he suffered a massive heart attack following which he underwent ventricular aneurysmectomy and quadruple aorto-coronary bypass surgery (open heart surgery for removal of the heart scar and bringing about new source of blood to the heart) utilizing saphenous vein conduits. He was maintained on digitalis and diuretics and resumed his activities with minor limitations. In 1984 he started to experience exertional angina (chest pain caused by limited blood flow to the heart arteries). Between 1984 and 1988 he underwent multiple procedures with balloon angioplasty to correct stenosis (narrowing) of each of two bypass grafts and two native coronary arteries. In 1992 he suffered an acute inferior myocardial infarction (heart attack) complicated by ventricular fibrillation and high grade AV block (major disruption of the heart's electric system and increased irritability). Testing showed a severely damaged heart with poor pumping function, total occlusion of all native coronary arteries, total occlusion of the vein grafts to two of the three coronary arteries along with diffuse disease in the remaining graft. He underwent repeat aorto-coronary bypass surgery. On the fifth post-operative day he developed hypotensive monomorphic ventricular tachycardia (fast, potentially lethal heart rhythm) and an AICD (artificial implantable cardiac device to shock the heart out of disordered rhythm) pacing unit was deemed necessary. He was placed on combination therapy with a multitude of medicines to control heart failure and help prevent disordered heart rhythm.

Following a protracted recovery period he showed satisfactory functional improvement and continued his daily activities without many limiting symptoms.

Between 1992 and 1998 he was hospitalized two times; once because of pneumonia and heart failure in 1994 and once because of severe bleeding from a stomach ulcer, requiring long-term therapy of a medication to control stomach acid production. In addition, he developed a hypothyroid state related to one of the medicines (Amiodarone) and was placed on thyroid hormone replacement therapy.

In 1996, he was diagnosed with prostate cancer for which he received radiation therapy. In 1997 the cancer was found to have spread into EF's bones and antitestosterone agents were added to the regimen. In 1998 he showed steady decline in his health with deteriorating kidney function, anemia, and further spreading of cancer to his lungs. The patient developed worsening of heart failure and required ever-increasing doses of diuretics.

All through the six years since he had the AICD, there was no evidence that the unit discharged when interrogated at regular intervals, meaning that the patient did not suffer a potentially lethal irregularity of the heartbeat.

Because of recent marked deterioration of health as well as heart failure, EF was enrolled in hospice care. Comfort measures were initiated and a Do Not Attempt Resuscitation order was entered into his chart.

In September 1998, EF was taken to the emergency room because of repeated discharge of the AICD (electric shock from the implanted device), causing immense pain for the patient and extreme anxiety among family members.

The Ethical Dilemma

You attend to the patient in the emergency room and consider the following options:

1. The patient is dying, and sooner or later these shocks will cease anyway.
2. Sedate the patient with large doses of morphine or resort to unconscious sedation with Midazolam Hcl (Versed) or light anesthesia.
3. Deactivate the AICD device externally if possible and if unsuccessful, open the AICD pocket and cut the pacing wires, knowing that such an act will lead to the patient's death.

The third choice is the proper choice. The second choice is a less desirable substitute.

Discussion

This patient with advanced, unresponsive cancer, end-stage heart disease, and progressive renal failure was appropriately placed in hospice care to ensure comfort and preserve dignity.

An intervention that would deliberately cause death or hasten the moment of dying is illegal. On the other hand, an intervention that interferes with the natural process of dying would be inhumane. In this particular patient, repeated firing from the AICD unit not only interfered with the natural process of dying but, more importantly, has caused the patient undue discomfort and the family unnecessary anguish. The objective of palliative care is patient comfort, even if that hastens the moment of dying.[11] Therefore, deactivation of the AICD should be undertaken as soon as possible. Certain AICD units can be deactivated by external place-ment of a magnet over the site of the generator. If that fails to achieve the desired objective, and assuming that an expert cannot be immediately available to reprogram the unit to a nonsensing mode, the pacing wire should be cut by a scalpel or scissors through a small incision.

We emphasize that in this case the objective of any intervention is to alleviate the patient's suffering. Even though the patient will inevitably die, the intervention is not intended to cause death. To make one die is ethi-cally and legally wrong. To let one die is not and, in this case, is the right thing to do. It may be prudent to deactivate AICD units, after obtaining the patients' consent, in patients whose condition has deteriorated consid-erably and who are in the process of dying.

In the previous case study, we presented a patient whose life was de-pendent on permanent pacing. The patient's surrogate asked that the pace-maker be removed or reprogrammed to hasten the death of a demented patient. We argued that such an intervention is ethically wrong based on the principle of nonmalefiscence. In the first case study we presented a patient with an AICD asked to deactivate the unit so that it would not interfere with the natural process of dying when the patient's moment comes. We argued that such an intervention is justified when based solely upon the patient's poor physiologic status and provided that the patient's request does not represent a case of potentially reversible depression.

We hope that by discussing these patients, the reader has a better view of difficult situations that may arise in the routine follow-up of pacemaker patients.

CASE STUDY #4

***The Ethical Issue:** A citizen from abroad develops acute myocardial infarction, heart failure, and renal failure requiring chronic dialysis, asks for asylum in the United States for lack of optimal treatment in his home country.*

A sixty-nine-year-old man is in the United States on a tourist visa, visiting family who had recently emigrated to the United States. During his visit he develops progressive lower extremity edema (swelling), weakness, and shortness of breath. He presents to the emergency room of a local hospital, where he is diagnosed with congestive heart failure and probable anterolateral myocardial infarction (heart attack). There are also concerns about underlying hypertension, diabetes, and renal (kidney) function. In the emergency room his blood pressure is noted to be 178/105, blood glucose 268, and creatinine 9.4. He is admitted to the hospital.

An extensive medical evaluation over the next week reveals moderate-to-severe diffuse multivessel coronary artery disease with severe heart failure due to a hardening of the arteries and high blood pressure. Additionally, his kidney function remains severely compromised as reflected by serum creatinines no better than the 7–8 range. He is placed on kidney dialysis. Nephrology opinion is that the man suffers from chronic renal failure secondary to uncontrolled long-standing diabetes and hypertension with further exacerbation secondary to his poor heart condition. The patient's blood pressure and blood sugars remain problematic throughout hospitalization, eventually requiring multiple medications, including insulin. There is also evidence of complications involving eye and leg arteries. Further history elicited from the patient and his family supports the diagnosis of chronic, uncontrolled disease.

Nine days after admission, the patient's medical state has been optimized and it is determined that he has reached his maximal benefit from hospitalization. He requires kidney dialysis three times a week because of his end-stage disease. As he is prepared for discharge, the patient and his family express concern about his long-term care. The patient's travel visa is soon to expire, necessitating his return to his homeland. They are concerned about the extremely limited availability of renal dialysis there, especially given their somewhat limited financial means. They request the patient be permitted to remain in the United States based on his need for life-sustaining renal dialysis.

The Ethical Dilemma

Given this scenario, the physician should

1. Require the patient to obtain appropriate visa to enable him to remain in the United States for optimal care.
2. Assist the patient through whatever means to obtain a permanent visa status as an alien citizen.

3. Optimize the patient's treatment for now and have the patient and family handle the legality of the visa status.

The proper answer is 3.

Discussion

On its face such a vexing problem can present a confusing, even heart-wrenching experience for the treating professional team. It challenges the core values of medicine of devotion to the patient's best interests, life, and well being. On the other hand, different societies have different priority standards for medical care based on economic logistics.

For example, according to the "willing to pay" standard, the United States spends $2.5 million to prevent one death caused by a road accident. By contrast, Portugal spends $20,000 per one life saved. By the same token there are three times as many elderly patients per thousand on dialysis in the United States as there are in Britain. Furthermore, the cost of health care for per citizen in the United States is nearly three times that of a British citizen ($4,100 versus $1,400). Also, the basic premise of distributive justice by which all citizens are eligible for the same basic health care varies enormously from one country to another. Societal goods are privileges offered to citizens based on the collective wealth of the country, its socioeconomic status, and laws.

In this patient's case, the treating team has done what is expected of it. The long-term care of a noncitizen is beyond the responsibility of health-care professionals. It is up to the patient and family to pursue whichever lawful avenue they deem appropriate to ensure further health care.

CASE STUDY #5

The Ethical Issue: An elderly patient declines cardiac surgery under optimal circumstances yet undergoes cardiac surgery when in extremis.

WB was an eighty-six-year-old Hispanic widow and mother of six children. At the time of her first hospital admission, her history indicated that she had been relatively healthy all her life and rarely took medicines. A few years earlier, she was found to have mild hypertension (high blood pressure) and was started on medication, which she took for only four months. She was unaware of her serum cholesterol level, was never diagnosed with diabetes, and never smoked.

Over the past three months, she had been troubled with attacks of epigastric (stomach area) discomfort, mostly after heavy meals or when she became upset. These attacks became more frequent, more severe, and sometimes nocturnal. Lately, she had been awakened from sleep with epigastric discomfort, shortness of breath, and excessive sweating. These attacks, which used to last only a few minutes, persisted almost half an hour and were associated with a sense of impending death.

Physical examination revealed blood pressure 150/92 mm Hg, heart rate 76, and respiration rate 20/minute. There was no discernible evidence of heart failure. Examination of the heart revealed questionable heart enlargement. There were signs of severe narrowing of the aortic valve (heart valve separating the left ventricle and aorta). The rest of the physical examination was unremarkable. The electrocardiogram was abnormal and showed evidence of severe left ventricular hypertrophy (enlargement) with left atrial enlargement. Lung examination showed no evidence of congestion. Chest radiograph showed aortic valve calcification and borderline left ventricular enlargement. An echocardiogram confirmed severe calcific aortic valve stenosis (narrowing) and decreased left ventricular contraction power suggesting early signs of heart failure.

The consulting cardiologist recommended further evaluation in anticipation of open heart surgery. The patient declined on the basis that "I have lived a long life and I am too old for open heart surgery." Efforts by her primary physician to persuade her to undergo the necessary testing were fruitless. The patient was given antianginal medications to relieve her discomfort.

Three weeks later she was brought to the emergency room in acute heart failure. The electrocardiogram showed a massive heart attack. An emergency evaluation with cardiac catheterization (the test she declined previously) showed severe narrowing of all arteries supplying the heart and confirmed the presence of severe narrowing of the aortic valve. Unfortunately, the contraction power of the heart had declined to half of what it had been three weeks earlier.

A discussion with family members resulted in emergency aorto-coronary bypass surgery and aortic valve replacement with a bioprosthesis (tissue valve). The postoperative course was complicated by persistent poor heart function, lung congestion (indicating heart failure), in addition to recurrent atrial fibrillation (disordered heart rhythm). Eventually, the patient showed signs of kidney failure and permanent damage to her lungs.

The patient never regained consciousness. Her cardiac (heart) status never improved in spite of intraaortic balloon assist. She died two weeks later.

The Ethical Dilemma

- Was the primary care physician at fault for not insisting on open heart surgery during the first hospital admission?
- Was it wrong for the treating team to proceed with cardiac catheterization and open heart surgery on the second admission?
- What if the family insisted that the reluctant physician "do something"?

Discussion

This case represents one of the difficult—yet not unusual—dilemmas in medical practice: A patient refuses treatment when the results would likely be favorable and asks for it under much less favorable circumstances. In this case, the chances of success of aortic valve replacement and aorto-coronary bypass surgery were favorable on the first hospital admission and were dismal at the time of surgery.

One may argue that a competent adult patient has the right to refuse potentially beneficial treatment. Also, patients have the right to change their mind. Further, when patients are not competent to make the decision for themselves this right is conferred to the surrogate to make a "substitute judgment" on behalf of the patient.

Therefore, on its face, this patient's treatment did not violate prevailing ethical precepts. It is our view, however, that this patient could have been better served if the treating team spent more time educating the patient and family about the sequellae of their initial decision to refuse surgery, and to arrive at a treatment plan covering all contingencies.

In the presence of moderately severe narrowing of the aortic valve, episodes of prolonged angina at rest should have alerted the treating team to the likelihood of associated severe coronary artery disease. The patient and family should have been informed that an acute myocardial infarction (heart attack) was imminent and that the chances of surgical success would become greatly diminished with this complication. At that point, if the patient, while competent to make decisions and fully informed about outcomes, voluntarily decides against surgery, it would have been appropriate to ensure that such a refusal also covers any foreseeable complications. This patient's course was predictable. Proper consent or refusal should have been more comprehensive in the first place.

CASE STUDY #6

The Ethical Issue: The wife of a hopelessly terminal patient asks physicians to hasten the moment of death.

Mr. BC, a sixty-seven-year-old industrialist with a long history of smoking, hypertension (high blood pressure), diabetes mellitus, and hyperlipidemia (high cholesterol) was brought to the emergency room with an acute inferior myocardial infarction (heart attack) complicated by interruption of the electric impulse in the heart.

Initially, he was hypotensive (had low blood pressure) with signs of low cardiac output, which improved with a temporary artificial pacemaker. He received a clot busting medicine. The chest pain subsided after one hour, suggesting that the previously blocked artery had opened up.

On the third hospital day, he developed chest tightness and acute pulmonary edema (acute heart failure) associated with manifestations of hypoperfusion (weak heart pumping). Physical examination revealed engorged neck veins, wet lungs, and congested liver as well as a loud systolic murmur over the heart. An echocardiogram showed a ventricular septal defect (a hole between the two sides of the heart).

The patient was placed on assisted ventilation and was immediately taken to the cardiac catheterization laboratory. An intraaortic balloon was inserted to assist heart function. Angiogram showed severe narrowing of all his coronary arteries. The pumping function of the heart was noted to be severely depressed.

The patient was taken to the operating room for immediate surgery. The operation proved to be extremely difficult due to fragility of the myocardium (heart muscle) at the infarction site as well as the large size of the hole between the heart chambers.

After surgery, the patient continued to have low cardiac output with anuria (no urine output by the kidneys) and insufficient blood flow to various organs, causing serious complications and beginnings of gangrene in one leg.

The patient never woke up and showed decerebrate posturing (seizure activity). Contrast computerized tomography (CT) brain scan showed extensive cortical necrosis in both cerebral hemispheres (extensive brain damage), and the electroencephalogram showed slow brain wave activity.

It became clear that the patient was beyond salvage, and his wife ordered discontinuation of life support. The patient could breathe on his own but remained comatose. Artificial feeding and hydration were discontinued, and the treating physician wrote an order for morphine as needed to alleviate seizures. The patient's wife became exceedingly hostile because the patient continued to have seizures and she demanded that the patient be given increasingly large doses of morphine. With every passing day, she became accusative and confrontational because she hated to see her husband linger in this "undignified" state. The nurse assigned to the patient, a devout Roman Catholic, resented giving the patient morphine since he was feeling no pain.

Discussion

This patient's care during life and until discontinuation of assisted ventilation was exemplary.[12] Once it was determined that life-support measures served only to prolong the process of dying, it was appropriate to disconnect the patient from the ventilator.

Many physicians, including specialists, prefer to sedate patients prior to discontinuing assisted ventilation. The sight of a suffocating patient can be difficult to tolerate not only by family members, but also by experienced physicians. The patient was weaned successfully from the ventilator, but the wife could not tolerate watching decerebrate gesturing (special form of seizure activity) and, to her, it was cruel to leave the patient in this state.

Allowing nature to take its course was done through cessation of feeding and hydration. Such cessation would lead to death in one to two weeks. The end was expected to come sooner rather than later because of the patient's renal failure. Additionally, once palliative terminal care is deemed appropriate, terminal sedation can be achieved through increasing doses of medication until total sedation is achieved.[13]

The nurse's resentment of morphine administration to this patient is not groundless. The patient is unconscious and should not be suffering any pain. Orders for morphine to be given "as needed" places the onus on the nurse to interpret the appropriateness of morphine administration. In this case, the treating physician deemed it necessary to abolish seizure activity because of the family's discomfort and out of respect for the dying patient. Therefore, it was incumbent on the physician to prescribe the dose of morphine sufficient to abolish seizures. The physician should not have left this as an ad hoc order subject to interpretation by the nursing staff.

The physician had to indicate in the patient's records that the reason for giving increasing doses of morphine, or any other form of sedation, is to preserve the patient's dignity. Furthermore, the treating physician had a duty to explain to the wife that the physician's role is not to "make die" but to "let die" in comfort and dignity. As previously mentioned, to "make die" is unlawful and subject to prosecution.

In these situations, one may argue that treatment with large doses of sedation is appropriate to preserve the patient's dignity when it is not aimed at alleviating pain. Predictably, this will also hasten death. The doctrine of *double effect* is ethically acceptable. The physician should explain his plan to the nurse taking care of the patient. If, in spite of all, the nurse feels she could not administer sedation with a clear conscience, care for the patient should be given to another nurse.

CASE STUDY #7

The Ethical Issue: A patient with clear advance instructions to forgo placement on a ventilator dies after several weeks of intensive care.

Mr. JW, a seventy-six-year-old gentleman who smoked three packs a day for over fifty years, developed severe emphysema and has been maintained on nasal oxygen around the clock. He has been wheelchair-bound for the past two years and continues to smoke.

Recently he was admitted to the intensive care unit and was placed on assisted ventilation for treatment of pneumonia and deterioration of lung function. He was weaned off the ventilator with great difficulty.

Dr. Smith: "Mr. JW, you know you have severe emphysema. This time we were lucky to have been able to wean you off the ventilator success-fully. You will need to stay on your oxygen permanently and continuously."

JW: "I know that. I've become so weak that I can't move anymore. I can't even finish a few words without getting short of breath."

Dr. Smith: "This time you have to stop smoking. It's killing you."

JW: "I know that, doc. But, I cannot and will not stop smoking now. It is the only remaining source of enjoyment in my life. I don't want to offend you but I don't want to ever be placed on a ventilator again. If there is a next time . . . please let me go."

Dr. Smith: "Is this your firm and unequivocal choice?"

JW: "Absolutely." JW turned to his wife, "Honey, that is what I want." His wife nodded in understanding and agreement.

The treating physician entered a comprehensive note in the patient's medical records and a DNAR (Do Not Attempt Resuscitation) order sticker was placed on the cover.

Four months later, JW was brought to the emergency room *in extremis*: suffocating, in severe chest pain, and drenched in sweat.

Wife: "Doctor, he's dying . . . do something!"

Dr. Jones: "He needs to be placed on a ventilator."

Wife: "Anything; he's dying."

JW was intubated and placed on full assist ventilation. Dr. Smith took over the patient's care. JW was found to have sustained a massive anterior myocardial infarction (heart attack) with cardiogenic shock, leading to ces-sation of kidney function. He was sustained in intensive care, developed a massive stroke, multiorgan failure, and systemic infection, with death coming a few weeks later. During these weeks, Dr. Smith followed the wife's instructions to persevere with the treatment to the very end.

The Ethical Dilemma

- Was Dr. Jones wrong to intubate JW and place him on the ventilator?
- Was the wife's cry to "do something" a rescission of the prior clear instructions from the patient to "please let me go"?
- What is the best way to deal with such situations?

Discussion

Chances are Dr. Jones did not know about the prior conversation between Dr. Smith and the patient. In this case, Dr. Jones did exactly what was expected of him. However, had he known the patient or known about the prior clear instructions from the patient, he should have followed a different course. His charge would have been to alleviate the patient's suffering rather than offer life-sustaining intervention. A nonrebreathing mask with 100 percent oxygen in addition to IV opiates would have been the appropriate intervention. This could have been initiated, the patient made comfortable, and then the physician would have had a quiet conversation with the wife. Legal precedent establishes that the patient's verbally expressed wishes are binding, even if the patient has not executed a living will.[14] This patient had his wishes known verbally and in writing. On the other hand, the wife, as the patient's appointed surrogate, has an implied right to override the patient's own expressed wishes since the patient is no longer competent to sustain his own.[15]

When Dr. Smith took over the care of the patient in the ICU, he should have discussed the situation at length with the wife. Life support could have been terminated earlier when it was discovered that the patient had a massive myocardial infarction (heart attack), or after a few days when it became clear that he had developed multi-organ failure, or even after he developed a stroke. It was not proper to persist with all forms of life support given the patient's terminal premorbid condition and the patient's clear verbal directive. A meaningful relationship between the treating physician and the patient's family could have prevented unnecessary and unwanted death-prolonging interventions.

This case further illustrates the need to readily identify patients who have advance directives asking not to be resuscitated, either written or verbal. A readily identifiable medical alert necklace or bracelet would have prevented subjecting this patient to an unwanted terminal technological nightmare.

CASE STUDY #8

The Ethical Issue: A medically impaired patient is determined to operate an automobile against his physicians' advice.

JV is a seventy-nine-year-old man with a history of multiple myocardial infarctions, critical aortic stenosis (severe narrowing of the aortic heart valve; valve area 0.6 cm²), chronic obstructive pulmonary disease (emphysema), terminal laryngeal (voice box) squamous cell cancer, considerably dilated aorta (diameter 8.3 cm) and bradycardia-induced syncope (loss of consciousness from a slow heart beat). Past medical history indicated that the patient had undergone radiation therapy for prostate cancer with resultant radiation proctitis (inflamed rectum). He was informed by the oncologist that he has six months to a year to live due to cancer of the voice box. He was brought to the emergency department complaining of chest pain typical of his usual angina.

He was admitted to the coronary care unit where an acute heart attack was ruled out by laboratory testing. His symptoms improved on intravenous heparin and nitroglycerin, but the hospital course was complicated by hemodynamically significant hematochezia (loss of blood in the stool) requiring emergent heater probe therapy of the rectum. The hemoglobin stabilized after several transfusions.

After the patient's chest pain and loss of blood in the stool resolved, the patient asked to be sent home. As he was considered not to be a candidate for surgery for his considerably dilated aorta, he was discharged, presumably to the care of his family. As the intern involved in JV's care was walking in the hospital parking lot, he noticed the patient getting into the driver's seat of a truck. Despite multiple attempts to convince the patient to have someone drive him home, he insisted upon driving himself. He even informed his caretaker that he would continue driving in the future and remained adamant in his decision.

The Ethical Dilemma

This patient has clearly decided to drive regardless of the fact that he has two serious health conditions, each of which may lead to sudden death:

- Significantly dilated aorta about to rupture and
- Episodes of severe heart slowing causing him to lose consciousness.

The physicians involved in his care should:

1. Honor his wishes and allow him to drive as he wishes during his last few months of life.
2. Inform hospital security of this patient's desires and have him removed from his vehicle.
3. Have the patient escorted home by the appropriate authorities and notify the Department of Motor Vehicles in order to have his license revoked.

Discussion

By enjoying the advantage of independent transportation, drivers also accept the responsibility of operating their vehicles safely. When people violate this contract and operate their vehicles unsafely by speeding or driving while intoxicated, our society has enacted laws that restrict these drivers from operating a vehicle in order to protect other citizens.

Likewise, when a physician diagnoses a medical condition that would prohibit a person from driving safely, the medical practitioner should inform the patient that he can no longer operate a vehicle reliably. The patient is expected to refrain from driving until his illness is treated or resolved. A dilemma arises when these standards are violated. What are physicians' moral and legal responsibilities when a patient insists on enjoying the privilege of independent transportation at societal hazard? How can the concepts of beneficence and compassion for the patient be reconciled with the physician's duty to society as a whole? Lastly, how can a doctor, sworn to be a patient advocate above all else, constrain a patient's independence against his wishes? Florida law, as well as the laws in most other states, stipulates that "Any physician, person, or agency having knowledge of any licensed driver's or applicant's mental or physical disability to drive . . . is authorized to report such knowledge to the Department of Highway Safety and Motor Vehicles. . . . The reports authorized by this section shall be confidential." The law also provides for protection against liability for the reporting of individuals, in that "No civil or criminal action may be brought against any physician, person, or agency who provides the information."[16]

The initial report is reviewed by a medical advisory board that decides whether to allow the patient to continue driving or revoke his or her license. In other words, practicing physicians in the state of Florida do not make the decisions to nullify a patient's driver's license; they merely report potentially hazardous drivers to the medical advisory board.

The word *authorized* in the Florida statute means that reporting individuals are permitted rather than obligated to notify state agencies. In contrast, the state of Georgia has passed a law stating that physicians and optometrists are "required to report to the Department of Public Safety the name of every person over 15 years of age diagnosed as having a disorder characterized by a lapse of consciousness or other mental or physical disability."[17] This significant difference in legal requirements from state to state underlines the importance that physicians become aware of the laws for reporting impaired drivers in their respective states. When physicians fail to comply with state laws and do not counsel their medically impaired patients to restrict their driving, they leave themselves liable to legal action. In a well-publicized landmark case in California (*Tarasoff* v. *Regents of the University of California*), a patient informed his mental health practitioner of his intent to harm others, but the clinician did not alert the authorities. When this patient committed murder, the psychotherapist was found liable because he did not warn the patient's intended victims. In a majority decision the California Supreme Court admonished "The protective privilege [of confidentiality] ends where public peril begins." The ruling extended to bodily disease as well as mental illness when it determined that "A doctor treating physical illness bears a duty . . . to give warnings" as well.[18]

In the even more relevant case of *Freese* v. *Lemmon*, the law established a physician's liability if he fails to warn and counsel patients as to the possible effect their disease may have on their driving ability. In this case, a newly diagnosed epileptic was not counseled by his physician to discontinue driving. The patient later suffered a seizure while driving and struck a pedestrian. The court deemed the physician guilty of malpractice.[19]

In addition to the legal precedents concerning medically impaired drivers, a higher moral obligation exists for physicians. A virtuous or ethical physician cannot relinquish his obligation to society in order to satisfy his patient's wishes in the name of beneficence. One could even make the argument that preventing a medically impaired driver from operating a vehicle is beneficent to the patient, since any accident caused by the patient's medical condition certainly increases his risk of traumatic injury or death. Deciding to limit the driving of medically hazardous patients is not a determination to be taken lightly; moreover, it must be based on factual data. Medical illnesses are responsible for less than 6 to 7 percent of all motor vehicle accidents.[20] Furthermore, studies have shown that few of the collisions caused by natural deaths of drivers result in serious injury.[21]

In this case, rupture of an abdominal aortic aneurysm is almost always preceded by warning symptoms of abdominal, back, or chest pain. Even that the aorta was considerably dilated and rupture is imminent by itself may not cause as much concern as the fact that the patient is prone to sudden death from cessation of heart beating. Sudden cardiac arrest from cessation of the electric signal to the heart is rarely abrupt and without warning symptoms of chest pain, lightheadedness, or palpitations. The vast majority of patients with advanced heart disease may indeed be allowed to drive as long as they are educated to pull over as soon as they experience warning symptoms. Of course, upon counseling a medically impaired patient regarding safe driving, it is imperative that treating physicians document their instructions in the chart for future reference if needed.

In the rare events of patients with conditions that clearly and unequivocally preclude safe driving refuse to follow their physician's recommendations, the physician may be compelled to notify state authorities in the interest of public safety. Physicians are justified in curbing individual patients' freedoms to ensure the security of the community.

CASE STUDY #9

The Ethical Issue: "Everyone knew he would not have wanted to live like this . . . but his advance directive was not clear about his wishes."

Mr. Howard was seventy-eight years old when his wife of fifty-four years died a painful and protracted death from disseminated myeloma (a highly malignant form of cancer). His grief was intense and his bereavement prolonged. As a commanding figure, a senior financial officer of a large corporation before his retirement twelve years prior, and a lay leader in his church, Mr. Howard was a man of faith and enjoyed many outdoor activities. Just a few months before his wife's death, he played eighteen holes of golf at least three times weekly and, weather permitting, took an hour-long stroll with his wife on the beach every evening. He was healthy except for mild hypertension (high blood pressure) controlled by medicine that he took daily.

Following his wife's death, he became a different person: quiet and morose with minimal interest in mingling with others. His three daughters attempted unsuccessfully to persuade him to travel, find a social companion, or become more involved in church affairs. His standard answer was "You have your life ahead of you; I had mine, and I look forward to being with your mother." The suggestion to see a psychiatrist for help was met with hostility. He made his wishes further known by executing a living will stating "When I am permanently disabled because of injury or sickness and my death is imminent and unavoidable, I ask that my life not be prolonged."

It seems that Mr. Howard stopped taking his blood pressure medication. Less than six months later, he suffered a massive left hemispherical stroke that left him with total right hemiplegia (paralysis of the right side of the body), aphasia (inability to speak), and inability to swallow. He received artificial feeding and hydration through a nasogastric tube. His oldest daughter, the appointed surrogate, cared for him in her house with the use of outside help.

Over the ensuing two years, Mr. Howard had to be hospitalized seven times because of aspiration pneumonia (because of his inability to swallow foods). This time was particularly difficult. He was taken to the emergency room with a temperature of 102°F, hypoxia, and severe respiratory distress. He was promptly intubated, placed on assisted ventilation and intravenous antibiotics. His left side had to be restrained to prevent him from pulling out the endotracheal (air pipe) tube. Clearly, Mr. Howard was angry and resentful although his aphasia precluded him from expressing himself plainly.

The patient's daughter asked to speak with the treating physician. Tearful and choking in her own words, she said, "I know my father would not have wanted all of this. He executed a living will to avoid this very situation."

The physician replied, "But pneumonia is reversible and his living will specifically calls for withholding treatment only when death is unavoidable." He added that as an appointed surrogate she had the right to refuse mechanical ventilation for her father should the need arise in the future.

Mr. Howard's daughter responded "My dilemma is that I am Catholic and cannot refuse treatment that keeps him alive. On the other hand, I know in my heart that he would have never agreed to be placed on the ventilator. Furthermore, one of my other sisters has said she will never speak to me again if I let him die!"

The Ethical Dilemma

Based on the patient's history and advance directive, the physician involved in his care should:

1. Continue treatment of his pneumonia with mechanical ventilation.
2. Extubate the patient (remove the patient from the ventilator) and provide comfort measures only since it appears that the patient would not have wanted to be on a ventilator.
3. Inform the patient's daughter that she, as the appointed surrogate, should make decisions limiting the patient's end-of-life care based on the instructions he had previously given her.

Discussion

In this case, the physician's role is only to advise, understand, and cooperate with sensitivity and wisdom. The doctor's conduct was proper in this situation. Pneumonia is a reversible disease and hemiplegia (stroke), even when severe, is not a terminal illness. The physician's notions about quality of life have no relevance to how this patient should be treated. On the other hand, the patient's unique wishes are understandable and can be conveyed only by the patient himself or his appointed surrogate.

It is true that every adult with a sound mind has the right to forgo potentially useful medical treatment. This right is grounded in the American Constitution and is part of the right to life and liberty.[22]

The patient's present inability to articulate his wishes is clearly an enormous impediment. Every effort should be made by the family, aided by the patient's priest if available, to fulfill the patient's true wishes. Of course, the timing and style of presenting these questions should be chosen carefully. The patient may be asked questions, shown diagrams, and asked to indicate his preference using his unparalyzed left hand. Should that effort prove futile, the whole family must revisit the issue in the presence of trusted others who knew the patient well. The oldest daughter, being the appointed surrogate by the patient, should be given explicit instructions after careful review of all facts. Unless the surrogate is able to give clear directions to the treating physician not to initiate artificial ventilation, the family should expect continuance of the same treatment even though the prevailing sentiment is that the patient would not have opted for it.

However, in this case, it would have been easy to conclude that the patient would have not consented to life support even on a temporary basis. A proxy judgment by the patient's appointed surrogate is a good match with the patient's wishes only if it is guided by specific instructions from the patient. These instructions may be written or verbal. The duty of relating the patient's previously expressed wishes to the physician falls upon the family members via the patient's chosen surrogate.

On a larger scale, this case represents one of the major weaknesses of currently available advance directives (AD). Individuals execute ADs in order to spare them indignity and pain during their last chapter of life when they become unable to make or articulate their own decisions. Unfortunately, with few exceptions, generic ADs have been transformed into legal documents that focus on life's terminal stage when death is imminent. They typically do not address chronic, nonterminal medical problems that severely impair patients' quality of life, such as a massive stroke with loss of speech and inability to walk, or severe dementia. Advance directives are sometimes an impediment to withhold unwanted treatment when the patient is no longer able to express his wishes.[23]

Currently, the majority of advance directives list patient preferences for the final page in a patient's life when the patient's demise is inevitable. Instead, advance directives should emphasize the last chapter of life by describing desired options within specific medical scenarios that may render the patient unable to care for himself, interact with others, or enjoy the richness of living.

CASE STUDY #10

The Ethical Issue: A "slow code" is suggested in response to a critical situation involving a patient with multiple medical problems.

SH is a seventy-year-old female with a history of ischemic cardiomyopathy (poor heart function due to hardening of the arteries), chronic atrial fibrillation (disordered heart rhythm), metastatic thyroid cancer, renal (kidney) insufficiency, diabetes mellitus type 2, and chronic obstructive pulmonary disease (emphysema). Recently she has shown signs of progressive dementia. After a prolonged pneumonia requiring tracheostomy (tube placed surgically in the air pipe), the patient was admitted to an extended care facility secondary to her dependence on mechanical ventilation.

On the patient's first evening in the new facility, she suffered cardiopulmonary arrest (cessation of breathing and heart beat) when her tracheostomy tube was dislodged during her bath. A code blue was called. When the physicians responding to the code arrived at the bedside, a nurse filled them in on the patient's complicated medical history. There were no Do Not Resuscitate (DNR) orders on the chart. The surgeon on call was notified, but he was already busy with another emergency in a different hospital. The nurse then suggested that the physicians initiate a "slow code," that is, a partial, half-hearted attempt at CPR, in light of the patient's multiple medical problems and subsequent poor prognosis.

The Ethical Dilemma

Based on the patient's history and current situation, the physicians involved in her care should:

1. Initiate cardiopulmonary resuscitative (CPR) measures and aggressively treat the patient.
2. Terminate resuscitative efforts after a brief trial of chest compressions and intravenous medications (i.e., a "slow code").
3. Determine that CPR is futile and thus not indicated in the patient with terminal cancer and multiple other medical problems.

Discussion

Over the past few decades, cardiopulmonary resuscitation has evolved from a process utilized only for select instance acute cardiac arrest such as with electrocution, heart attack, or anesthesia to a default ritual performed in all cases of cardiopulmonary arrest. In the United States, CPR is traditionally employed for every patient during their final moments unless explicitly declined by the patient or his or her family, despite the low success rate of CPR in the hospital setting.[24]

Although every patient who desires CPR in the event of cardiopulmonary arrest receives resuscitative efforts, some attempts at restoring physiologic homeostasis (satisfactory response) in arresting patients are performed in an unhurried or abridged fashion. These endeavors are referred to in the discreet vernacular of medicine as slow codes. Slow codes, also referred to as light blue or partial codes, are frequently performed on patients with dementia, advanced terminal illnesses, persistent vegetative states, or patients in whom recovery of functional quality of life is not anticipated. Unfortunately, the decision to implement a slow code is often made unilaterally by the treating physician without input from family members.

An ethical dilemma develops when severely compromised patients without clear advance directives develop cardiopulmonary arrest and the ancillary staff suggests a slow code. When, if ever, should physicians initiate a slow code? What type of patient is benefited by a slow code? And lastly, why do doctors initiate a slow code for patients whose wishes are to undergo full resuscitation?

The American College of Physicians has determined that "If DNR [Do Not Resuscitate] orders are not written, it is unethical for physicians and nurses to perform half-hearted resuscitation efforts."[25] When medical staff decide to initiate slow codes, they are not only circumventing a clear decision concerning patient requests, but they are also violating the written ethical guidelines of their own profession. Ideally, physicians should appropriately address patients' wishes regarding end-of-life issues with patients or their families, and CPR at the end of life should be carried out aggressively or not at all.

Patients benefit little, if any, from slow codes. The low success rate of in-hospital cardiopulmonary resuscitation is further decreased when arrest situations are not treated assertively in a timely fashion. Patients who undergo slow codes experience the worst of both scenarios; they not only endure the pain and indignity of cardiopulmonary resuscitation, but also they do not receive the full benefits that a more vigorous resuscitation might offer.

Some health-care practitioners perform slow codes for fear that an honest discussion of the patient's prognosis with the family will make the patient's relatives feel that the physician is "giving up" on their loved one. It also represents an attempt at self-preservation; doctors are apprehensive that after the patient's demise, the anger associated with the family's normal grieving process may then be directed at the treating physician. The concern of legal retribution is very real, and litigation can be painful to both health-care providers and patients' families. Doctors may see a slow code as a convenient way out for both parties.

One strategy to alleviate the family's concern that physicians have stopped trying to save their loved one is for the physician to describe in lay terminology all that he or she is still doing for the patient (e.g., anticoagulation, arrhythmia treatment and prophylaxis, pressor support, airway protection, etc.). The list is usually quite long for critically ill patients and should be emphasized to allay the relatives' fears of physician abandonment.

Other authors have suggested that the performance of cardiopulmonary resuscitation has become a "ritualistic comforting hand on the shoulder of a grieving family member."[26] But in actuality, a literal comforting hand and gentle words of consolation are much more effective, and honest assurance will mean more to bereaved family members than half-hearted chest compressions and abbreviated drug therapy.

The difficulties inherent in explaining the impending death of a loved one are compounded by having to translate medical terminology into lay terms. Relatives whose comprehension and judgment are understandably clouded by emotion and the lack of physician training in discussing end-of-life issues can also make communication difficult between doctors and their patients' families. Slow codes may represent an effort by some physicians to avoid these challenging discussions.

Finally, there exist some families who desire medically unrealistic care of their terminally ill loved ones. This occurs despite the best physician-family rapport, the best explanation of the patient's grim prognosis, or the most prompt and thorough discussion of the family's fears concerning death. The solution to this dilemma is to change the default position unique to the United States of providing resuscitative efforts to every dying patient unless otherwise requested.[27] Physicians must realize that their vast armamentarium of resuscitative interventions are effective in only a minority of cases, and that a model of performing cardiopulmonary resuscitation only on those patients who have a likelihood of meaningful recovery should be adopted.[28]

Slow codes are expensive, unethical, and are almost always futile. They benefit no one, and they rob terminally ill patients of their exit from this life with dignity. They should be abandoned. We should select patients likely to receive meaningful benefit from serious resuscitative efforts and treat them accordingly. Terminally ill patients should be provided comfort care and other interventions more useful than chest compressions, cardioversion, and epinephrine.

CASE STUDY #11

The Ethical Issue: A patient insists on oral feeding against evidence that it may cause pneumonia.

JW is a very nice ninety-two-year-old lady who has lead a semi-independent life in an assisted living facility. She has been healthy all her life except for the last year when she was hospitalized three times because of heart failure exacerbated by episodes of pneumonia. Left ventricular (heart) failure was deemed to be due to moderately severe calcific aortic valve disease with both aortic stenosis (narrowing; valve area 0.8 cm^2) and moderately severe aortic regurgitation (leaking).

The patient executed an advance care plan in which she chose to forgo CPR and all life-prolonging measures, including artificial feeding and hydration. She appointed her only daughter to be her surrogate in case she became incompetent.

During the last hospitalization the daughter accepted placing her mother on assisted ventilation reluctantly and only after physicians assured her that they expected her to be weaned off the ventilator as soon as the pneumonia was cured. Subsequent to weaning off the ventilator, a swallowing study showed impaired function of JW's throat muscles and a propensity toward the passage of food or drink into her windpipe.

The treating physician recommended a feeding tube, which the patient and her daughter objected to. The patient asked that she continue to be fed orally. Specifically, she asked for an ice cream cone.

The Ethical Dilemma

Should the physician

1. insist that no food or drink be offered orally?
2. insist on tube feeding or else relinquish the patient's care to another physician?
3. go ahead and give the patient the ice cream cone she asked for, knowing that it may result in aspiration?

The proper answer is 3, provided that the physician explains in great detail the consequences of this decision. Also, he should make certain that the patient elect to forgo treatment of pneumonia resulting from aspiration, including the possibility of assisted ventilation. Further, the treating physician should record this information into the patient's chart and should enter a "Do Not Attempt Resuscitation" order in the chart. It is desirable to have the patient's nurse included in such discussions.

Discussion

The principle of sovereignty over one's own body has been recognized by the courts and ethicists for decades.[29] Not to respect an informed patient's expressed wishes constitutes the criminal offense of battery.

In certain instances, however, it is the duty of the treating physician to verify the validity of the patient's decision to forgo a potentially beneficial medical intervention. The patient has to be fully aware of the consequences of his or her decision. Also, the patient has to have the capacity to discern between options and that the patient's decision to forgo treatment is spontaneous and uncoerced. That way the treating physician is sure that the three legs of informed consent have been satisfied (i.e., full disclosure, competence, and the exercise of free will).[30] It must be emphasized that the right to refuse treatment extends to the patient's appointed surrogate. The physician has an obligation to abide by choices made on the patient's behalf by the appointed surrogate as if they were the patient's own expressed choices. There is one caveat: This general principle does not apply when the surrogate's decision is malicious, reflects poor understanding, or serves the surrogates' own self-interests.

In this case, JW lived a full life, came to terms with her own mortality, and elected to die without any more medical intervention. Her decision may not be readily appreciated by her young interventionalist. However, it is JW's life, after all. If an ice cream cone brings her a moment of pleasure before life's sunset, so be it!

CASE STUDY #12

The Ethical Issue: The patient's pneumonia required assisted ventilation. After weaning, a second intubation is necessary. The patient's "living will" asks for **no** *artificial life support.*

MM is a seventy-six-year-old renowned physician leader. He has been recognized worldwide for his teaching skills, humanitarian endeavors, and compassion. Recently, he was diagnosed with prostate cancer with metastases. This prompted him to execute an advance directive in which he indicated that, in case of incompetence or incapacity, he would not wish to be maintained on life-prolonging artificial means.

MM has been quite healthy all his life, except for elevated blood pressure requiring a multitude of medications, until he was afflicted with prostate cancer. Radiation therapy and testosterone antagonists rendered him somewhat weak but by no means an invalid. MM developed acute pneumonia, became deficient in oxygen and required assisted ventilation. After a few days of antibiotic treatment he was weaned off the ventilator machine. He did fairly well initially, but was obviously weak. A couple of days later he relapsed. He developed fever, became confused, and showed a significant drop in blood oxygen and the family had to consider whether to place him back on artificial ventilation.

One of the children, the appointed surrogate, insisted that his father explicitly asked not to receive artificial life-prolonging measures. The rest of the family wanted their loved one to be treated aggressively. The family asked to have a conference with the treating team to discuss their decision.

The Ethical Dilemma

As the treating physician, you should

1. go along with the appointed surrogate (the patient's son) in that only comfort measures be applied;
2. argue vehemently in favor of placing MM on artificial ventilation, since there is an excellent chance for recovery; or
3. take a neutral stand and ask the family to resolve the matter among themselves.

The proper answer is 2.

Discussion

This case demonstrates one of the problems inherent in advance directives, particularly when they are written in general, nonspecific language such as, "I don't want life-prolonging measures through heroic interventions or artificial means."

Most individuals who execute advance directives expect them to apply when death is imminent and unavoidable or when there is no reasonable chance for a meaningful recovery. MM's chances for cure were substantial and assisted ventilation should be viewed as a temporary means to bring the patient back to health and not as a measure that serves only to prolong the process of dying.

It is the physician's duty to make sure that the patient's surrogate and the rest of the family understand fully the probabilities for improvement with and without a certain intervention. A blind application of a poorly worded advance directive can be disastrous. In all circumstances, the physician has to follow the spirit and not necessarily the letter of the document. The shortcomings of advance directives are many. A minority of citizens execute advance directives. The documents are not yet fully integrated in the medical records of patients. Further, most advance directives are written in general, nonspecific language that rarely applies to the patient's condition and physicians are often at a loss trying to decipher at what stage of the patient's illness an advance directive should be considered.[31]

Because of these shortcomings, proper advance care planning should be medical-scenario specific. We recommend that it is best done in consultation with the patient's primary physician and that appointed surrogates be fully informed about the patient's choices.

CASE STUDY #13

The Ethical Issue: A patient explicitly wanting to avoid a harsh death ends up with a horrific one.

PP, a sixty-two-year-old neurosurgeon with no prior history of significant health problems was an athlete, a pilot, and a mountain climber. He led a life of independence, travel, and adventure. PP experienced two episodes of atrial fibrillation (disordered heart rhythm). Each lasted for a few hours and aborted spontaneously. Clinical evaluation showed no evidence of structural heart disease and no evidence of hyperthyroidism. All PP needed to do was to rest and take a tranquilizer for the episodes to terminate spontaneously. He objected to any medication that would slow him down, even if it would help his medical condition.

A third episode of atrial fibrillation was followed by cerebral thromboembolism (a clot going to the brain) manifested by asphasia (a loss of speech) and right hand weakness (stroke). PP was placed on Coumadin (a blood thinner) and the neurologic deficit resolved almost completely.

PP returned to work a full schedule. He made it unequivocally clear to his family and treating physicians that he would never want to live a dependent life in which he could not communicate intelligently with others or take care of himself. He was forceful in expressing his fear of incapacity and demanded that all pledge to him to honor his wishes if ever he developed another stroke.

Subsequent to the initial stroke, PP had no other major health problems, although he hardly tolerated the limitations on his lifestyle imposed by Coumadin therapy.

At age sixty-five PP suffered a seizure attack, which was initially thought to be due to another clot originating from the heart as a complication of an undetected episode of disordered heart rhythm. Evaluation with a CT brain scan and MRI showed a brain tumor and a biopsy revealed it to be a malignant glioma. PP's condition deteriorated quickly. He became confused and combative, and required large doses of anticonvulsants to combat incessant seizure activity.

The Ethical Dilemma

What is the best treatment for this patient with clear directives?

1. Euthanasia.
2. Order not to attempt resuscitation and let nature take its course.
3. Request an anesthesia consultation to undertake terminal unconscious sedation (by giving the patient a medicine by vein to render the patient unconscious) and cease the administration of feeding and hydration.

The correct answer is 3.

Discussion

Euthanasia (mercy killing), by which the physician intentionally ends the life of a patient in order to put an end to his suffering, is illegal in the United States. Even if the intent is to spare the patient a harsh death and replace it with an easier one, the intent does not justify the deed. Furthermore, the U.S. Supreme Court has ruled that citizens do not have a constitutional liberty right to assisted suicide by which the patient himself controls the act of terminating his or her own life by swallowing a prescribed sedative in a dose large enough to ensure one's death.[32] The state of Oregon is the only state in the Unites States that has elected to permit physician-assisted suicide. The Oregon Death with Dignity Act of 1997 allowed physicians to prescribe lethal medication provided certain conditions are satisfied. This patient neither lived in Oregon nor was he lucid enough to ask for or self-administer the lethal medicine.

Asking for a Do Not Attempt Resuscitation order while persevering with life support in this patient would fall short of the pledge already made to the patient by his family and treating physician. It would not spare the patient the indignity he so dreaded.

In this particular case, terminal unconscious sedation and cessation of artificial feeding and hydration is the treatment of choice. Such a dramatic measure requires the assistance of an anesthesiologist. The patient is sedated to unconsciousness to relieve severe physical suffering, terminal delerium, and seizure activity. Terminal sedation is considered to be a combination of withdrawal of life support as well as aggressive palliation of symptoms.[33] Most ethicists find this intervention acceptable, subject to restrictions and safeguards. As opposed to physician–assisted suicide, the intent in terminal unconscious sedation is to obtain symptom relief; death is an unintended but inevitable result. On the other hand, in physician–assisted suicide the intention is to end the life of a patient in order to achieve permanent symptom relief. The subtle difference between unconscious sedation and physician–assisted suicide may seem a confusing technicality since both lead to permanent relief of harsh symptoms with death as the foreseen end result. But this is where the line is drawn by law and widely accepted ethical precepts . . . at least for now.

CASE STUDY #14

The Ethical Issue: After the death of his appointed surrogate, a demented, senile patient is caught in a whirlwind of medical decision making.

JW was ninety-two years old when he was admitted to the hospital in acute heart failure for which he had been intubated and placed on assisted ventilation. Review of his medical records showed that he had been diagnosed with narrowing of the aortic valve six years earlier.

A repeat ultrasound evaluation of the heart was of poor technical quality and was therefore inconclusive. It suggested, however, severe aortic valve calcification and poor left ventricular systolic function (weak heart muscle). Laboratory tests revealed moderately severe kidney failure with a creatinine level of 3.6, severe anemia with a hemoglobin of 6.7 (severe blood loss), and a hemocult positive stool indicative of gastrointestinal bleeding.

JW had executed a living will five years earlier in which he asked to forgo heroic intervention or life-prolonging artificial means. He appointed his only surviving daughter to be his surrogate. However, the patient's appointed surrogate died from disseminated breast cancer a year before

JW's present hospital admission. Because the patient's daughter had been his caretaker, JW was placed in a nursing home. Recently, he was described as being confused, lonesome, and depressed, and requiring total care.

After JW was admitted to the intensive care unit, decision making was relegated to his six grandchildren. While in the hospital JW was seen by a cardiologist who recommended transesophageal echocardiography (ultrasound imaging of the heart through the esophagus) and possible right and left cardiac catheterization with coronary arteriography in order to better evaluate the cardiac (heart) status.

A gastroenterologist advocated a specialized test (endoscopy) to visualize the inside of the patient's colon in order to assess for the origin of gastrointestinal bleeding—suspecting a colon cancer (the patient had prior history of colon polyps). A nephrologist advised to undertake cystoscopy, a specialized procedure to visualize the inside of the urinary bladder and renal (kidney) ultrasound examination because of suspicion that the patient might have bladder neck obstruction that contributed to impaired kidney function. The pulmonologist suggested that there was little hope of being able to wean JW off the ventilator without addressing the patient's cardiac (heart) problems.

The patient's grandchildren, overwhelmed and bewildered, could not agree among themselves on which course to take. They asked to have a conference to help them through the decision-making process.

The Ethical Dilemma

If you were the physician, should you

1. tell them that the physician's job is to give an accurate and honest evaluation of the medical status of the patient but that further decisions are entirely up to them?
2. advocate proceeding with various tests recommended by the numerous consulting physicians to obtain more information about the cardiac status, assess the cause of GI bleeding, and undertake the urologic evaluation before any sensible decision can be made?
3. recommend palliative care only, citing the following reasons?
    a.   The patient is clearly at the sunset of his life, he is senile and demented and suffers from multiple organ failure;
    b.   Although the patient's living will does not specifically apply to

the patient's present condition, its spirit dictates restraint in recommending intrusive, nonbeneficial care; and

c. No procedure is without its own complications (e.g., cardiac
    catheterization will certainly accentuate renal failure). Further-
    more, the patient is not a candidate for aortic valve replacement
    (heart surgery) or repair. Therefore, information obtained from
    various testing is unlikely to influence the treatment plan.

The proper answer is 3.

Discussion

Physicians should not offer an intervention that is not likely to benefit a
patient. By the same token patients and their families should not expect an
intervention deemed useless by rational medical standards.

Difficulty arises when a proposed intervention is potentially of a marginal benefit to the patient. In JW's case it can be argued that transesophageal echocardiography, colonoscopy, and cystoscopy do not carry a
significant risk and will establish the proper diagnosis. Indeed, this is not
an unreasonable argument. The problem is that each of these procedures
may call for a certain subsequent intervention, such as removal of colonic
polyps or transurethral resection of the prostate that carries some risks
without the promise of a measurable total benefit to the patient.

Withholding medical interventions of questionable utility may be
appropriate if it satisfies any one of three standards:

- Clear and convincing evidence that the patient does not want the
  intervention.
- Substitute judgment by a legally acceptable individual speaking on
  behalf of an incompetent patient.
- The patient's best interest is served by withholding the proposed
  intervention.

The clear and convincing evidence standard is satisfied if the patient has
an advance directive that clearly pertains to the patient's present condition or
if the patient has given oral instructions to forgo a certain intervention.

The substitute judgment standard is satisfied through a surrogate previously appointed by the patient to make decisions on his behalf once the patient has become unable or incapable of making such decisions. The same power is conferred to a court-appointed guardian or proxy for the patient.

In many instances, physicians have to make treatment decisions based on the patient's best interest standard.

In this case, the patient's advance directive was not conclusive, albeit suggestive of the patient's sentiments, and the patient's appointed surrogate predeceased the patient. In these difficult and vexing situations the physician has to weigh carefully the following questions:

- What is a probability of a meaningful recovery?
- Given the most realistic scenario, will the patient's quality of life be materially and measurably improved?
- What is the likely duration of such a benefit versus the duration of the recovery process?
- What are the possible cumulative risks to the patient from these interventions?

In other words, an experienced physician should be able to weigh the possibility, magnitude, and duration of benefiting the patient versus the risk and cost (human and otherwise) of an intervention. Physicians have to consider the patient's total health status and unique choices and not as comprised of multiple organ systems, each of which is attended to by an organ expert.

If the possible benefits do not outweigh the risks, the treating physician has a moral obligation to recommend against further intervention.[34] Physicians have to accept the finitude of life. It is when death is accepted as the concrete a priori of medical experience that physicians will come to terms with the unalterable truth that medicine is, likewise, a perishable good with its own inherent limits.

CASE STUDY #15

The Ethical Issue: A nonterminally ill cardiac patient opts for a high-risk heart procedure but insists not to receive CPR in the event of cardiac arrest during the procedure.

BL is a seventy-two-year-old retired executive. BL comes from a family with a strong history of premature coronary artery disease. At age fifty-six BL underwent quadruple bypass graft surgery. Over the following twelve years, BL underwent six coronary arteriograms and four balloon angioplasty procedures. A repeat bypass surgery was undertaken at age sixty-eight with two new grafts to two of the three coronary (heart) arteries. The third coronary artery was noted to be a large vessel and the prior bypass graft to its two large branches was noted to have only mild disease and, therefore, was not replaced.

BL was very health-conscious. He became vegetarian, exercised regularly, watched his weight religiously, and his total cholesterol value became satisfactory.

BL's younger brother, a professional pilot, suffered a cardiopulmonary arrest at age fifty-eight. He was resuscitated and placed on a ventilator but remained unconscious and eventually assisted ventilation was discontinued after several weeks. Overtaken by grief and shaken by the tragedy of his brother's death, BL executed all necessary documents making sure that he would not receive CPR in the event he suffered a cardiac arrest.

Four years after the second aortocoronary bypass operation, BL started to experience recurring angina pectoris. His exercise tolerance deteriorated. An exercise nuclear scan showed a large area of decreased blood flow involving the territory supplied by the one artery not bypassed during the last surgery. Heart function was noted to be only slightly impaired.

Coronary arteriograms and bypass graft angiograms (procedure by which a contrast agent is injected selectively in each of these vessels) showed a 90 to 95 percent narrowing extending over a long segment in the proximal one-third of the vein graft to the large coronary artery that did not need bypassing during the last heart surgery.

You discuss the findings with BL and you recommend the use of an injectable antiplatelet agent with multiple stent (a meshed coil inserted over a balloon to open up the graft and prevent it from collapsing back) deployment. You emphasize that the procedure carries a much higher than average risk of a heart attack or even sudden death due to disordered heart rhythm. You share with BL that the higher risk is due to the age of the graft (sixteen years) and the extent and nature of the narrowing.

BL agrees to undergo the procedure provided that no attempt to resuscitate him would be undertaken should he develop a cardiac arrest. You spend enough time trying to persuade him to change his mind. You emphasize that cardiac arrest during this procedure is not a rare occurrence and that most patients are easily converted back to normal rhythm. The patient is adamant about his demand.

The Ethical Dilemma

Given these circumstances should you:

1. refuse to do the procedure and give the patient medical treatment in view of his unreasonable intransigence?
2. undertake the procedure with all necessary precautions to minimize the likelihood of ventricular fibrillation (even to the extent of using circulatory support)?
3. transfer the patient's care to another physician, indicating that you do not wish to undertake an unnecessarily high risk of procedure-related mortality?

The proper answer is 2. Some physicians may opt for 3.

Discussion

This case represents a rare but a real challenge that frustrates the physician's sacred duty to be beneficent and nonmalefiscent toward his patient and the patient's right to forgo a life-saving intervention, a decision that may be judged unwise and even irrational. The physician's dilemma is further compounded by the fact that death induced by a therapeutic intervention represents a procedure-caused (iatrogenic) complication and will taint the physician's record.

Some studies cite serious or fatal procedure-related complications in 4 to 9 percent of hospitalized patients.[35] In one retrospective series 14 percent of cardiac arrests were deemed to be due to such an event.[36] In an article titled "DNR in the OR," R. M. Walker argued that Do Not Resuscitate orders should not be rescinded when terminally ill patients undergo palliative surgery.[37] Walker argued that physicians' moral concerns about hastening the patient's death may be assuaged by

- emphasizing the patient's acceptance of operative mortality risk;
- viewing matters as analogous to surgery on Jehovah's Witnesses who refuse life-saving transfusions;
- viewing the patient's intraoperative death as a double effect, that is, an unintended negative effect that is linked to the performance of a good act; and
- distinguishing this from assisted suicide in which the intent is to end the life of a patient.

In a more recent review, D. Casarett and L. F. Ross argue against over-riding a patient's refusal of treatment after an iatrogenic complication.[38] The authors assert that no ethical principle of first do no harm should accommodate the patient's own perspective of quality of life and dignity. The authors underscore that even when resuscitation of iatrogenic cardiac arrest is likely to succeed it must never be a reason to undermine a competent individual's rights. Furthermore, the physician's intervention, under these circumstances, should not be viewed as the most important factor in the chain of events that ultimately lead to the patient's death.

Importantly, these authors cite instances in which the patient's prior directive can be overridden. Resuscitation would be appropriate if there were reason to believe that it would be consistent with the patient goals. In Case Study #2 we described a patient who executed a living will asking for no CPR. The patient suffered disordered rhythm of the upper heart chambers (atrial fibrillation) and the medicine given to correct this condition caused a more serious rhythm disorder called ventricular fibrillation. Cardioversion (electric shock to restore normal heart rhythm) was appropriately administered. When discussion about possible complications is inadequate, a patient with nonterminal condition who suffers an unforeseen cardiac arrest should be resuscitated, despite the patient's advance directives. It must be emphasized that physicians have a duty to discuss with their patients treatment goals and potential complications. On the other hand, it is unrealistic to expect physicians to cover all contingencies in adequate detail with every intervention. At all times, components of the discussion have to be documented in the patient's chart. In this particular case, however, a full discussion about possible complications of the planned procedure was undertaken. The patient remained insistent about his choice of no CPR in the case of cardiac arrest.

To quote noted ethicist Dr. H. T. Englehardt, taking freedom seriously means acknowledging the rights of competent individuals to dispose of their lives in ways that others may judge imprudent.[39]

CASE STUDY #16

The Ethical Issue: A child with disseminated cancer continues to be subjected to painful medical interventions after it has become clear that the treatment has failed.

VQ, an eight-year-old boy, was diagnosed with a virulent form of cancer involving the left thigh bone (femur), which had spread to the lungs. VQ underwent left hip disarticulation for removal of the left lower extremity. Soon thereafter, he received a high dose antimitotic combination therapy and became a candidate for bone marrow transplantation. All of this required a multitude of evaluations, procedures, and treatment side effects that had their toll on little VQ. Fortunately VQ had a supportive family: a dedicated father, a loving mother, and a younger sister. All of them urged the treating physicians to go all the way and never to waver, even if the odds were stacked against little VQ.

Bone marrow transplant didn't take in spite of antirejection drugs and large doses of steroids. Little VQ developed recurrent episodes of systemic infection, the last of which caused bilateral bronchopneumonia with a highly virulent organism requiring placement on assisted ventilation and the use of large doses of parenteral antibiotics. As a result, kidney function deteriorated seriously, requiring peritoneal dialysis. Pulmonary functions continued to deteriorate and VQ required intermittent positive pressure ventilation. In addition, anticancer agents caused deterioration in left ventricular (heart muscle) function and culminated in heart failure. This contributed to deteriorating lung function.

VQ became ventilator dependent and a tracheostomy was undertaken to enable proper care of his respiratory passages.

VQ developed systemic fungal infection, causing a brain abscess, weakness of the left side of the body, and seizure activity. The family had a conference with the treating physicians who conveyed a gloomy picture to the family.

"Is there any hope at all?" "There is little hope," the physician said. "If we are able to eradicate the fungal infection and are successful with another bone marrow transplant, the patient can be maintained on dialysis and then receive a heart/lung transplant."

The family insisted the doctors not give up and pursue this plan vigorously. However, VQ's systemic fungus infection could not be eradicated and the little boy died after several months of relentless, aggressive medical interventions.

The Dilemma

Was the physician's final representation accurate or was it a convenient way to avoid the very difficult situation of how to bring unwelcome news to a loving family?

Discussion

False hopes lead to unrealistic expectations and ultimately to devastatingly painful disappointment. Each year about 12,400 children in the United States are diagnosed to have cancer. Thanks to enormous scientific progress over the past three decades, overall survival improved from 10 percent to over 70 percent.

As in many other medical disciplines technologic advances have outpaced our ability to deal with children who do not respond favorably to various aggressive interventions. In other words, breathtaking scientific advances have rendered a death of a child an unacceptable failure.[40] A recent study by J. Wolfe et al. shows that children who die of cancer, systematically, receive aggressive treatment at the end of life and that many have substantial, uncontrollable suffering in the last month of life.[41] The authors surveyed 103 parents of children who died of cancer between 1990 and 1997 and who were cared for at Children's Hospital in Boston, and/or the Dana Farber Cancer Institute. The psychological and emotional burdens of giving up make it extremely difficult, often impossible for parents to abandon hope and perseverance in the pursuit of cure, even if that becomes clearly elusive. Death coming after a long life can be sad. Death of a child is nothing short of devastating. While hospice care is gaining acceptance for the management of dying adults, it is hardly ever sought in the care of dying children. Furthermore, children dying of chronic disease require difficult and highly specialized care to assist them in dealing with pain, suffering, intrusive procedures, side effects of interventions, and the inevitable sense of helplessness. The importance of proper nutrition and family involvement add to the complexity.

Early involvement by highly skilled, well-trained, specialized teams not only would ensure proper palliative care but also is paramount in assisting parents in making painful but necessary decisions of when life-prolonging interventions should cease. There is a societal need to change our perception by physicians, other care givers and families that discontinuing aggressive care means that they are giving up and, in effect represents failure.

CONCLUSION

In this chapter, I have shared stories of some of my patients. No number of stories would suffice to cover the wide spectrum of dying. In fact, every patient has a unique and different image colored less by the patient's illness and more by the patient's reaction to his predicament; the threat of an imminent death, a life cut short before its time, and slashed hopes. The picture is further influenced by the patient's understanding of his illness, psychosocial support system, spiritual beliefs, and the level of patient's trust in the treating physician/team.

Lack of experience precludes me from presenting enough examples of dying at a young age. In 1960, while in training at Hammersmith Hospital in London, I was given the responsibility as a junior physician on the heart surgery ward, which dealt with children born with heart defects. I cannot count how many times I spent my nights weeping over the loss of one of my patients and how my mentor, Professor John Goodwin, used to admonish me, "you need to keep an emotional arm's length from your patients." Since then numberless vicarious encounters with dying might have immunized me but not when it comes to children. I must relinquish the painful subject of the dying young to some other, better-qualified author.

GLOSSARY

ACTIVE EUTHANASIA: Administering a medicine in a large enough dose with the intent to cause death and end suffering.

ACTIVE INVOLUNTARY EUTHANASIA: Administering a medicine with the intent to end a life *without* the patient's asking for it.

ACTIVE VOLUNTARY EUTHANASIA: Administering a medicine with the intent to end a life *with* the patient's asking for it.

ADVANCE CARE PLAN: A legally binding document executed by a competent adult patient with instructions about the person's choices for medical treatments that apply when the person becomes unable to express his or her choices.

ADVANCED DEMENTIA: A condition in which the patient is generally awake and able to respond but is confused as far as time, place, and names with impaired memory, vocabulary, and ability to reason because of deterioration of brain function not due to medication or a transient or reversible condition.

ASSISTED SUICIDE: Assisting a patient to take his or her own life by providing a prescription or medicine in a dose sufficient to cause death.

AUTONOMY: A principle that gives to the competent adult individual the right of self-determination and to have full control over decisions related to invasion of the body.

BENEFICENCE: The principle that the physician should be the patient's advocate under all circumstances. The patient's well-being should be placed above the physician's self-interest.

CENTRAL REGISTRY: A computer-based data bank in which the names and identification of patients executing a living will is stored and can be readily retrieved.

COMA: Total unawareness of self and environment with no periods of awakening; may be deep with total lack of response or less deep when some reflex response can be evoked with stimulation.

COMPETENCE TO MAKE MEDICAL TREATMENT DECISIONS: Not necessarily equivalent to legal competence, it stipulates that the patient is able to understand, evaluate, and choose a treatment.

CPR (CARDIOPULMONARY RESUSCITATION): Resuscitation through the use of electric shock to the heart and artificial ventilation with or without external chest compressions. This is employed in the treatment of cessation of heart or lung function.

DNR (DO-NOT-RESUSCITATE) ORDER: An indication that for medical reasons or a terminal condition CPR is inappropriate in the event of cessation of the heartbeat or breathing.

DNAR (DO NOT ATTEMPT RESUSCITATION) ORDER: A better term than DNR, which may give the impression of abandoning the patient.

HIGH BRAIN DEATH: Loss of high brain functions that define a person: decision making, passions, and reason.

INFORMED CONSENT: The patient agrees to a certain medical intervention based on his or her evaluation of all relevant information about the procedure, alternatives, and the competence of the treating team.

LIVING WILL: A legal document by which the patient states his or her preference to forgo life-sustaining treatment during terminal illness or a terminal state of unconsciousness.

NONMALEFICENCE: Meaning "first do no harm," this principle is the first law in the practice of medicine.

PASSIVE EUTHANASIA: To terminate artificial means of life support in order to allow the natural process of death to take its course.

PATERNALISM: Forced decision making without adequate information or consent from the patient.

PATIENT'S BEST-INTEREST STANDARD: To apply treatment as judged to be in the patient's best interests in accordance to competent medical standards and rational prevailing societal sentiments.

PATIENT SELF-DETERMINATION ACT: Part of Budget Reconciliation Act of 1990, PL 101-508, sections 4206, 4751; a federal law, implemented in December 1991, that requires institutions to notify patients about the availability of formal advance directives.

PERMANENT VEGETATIVE STATE: Irreversible vegetative state due to severe injury or acute oxygen deprivation to progressive degenerative metabolic or developmental brain disorder.

PERSISTENT VEGETATIVE STATE: A vegetative state that has persisted for a period of time (three months when caused by disease and twelve months after head injury).

PROXY FOR HEALTH-CARE DECISIONS: Many living will legislations allow for the appointment of a proxy decision maker to make health-care decisions when the patient is no longer competent to make them.

SHARED DECISION MAKING: A competent adult individual has the ultimate right to accept or refuse medical treatment even if that decision is deemed irrational or harmful.

SUBJECTIVE STANDARD: A method of medical decision making in which there is clear and convincing evidence that the medical decision to be implemented is exactly what an incompetent or unconscious patient would have chosen for himself or herself.

SUBSTITUTE JUDGMENT STANDARD: To implement the recommendation of an appointed guardian or family member as a substitute for the patient's own judgment.

VEGETATIVE STATE: Unawareness of self and environment with sleep-wake cycles and with either complete or partial preservation of brain-stem autonomic functions.

WHOLE BRAIN DEATH: Disappearance of all brain functions including the primitive autonomic functions of the brain stem. The brain produces no spontaneous electric activity.

APPENDIX

ADVANCE CARE PLANNING

In order to ensure that one's own choices for medical treatment are honored when life approaches its close, one has to choose the right document. Characteristics that make the document more effective include

- brevity; a redundant multi-page document tends to get lost.
- medical-scenario–specific language; documents written in legalese or as general statements are almost irrelevant in guiding medical treatment.
- language that is understood by the public and that is acceptable to medical professionals.
- easy retrievability; in order to achieve this objective, national Advance Care Plan repositories need to be established and mechanisms for immediate availability developed. Efforts are underway to achieve this goal.
- easy tranference and renewal among different states and legal acceptability across state lines. These requisites are self-evident. They could be facilitated by the impending enactment of the uniform health decisions act.
- easy integration into the patient's medical record.

Certain statements are problematic, such as, "when I have a *terminal, irreversible* illness with *no hope* for my recovery, I don't want my life sustained by *heroic measures* or *artificial means*." The word *terminal* can have many interpretations; patients with advanced Alzheimer's disease, as well as those suffering from other chronic debilitating conditions can linger for years.

The term *irreversible* creates a good deal of misunderstanding; patients with advanced, chronic diseases often die from a potentially reversible condition such as pneumonia. A document worded this way may be interpreted to mean that the incidental "potentially reversible" pneumonia should be treated aggressively. Routinely, patients with advanced medical conditions are placed on ventilators and receive interventions aimed at curing another incidental ailment such as pneumonia, heart attack, or a newly discovered cancer.

An Advance Care Plan should be clear about whether one wants such an aggressive treatment of the potentially lethal incidental disease or whether one wishes to have nature take its course without interference, except for that which produces comfort.

The "no hope" statement requires the "absolute" standard and often produces the exact opposite of the person's desired choice. Doctors tend to interpret the document to mean that they should make certain that all medical interventions are exhausted. The more practical "beyond reasonable doubt" standard should be the guiding post.

"Heroic measures," no doubt, have some special meaning to lay individuals. Applying an electric jolt to the heart or undertaking resuscitation efforts may seem heroic to the public. Often, they are viewed differently by members of the medical profession.

The "artificial means" statement is almost meaningless when it comes to medical management. Almost all major medical interventions are possible only because of artificial machines, gadgets, or tubes.

On the one hand, most of the public has poor understanding of medical jargon. On the other hand, physicians are disassociated from the public's perception of medical terminology prevalent in scientific publications and textbooks. Advance medical care planning documents have to provide the bridge that facilitates communication between patients (or would-be patients) and physicians. Furthermore, the document has to be easy to understand by citizens at all levels of education beyond the eighth grade.

The Project GRACE task force on advance care planning discovered, through testing of various versions of the Advance Care Plan, that the size and format of the document are important. The Project GRACE Advance Care Plan document is the size of medical record observation notes, as well as laboratory, X-ray, and EKG reports.

Project GRACE developed, tested, and modified its plan to satisfy all of these and other requirements.

In its present form, the Project GRACE Advance Care Plan goes a long way toward enhancing the chances that citizens' choices for medical treatment during the last chapter of life are duly honored.

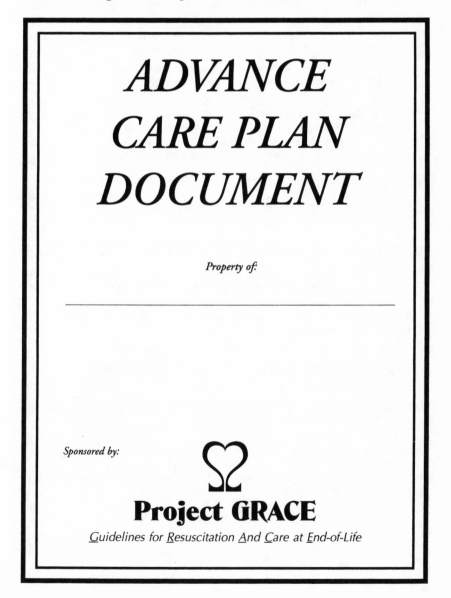

ADVANCE CARE PLAN DOCUMENT

Property of:

_____

Sponsored by:

Project GRACE

Guidelines for Resuscitation And Care at End-of-Life

GUIDELINES

(Use the following list as a reference when answering the questions to the right)

Illness/Conditions

- **Unconscious State (Permanent Vegetative State):** Patient is totally unaware with little chance of ever waking up

- **Permanent Confusion:** Patient is unable to remember, understand or make decisions. He/She does not recognize his/her loved ones or have a clear conversation with them.

- **Total Dependence:** Patient is unable to talk clearly or move by him/herself. He/She depends on others for feeding and hygiene. Patient's condition cannot be helped by rehabilitation or any other means.

- **End-Stage Disease:** This illness has reached its final stages in spite of full treatment.
  Example: • Widespread cancer that cannot be helped with treatment
  • Badly damaged heart and lungs. The patient needs oxygen around the clock and cannot make any effort without feeling suffocation.

Treatment Choices

- **CPR (Cardiopulmonary Resuscitation):** To make the heart beat again and the patient to start breathing after it has stopped. Usually this involves electric shock and/or use of a breathing machine.

- **Life support:** Use of machines that breathe in place of the lungs and/or take on the job of other organs.

- **Surgery, blood transfusion, antibiotics:** These treatments deal with a new condition but will not help the main illness.

  Examples: an unconscious or confused patient develops cancer or a heart attack or patient with End-Stage Disease develops a pneumonia.

- **Tube feeding:** Use of tubes to deliver food and water in the stomach or into a vein in a patient who cannot swallow

End of life issues are of concern to each of us and doctors alike. Every adult has the right to choose the manner of treatment they will receive.

Adequate control of pain and suffering, comfort care and access to hospice services are the right of every individual. Doctors have learned that it may be futile and painful to keep some individuals alive at all costs and by every known method. Florida law requires that the patient's end-of-life directions, if clearly expressed, should be followed.

Project GRACE Advance Care Plan

I_____ want to choose how I will be treated by my doctors and other health care providers during the last days of my life. I do not want to suffer unnecessarily and I do not want to be kept on machines that will serve only to delay the time of my death. My choices about treatments which have little chance of making my condition better, if I am unable to make my own decisions, are below. Checking yes means I want the treatment. Checking no means I do not want the treatment.

Illness/Conditions   Treatment Choices

	CPR*		Life Support		Surgery Blood/Antibiotics		Tube Feeding	
	Yes	No	Yes	No	Yes	No	Yes	No
Unconscious State:	☐	☐	☐	☐	☐	☐	☐	☐
Permanent Confusion:	☐	☐	☐	☐	☐	☐	☐	☐
Total Dependence:	☐	☐	☐	☐	☐	☐	☐	☐
End Stage Disease:	☐	☐	☐	☐	☐	☐	☐	☐

Other Instructions: _____

_____

_____

*Answering **NO** to the above CPR questions constitutes a Do Not Attempt Resuscitation Order. (The State of Florida requires an additional form be completed.)

After my death, I do _____ I do not _____ wish to donate my organs for the benefit of others.

I agree _____ or do not agree _____ to include this Advance Care Plan in the Central Registry.

Choice of Surrogate for Health Care Affairs

When I am unable to make my own choices and my condition is not clearly covered by this document, I appoint the following person(s) to make treatment choices for me:

Designate: **Alternate:**

Name_____ Tel. No (___)_____   Name_____ Tel. No. (___)_____

Address _____   Address _____

I hereby hold harmless my physicians and any other health care providers who render care or withhold care from me in good faith, if they reasonably believe such action(s) is/are consistent with my wishes as expressed in this document. I further request that my family and anyone acting on my behalf follow my wishes and directives and take whatever steps are necessary, including legal action, to ensure that my wishes and directives are carried out. I direct my Power of Attorney or Trustee holding funds on my behalf to make such funds available to my healthcare surrogate or anyone acting on my behalf to ensure that my wishes, as expressed herein, are carried out.

Print Name_____   **Signature**_____

Social Security Number_____   Tel. No (_____) _____

Address _____

Dated: _____

Witness - Print Name_____   **Signature** _____

Address_____

Witness - Print Name_____   **Signature** _____

Address _____

(One witness cannot be an heir, blood relative or health care provider.)

<u>WHAT TO DO WITH THIS ADVANCE CARE PLAN DOCUMENT</u>

Give a copy to your physician(s)

Keep a copy in your personal files where it is accessible to others

Tell your closest relatives what is in the Advance Care Plan document

Give a copy to your Health Care Surrogate

For inquiries:
Project GRACE • 1311 N. Westshore Blvd. #107 • Tampa, FL 33607
Toll Free 1-877-994-7223• Office (813) 281-2324 • Fax (813) 281-0295 • Cell (813) 205-2517
www.p-grace.org

NOTES

❦

FOREWORD

1. H. D. McIntosh, "Attaining and Maintaining Autonomy," in *Clinical Cardiology in the Elderly*, ed. Elliot Chesler (Armonk, N.Y.: Futura Publishing Co., Inc., 1994), pp. 547–63.

2. Ibid.

PROLOGUE

1. E. Kübler-Ross, *Death, the Final Stage of Growth* (Englewood Cliffs, N.J.: Prentice Hall, 1975), p. 161.

2. E. A. Stead, Jr., *What This Patient Needs Is a Doctor*, ed. Galen S. Wagner, Bess Cebe, and Marvin P. Rozear (Durham, S.C.: Carolina Academic Press, 1978).

INTRODUCTION

1. Quoted from "Who Owns Medical Technology?" *Lancet* 345 (1995): 1126.

2. B. Starfield, "Is US Health Really the Best in the World?" *Journal of the American Medical Association* 284 (2000): 483–85.

3. L. L. Basta and H. D. McIntosh, "Project GRACE (Guidelines for Resuscitation And Care at End-of-Life)," *Clinical Cardiology* 23 (2000): Suppl. II.

CHAPTER 1

1. J. M. Steckelberg et al., "Werner Forsmann (1904–1979) and His Unusual Success Story," *Mayo Clinic Proceedings* 54 (1929): 746–48.

2. S. Radner, "An Attempt at Roentgenologic Visualization of Coronary Blood Vessels in Man," *Acta Radiologica* 26 (1945): 497–502.

3. D. D. Schocken, M. I. Arrieta, and P. E. Leaverton, "Prevalence and Mortality Rate of Congestive Heart Failure in the United States," *Journal of American College of Cardiology* 20 (1992): 301–306.

4. M. C. Weinstein et al., "Forecasting Coronary Artery Disease: Incidence, Mortality and Cost," *American Journal of Public Health* 77 (1987): 1417–26.

5. P. Aries, *The Hour of Death* (New York: Vintage Books, 1981).

6. *Health US* (Hyattsville, Md.: National Center for Health Statistics, 1999), p. 9.

7. J. R. Jude and J. O. Elam, *Fundamentals of Cardiopulmonary Resuscitation* (Philadelphia: Davis Co., 1965).

8. B. Lown, R. Amarsingham, and J. Newman, "New Method for Terminating Cardiac Arrhythmia: Use of a Synchronized Capacitor Discharge," *Journal of the American Medical Association* 182 (1962): 548–55.

9. "Ad Hoc Committee of the Harvard Medical School to Examine the Definition of Brain Death: A Definition of Irreversible Coma," *Journal of the American Medical Association* 205 (1968): 337–40.

10. President's Commission for the Study of Ethical Problems in Medicine and Biomedical and Behavioral Research, *Defining Death: Medical, Legal, and Ethical Issues in the Determination of Death* (Washington, D.C.: U.S. Government Printing Office, 1981).

11. S. Youngner and E. T. Bartlett, "Human Death and High Technology: The Failure of the Whole-Brain Formulations," *Annals of Internal Medicine* 99 (1983): 252–58.

12. Multi-Society Task Force on PVS, American Academy of Neurology, "Medical Aspects of the Persistent Vegetative State, Part 1," *New England Journal of Medicine* 330 (1994): 1572–79.

13. Ibid.

14. American Neurological Association Committee on Ethical Affairs, "Persistent Vegetative State: Report of the American Neurological Association Committee on Ethical Affairs," *Annals of Neurology* 33 (1993): 386–90.

15. D. Black et al., "Permanent Vegetative State, Addendum to a Review by a Working Group," *Journal of the Royal College of Physicians of London* 31 (1997): 260.

16. J. Naslund et al., "Correlation between Elevated Levels of Amyloid B. Peptide in the Brain and Cognitive Decline," *Journal of the American Medical Association* 283 (2000): 1571–77.

17. M. N. Rossor, "Catastrophe, Chaos, and Alzheimer's Disease," *Journal of the Royal College of Physicians of London* 29 (1995): 412–18.

18. R. S. Morrison and A. L. Siu, "Survival in End-Stage Dementia Following Acute Illness," *Journal of the American Medical Association* 284 (July 5, 2000): 47–52.

19. Black et al., "Permanent Vegetative State."

CHAPTER 2

1. Plato, *The Republic*, trans. G. M. Grube (Indianapolis: Hackett Publishing, 1981), pp. 76–77.

2. Quoted in S. J. Reiser, A. J. Dyuck, and W. J. Curran, *Ethics in Medicine: Historical Perspectives and Contemporary Concerns* (Cambridge, Mass.: MIT Press, 1977), pp. 6–7.

3. F. W. Peabody, "The Care of the Patient," *Journal of American Medical Association* 88 (1927): 877–81.

4. K. R. Mitchell, I. H. Kerridge, and R. J. Lovat, "Medical Futility, Treatment Withdrawal and the Persistent Vegetative State," *Journal of Medical Ethics* 19 (1993): 71–76.

5. Council on Scientific Affairs and Council on Ethical and Judicial Affairs, American Medical Association, "Persistent Vegetative State and the Decision to Withdraw or Withhold Life Support," *Journal of American Medical Association* 263 (1990): 426–30.

6. American Neurological Association Committee on Ethical Affairs, "Persistent Vegetative State: Report of the American Neurological Association Committee on Ethical Affairs," *Annals of Neurology* 33 (1993): 386–90.

7. Medical Ethics Committee of the British Medical Association, "Treatment of Patients in Persistent Vegetative State," *Proceedings of the British Medical Association* (September 1992).

8. United States Bishops Committee, "Statement on Nutrition and Hydration," *Cambridge Quarterly of Health Care Ethics* 2 (1993): 341.

9. T. E. Quill, R. Dresser, and D. W. Brock, "The Rule of Double Effect—A Critique of Its Role in End-of-Life Decision Making," *New England Journal of Medicine* 337 (1997): 1768–71.

10. J. T. Mangan, "An Historical Analysis of the Principle of Double Effect," *Theological Studies* 10 (1949): 41–61.

11. *Washington* v. *Glucksberg*, 117 S. Ct. 2258 (1997).

12. R. A. Burt, "The Supreme Court Speaks: Not Assisted Suicide but a Constitutional Right to Palliative Care," *New England Journal of Medicine* 337 (1997): 1234–36.

13. J. J. Fins, "Futility in Clinical Practice," *Journal of American Geriatric Society* 42 (1994): 861–65.

14. D. Callahan, *The Troubled Dream of Life: Living with Mortality* (New York: Simon & Schuster, 1993).

15. R. M. Veatch, "Why Physicians Cannot Determine if Care Is Futile," *Journal of the American Geriatric Society* 42 (1994): 871–74.

16. H. Brody, "The Physician's Role in Determining Futility," *Journal of the American Geriatric Society* 42 (1994): 875–78.

17. J. D. Lantos, "Futility Assessments and the Doctor-Patient Relationship," *Journal of the American Geriatric Society* 42 (1994): 868–70.

18. L. S. Schneiderman, "The Futility Debate: Effective versus Beneficial Intervention," *Journal of the American Geriatric Society* 42 (1994): 883–86.

19. S. J. Youngner, "Applying Futility: Saying No Is Not Enough," *Journal of the American Geriatric Society* 42 (1994): 887–89.

20. P. R. Helft, M. Siegler, and J. Lantos, "The Rise and Fall of the Futility Movement," *New England Journal of Medicine* 343 (2000): 293–96.

CHAPTER 3

1. M. H. Weil, "Alternatives to Rationing, in Brooking's Dialogues on Public Policy," in *Rationing of Medical Care for the Critically Ill* (Washington, D.C.: The Brookings Institution, 1989), pp. 17–23.

2. D. G. Smith, "Neonatal Intensive Care: How Much Is Too Much?" *Medical Ethics* 5 (1990): 13–14.

3. F. W. Peabody, "The Care of the Patient," *Journal of the American Medical Association* 88 (1927): 877–81.

4. T. E. Quill, "Doctor I Want to Die. Will You Help Me?" *Journal of the American Medical Association* 270 (1993): 870–73.

CHAPTER 4

1. Hesiod, *The Homeric Hymns and Homerica*, trans. H. G. Evelyn White (New York: Putnam, 1920), pp. 440–41.

2. J. G. Frazer, *Apollodorus: The Library* (New York: Putnam, 1921), pp. 22–34.

3. H. P. Liss, "A History of Resuscitation," *Annals of Emergency Medicine* 15 (1986): 65–72.

4. K. J. Tucker et al., "Cardiopulmonary Resuscitation: Historical Perspectives, Physiology, and Future Directions," *Archives of Internal Medicine* 154 (1994): 2141–50.

5. G. W. Crile, *Anemia and Resuscitation* (New York: D. Appleton & Co., 1914), pp. 15–32.

6. W. B. Kouwenhoven and O. R. Langworthy, "Cardiopulmonary Resuscitation: An Account of 45 Years of Research," *Johns Hopkins Medical Journal* 132 (1973): 186–93.

7. W. B. Kouwenhoven, "The Development of the Defibrillator," *Annals of Internal Medicine* 71 (1969): 449–58.

8. B. Lown, R. Amarsingham, and J. Newman, "New Method for Terminating Cardiac Arrhythmia: Use of Synchronized Capacitor Discharge," *Journal of the American Medical Association* 182 (1962): 548–55.

9. J. R. Jude and J. O. Elam, *Fundamentals of Cardiopulmonary Resuscitation* (Philadelphia: F. A. Davis Co., 1965).

10. "Optimum Care for Hopelessly Ill Patients, a Report of the Clinical Care Committee of the Massachusetts General Hospital," *New England Journal of Medicine* 7 (1976): 362–64; M. T. Rabkin, G. Dillerman, and N. R. Rice, "Orders Not to Resuscitate," *New England Journal of Medicine* 7 (1976): 364–66.

11. L. Basta et al., "Cardiopulmonary Resuscitation in the Elderly: Defining the Limits of Appropriateness," *American Journal of Geriatric Cardiology* (1998): 46–55.

12. S. J. Diem, J. D. Lantos, and J. A. Tulsky, "Cardiopulmonary Resuscitation on Television: Miracles and Misinformation," *New England Journal of Medicine* 334 (1996): 1578–82.

13. A. Wagg, M. Kininirons, and K. Stewart, "Cardiopulmonary Resuscitation: Doctors and Nurses Expect Too Much," *Journal of the Royal College of London* 29 (1995): 20–24.

14. D. J. Murphy et al., "The Influence of Probability of Survival on Patients' Preferences Regarding Cardiopulmonary Resuscitation," *New England Journal of Medicine* 330 (1994): 545–49.

15. R. G. Shashy et al., "Attitudes of the Informed Elderly Lay Public Toward Cardiopulmonary Resuscitation at the End-of-Life," *Disability* 8 (1999): 11–19.

16. R. Baker, *Beyond Do-Not-Resuscitate Orders,* Brookings Dialogues on Public Policy. Rationing of Medical Care for the Critically Ill (Washington, D.C.: Brookings Institution, 1989), pp. 52–63.

17. *In re Doe,* Civ. Action No D–93064 (Fulton County, Ga., 1991).

18. D. B. Waisel and R. D. Truog, "The Cardiopulmonary Resuscitation-Not-Indicated Order: Futility Revisited," *Annals of Internal Medicine* 122 (1995): 304–308.

19. K. Plunkitt, F. Matar, and L. Basta, "Therapeutic CPR or Consent DNR—A Dilemma Looking for an Answer," *Journal of the American College of Cardiology* 32 (1998): 2095–97.

20. M. Davis et al., "Stability of Choices about Life Sustaining Treatments," *Annals of Internal Medicine* 120 (1994): 567–73.

21. J. Hardwig, "The Problem of Proxies with Interests of Their Own: Toward a Better Theory of Proxy Decisions," *Journal of Clinical Ethics* 4 (1991): 41–46; A. B. Seckler et al., "Substituted Judgment: How Accurate Are Proxy Predictions?" *Annals of Internal Medicine* 115 (1991): 92–98.

22. Support Principal Investigators, "A Controlled Trial to Improve Care for Seriously Ill Hospitalized Patients: The Study to Understand Prognosis and Preferences for Outcomes and Treatment (SUPPORT)," *Journal of the American Medical Association* 274 (1995): 1591–98.

23. Council on Ethical and Judicial Affairs, American Medical Association, "Guidelines for Appropriate Use of Do Not Resuscitate Orders," *Journal of the American Medical Association* 265 (1991): 1868–71.

24. J. R. Mitchell, I. H. Kerridge, and R. J. Lovat, "Medical Futility, Treatment Withdrawal and the Persistent Vegetative State," *Journal of Medical Ethics* 19 (1993): 71–76.

25. *In the Matter of Shirley Dinnerstein* (Mass. App. 380 N.E. 2d 134, 1978).

CHAPTER 5

1. Council on Ethical and Judicial Affairs, American Medical Association, "Decisions Near the End of Life," *Journal of the American Medical Association* 267 (1992): 2229–33.

2. R. Gillon, "Euthanasia, Withholding Life-Prolonging Treatment and Moral Differences between Killing and Letting Die," *Journal of Medical Ethics* 14 (1988): 115–17.

3. Lord Browne-Wilkinson, Letter in *Airedale NHS Trust (Respondents)* v. *Bland* (Judgment, 1993), pp. 24–33.

4. R. J. Waller, *Old Songs in a New Café* (New York: Warner Books, 1994), p. 38.

5. Council on Ethical and Judicial Affairs, American Medical Association, "Decisions Near the End of Life," *Journal of the American Medical Association* 267 (1992): 2229–33.

6. *Biolaw* Special Section, "Assisted Suicide" (Bethesda, Md.: University Publications of America, 1994), pp. 103–106.

7. M. S. Ewer, "The Suicide Device: Does It Really Matter Who Pushes the Button?" *Internal Medicine World Report* 5 (1990): 7.

8. *Biolaw* Special Section, "Assisted Suicide."

9. "Kevorkian Aids in 2 More Suicides: Total Is 15," *New York Times* (February 19, 1993), p. A10.

10. *Final Report of the Michigan Commission on Death and Dying* (Lansing: Michigan Death and Dying Commission, 1994).

11. G. J. Annas, "Physician-Assisted Suicide—Michigan's Temporary Solution," *New England Journal of Medicine* 328 (1993): 1573–76.

12. *Rodriguez* v. *British Columbia* (Attorney General, No. 23476, British Columbia, Superior Court, September 30, 1993).

13. *Nancy B.* v. *l'Hotel-Dieu de Quebec* (R.J.Q., 1992), 361 (Superior Court).

14. E. J. Emanuel, "Euthanasia: Historical, Ethical, and Empiric Prospectives," *Archives of Internal Medicine* 154 (1994): 1890–1900.

15. Quoted in ibid.

16. Ibid.

17. Ibid.

18. Quoted in E. J. Emanuel, "The History of Euthanasia: Debates in the United States and Britain," *Annals of Internal Medicine* 121 (1994): 793–802.

19. Ibid.

20. A. Hocke and K. Binding, "Permitting the Destruction of Unworthy Life. Its Extent and Form," *Issues of Law and Medicine* 8 (1992): 231–65.

21. "Euthanasia: To Cease upon the Midnight," *Economist* 332 (1994): 21–23; R. Fenigsen, "The Netherlands: New Regulations Concerning Euthanasia," *Issues in Law and Medicine* 9 (1993): 167–73.

22. T. E. Quill, "Death and Dignity: A Case of Individualized Decision-Making," *New England Journal of Medicine* 324, no. 10 (1991): 691–94; C. Dyer, "Rheumatologist Convicted of Attempted Murder," *British Medical Journal* 325 (1992): 731.

23. D. W. Brock, "Voluntary Active Euthanasia," *Hastings Center Report* 22 (1992): 10–22.

24. R. A. Knox, "Poll: Americans Favor Mercy Killing," *Boston Globe* (November 3, 1991), sec. 1, p. 22.

25. M. Dean, "Politics of Euthanasia in U.K.," *Lancet* 345 (1995): 714.

26. *Cruzan v. Director* (497 U.S. 261, 1990).

27. Statistics Netherlands, *The End of Life in Medical Practice* (The Hague: SDU Publishers, 1992); M. A. de Watcher, "Active Euthanasia in the Netherlands," *Journal of the American Medical Association* 262 (1989): 3316–19.

28. de Watcher, "Active Euthanasia in the Netherlands."

29. "The Dutch Way of Dying," *Economist* 332 (1994): 23; "Netherlands. Biomedical Ethics," in *Biolaw* (Bethesda, Md.: University Publications of America, 1994), p. 47.

30. "The Dutch Way of Dying," p. 23.

31. "California's Proposition 161 and Physician-Assisted Dying," in *Biolaw* (Bethesda, Md.: University Publications of America, 1993), pp. 11–15.

32. Ibid.

33. "Oregon's Ballot Measure," *Legal Issues in Medicine* 331 (1994), p. 1241.

34. Quill, "Death and Dignity," pp. 691–94.

35. Dyer, "Rheumatologist Convicted," p. 737.

36. Ibid.

37. T. E. Quill, C. K. Cassel, and D. E. Meier, "Care of the Hopelessly Ill: Proposed Clinical Criteria for Physician-Assisted Suicide," *New England Journal of Medicine* 327 (1992): 1380–84.

38. "Suicide: A Difficult Road for People with AIDS," *New York Times* (June 14, 1994), pp. C1+.

39. F. G. Miller and J. C. Fletcher, "The Case for Legalized Euthanasia," *Perspectives in Biology and Medicine* 36 (1993): 159–76.

40. *Compassion in Dying v. State of Washington U.S. District Court* (Washington and Seattle, 1994), in *Biolaw,* Special Section (June 1994).

41. Ibid.

42. *Casey v. Planned Parenthood,* 14 F. 3d, 848 (1994).

43. *Washington v. Glucksberg,* 117 S. Ct. 2258 (1997).

44. Oregon Death with Dignity Act, Oregon Revised Statutes § 127: 800–897 (1997).

45. L. Ganzini et al., "Physicians' Experiences with the Oregon Death with Dignity Act," *New England Journal of Medicine* 342 (2000): 557–63.

46. A. D. Sullivan, K. Hedberg, and D. Fleming, "Legalized Physician-Assisted Suicide in Oregon—The Second Year," *New England Journal of Medicine* 342 (2000): 598–604.

47. D. L. Willems et al., "Attitudes and Practices Concerning the End-of-Life, a Comparison between Physicians from the United States and from The Netherlands," *Archives of Internal Medicine* 160 (2000): 63–68.

48. "Dutch Parliament Passes Bill Legalizing Euthanasia," Associated Press release, November 28, 2000.

49. Ibid.

50. C. J. Williams, "Netherlands OKs Assisted Suicide," *Los Angeles Times*, April 11, 2001, sec. A.

51. Ibid.

52. Ibid.

53. L. A. Roscoe, L. J. Dragovic, and D. Cohen, "Dr. Jack Kevorkian and Cases of Euthanasia in Oakland County, Michigan, 1990–1998," *New England Journal of Medicine* 343, no. 23 (2000): 1735–36.

54. K. M. Foley, "Competent Care for the Dying Instead of Physician-Assisted Suicide," *New England Journal of Medicine* 336 (1997): 54–58.

55. E. D. Pelligrino, "Ethics," *Journal of the American Medical Association* 270 (1993): 202–203.

56. K. F. Langendoen, "The Clinical Management of Dying Patients Receiving Mechanical Ventilation: A Survey of Physician Practice," *Chest* 106 (1994): 880–88.

57. L. Schostak, "Jewish Ethical Guidelines for Resuscitation and Artificial Nutrition and Hydration of the Dying Elderly," *Journal of Medical Ethics* 20 (1994): 93–100.

58. "The Final Autonomy," *Lancet* 346 (1995): 259.

CHAPTER 6

1. D. Callahan, "Limiting Health Care for the Old," in *Aging and Ethics*, ed. N. Jecker (Totowa, N.J.: Humana Press, 1991), pp. 219–26.

2. National Center for Health Statistics, "National Hospital Discharge Survey. Advance Data from Vital and Health Statistics. 1986 Summary," (Hyattsville, Md., Public Health Service, DHHS Publication No. 145 [PHS] 87–1250, 1987), pp. 1–16.

3. V. R. Fuchs, *The Future of Health Policy* (Cambridge, Mass.: Harvard University Press, 1993).

4. B. Starfield, "Is US Health Really the Best in the World?" *Journal of the American Medical Association* 284, no. 4 (2000): 483–85.

5. L. Kohn, J. Corrigan, and M. Donaldson, *To Err Is Human: Building a Safe Health System* (Washington, D.C.: National Academy Press, 1999).

6. Starfield, "Is US Health Really the Best in the World?"

7. World Health Report 2000. Available at http://www.who.int/whr/2000/en/report.htm; accessed June 28, 2000.

8. J. E. Dalen, "Health Care in America: The Good, the Bad, and the Ugly," *Archives of Internal Medicine* 160 (2000): 2573–76.

9. A. L. Caplan, "Straight Talk about Rationing," *Annals of Internal Medicine* 122 (1995): 795–96.

10. S. T. Bruner, D. R. Waldo, and D. R. Makusick, "National Health Expenditure Projection through 2030," *Health Care Financing Review* 14 (1992): 14–29.

11. M. Gillick, "The High Cost of Dying: A Way Out," *Archives of Internal Medicine* 154 (1994): 2134–37.

12. R. D. Lamm, *America in Decline* (Denver: The Center for Public Policy and Contemporary Issues, University of Denver, 1990).

13. N. Daniels, *"Am I My Parents' Keeper? An Essay on Justice between the Young and Old"* (New York: Oxford University Press, 1988), pp. 40–65, 88–102.

14. H. T. Engelhardt and M. A. Rie, "Intensive Units' Scarce Resources and Conflicting Principles of Justice," *Journal of the American Medical Association* 225 (1986): 1162–65.

15. D. C. Hadron, "Setting Health Care Priorities in Oregon: Cost Effectiveness Meets the Rule of Rescue," *Journal of the American Medical Association* 265 (1991): 2218–25.

16. P. T. Menzel, "Paying the Real Costs of Lifesaving," in *Aging and Ethics*, ed. N. Jecker (Totowa, N.J.: Humana Press, 1991), pp. 285–305.

17. K. M. Rowan et al., "Intensive Care Society's APACHE II Study in Britain and Ireland II: Outcome Comparisons of Intensive Care Units after Adjustment for Case Mix by the American APACHE II Method," *British Medical Journal* 309 (1993): 977–81.

18. S. Atkinson et al., "Identification of Futility in Intensive Care," *Lancet* 344 (1994): 1203–1206.

19. L. Churchill, *Rationing Health Care in America* (South Bend, Ind.: Notre Dame University Press, 1988).

CHAPTER 7

1. K. Ritchie, "Mental Status Examination of an Exceptional Case of Longevity," *British Journal of Psychiatry* 166 (1995): 229–35.

2. U. Gleichman et al., "Treatment of Cardiovascular Disease on the Elderly in Germany," *American Journal of Geriatric Cardiology* 4 (1995): 34–41.

3. J. McCue, "The Naturalness of Dying," *Journal of the American Medical Association* 273 (1995): 1039–43.

4. P. Aries, *The Hour of Our Death* (New York: Vintage Books, 1981).

5. R. D. Lamm, *America in Decline* (Denver: Center for Public Policy and Contemporary Issues, University of Denver, 1990), p. 18.

6. D. Callahan, "Necessity, Futility and the Good Society," *Journal of the Geriatric Society* 42 (1994): 866–67.

7. D. Callahan, *Setting Limits: Medical Goals in an Aging Society* (New York: Simon & Schuster, 1993).

8. D. Callahan, "Limiting Health Care for the Old," in *Aging and Ethics*, ed. N. Jecker (Totowa, N.J.: Humana Press 1991), pp. 225–26.

CHAPTER 8

1. Lord Mustill, Letter in *Airedale NHS Trust (Respondents)* v. *Bland* (acting as his guardian *ad litem*) (Appellant). Judgment, February 4, 1993, pp. 33–48.

2. F. W. Peabody, "The Care of the Patient," *Journal of the American Medical Association* 88 (1927): 877–81.

3. R. M. Rilke, *Selected Poems of Rainer Maria Rilke: A Translation from German and Commentary by Robert Bly* (New York: Harper & Row, 1979), p. 119.

4. J. P. Lizza, "Persons and Death: What's Metaphysically Wrong with Our Current Statutory Definition of Death?" *Journal of Medicine and Philosophy* 18 (1993): 351–74.

5. A. Halevy and B. Brody, "Brain Death: Reconciling Definitions, Criteria, and Tests," *Annals of Internal Medicine* 19 (1993): 519–25.

6. A. L. Caplan, "Straight Talk about Rationing," *Annals of Internal Medicine* 122 (1995): 795–96.

7. "Efficacy of the Patient Self-Determination Act," in *Biolaw*, "Death and Dying" (Bethesda, Md.: University Publications of America, 1994), p. 171; E. J. Emanuel et al., "How Well Is the Patient Self-Determination Act Working?" *American Journal of Medicine* 95 (1993): 619–28.

8. J. S. Tobias and R. L. Soulami, "Fully Informed Consent Can Be Needlessly Cruel," *British Medical Journal* 307 (1993): 1435–39.

9. L. Forrow, R. M. Arnold, and L. S. Parker, "Preventative Ethics: Expanding the Horizons of Clinical Ethics," *Journal of Clinical Ethics* 4 (1993): 287–93.

10. "Public Uses Denmark's Living Will," *British Medical Journal* 306 (1993): 413–15.

11. M. A. Strosberg, I. O. Fein, and J. D. Carroll, eds., *Rationing of Medical*

Care for the Critically Ill (Washington, D.C.: Brookings Institution, Dialogs in Public Policy, 1986).

12. Alexis de Tocqueville, *Democracy in America: The Henry Reeve Text*, vol. 2 (New York: Vintage Books, 1945), p. 185.

13. A. Einstein, "From Living Philosophies," in *Living Philosophies*, ed. Clifton Fadiman (New York: Doubleday, 1990), p. 3. (Original published in 1931.)

CHAPTER 9

1. I. Kutner, "Due Process of Euthanasia: The Living Will, a Proposal" *Indiana Law Journal* (1969): 44.

2. See *Schloendorff* v. *Society of New York Hospitals*, 211 N.Y. 128, 105 N.E. 93, 1914.

3. *Brophy* v. *New England Sinai Hospital, Inc.* (497 N.E. 2d 626, MA, 1986).

4. G. Annas, "Nancy Cruzan and the Right to Die," *New England Journal of Medicine* 323 (1990): 670–73.

5. *Cruzan* v. *Director* (497 U.S. 261, 1990), quoted in A. Miesel, "A Retrospective on Cruzan," *Law, Medicine, and Health Care* 20 (1992): 340.

6. Ibid.

7. J. Cohen-Mansfield, J. A. Droge, and N. Billig, "The Utilization of the Durable Power of Attorney for Health Care among Hospitalized Elderly Patients," *Journal of the American Geriatric Society* 39 (1991): 1174–78; J Cohen-Mansfield et al., "The Decision to Execute a Durable Power of Attorney for Health Care and Preferences Regarding the Utilization of Life-Sustaining Treatments in Nursing Home Residents," *Archives of Internal Medicine* 151 (1991): 289–94.

8. A. Meisel, *Cruzan v. Director. The Right to Die* (New York: Wiley Law Publications, 1989, in 1994 supplement), p. 25.

9. *Airedale NHS Trust (Respondents)* v. *Bland*, Judgment, February 4, 1993. 2 WLR 316, 343, per L. J. Burler-Sloso.

10. Supreme Judicial Court of Massachusetts in *Superintendent of Belchertown State School* v. *Saikewicz* (370 N.E. 2d, 1977), p. 428.

11. Lord Lowry, letter in *Airedale NHS Trust (Respondents)* v. *Bland* (Acting by his guardian *ad litem*) (Appellate) Judgment, February 4, 1993, pp. 33–48.

12. *Barber* v. *Superior Court of State of California* (Cal. Rptr., 1983).

13. *In re Spring* 380 Mass. 629 405 N.E. 2d 115, 119 (1980).

14. A. Meisel, "The Legal Consensus about Forgoing Life-Sustaining Treatment: Its Status and Its Prospects," *Kennedy Institute of Ethics Journal* 2 (1992): 309–12.

15. *In re Wanglie* No. PX–91–283 (4th District Court, Hennepin County, Minn., 1991).

16. A. Meisel, *In Evans v. Bellevue Hospital. The Right to Die* (New York: Wiley Law Publications, 1989).

17. *Superintendent of Belchertown State School* v. *Saikewicz*, p. 428.

18. "Hospital Appeals Decision on Treating Anencephalic Baby," *Hospital Ethics* 9 (1993): 6–7.

19. *In the Matter of Baby K*, No. CIV A. 93–104–1 (Ed VA: 7 July 1993).

20. "Netherlands," in *Biolaw,* "Biomedical Ethics" (Bethesda, Md.: University Publications of America, 1994), p. 47; "Denmark," in *Biolaw* "Biomedical Ethics" (Bethesda, Md.: University Publications of America, 1993), pp. 43–44.

CHAPTER 10

1. S. Bok, "Personal Directions for Care at the End of Life," *New England Journal of Medicine* 7 (1976): 367–68.

2. L. L. Emanuel et al., "Advance Directives: Stability of Patients' Treatment Choices," *Archives of Internal Medicine* 154 (1994): 209–17.

3. M. R. Wicclair, *Ethics and the Elderly* (New York: Oxford University Press, 1993).

4. J. Hardwig, "The Problem of Proxies with Interests of Their Own: Toward a Better Theory of Proxy Decisions," *Journal of Clinical Ethics* 4 (1991): 41–46.

5. L. Emanuel, "Advance Directives: What Have We Learned So Far?" *Journal of Clinical Ethics* 4 (1993): 8–16; L. L. Emanuel, "Advance Directives: Do They Work?" *Journal American College of Cardiology* 25 (1995): 35–38.

6. W. A. Knaus et al., "The SUPPORT Prognostic Model: Objective Estimates of Survival for Seriously Ill Hospitalized Adults," *Annals of Internal Medicine,* 22 (1995): 191–203; J. M. Teno et al. "Do Formal Advance Directives Affect Resuscitation Decisions and the Use of Resources for Seriously Ill Patients?" *Journal of Clinical Ethics* 5 (1994): 23–30.

7. J. M. Teno et al., "Do Advance Directives Provide Instructions That Direct Care?" *Journal of American Geriatric Society* 45 (1997): 508–12.

8. P. A. Singer, D. K. Martin, and M. Kelner, "Quality End-of-Life Care, Patients' Perspectives," *Journal of American Medical Association* 281 (1999): 163–68.

9. Ibid.

CHAPTER 11

1. J. H. Sammons, *Inside Medical Washington* (Knoxville, Tenn.: Whittle Direct Books, 1991), pp. 5–6.

2. Editorial, "Case Management: A Disastrous Mistake," *Lancet* 345 (1995): 399–401.

3. H. Nelson, "California's Anguished Doctors Revolt," *Lancet* 345 (1995): 716.

4. L. R. Kass, *Neither for Love nor Money: Why Doctors Must Not Kill* (Washington, D.C.: Public Interest, published by National Affairs, 1989), pp. 25–46.

5. Quoted in L. L. Basta, "Sorcery and Scientific Medicine in Ancient Egypt," *Journal of the Oklahoma State Medical Association* 69 (1976): 173–80.

6. E. J. Edelstein and L. Edelstein, *Asclepius: A Collection and Interpretation of the Testimonies*, vol. 2 (Baltimore, Md.: Johns Hopkins Press, 1945), p. 7.

7. J. E. Bailey, "Asklepios: Ancient Hero of Medical Caring," *Annals of Internal Medicine* 124 (1996): 257–63.

8. Plato, *The Republic*, trans. G. M. Grube (Indianapolis: Hackett Publishing Co., 1992).

9. *Hippocrates* (6 vols.), trans. W. H. S. Jones. The Loeb Classical Library (Cambridge, Mass.: Harvard University Press, 1988). (Originally published in 1923.)

10. E. D. Pellegrino and D. C. Thomasma, *A Philosophical Basis of Medical Practice* (Oxford: Oxford University Press, 1981).

11. M. Dean, "Politics of Euthanasia in UK," *Lancet* 345 (1995): 714.

12. M. Chiswick, "The Science of Making Mistakes," *Lancet* 345 (1995): 871–72.

13. J. S. Haas, J. S. Weissman, and P. D. Cleary, "Discussion of Preferences for Life-Sustaining Care by Persons with AIDS: Predictors of Failure in Patient-Physician Communication," *Archives of Internal Medicine* 153 (1993): 1241–48.

14. D. G. Larson and D. R. Tobin, "End-of-Life Conversations: Evolving Practice and Theory," *Journal of the American Medical Association* 284 (2000): 1573–78.

15. Bailey, "Asklepios."

16. A. Campbell et al., *Medical Ethics* (New Zealand: Oxford University Press, 1997), p. 28.

17. L. R. Bristow et al., "Patient-Physician Covenant," *Journal of the American Medical Association* 273 (1995): 1553.

CHAPTER 12

1. American Medical Association, Council on Ethical and Judicial Affairs, "Decisions Near the End of Life," *Journal of the American Medical Association* 267 (1992): 2229–33; American Medical Association, Council on Scientific Affairs, "Good Care of the Dying Patient," *Journal of the American Medical Association* 275 (1996): 474–78. American Board of Internal Medicine, End-of-Life Patient Care Project Committee, *Caring for the Dying: Identification and Promotion of Physician Competence* (Philadelphia: American Board of Internal Medicine, 1996).

2. T. E. Quill, B. C. Lee, and S. Nunn, "Palliative Treatments of Last Resort. Choosing the Least Harmful Alternative," *Annals of Internal Medicine* 132 (2000): 488–93.

3. *Quill v. Vacco* 80 F. 3d 716, 729 (1996).

4. J. Lynn, "Measuring Quality of Care at the End-of-Life: A Statement of Principles," *Journal of the American Geriatric Society* 45 (1997): 526–27.

5. R. S. Morrison et al., "The Hard Task of Improving the Quality of Care at the End-of-Life," *Archives of Internal Medicine* 160 (2000): 743–47.

6. D. Callahan, "Death and the Research Imperative," *New England Journal of Medicine* 342 (2000): 654–56.

7. M. Foucault, *The Birth of the Clinic: An Archeology of Medical Perception* (New York: Vintage Books, 1994), p. 197.

CHAPTER 13

1. This chapter contains valuable contributions from the following authors: Co-editor, Henry D. McIntosh; Education Implementation, William Leonard; Advance Care Planning, Michael D. D. Geldart, Ron Shashy, and Irvin Kalb; Medical Futility, W. Daniel Doty and Robert M. Walker; Palliative Care, Ronald Schonwetter, Lula Redmond, Janice Lowell, Lori Roscoe, Susan Bruno, and David McGrew. A portion of this chapter was published in a special supplement of *Clinical Cardiology*, v. 23 (February 2000), Supplement II.

2. W. Leonard, "Project GRACE: Summary of Task Forces I, II, and III, and Report of Task Force IV Education and Implementation," *Clinical Cardiology*, v. 23 (February 2000): Suppl. II, pp. 26–28.

3. M. Geldart, R. Shashy, and I. Kalb, "Project GRACE: Advance Care Planning," *Clinical Cardiology*, v. 23 (February 2000): Suppl. II, pp. 17–20.

4. R. Schonwetter et al., "Project GRACE: Palliative Care," *Clinical Cardiology*, v. 23 (2000): Suppl. II, pp. 21–25.

5. P. A. Singer, D. K. Martin, and M. Kelner, "Quality End-of-Life Care, Patients' Perspectives," *Journal of American Medical Association* 281 (1999): 163–68.

6. J. M. Teno et al., "Do Advance Directives Provide Instructions That Direct Care?" *Journal of the American Geriatric Society* 45 (1997): 508–12.

7. W. D. Doty and R. M. Walker, "Project GRACE: Medical Futility," *Clinical Cardiology*, v. 23 (February 2000): Suppl. II, pp. 6–16.

8. L. L. Basta, " 'The Universal Living Will,' A Third Generation Advance Directive," copyright Library of Congress TXU 685–553, January 9, 1995.

9. *Schloendorff v. Society of New York Hospital* 211 N.Y. 125, 105 N.E. 92 (1914).

10. *Cruzan v. Director* 110 S. Ct. 2851 (1990).

11. *Bouvia v. Superior Court*, 225 Cal. Rptr. 287 (Cal. App. 1986).

12. J. Areen, "The Legal Status of Consent Obtained from Families of Adult Patients to Withhold or Withdraw Treatment," *Journal of the American Medical Association* 258 (1987): 229–35.

13. S. S. Sanbar et al., *Legal Medicine*, 4th ed. (St. Louis, Mo.: Mosby, 1988), pp. 359–61.

14. "Hippocratic Corpus: The Art," in *Ethics in Medicine: Historical Perspectives and Contemporary Concerns*, ed. S. J. Reiser, A. J. Dyck, and W. J. Curran (Cambridge, Mass.: MIT Press, 1977), pp. 6–7.

15. Plato, *The Republic*, trans. G. M. Grube (Indianapolis, Ind.: Hackett Publishing, 1981), pp. 76–77.

16. "Final Report, Panel for the Study of End-of-Life Care" (Tallahassee, Fla.: Pepper Institute on Aging and Public Policy, Florida State University, 1999), p. 13.

17. F. H. Marsh and A. Staver, "Physician Authority for Unilateral DNR Orders," *Journal of Legal Medicine* 12 (1991): 115–65; L. J. Blackhall, "Must We Always Use CPR?" *New England Journal of Medicine* 317 (1987): 1281–85; R. T. Layson and T. McConnell, "Must Consent Always Be Obtained for a Do-Not-Resuscitate Order?" *Archives of Internal Medicine* 156 (1996): 2617–20.

18. K. Plunkitt, F. Matar, and L. Basta, "Therapeutic CPR or Consent DNR—A Dilemma Looking for an Answer," *Journal of the American College of Cardiology* 32 (1998): 2095–97.

19. Sanbar et al., *Legal Medicine*.

20. J. F. Drane and J. L. Coulehan, "The Concept of Futility: Patients Do Not Have a Right to Demand Medically Useless Treatment," *Health Progress* 74 (December 1993): 28–32.

21. Omnibus Reconciliation Act of 1990, Pub. L. 101–508 §§ 4206, 4751, 104 Stat. 1388, codified at 42 U.S.C. §§ 1395 cc(a)(1)(Q), 1395mm(c)(8), 1395cc(f), 1396a(a)(57), (58), 1396a(w). See also regulations at 57 Fed. Reg. 8194–8204 (March 6, 1992).

22. Sanbar et al., *Legal Medicine*.

23. Ibid.

24. P. S. Appelbaum and T. Grisso, "Assessing Patients' Capacities to Consent to Treatment" *New England Journal of Medicine* 319 (1988): 1635–38 (published erratum appears in 320 [1989]: 748); Hastings Center, *Guidelines on the Termination of Life-Sustaining Treatment and the Care of the Dying* (Bloomington: Indiana University Press, 1987), p. 141; California Health & Safety Code 7188 (West Supp. 1996); Oregon Revised Statutes ch. 127.515(4)(e) (Supp. Part 2, 1994); M. L. Osborne, "Physician Decisions Regarding Life Support in the Intensive Care Unit," *Chest* 101 (1992): 217–24.

25. A. U. Rivin, "Futile Care Policy. Lessons Learned from Three Years' Experience in a Community Hospital," *Western Journal of Medicine* 166 (1997): 389–93 (published erratum appears in 167 [1997]: 53); A. Halevy and B. A. Brody, "A Multi-Institutional Collaborative Policy on Medical Futility," *Journal of the*

American Medical Association 276 (1996): 571–74; M. A. Eloubeidi, J. W. Swanson, and J. Sugarman, "North Carolina Hospitals' Policies on Medical Futility," *North Carolina Medical Journal* 56 (1995): 420–22; D. E. Vawter, "The Houston Citywide Policy on Medical Futility," *Journal of the American Medical Association* 276 (1996): 1549–50; L. R. Churchill, "The Ethical Issues of Futility from a Community Perspective," *North Carolina Medical Journal* 56 (1995): 424–26; "Consensus Statement of the Society of Critical Care Medicine's Ethics Committee Regarding Futile and Other Possibly Inadvisable Treatments," *Critical Care Medicine* 25 (1997): 887–91; S. B. King III et al., "Task Force 2: Application of Medical and Surgical Interventions Near the End of Life," *Journal of the American College of Cardiology* 31 (1998): 933–42.

26. R. Halliday, "Medical Futility and the Social Context," *Journal of Medical Ethics* 23 (1997): 148–53; R. E. Cranford, "Medical Futility: Transforming a Clinical Concept into Legal and Social Policies," *Journal of the American Geriatrics Society* 42 (1994): 894–98.

27. P. Aries and P. M. Ranum, trans., *Western Attitudes toward Death: From the Middle Ages to the Present* (Baltimore: Johns Hopkins University Press, 1974).

28. R. M. Walker et al., "Living Wills and Resuscitation Preferences in an Elderly Population," *Archives of Internal Medicine* 155, no. 2 (1995): 171–75.

29. P. H. Ditto et al. "Fates Worse than Death: The Role of Valued Life Activities in Health-State Evaluations," *Health Psychology* 15, no. 5 (1996): 332–43; J. M. Potter, D. Stewart, and G. Duncan, "Living Wills: Would Sick People Change Their Minds?" *Postgraduate Medical Journal* 70, no. 829 (1994): 818–20; D. R. Watson et al., "The Effect of Hospital Admission on the Opinions and Knowledge of Elderly Patients Regarding Cardiopulmonary Resuscitation," *Age & Aging* 26, no. 6 (1997): 429–34; K. E. Rosenfeld et al., "Factors Associated with Change in Resuscitation Preference of Seriously Ill Patients. The SUPPORT Investigators. Study to Understand Prognoses and Preferences of Outcomes and Risks of Treatments," *Archives of Internal Medicine* 156, no. 14 (1996): 1558–64.

30. "A Definition of Irreversible Coma. Report of the Ad Hoc Committee of the Harvard Medical School to Examine the Definition of Brain Death," *Journal of the American Medical Association* 205 (1968): 337–40; President's Commission for the Study of Ethical Problems in Medicine and Biomedical and Behavioral Research, *Defining Death: Medical, Legal and Ethical Issues in the Determination of Death* (Washington, D.C.: U.S. Government Printing Office, 1981).

31. L. L. Kirkland, "Family Refusal to Accept Brain Death and Termination of Life Support: Physician Responsibility," *Journal of Clinical Ethics* 2 (1991): 171; A. M. Harrison and J. R. Botkin, "Can Pediatricians Define and Apply the Concept of Brain Death?" *Pediatrics* 103 (1999): 82.

32. K. R. Mitchell, I. H. Kerridge, and T. J. Lovat, "Medical Futility, Treatment Withdrawal and the Persistent Vegetative State," *Journal of Medical Ethics* 19 (1993): 71–76.

33. S. J. Youngner and E. T. Bartlett, "Human Death and High Technology:

The Failure of the Whole-Brain Formulations," *Annals of Internal Medicine* 99 (1983): 252–58; R. M. Veatch, "The Impending Collapse of the Whole-Brain Definition of Death" *Hastings Center Report* 23 (1993): 18–24 (published erratum appears in 23 [1993]: 4).

34. L. Gostin and R. F. Weir, "Life and Death Choices after *Cruzan*: Case Law and Standards of Professional Conduct," *Milbank Quarterly* 69 (1991): 143–73.

35. J. Areen, "Advance Directives Under State Law and Judicial Decisions," *Legal Medicine and Health Care* 19 (1991); Harrison and Botkin, "Can Pediatricians Define and Apply the Concept of Brain Death?" p. 92.

36. J. A. Robertson, "Second Thoughts on Living Wills," *Hastings Center Report* 21 (1991): 6–9; M. D. D. Geldart, I. Kalb, and R. Shashy, "Advance Care Planning," *Clinical Cardiology* 23 (February 2000): Suppl. II.

37. R. M. Walker, "Ethical Issues in End-of-Life Care," *Cancer Control* 6 (1999): 162–67.

38. S. H. Miles, "Informed Demand for 'Non-Beneficial' Medical Treatment," *New England Journal of Medicine* 325 (1991): 512–15.

39. E. J. Emanuel et al., "Assistance from Family Members, Friends, Paid Care Givers, and Volunteers in the Care of Terminally Ill Patients," *New England Journal of Medicine* 341 (1999): 956–63.

40. A. A. Scitovsky, "The High Cost of Dying: What Do the Data Show?" *Milbank Quarterly* 62 (1984): 591–608; S. J. Youngner, "Who Defines Futility?" *Journal of the American Medical Association* 260 (1988): 2094–95; L. J. Schneiderman, N. S. Jecker, and A. R. Jonsen, "Medical Futility: Its Meaning and Ethical Implications," *Annals of Internal Medicine* 112 (1990): 949–54.

41. L. Chelluri, A. Grenvik, and M. Silverman, "Intensive Care for Critically Ill Elderly: Mortality, Costs, and Quality of Life. Review of the Literature," *Archives of Internal Medicine* 155 (1995): 1013–22.

42. M. J. Brenner, "The Curative Paradigm in Medical Education: Striking a Balance between Caring and Curing," *The Pharos* (Summer 1999): 4–9.

43. A. N. Ramsetty, "Walking Through the Valley of the Shadow of Death: A Student's Perspective on Death and the Medical Profession," *The Pharos* (Summer 1999): 11–15.

44. Hastings Center, *Guidelines on the Termination of Life-Sustaining Treatment and the Care of the Dying* (Bloomington: Indiana University Press, 1987).

45. J. H. Miles, "Medical Futility," *Legal Medicine and Health Care* 20 (1992): 310–15.

46. Youngner, "Who Defines Futility?"

47. *In the Matter of Baby K*, 832 F. Supp. 1022 (E.D.Va. 1993).

48. American Academy of Neurology, Multi-Society Task force on PVS, "Medical Aspects of the Persistent Vegetative State, Part 1," *New England Journal of Medicine* 330 (1994): 1572–79.

49. W. A. Knaus et al., "The SUPPORT Prognostic Model. Objective Estimates of Survival for Seriously Ill Hospitalized Adults. Study to Understand Prog-

noses and Preferences for Outcomes and Risks of Treatments," *Annals of Internal Medicine* 122 (1995): 191–203; S. Lemeshow et al., "Mortality Probability Models (MPM II) Based on an International Cohort of Intensive Care Unit Patients," *Journal of the American Medical Association* 270 (1993): 2478–86; K. M. Rowan et al., "Intensive Care Society's APACHE II Study in Britain and Ireland—I: Variations in Case Mix of Adult Admissions to General Intensive Care Units and Impact on Outcome," *British Medical Journal* 307 (1993): 972–77.

50. A. Wagg, M. Kinirons, and K. Stewart, "Cardiopulmonary Resuscitation: Doctors and Nurses Expect Too Much," *Journal of the Royal College of Physicians of London* 29 (1995): 20–24.

51. S. J. Diem, J. D. Lantos, and J. A. Tulsky, "Cardiopulmonary Resuscitation on Television. Miracles and Misinformation," *New England Journal of Medicine* 334 (1996): 1578–82.

52. L. Basta et al., "Cardiopulmonary Resuscitation in the Elderly: Defining the Limits of Appropriateness," *American Journal of Geriatric Cardiology* 7 (1998): 46–55.

53. R. S. Schonwetter et al., "Resuscitation Decision Making in the Elderly: The Value of Outcome Data," *Journal of General Internal Medicine* 8 (1993): 295–300.

54. "Standards for Cardiopulmonary Resuscitation (CPR) and Emergency Cardiac Care (ECC). V. Medicolegal Considerations and Recommendations," *Journal of the American Medical Association* 227 (1974): Suppl., pp. 864–68.

55. American Medical Association, Council on Ethical and Judicial Affairs, "Guidelines for the Appropriate Use of Do-Not-Resuscitate Orders," *Journal of the American Medical Association* 265 (1991): 1868–71.

56. J. R. Curtis et al., "Use of the Medical Futility Rationale in Do-Not-Attempt-Resuscitation Orders," *Journal of the American Medical Association* 273 (1995): 124–28; N. S. Jecker and L. J. Schneiderman, "When Families Request That 'Everything Possible' Be Done," *Journal of Medical Philosophy* 20 (1995): 145–63.

57. R. M. Walker et al., "Physicians' and Nurses' Perceptions of Ethics Problems on General Medical Services," *Journal of General Internal Medicine* 6 (1991): 424–29.

58. J. Tsevat et al., "Health Values of Hospitalized Patients 80 Years or Older. HELP Investigators. Hospitalized Elderly Longitudinal Project," *Journal of the American Medical Association* 279 (1998): 371–75; M. B. Hamel et al., "Patient Age and Decisions to Withhold Life-Sustaining Treatments from Seriously Ill, Hospitalized Adults. SUPPORT Investigators. Study to Understand Prognoses and Preferences for Outcomes and Risks of Treatment," *Annals of Internal Medicine* 130 (1999): 116–25.

59. J. H. Karlawish, T. Quill, and D. E. Meier, "A Consensus-Based Approach to Providing Palliative Care to Patients Who Lack Decision-Making Capacity. ACP-ASIM End-of-Life Care Consensus Panel. American College of Physicians-

American Society of Internal Medicine," *Annals of Internal Medicine* 130 (1999): 835–40.

60. J. D. Lantos et al., "The Illusion of Futility in Clinical Practice," *American Journal of Medicine* 87 (1989): 81–84; 42 (1994): 868–70.

61. J. D. Lantos, "Futility Assessments and the Doctor-Patient Relationship," *Journal of the American Geriatrics Society* 42 (1994): 870.

62. Fl. Stat. 765.101(1)

63. SUPPORT Principal Investigators, "A Controlled Trial to Improve Care for Seriously Ill Hospitalized Patients: The Study to Understand Prognoses and Preferences for Outcomes and Risks of Treatments (SUPPORT)," *Journal of the American Medical Association* 274 (1995): 1591–98.

64. T. Iwashyna and N. Christakis, "Attitude and Self-Reported Practice Regarding Hospice Referral in a National Sample of Internists," *Journal of Palliative Medicine* 1 (1998): 241–48.

65. Task Force on Palliative Care, LAST ACTS Campaign, Robert Wood Johnson Foundation, "Precepts of Palliative Care," *Journal of Palliative Medicine* 1 (1998): 109–12.

66. J. Billings, "What Is Palliative Care?" *Journal of Palliative Medicine* 1 (1998): 73–81.

67. U.S. Healthcare, Inc., "CHF Disease Management Program," USQA, 1996.

68. A. L. Back et al., "Physician-Assisted Suicide and Euthanasia in Washington State: Patient Requests and Physician Responses," *Journal of the American Medical Association* 275 (1996): 919–25.

69. J. H. Brown et al., "Is It Normal for Terminally Ill Patients to Desire Death?" *American Journal of Psychiatry* 143 (1986): 208–11; H. M. Chochinov et al., "Desire for Death in the Terminally Ill," *American Journal of Psychiatry* 152 (1995): 1185–91; W. Breitbart, B. D. Rosenfeld, and S. D. Passik, "Interest in Physician-Assisted Suicide among Ambulatory HIV-Infected Patients," *American Journal of Psychiatry* 153 (1996): 238–42.

70. M. Angell, "The Supreme Court and Physician-Assisted Suicide—The Ultimate Right," *New England Journal of Medicine* 336 (1997): 50–53.

71. S. Grond et al., "Validation of the World Health Organization Guidelines for Cancer Pain Relief during the Last Days and Hours of Life," *Journal of Pain Symptom Management* 6 (1991): 411–22; K. M. Foley, "The Relationship of Pain and Symptom Management to Patient Requests for Physician-Assisted Suicide," *Journal of Pain Symptom Management* 6 (1991): 289–97; R. Portenoy and N. Coyle, "Controversies in the Long-Term Management of Analgesic Therapy in Patients with Advanced Cancer," *Journal of Pain Symptom Management* 5 (1990): 307–19; J. M. Cain and B. J. Hammes, "Ethics and Pain Management: Respecting Patient Wishes," *Journal of Pain Symptom Management* 9 (1994): 160–65; E. D. Pellegrino, "Compassion Needs Reason Too," *Journal of the American Medical Association* 270 (1993): 874–75.

72. R. A. Burt, "The Supreme Court Speaks—Not Assisted Suicide but a Constitutional Right to Palliative Care," *New England Journal of Medicine* 337 (1997): 1234–36.

73. Nationwide Gallup survey conducted for National Health Organization in fall 1996.

74. National Center for Health Statistics, Monthly Vital Statistics Report, September 30, 1996; D. B. Brock and D. J. Foley, "Demography and Epidemiology of Dying in the US with Emphasis on Death of Older Persons," *Hospice Journal* 13, nos. 1, 2 (1998): 49–60.

75. A. Sankar, *Dying at Home: A Family Guide for Caregiving* (Baltimore: Johns Hopkins University Press, 1991), pp. 33–40.

76. J. A. Billings and S. Block, "Palliative Care in Undergraduate Medical Education: Status Report and Future Directions," *Journal of the American Medical Association* 278 (1997): 733–38.

77. T. P. Hill, "Treating the Dying Patient: The Challenge of Medical Education," *Archives of Internal Medicine* 155 (1995): 1265–69.

78. E. J. Emanuel and L. L. Emanuel, "The Economics of Dying," *New England Journal of Medicine* 330 (1994): 540–44.

79. D. Kidder, K. Merrell, and D. Dohan, *Medicare Hospice Benefit Program Evaluation: Final Summary Report* (Baltimore: U.S. Department of Health and Human Services, Health Care Financing Administration, January 21, 1989); Health Care Financing Administration, "Medicare and Medicaid Statistical Supplement," *Health Care Financing Review* (1997); D. Kidder, "Hospice Services and Cost Savings in the Last Weeks of Life," in *The Hospice Experiment*, ed. V. Mor, D. S. Greer, and R. Kastenbaum (Baltimore: Johns Hopkins Univeristy Press, 1988), pp. 69–87; D. Kidder, "Hospice: Does It Still Save Medicare Money?" *Journal of Palliative Medicine* 2 (1998): 151–54; D. Hurley, "New Study Shows Hospice Benefit Saves Medicare Money," *National Hospice Organization News*, April 26, 1995.

80. E. S. Cassell, "The Nature of Suffering and the Goals of Medicine," *New England Journal of Medicine* 306 (1982): 639–45.

81. I. Byock, "Hospice and Palliative Care: A Parting of Ways or a Path to the Future?" *Journal of Palliative Medicine* 2 (1998): 165–76.

82. D. Pendley and R. White, "Applying Hospice Principles in the Palliative Care Debate," *American Journal of Hospice and Palliative Care* (January/February 1999): 412–15; D. E. Weissman, "Consultation in Palliative Medicine," *Archives of Internal Medicine* 157 (1997): 734–37.

83. American Medical Association, *Physicians' Current Procedural Terminology* (Chicago: American Medical Association, 1998), pp. 9–42.

84. R. S. Schonwetter, W. Hawke, and C. F. Knight, eds. *Hospice and Palliative Medicine Care Curriculum and Review Syllabus* (Dubuque, Iowa: American Academy of Hospice and Palliative Medicine, Kendall/Hunt Publishing Company, 1999).

CHAPTER 14

1. *Cantebury* v. *Spence* 464 A.F. 2d 772 (D.C. Cir.), cert. denied, 409 U.S. 1064, 1972.

2. *Conservatorship of Drabick*, 245 Cal. Rptr. 840 (Ct. app.), Cert. denied, 488 U.S. 958, 1988.

3. R. Weir, *Physician Assisted Suicide* (Bloomington: Indiana University Press, 1997).

4. *Rodriguez* v. *British Columbia (Attorney General)* No. 23476, British Columbia Superior Court, September 30, 1993.

5. *Nancy B.* v. *L'Hotel-Dieu de Quebec* (R.J.Q. 1992) 361 (Superior Court).

6. *Washington* v. *Glucksberg* 117 S. Ct. 2258, 1997.

7. L. O. Gostin, "Deciding Life and Death in the Courtroom from Quinlan to Cruzan, Glucksberg and Vacco—A Brief History and Analysis of Constitutional Protection of the Right to Die," *Journal of the American Medical Association* 278 (1997): 1523–28.

8. W. H. S. Jones, trans., *Hippocrates,* Loeb Classical Library (Cambridge, Mass.: Harvard University Press, 1923–1988).

9. J. G. Ouslander, A. J. Tymchuk, and B. Rabhar, "Healthcare Decisions among Elderly Long-Term Care Residents and Their Potential Proxies," *Archives of Internal Medicine* 149 (1989): 1367–1723.

10. A. B. Seckler et al., "Substituted Judgment—How Accurate Are Proxy Predictions?" *Annals of Internal Medicine* 115 (1991): 92–98; J. Hardwig, "The Problem with Proxies with Interests of Their Own: Toward a Better Theory for Proxy Decision," *Journal of Clinical Ethics* 4 (1991): 41–46.

11. R. Lipsyle, *In the Country of Illness: Comfort and Advice for the Journey* (New York: Alfred A. Knopf, Inc., 1998).

12. L. L. Basta and J. Tauth, "High Technology Near the End of Life, Setting Limits," *Journal of the American College of Cardiology* 28 (1996): 1623–30.

13. D. P. Sulmasy and J. Lynn, "End of Life Care," *Journal of the American Medical Association* 277 (1997): 1854–55.

14. *Brophy* v. *New England Sinai Hospital, Inc.*, 497 N.E. 2d 626 (Mass. 1986).

15. A. B. Sickler et al., "Substituted Judgment: How Accurate Are Proxy Predictions?" *Annals of Internal Medicine* 115 (1991): 92–98; M. Davis et al., "Stability of Choices about Life Sustaining Treatments," *Annals of Internal Medicine* 120 (1994): 567–73.

16. Florida Statutes Section 322.126(2),(3). State of Florida Dept. of Highway Safety and Motor Vehicles.

17. S. Zoukis, "Reporting Medically Impaired Drivers," *Journal of the Medical Association of Georgia* 65, no. 4 (1976): 129–30.

18. *Tarasoff* v. *Regents of the University of California* (California Supreme Court) Cal. Rptr. 129, 1974.

19. *Freese* v. *Lemmon,* Iowa N.W. 2d 576 (1973).

20. Florida Dept. of Highway Safety and Motor Vehicles, *Florida Traffic Crash Facts* (Florida Dept. of Highway Safety and Motor Vehicles, 1997), p. 21.

21. B. J. Peterson and C. S. Petty, "Sudden Natural Death among Automobile Drivers," *Journal of Forensic Science* 7 (1962): 274–85; J. M. Trapnell and H. D. Greoff, "Myocardial Infarction in Commercial Drivers," *Journal of Occupational Medicine* 5 (1963): 182–84.

22. *Superintendent of Belchertown State School* v. *Saikewicz*, 370 N.E. 2d 417 (Mass. 1977); *In re Storar*, 420 N.E. 2d 64 (N.Y.), cert. denied, 454 U.S. 858 (1981); *Brophy* v. *New England Sinai Hospital, Inc.*; *Union Pacific Railway Co.* v. *Botsford*, 141 U.S. 250, 251 (1891).

23. L. L. Basta, "Does the Living Will Deserve to Live?" in *A Graceful Exit: Life and Death on Your Own Terms* (New York and London: Plenum Press, 1996), pp. 205–20.

24. A. P. Schneider II, D. J. Nelson, and D. O. Brown, "In-Hospital Cardiopulmonary Resuscitation: A 30-Year Review," *Journal of the American Board of Family Practice* 6 (1993): 91–101; M. Saklayen, H. Liss, and R. Markert, "In-Hospital Cardiopulmonary Resuscitation: Survival in One Hospital and Literature Review," *Medicine* (Baltimore) 74 (1995): 163–75; F. J. Landry, J. M. Parker, and Y. Y. Phillips, "Outcome of Cardiopulmonary Resuscitation in the Intensive Care Setting," *Archives of Internal Medicine* 153 (1992): 2305–2308; D. J. Murphy et al., "Outcomes of Cardiopulmonary Resuscitation in the Elderly," *Annals of Internal Medicine* 111 (1989): 190–205.

25. "ACP Ethics Manual, 3d ed." *Annals of Internal Medicine* 117 (1992): 947–60.

26. E. Segal, T. Halamish-Shani, "The Slow Code (Correspondence)," *New England Journal of Medicine* 338, no. 26 (1998): 1921.

27. M. Mello and C. Jenkinson, "Comparison of Medical and Nursing Attitudes to Resuscitation and Patient Autonomy between a British and an American Teaching Hospital," *Social Science Medicine* 46, no. 3 (1998): 415–24.

28. K. Plunkitt, F. Matar, and L. L. Basta, "Therapeutic CPR or Consent DNR?" *Journal of the American College of Cardiology* 7, no. 6 (1998): 46–54.

29. *Schloendorff* v. *Society of New York Hospital*, 211 N.Y. 125, 105 N.E. 92 (1914).

30. J. Acreen, "The Legal Status of Consent Obtained from Families of Adult Patients to Withhold or Withdraw Treatment," *Journal of the American Medical Association* 258 (1987): 229–35.

31. J. M. Tens et al., "Do Advance Directives Provide Instructions that Direct Care?" *Journal of the American Geriatric Society* 45 (1997): 508–12.

32. M. Angell, "The Supreme Court and Physician-Assisted Suicide—The Ultimate Right," *New England Journal of Medicine* 336 (1997): 50–53.

33. T. E. Quill, B. Lo, and D. W. Brock, "Palliative Options of Last Resort: A Comparison of Voluntary Stopping Eating and Drinking, Terminal Sedation,

Physician-Assisted Suicide and Voluntary Active Euthanasia," *Journal of the American Medical Association* 278 (1997): 2099–104.

34. K. M. Foley, "Competent Care for the Dying Instead of Physician-Assisted Suicide," *New England Journal of Medicine* 336 (1997): 54–58.

35. T. A. Brenan et al., "Incidence of Adverse Events and Negligence in Hospitalized Patients—Results of the Harvard Medical Practice Study 1," *New England Journal of Medicine* 324 (1991): 370–76; K. Steel et al., "Iatrogenic Illness on a General Medical Service at a University Hospital," *New England Journal of Medicine* 304 (1981): 638–42; E. M. Schimmel, "The Hazards of Hospitalization," *Annals of Internal Medicine* 60 (1964): 100–10.

36. S. E. Bedell et al., "Incidence and Characteristics of Preventable Iatrogenic Cardiac Arrests," *Journal of the American Medical Association* 265 (1991): 2815–20.

37. R. M. Walker, "DNR in the OR. Resuscitation as an Operative Risk," *Journal of the American Medical Association* 266 (1991): 2407–12.

38. D. Casarett and L. F. Ross, "Overriding a Patient's Refusal of Treatment after an Iatrogenic Complication," *New England Journal of Medicine* 336 (1997): 1908–10.

39. H. T. Englehardt, "Freedom vs. Best Interest: A Conflict at the Roots of Health Care," in *Day's Case: Essays in Medical Ethics and Human Meaning*, by L. D. Kliever (Dallas: Southern Methodist University Press, 1989), pp. 79–96.

40. P. G. Ries et al., eds., *Cancer Incidena of Survival among Children and Adolescents: United States SEER Program. 1975–1995* (Bethesda, Md.: National Institute of Health, 1999 [NIH Publication 99–4649]).

41. J. Wolfe et al., "Symptoms and Suffering at the End of Life in Children with Cancer," *New England Journal of Medicine* 342 (2000): 326–33.

INDEX

NARRAGANSETT PUBLIC LIBRARY
35 KINGSTOWN ROAD
NARRAGANSETT, RI 02882